# IN SEARCH OF
# FLINT McCULLOUGH
## and
# ROBERT HORTON

*The Man*
*Behind The Myth*

*By*
*Aileen J. Elliott*

Published in the USA by:
BearManor Media
1317 Edgewater Dr #110
Orlando, FL 32804
www.bearmanormedia.com

Perfect ISBN 978-1-62933-791-3
Case ISBN 978-1-62933-792-0
BearManor Media, Orlando, Florida
Printed in the United States of America
Book design by Robbie Adkins, www.adkinsconsult.com

*Cover Photo: Robert Horton as Flint McCullough. 1958.*
*NBC promotional photograph.*

*For my beloved twin sister, Penelope Jane Simone,*

*With eternal thanks and indebtedness to her for her*

*incisive advice, endless encouragement and*

*unwavering support.*

*1947 ~ 2018*

*Robert Horton as Flint McCullough. 1958. NBC promotional photograph.*

# TABLE OF CONTENTS

# ACKNOWLEDGMENTS

I have had invaluable help from close friends of Robert Horton's, as well as having acquired details of his life through the sale of his personal memorabilia. I am grateful to have these items; scrapbooks, photograph albums, letters, telegrams, diplomas, graduation certificates, a handful of books which came from his own library, his high school yearbook *The Sentinel*, from The Harvard School, dated 1942, his U.S. Coast Guard records, his Pilot's Log which records the flights he made between 1961 and 1994, his own annotated script of NBC's *This Is Your Life* which was recorded on January 18, 1961 and aired on January 22, and a guest book kept by Marilynn Horton between the years 1977 and 1980. All of these have helped me piece together his life and have contributed enormously to the veracity underlying the many so-called life stories published about him when he became truly famous as Flint McCullough in Wagon Train, as well as providing much needed information about him, and clues as to who he was, and what he was doing, especially in his formative years.

I have also compiled my own personal collection of photographs, playbills and magazines which have provided me with a great deal of information, from the "snipes" on the back of promotional photographs to the profiles in the playbills and the enormous number of articles written about Bob as he pursued his career. I must acknowledge the various writers of these articles, from "anonymous" to those named. While I have had to distill much of those contemporary writings in order to discern truth from fiction, or at least, some "colorful" writing, their contribution must be noted. Syndicated columnists such as Hedda Hopper and Louella Parsons appeared in national and local publications on a regular basis, and much of what was written was picked up, reworked and published by others. That soon became obvious to me. I gave credence to that which seemed most reliable and authentic. There was a considerable amount of speculative rubbish written, as well as some outright untruths.

Betty Burris, a long-time fan of Bob's who also served for many years in several capacities in his American fan club and who became a personal friend, put together and kept a scrapbook about Bob from the mid-Fifties through to the late Eighties, when she died. I refer to it as the *Burris Scrapbook*. She left instructions, pasted inside the front cover of the book, that it be sent to Robert Horton upon her death. This duly happened and Robert Horton, in turn, gave the scrapbook to the woman who, in 1990, became "the joy of his life". She subsequently, and without hesitation, loaned me the scrapbook when I contacted her in regard to the biography I was writing. It was a generous thing to do, and she left it with me for as long as I needed it. It proved to be full of information, albeit frustratingly lacking in identification such as dates, publication titles and writer's names. Those, it seems, were of little consequence to Betty, but I was able, in some cases, to cross-reference those articles with some from other sources I acquired, or had access to, memorabilia which belonged to Robert Horton. These very personal items, the letters, telegrams and a number of Horton's own photograph albums and scrapbooks have aided me considerably in piecing together Bob's early career, the years which preceded his meteoric rise to fame as Flint McCullough. One, a large, thick red leather scrapbook was clearly Robert's overall, pre-eminent collection of his most mean-ingful memorabilia. The *Red Book* covers his career from its earliest events through to the 1990s. It contains letters, telegrams, clippings, photographs, playbills, and critiques, an altogether deeply personal collection. Two scrapbooks in particular clarified and helped put in order his life at university and his first efforts in the theater. I refer to them as *Scrapbook I* and *Scrapbook II*. In all there were seven albums and scrapbooks and they are so referred to (*Scrapbook I - Scrapbook VII*) within the narrative as well as the Notes and Bibliography at the end of this book. Another very useful source was the vast number of newspaper and magazine clippings kept by various clippings services, covering Bob's *Wagon Train* years between 1957 and 1962 and which were given to Bob during that period. After that time, though there are clippings, playbills and some photographs in folders covering his stage career in the 1970s and 1980s, the impression given is that keeping a record of his career, or Marilynn's, in any great care or detail ceased to be of much importance to him.

I could not have built a record of his years without these things. If I have made mistakes, or misunderstood any matters within these contexts, I accept the responsibility totally. I have done my best to reconstruct Robert Horton's life as truthfully as possible, at all times with a real respect and admiration for a man who was true to himself, stood up for himself and all he believed in, and remained, always, a real, if flawed human being to the end of his days. None of which detracts from all of his talents, virtuosity, humanity and overall decency.

The collection I have of his work, from every *Wagon Train* episode in which he appeared, every episode of *A Man Called Shenandoah*, his movies, from the uncut version of *A Walk in the Sun* to *The Green Slime*, his television movies, much of his other television work, some of his nightclub and stage show acts, some panel show appearances (those which are extant today), all of his recordings and a vast array of magazines, articles, interviews, advertisements and clippings represent the other major sources from which I have been able to draw and compile the information which forms the basis for Robert Horton's story. The website compiled by Alicia Williams with Horton's eventual consent around 2002 has been useful inasmuch as I have been able to check and compare my own research against it. It is, however, by no means totally comprehensive and contains no personal information about the man's life beyond the basic statistics of birth, a marriage (to Marilynn Bradley) and his date of death. Furthermore, the source of much of that information was Robert Horton himself and he undoubtedly referred to his own memorabilia, the same memorabilia I have been privileged to acquire or review in depth.

Above all, the help I've received from people in his life must be acknowledged and thanked. The most significant contributions to this book have been made by Bob's friends. First and foremost is the woman he called the love of his life, and with whom he shared a deep and visceral friendship for over twenty-six years. Her wish is to remain anonymous, although she agreed to the use of the initials

"K.M." when being referred to within the story, for ease of reading and clarity. They are not her initials, but they have a significance within her story and her friendship with Robert Horton. Barbara and Will Hutchins, who became Bob's greatly valued friends in the late Eighties and Boyd Magers, who did likewise and helped Bob recognize, like it or not, that he meant a great deal to people through his depiction of the scout, Flint McCullough, in *Wagon Train*. Toby Wolfe, a friend of latter years, who recognized in Bob a heart yearning after greater things than *Wagon Train* could offer also contributed much about Bob's final years. Jan Shepard, who validated all I had thought about Robert Horton through her tales of her friendship with this mercurial being in their later years. Eugenia Fredricksen, his book-writer friend of the last two and a half years of his life helped my understanding of that unsettled period. Betty Marvin, who honestly replied to my inquiries about Bob and who, when I met and talked with her about him, lit up with pleasure and animation in her recollections of him. Two family members made considerable contributions; his younger niece, Joan Horton Evans, and his eldest nephew, Creighton C. Horton, II. I thank them profoundly for their honesty and willingness to share their stories as well as family photographs. Others who helped me deserve a mention; David Kestenbaum, Theodore Hovey, Cindy Robbins, Inga Swenson, Dwayne Epstein, David Ritter, Asi Livyatan, Brett Homenick, Maxine Hanson, Valerie Yaros, Lou Valentino, Bruce Boxleitner, Allan Sasaki, Michael Hawley and Steve Harbeson.

The wholesale distribution of Robert Horton's Estate helped a great deal. However, Robert Horton's widow, Marilynn, sadly declined to participate in any way beyond wishing me "good luck" on two separate occasions.[1]

Robert Horton died on March 9, 2016. His ashes were interred at the Hollywood Forever Cemetery on April 22, 2016. There was no funeral, but this may have been in accordance with his own wishes. There is no memorial to him. I hope this can be changed.

Finally, one small nota bene: Creighton Horton II, during one of our conversations, observed that the name "Mead", in relation to his grandfather, is consistently misspelled, with an "e" at the end.

Letterhead from Mead Horton's company and his business cards are spelled "Mead". A copy of this letterhead with Chelta Horton's hand-writing contained in *Scrapbook I* bears this out, as does a company notebook in which she wrote down recipes.[2] All are spelled "Mead". However, in all the references to their younger son, named Meade Howard Horton, Jr., the name "Meade" is spelled with an "e" - high school diploma, Coast Guard records, UCLA diploma. Known to his family as Howard, Robert Horton used the name Robert Howard Horton officially and ignored the name Meade from the mid-Forties on. He disliked it intensely.[3] Robert Howard Horton is the name on his marriage certificate to Marilynn Bradley, and it is the name on the burial records of the Hollywood Forever Cemetery.

# PREFACE

During the years I have worked on this book, I have been asked, "Who are you writing about?" over and over again. I reached a point where all I did by way of response was to show the asker the picture of Robert Horton I have on my phone. Without exception, the reaction was a sharp intake of breath, followed by a look of recognition or of wonder, or both.

Robert Horton's story is fascinating and intriguing. It seemed he almost came from nowhere, blazed an iconic trail in *Wagon Train*, and then faded, inexplicably, from the entertainment scene. The truth is far more intricate, detailed and absorbing.

Like millions of other young girls and women, as well as boys, I fell in love with Flint McCullough when, at the age of thirteen, I saw him on our family's flickering black and white television screen. He affected me in a way which no-one else ever had. He made me realize that there was something unique, special and precious that went on between a man and a woman. I grew up, met my own loves, lived my own life. I forgot about Flint McCullough until one snowy winter's night in February 2011, when I saw his face, wreathed in his inimitable smile, gazing at me from the wide screen television on the family room wall. I fell in love all over again.

That face, and his wonderful voice, haunted me. Over forty-five years of living had gone by, yet there he was, casting his magic just as before. I knew I had to find out more about him, and so I embarked upon my quest to learn as much as I could about the man behind Flint McCullough, the man known as Robert Horton. I discovered that he was alive. That there was a website in his name, though not a functioning one. That countless people still followed his life and career and were in touch with him and remained his loyal, dedicated fans.

His story, however, seemed disjointed, somehow out of synch. What happened to him after *Wagon Train*? After I heard him sing for the first time, I found it hard to believe that the records he cut were so few. I stumbled across his Western festival appearances and discovered that even in his eighties he was handsome and full of magnetism. Then there was the story of his fabled love affair with a wife he still shared his life with and who, he proclaimed, he still cherished. Learning that he came from a Mormon background was just one more aspect to his character that demanded exploration.

Knowing he was alive I wanted very much to visit him, but for profound reasons I was unable to fulfill that wish. When I learned of his death five days after the event, I was shocked. By March 2016 I knew enough about the man to be shaken by the lack of interest in his passing. That triggered me into action. What I had thought about doing, writing about him, then became an obsession. Thus began my journey, a journey which has taken me from Pennsylvania to California, to New Mexico and Nebraska and New York. It has involved me in hundreds of hours of research, of piecing together a vast array of information, much of which came from the personal memorabilia collection of Robert Horton himself. Along the way I was introduced to many fine people who were Robert's good friends, some of whom have now become mine. Thank you, Bob. All of which has brought me to this point. I believe I understand a little better now how Robert Horton became the man he was, and why he never became the star he should have been. His huge talent was never acknowledged as it might have been and his days ended in deep sadness. Nothing can change the facts of his life, how he lived it and what ultimately happened to him. However, there are millions across the globe who still care about him and, I believe, want to know more about him. They want to know about the man who created their hero, Flint McCullough, and Robert Horton's story is, like the old saying about fact and fiction, a thousand times more interesting, riveting, fascinating and profound than that of the wagon train scout.

# PROLOGUE

"Flint McCullough," the handsome, romantic, intelligent and rugged *Wagon Train* scout who set women's pulses racing across the globe for five intense years between 1957 and 1962 was a Western character portrayed by the actor Robert Horton, a role which launched him into the stratosphere of stardom. It didn't happen overnight. Along the way, Horton met and overcame producers' and directors' lack of interest in, and respect for, his dedication to his art and his integrity as an actor. During an interview for *The Saturday Evening Post* in 1961 he said, notably,

"As it was left for me to develop the character, I naturally created a character that would be easiest for me to play." The writer of the piece went on, "In doing so, he endowed Flint with traits which he personally admires and practices - among them honesty, forthrightness, courtesy and an aversion to religious, racial and social discrimination." (*The Saturday Evening Post*, December, 1961, "Big Ego, Big Talent," by Robert Johnson).

Later, after he walked away from the role which brought him world-wide fame and adulation in order to follow the dictates of his own heart and pursue a career in musical theater, Charles Staff, a critic for an unidentified Indianapolis newspaper, wrote in July 1968 of his performance in a local theater production of *The Pajama Game*, "Robert Horton stars and one can only observe that it is curious he is not a bigger theatre personality than he already is. His success in New York in "110 in the Shade" and on television in "Wagon Train" is impressive but not relative to his gifts and talents. With his face, figure, voice and acting ability, he should be a matinee idol in the Broadway sense of that now probably passe term."

In December 1958, Harriet Van Horne, a syndicated columnist, wrote under various headlines, one of which appeared in the *New York World Telegram and Sun*, "Actor-Cowboy Reads Books Too," and went on "Astringently honest, pleasantly modest, Bob is the sort other actors call "the intellectual type." He reads, writes and thinks a lot. His range of interest is wide, his conversation informed and evocative."

These are but three of the myriad of descriptions I have come across in my quest to write Robert Horton's biography. It has been a singular quest, an endless attempt to get to the truth of his life, to find out what made the man tick, what molded his character - and why. Those traits specified in these three quotes speak volumes as to who Robert Horton truly was. Many years have passed since he was born. There were few contemporaries to consult, and his remaining family members were too young to know the facts of their famous relative's childhood and youth, or his nascent career in movies. However, the handful of true friends yet alive spoke of Bob in the same terms and confirmed much of what was written about him contemporaneously.

The loss to the entertainment world upon his death was and is significant. He was a blazing talent, endowed with incredible looks, a mercurial personality, a deep and resonant baritone voice, and an ability to convey all the feelings of the human experience with delicacy, subtlety and strength. He was the product of a family which at best might be described as indifferent to him. Because he was the man he was, there has been a great deal of "reading between the lines" to assess him, to reach conclusions about him. He was the victim of ill-timing, some of it his own, much of it out of his control. Even his birth might be seen as ill-timed. Was he ill-fated? Perhaps. In his own words, at some time later in life, he said, "Life has been one long party." In some ways maybe it was, but there are undeniably dark aspects to that life which run like deep black threads through a brilliantly colored tapestry.

There is no doubt that everything that molded him, everything that lived and breathed within him came about because of his struggle with himself, and his struggle against all the influences brought to bear upon him; his family, his background, his heritage. He responded to those influences by rebelling against them. His choice of career was so alien and shocking to his large, prosperous and influential family that he became, to all intents and purposes, its "black sheep". Their disdain and disapproval goaded him into a state of rebellion.

He struggled to be his own man; he refused to be a compliant, submissive, obedient son, either to his parents, or their heritage, or the expectations they had of him.

Because there are so few people alive today who knew Robert Horton and were close to him, finding out about his life has been something of an exercise in detective work. It has had its frustrations and disappointments, as well as some triumphs, but throughout my research I have been determined to do my best to state honestly what I have learned. Robert Horton was a complicated, complex individual, but there is no doubt that he was loved by millions across the world who never met him, and those who were fortunate enough to know him and were befriended by him speak eloquently of his warmth, sincerity and honesty. I have done my best to honor a man who, despite his great talent, was nevertheless just that - a man. He had his faults, but in the end he should be remembered for all that he brought to this world - light and love and beauty of a kind which is so often, for most of us, very hard to find.

# FOREWORD
## *By Boyd Magers*

I'd casually met and talked with Robert Horton a couple of times prior to the announcement that he would be a guest at an annual Wild West Film Festival in Sonora, California, to which I'd been a regular attendee and where I had moderated several celebrity panel discussions. Then, to my surprise, a few weeks before this event, I received a phone call from one of the festival organizers who told me, "We had assigned someone to introduce Mr. Horton at the banquet but when we told Mr. Horton, he abruptly and firmly stated, 'Who? Why don't you get someone who knows me and something about my career? Get Boyd Magers!'" Of course, I was honored to introduce Bob at the event, even to having a little fun in asking him to sing the theme to "A Man Called Shenandoah". He laughed it off, but did manage a line or two. The festival solidified our friendship which lasted for many visits in his beautiful home in Encino (one of only a few built by Western actor George Montgomery – now sadly torn down), and fun dinners along Ventura Boulevard. I also brought Bob to several Western Film Festivals back East where he enjoyed seeing old friends from the film industry and greeting fans. Over the years he shared with me many stories of his days on "Wagon Train" and "A Man Called Shenandoah" which I included in some of the books I've written. Perhaps a bit of a man unto himself, he was always gracious, amiable and lovingly engaging with my wife, Donna. Robert Horton leaves a void in ours and many others' lives. But I'm certain Aileen's amazingly diligent research into his life will help readers fill a bit of that void.

# PART I BOYHOOD
## Chapter 1

*My Ancestors Came West with Brigham Young*

It is indisputable that Robert Horton, or more properly, Meade Howard Horton, Jr. was born on July 29, 1924, at 12:07 pm in the maternity wing of the Good Samaritan Hospital in Los Angeles, California.[1] Much of the rest of his life has been subject to conjecture. Unraveling it has involved a great deal of painstaking research and some intriguing guesswork which has produced a considerable amount of reliable information, some fascinating insights and quite a few unanswered questions. What has been revealed is a life of complexity – triumph over adversity, immense achievement and a slide into obscurity, ending in deep, dark sadness.

Robert Horton gained enormous fame in his mid-thirties playing the role of wagon train scout Flint McCullough on the NBC hit television series *Wagon Train* which first aired in September 1957. Adored by millions of women across four continents, there was a time when he received over two thousand letters a month from his smitten fans and was written about endlessly in countless movie and television magazines. He was a favorite of Alfred Hitchcock's, being featured in more roles in the famous director's television series *Alfred Hitchcock Presents* than any other actor, and in the midst of this period, in 1960, he performed for the Queen of England at her command. Then, determined not to be typecast, he quit the role which had brought him such huge adulation and went on to a successful career in musical theater and nightclub venues for another twenty years. These momentous achievements were hard won. To appreciate how hard won, it is necessary to understand Robert Horton's background, how he was shaped by pressures and influences over which he had no control as a child and young man. It began with the Mormon family into which he was born and the heritage from which he was descended.

Though Robert himself seldom alluded to his ancestry, except once to say that "my ancestors came West with Brigham Young,"[2] he was, in fact, descended from a leading figure in the Mormon Church through his mother's line. Both his parents were Mormons whose families had settled in and around Salt Lake City in the mid-nineteenth century, but it was the McMurrins, his mother's family, who claimed prominence in the hierarchy of The Church of Latter-day Saints, specifically Joseph William McMurrin, Robert's maternal grandfather.

In his biography of Joseph McMurrin, which formed part of his Biographical Encyclopedia of the LDS Church, Andrew Jensen described Joseph McMurrin as one of the Church's most highly respected elders. Indeed, he was elected one of the First Seven Presidents of Seventy in October 1897 (being a person of general authority and responsibility within the Church as a whole), a position he held until his death in Los Angeles in 1932 where he had been sent around the turn of the century to help establish the Church there. Like most male Mormons he undertook missionary work in his teens, and though he lacked a formal education he learned many skills as a youth which he employed throughout his missions. He married Mary Ellen Hunter in April 1880 and together they had seven children. Their first daughter and fourth child was born in Cheltenham, England in 1888 during Joseph's second missionary term abroad. They named her Chelta, after the town, and it was she who became the mother of Robert Horton.[3] Joseph and Mary Ellen were known to the rest of the family as Papa and Mama Mac and were very much loved and revered by all. According to their great-granddaughter, Joan Evans, Robert had a great affection for both these grandparents, especially for his grandmother, Mama Mac.

Two stories about his famous grandfather would have fitted right in to any *Wagon Train* script. One, related in the Biographical Encyclopedia, described how Joseph McMurrin was shot by a U.S. Deputy Marshal in Salt Lake City in 1881, during a skirmish when the law was bent on finding and imprisoning Mormons for their practice of plural marriage. He survived.[4] The second story was related by his great-granddaughter, Joan, and concerned her grandmother, Chelta.

Around the time Chelta was twelve, and living on a ranch in Utah with her family, a band of Indians, probably Shoshone, approached the house while she was outside with her father. She wore trousers and her long auburn hair was loose. On spotting the Indians some distance away, Joseph McMurrin told Chelta to get a hat and pile her hair into it. The Indians approached, parleyed for a time, then one of them, pointing at Chelta asked, "That a girl?"

McMurrin politely but firmly replied, "No." Eventually the Indians rode off. Chelta asked her father why he had done and said what he had. Her father answered, "Because, if they knew you were a girl they might have taken you, and I could have done nothing about it!"

Despite growing up on a ranch in Utah, Chelta McMurrin was very aware of her ancestry and the social standing which went with it. Joan Evans described her grandmother as "very proper," "formal," and often "cold". Photographs of Chelta portray a handsome, stately, well-dressed woman and there is a distinct impression conveyed of her confidence in her position in society. Her second son Robert called her a "perfectionist," but not necessarily in a positive way. Perfectionism, he said, had its down side. This reference to his mother, in an article entitled "What Women Have Done For Me" *(Silver Screen, October 1959)* is telling. "Everything she did had to be right, perfect." He went on to credit her with his own desire to be perfect, a perfectionist in his chosen profession. "But being a perfectionist makes life difficult. Miserable sometimes." It is easy to understand that life with this perfectionist certainly was difficult and miserable sometimes, especially for a boy whose character was so different from hers.

The Hortons, on the other hand, had no such pedigree. Elijah Hortin, born in 1850 in Leamington, in Warwickshire, England, at some time emigrated to America and found his way to Utah. Somewhere along the line, "Hortin" became "Horton". He married Christobel Frazier, probably around 1873, for a daughter was born in 1874. This was the first of eight children born between 1874 and 1890. The second last, a son, was born in 1888 and named Mead Howard Horton.[5] The birth of their eighth child, a girl, in 1890, took the life of Christobel, and it fell to his older sister, Emma, then fourteen years old, to raise young Mead. The baby girl, Lilian, Elijah's eighth child, died a few months after her arrival into the world and in despair at the loss of his wife and last child, Elijah took to drink and died in 1915.[6]

This was the year that Mead Horton married Chelta McMurrin, on September 1.[7] They were both twenty-seven, old enough for a man to marry, but certainly rather old for a woman in those days. In fact, Chelta was almost seven months older than her husband. According to Joan Evans, Mead Horton was a "self-made man," and as a youth may have worked in the same mines in which his future father-in-law once toiled. She also spoke of his driving a stagecoach between Oakley and Park City, developing a love of horses which remained with him throughout his life. He was almost engaged to another young lady when he first set eyes on Chelta. He determined he wanted her, ended his engagement and successfully wooed Chelta. This represented a step up the social ladder for the stagecoach driver of humble origins. He embarked on a career in insurance after attending business school.[8] He was a determined type and ultimately developed a highly successful career in the industry. Their first child, a boy, was born in Salt Lake City in 1918, on September 11. It is interesting to note that, despite the large families on both the McMurrin and Horton sides of the family, Creighton Clark Horton, as they named their son, was not born until ten days following their third wedding anniversary.

Whatever the reason behind this, Creighton became the apple of his parents' eyes, a beautiful child, an obedient child. A child who did everything asked of him, and did it to perfection. At some time following his birth, the Hortons moved to Los Angeles where Mead went to work for New York Life, and established himself in offices located on Wilshire Boulevard. By the time their second child arrived on the scene, the Horton family occupied a very grand home on South Kingsley Drive not far from the affluent Hancock section of Los Angeles.[9] Glamorous in its own right, the mid-Wilshire district was home to the Ambassador Hotel which hosted the Academy Awards in 1930, 1931, 1932 and 1934 during the height of the district's association with Hollywood. It is not surprising, therefore, that the family was well aware of Hollywood's

*333 South Kingsley Drive, undated. Courtesy of the Horton family.*

influence even if it was an influence of which they disapproved. Mead Horton, however, was not above taking clients from the ranks of the Hollywood elite and numbered several iconic actors such as Harold Lloyd and Clark Gable in his portfolio.[10]

An elegant, palatial edifice, 333 South Kingsley Drive was situated on raised ground overlooking the road. Three graded flights of steps led up to a spacious arched porch-way which shaded the ground floor and the large main entrance. A wrap-around balcony encircled the entire second story, and ivy climbed up one side, covering a tall chimney. Trees gave privacy in the back, and the clipped lawn swept down in tiers to the sidewalk. This was home to the Hortons throughout their lives until it succumbed to developers' bulldozers after Mead Horton's death in 1972. It was the place that baby Meade Howard Horton, Jr., (named after his father at his mother's behest, although the name "Mead" was changed to "Meade" for their second son) was brought home to and where he was immediately consigned to the care of the live-in maid, a black widow woman named Mary Augustine.[11] There is no definitive explanation for the newborn being handed over to Mary Augustine. At this point Robert Horton's brother was six years older than him and his parents were both aged thirty-six, almost middle-aged in the Roaring Twenties. These ages and time spans matter, as does the act of relinquishing the infant almost totally into the care of a servant. They established a gulf between the little boy and his brother and parents from the very beginning.

# Chapter 2

## *That Strange Egg*

Why Chelta Horton had so little interest in her second son is difficult to understand, for he had her auburn hair, as well as her build and bone structure. Perhaps he represented other things which kept her from falling in love with him. Her younger granddaughter Joan, speaking of the wide differences between her father Creighton and her uncle, observed that pregnancy was not something her grandmother enjoyed. All of its side effects upset her, particularly the loss of her luxuriant hair.[1] Given the time lapse between the two births, it is possible that the second baby was unplanned, and his arrival resented. By the time he was born, his brother Creighton was thoroughly established in the hearts and minds of his parents. It seems he did not disturb the even tenor, order and tranquility of the comfortable household. A new baby certainly would, and he did.

Described by a family friend as "a strange egg they (the Hortons) had hatched,"[2] Meade Howard Horton, Jr. was known to the family as Howard, or Howie, though his brother nicknamed him "Babe" in his early years. Nicknames were a thing within the Horton family, according to Joan. A strange egg Howard may have been to his parents, but "Babe" was, in fact, a beautiful little boy, judging by early photographs of him. One in particular was taken when he was about fourteen months old. His thick, silky hair lies neatly about his well-shaped head, his eyes are large and dark, his mouth a perfect cupid's bow, the chin below so daintily curved it is hard to imagine it as the fine square jaw which would one day set millions of female hearts fluttering across the globe. These were the features of an angelic looking little boy who stared steadfastly at the camera, one dimpled knee revealed below his romper suit, one dimpled fist curled  beside a book.

Angelic, however, he most certainly was not. This "strange egg" was an individual, as different from anyone in the family into which he had been hatched as it was possible to be. His brother Creighton

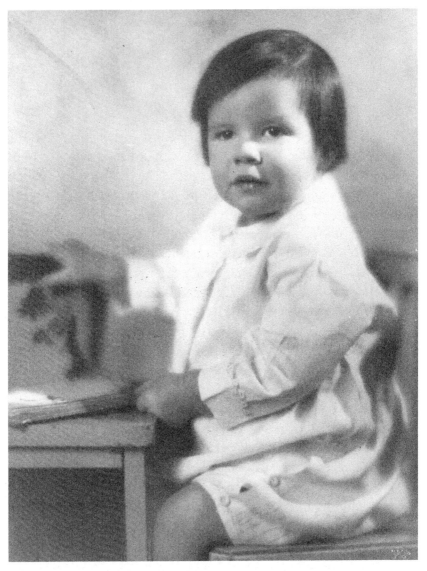

*Bob aged about fourteen months. Author's collection.*

no doubt felt the intrusion of his sibling, regardless of whether or not he felt usurped. In fact, his little brother never displaced Creighton from his position as the favored child, the perfect example of a perfect son. The two boys locked horns from the start. Oil and water, chalk and cheese, the differences between them were radical. Creighton was obedient, pliant, submissive. Howard, or "Robert" as he subsequently named himself, was a rebel, the complete antithesis of his brother. His thick red hair contrasted with the light brown shade of his brother's, his freckled skin contrasted with Creighton's clear complexion, but it was his personality which truly set him apart. As he grew up he determinedly followed his own path, despite at times wishing he could be more like his well-behaved brother. Wishing did not make it so, and there is no evidence to show that he ever made any kind of effort to comply with the dictates of his family. It is evident, however, that Robert's parents' relationship with their younger son was uneasy from the very beginning. Chelta, his mother, was particularly stiff and formal, and lacked, it seems, a natural maternal instinct. Handing a newborn infant into the care of a household maid is astonishing, and perhaps illustrates Chelta's lack of association with the role of motherhood and her second child. His father Mead Horton was, it seems, the quintessential male figurehead in this Mormon family. He held the reins, he drove the household. His age, his work responsibilities and possibly his incipient diabetes precluded him from close involvement with his sons.[3] Since Robert's brother was always a well-behaved child his relationship with his father was an easy, positive one. Robert was altogether different, and even as a toddler he often crossed his father as he determinedly sought to be himself.

Throughout his childhood, teenage years, young adulthood and manhood, there are repeated examples of his parents' inability to understand and relate to their second son which he himself refers to in numerous articles published at the height of his fame. There are a number of significant situations which spoke of a mystifying disregard his parents had for him. In addition, there are few, if any stories of "fun times" together as a family, no anecdotes of good times shared, and oddly, only a very few photographs have come to light from those early days. What is clear is that the auburn-haired, freckle-faced Robert never fitted in to his family's formal environment and that his parents maintained a distant attitude toward him as a child.[4]

The true guiding force in Robert's life from the time he was born until he was almost fourteen was Mary Augustine. It is not an exaggeration to say that she raised him from an infant to a young boy of thirteen, and as a man in his eighties, contemplating the business of writing his autobiography, and in answer to the question posed by his then putative collaborator Theodora "Toby" Wolfe, "How influential was Mary in your life?" he said that Mary was practically one hundred percent responsible for his care until the time she retired from the Horton household.[5]

In fact, Mary was Robert's whole life as he grew from a toddler to a little boy and finally to a teenager. She loved the child and he loved her, unconditionally. Mary herself referred to him as "her boy" and for all intents and purposes, he was. As a baby she fed him, dressed him and took care of him. As a toddler, she took him shopping and it was she who escorted him to his first school, Cahuenga Grammar School on South Hobart Boulevard, a few blocks from the Horton home on South Kingsley Drive. They had fun together, sang songs together and it was Mary who chastised him, when necessary, from threatening him with bogeymen, to spanking him. There were pats on the head, too, and much love from Mary, and it was Mary who met his emotional needs in a way which seemed to elude his parents.[6]

Mary Augustine's own story of raising Robert Horton came to the forefront of public knowledge as a result of her appearance on the legendary program, *This Is Your Life*, dedicated to Robert, recorded by NBC on Wednesday, January 18 and aired on Sunday, January 22, 1961. When Mary Augustine came on stage, Robert greeted her with such unalloyed joy, lifting her up, hugging her, whirling her about and setting her back on her feet that no-one who saw it could mistake the love which passed between them. Minutes before he had greeted his mother with a formal kiss and the words "You look magnificent," while his father got a handshake. The viewing public demanded to know more about the little black lady with a halo of white hair who meant so much to their hero. They had to wait for the August 1961 edition of *TV Movie Screen*, and an article entitled "Let Me Tell You About My Boy" written by Alice L. Tildesley, following an interview she conducted with Robert and Mary at the rest home where Mary lived at the time. This article, a lengthy one, enlarged on many of the references made within the television show and emphasized the closeness of the relationship between Mary and Robert. She encouraged his love of animals, aiding and abetting him in acquiring a string of stray cats and at least one stray dog. They were so close that when Mary left for her two days off each week, he wept so inconsolably at parting from her that, in the end, she took him with her on a regular basis. With her, amidst her surroundings, he was exposed to a different way of life, to different social mores, to different people. Robert credited this experience with fashioning his own tolerant and liberal views of society. Their interaction, and her love for him developed in him a deep affection for her and an understanding and appreciation for tolerance of race, upbringing and social standing which stayed with him throughout his life. Sadly, his family had other views, and this was yet another battleground upon which their differences were fought out.[7]

So-called life stories written about Robert Horton at the height of his career all play up his early childhood as being one of rebellion, accident, and illness. Rebellion, indeed, became something of a watchword for him, his personality, and describing who he was. Though many of the stories written about him may contain exaggeration and hyperbole, there is a consistent strain of truth which runs through them, and there is no doubt that as a little boy he displayed behavior which puzzled his straightlaced parents and earned him their disapproval. One thing which was true, and remained true throughout his life was that, as a highly intelligent individual he was easily bored, a fact which he made clear to Toby Wolfe, in their discussions regarding his memoirs. He described his life in that staid Mormon household as stultifying. Much has been made of the accidents he suffered as a little boy, and it is easy to suppose that he got into trouble because he sought stimulation. He admitted to having a relentless urge to "see what was round the corner," to refusing to do as he was told, to talking back to those in authority. In one of the many life stories written about him he said that he "ran away" as a toddler, making off on his tricycle, escaping from the confines and constraints of life at home.[8] He fought with his brother Creighton, who had his own circle of friends and no doubt found having his little brother tagging around after him tiresome. Some episodes illustrate the situation aptly. Robert related one such incident. Aged about three, he "clobbered" his brother's best friend with a roller skate. Why? He does not say, he simply says he did it and he must have inflicted enough damage to make the incident memorable.[9]

He was between three and four years old when he was knocked down by a car outside the Kingsley Drive house. At the time his parents were off traveling, so the only adult at home was Mary. There are two versions to this tale, one of which came from Creighton Horton's younger daughter, Joan. That version says that Creighton had crossed South Kingsley Drive and yelled at his little brother not to follow him, but little red-headed, rebellious Robert would not be told. He dashed out into the street where he was hit and run over by a car he did not see. Mary's version says that Creighton told Robert it was safe to cross the street, but that a street car blocked the little boy's view of the road. He ventured out and under the wheels of an unseen car. He was, he said "about as high as the headlights." No doubt the driver of the car did not see the child, either. Whichever version is correct, the result was the same. Robert Horton was literally run over by the car, suffering broken ribs, severe bruising and a concussion. Knocked unconscious he lay in the street. An ambulance was summoned, but when Mary began to climb into the vehicle to go with her charge to the hospital, she was deterred by the white ambulance crew. She had none of it. He was her baby and she was going to hospital with him.

"This is no poor white trash you're dealing with," she purportedly told them. They acquiesced. Meanwhile his parents had to cut short their trip and returned to find their son in a parlous state. Mary had returned to her household duties when the Hortons arrived, but their little boy cried and begged for her to be with him. He wanted her, and only her, not his parents, not his brother, but "Dee," (his own special name for Mary). His doctors realized that having Mary with him was vital to their small patient and so she was sent for. Once she was beside him, holding his hand and reassuring him, he settled and slowly but surely began to recover.[10]

There are any number of tales of Robert Horton's youthful accidents and injuries, many cited in the copious fan magazines published in the late Fifties and early Sixties, all of them using much the same basic material and re-writing it to suit themselves, but just how many mishaps there truly were will never be known. Robert Horton was undoubtedly the original source of that basic material though it's evident that some stories have been embellished and others simply made up for effect.[11] What is documented from his youth however, is a four-inch burn scar on his left shoulder, the result of his being burned by a blazing firecracker, a one-inch scar above his right eye, in all likelihood the head injury he suffered when he was run over, a hernia operation scar, an appendectomy scar and a twelve-inch scar which circled his left back and side and was the result of a major kidney operation he underwent at the age of thirteen.[12]

None of the other apocryphal tales related in the various "life story" magazines produced in the Fifties can be verified now, but the fall from a tree in the backyard of his home at the age of five was told by Mary in the aforementioned article "Let Me Tell You About My Boy." The broken arm he suffered, a compound fracture, was certainly real and it fell to Mary Augustine to administer the physical therapy prescribed, for somehow this was beyond his mother. Much to do with raising Robert was beyond his mother. It was Mary who was primarily responsible for helping to straighten that arm over agonizing months of rehabilitation, ensuring that he grew up unscarred by the break.

Other scars which Robert Horton bore throughout his life are less obvious, but just as real and arguably much more influential. They were the kind of scars inflicted by the attitudes adopted toward him by a family whose approval and love he craved, but never got. Emotionally he was isolated, alone. He was constantly compared to Creighton, who was good at everything he did, obedient to his parents' wishes, dedicated to their faith, and who could do nothing wrong, whereas Robert, according to himself, could do nothing right.[13]

The age difference between Robert and Creighton was a problem in and of itself, but it is clear that Creighton also saw his little brother as a nuisance rather than a cohort. He must have been aware of the different attitude his parents had toward their younger son, aware of the fact that his brother was principally cared for by the household maid. Creighton attended junior high school in Los

*Portent of the future. Aged about six. Courtesy of the Horton family.*

Angeles, but when he turned fifteen, he opted to go to military boarding school in Carlsbad, California where he attended the San Diego Army and Navy Academy, so for the first time the brothers were separated. Apparently, Creighton found life at home at this time "uncomfortable".[14] By then Robert was nine and if the separation troubled him he never said so. In later years he was quite

*Family outing, Griffith Park. L to R: Mead Horton, Creighton Horton, Bob, c. 1935. Courtesy of the Horton family..*

straight-forward about his relationship with his brother. "We were not close." "We never had anything in common," he said.[15]

Having chosen to go to boarding school at fifteen, Creighton Horton's presence was therefore less intrusive to Robert, but it did not go away altogether, nor did it put a stop to Creighton being constantly held up to him as an example he should follow. That merely antagonized Robert and was sure to trigger a rebellious outburst from him.[16]

School was another place where he fell foul of authority and his fiery temper got him into trouble, especially in junior high. Mary Augustine was quite clear that as a little child he did well, was always at the top of his class, but this state of affairs did not last. Robert was intelligent and capable of excelling but if he had no interest in a subject he did not exert himself. He was, he said, an "O.K. student, fair," but "if interested, very good."[17] Like most really intelligent people, if he was bored, he simply did not bother. As he grew, Mary was no longer required to accompany him to the Cahuenga Grammar School where he was a pupil and which he attended until he was twelve. Situated on South Hobart Boulevard, it was not too far for him to travel and he undoubtedly enjoyed the independence of making his way to and from school on his own.

Robert Horton was eleven years old in 1935 when the kidney problem from which he would suffer throughout his life first began to manifest itself. Again, various versions of its advent have been told, including a fight with Creighton during which the older boy shoved his little brother into the corner of a table in the house.[18] There is a version of how he was painfully incapacitated at the outset of a much-anticipated family trip to Boulder Dam. However it came about, he was severely affected, suffering acute pain and fevers brought on by infection. The problem, ultimately diagnosed as hydronephrosis was, in fact, congenital and affected his left kidney. The fight with his brother, therefore, may have exacerbated the condition. Whatever brought it on, and in order to avoid surgery, he underwent regular treatments known as cystoscopy to relieve fluid build-up and deter any infections. For a boy teetering on the brink of puberty, the treatments were embarrassing and painful and while they alleviated the condition they did not cure it. Astonishingly, he was left to face these sessions alone. Neither of his parents accompanied him. Robert Horton made his solitary way to the hospital every two weeks for two years by bus, underwent the treatments and came home, alone.[19]

The onset of his kidney trouble came at a particularly difficult time. Instead of working out his excess energy as he grew, he was treated like an invalid, made to be quiet, to stay indoors, and prevented from engaging in sport or boisterous games with friends. He should have been embarking on his high school life, but instead he spent long hours confined to the house. While this may have been standard treatment for ailments such as his at the time, its effect on his outlook was negative and long-lasting. He combated it in a number of solitary ways. He had always cared for animals, and he developed a keen interest in birds during this time. This was seen as an acceptable form of entertainment for a sickly child although just how it really came about is, again, like so much of his history, open to conjecture. An aviary was built in the backyard and at one time he cared for over sixty birds of one type or another. His Coast Guard records bear out this interest. On his first military application card[20] under "Hobbies" the words "Raises tropical birds" are written, and when his Estate was liquidated seventy-two years later a number of beautifully preserved macaws were offered for sale. Model airplanes also captured his boyish imagination and he occupied a lot of time in building them. It is hard to say which came first, an interest in flight or an interest in birds and aircraft, but the fact is that when he reached his early thirties he took up flying and ultimately became a highly proficient pilot amassing hundreds of hours in the air.

As well as raising birds and building model planes, Robert Horton also sought comfort in food. As a result he became a chubby boy whose good looks were blurred by a veil of fat. Food was a quick fix; it fed his boredom, it fed his loneliness and it fed his frustration. He was bluntly honest about this when he spoke of his youth, so much so that throughout his life he waged his own personal war against excess weight in himself and others.[21]

Creighton was in the midst of graduating from high school at the time the kidney complaint first manifested itself in his younger brother. He was preparing to head off to the University of Utah when the decision was made by Robert's doctors that the only solution to his problem was surgery, and the repair of the stricture causing his ailment finally took place. The surgery was major and lasted several hours. The twelve-inch scar on his torso bore lifelong testimony to this lengthy and complicated procedure. He was thirteen.

To a degree, the operation was successful. However, after two years of being told that all would be well, the fact that Robert had to undergo it at all made him distrustful and wary of anything he was told about his condition, and about anything he was subjected to by his family and other authority figures. It was around this time that he declared he had no time for his family's religion, and he refused to join their church.[22] This was hardly surprising given all he had experienced to this point in his short life, as well as his own innate intelligence. At this incredibly vulnerable time, the only person he felt he could turn to left the Horton household. Mary Augustine retired and Robert Horton was on his own.

There is a clue as to what may have happened as a stop-gap measure when Mary Augustine retired. Robert Horton, aged thirteen years and two months, wrote to his father from the Pacific Military Academy in Culver City on October 7, 1937. With a return address stating "After Five Days Return to Cadet H. Horton, Pacific Military Academy, Culver City, Calif." the letter was addressed to Mr. M. H. Horton at the Hotel Utah in Salt Lake City. It's probable that Robert Horton's father, together with Chelta, had accompanied their elder son Creighton to settle him into his first year at the University of Utah in Salt Lake City. Robert could not be left behind, alone, at his age and his health also dictated that he be in someone's care. Perhaps his behavior dictated this as well. At all events, he was certainly a boarder there when he wrote the letter, although his attendance at this school was not listed on his Coast Guard records, so it is safe to assume that it was of short duration. The school ideals were listed as "high scholastic standards, physical development, military science and training for purposes of discipline, administration, uniformity and the development of leadership, moral character and training, responsibility of citizenship and Americanism." The annual fee for a boy to board at the Academy in 1937 was about $1,000. There is no way now to be certain about the situation, other than the letter which places Robert Horton at this school in October 1937.[23] He may have spent a year there, or more, or less, but he was certainly a pupil at John Rice Burroughs Junior High by 1939, which he attended on a normal, every-day basis.

Between his low threshold for boredom and his keen awareness of the fact that he simply did not fit in, it is quite logical that he found himself at odds with his family and his heritage. Their attitude toward him created a huge insecurity within him and all his life he struggled to gain their approval, if not their love. He must have been acutely aware of a different standard employed in his upbringing. He was closer to Mary Augustine in every way than to his parents or his brother, yet he must have wanted desperately to have the same depth of relationship with his family members.

He was seldom quoted negatively in regard to his parents, but by the same token what he did say is not imbued with overweening love. In a solid piece of writing by Beverly Linet, a long-time friend of Horton's, entitled "Secret Confessions," *TV Star Parade*, April 1959, at the end of a list of "likes" he mentions his parents. Then, in a list of "dislikes" immediately following, he cites "parents who make no effort to understand their children." This is just one example of the contradictory nature of his relationship with his parents. Throughout his life he talked about being "mis-understood," an observation which is clearly the result of personal experience. He says very little about his early childhood, or his relationship with his mother and father and the impression given is one of formality, even distance. He refrains from direct criticism, however, even in the matter of his mother's lack of interest in helping him recuperate from the multiple fracture of his arm. He excuses her on the grounds that to participate in his rehabilitation would cause her too much suffering. He says nothing in regard to her sending him off on his own to undergo the painful kidney treatments he endured for nearly two years. He did speak candidly about his relationship with his brother, and it is clear from numerous references to it that Robert Horton felt overshadowed by Creighton, and inadequate by comparison to him. He speaks of his mother's perfectionism, even allows that he inherited that trait from her, but he qualifies that by saying it made life difficult. His father comes across as rather remote, something of a disciplinarian and lacking in any ability to understand his younger son.

Referred to as "self-made" by his granddaughter Joan, Mead Horton was extremely successful as an agent for the New York Life Insurance Company, and indeed became president of the Life Underwriters Association in Los Angeles. He sold the first million-dollar policy to an actor, the great Harold Lloyd, and counted Clark Gable as one of his clients, the same man his younger son would one day be likened to at the start of his short-lived movie career.[24] So successful and valued was Mead Horton by the company that when he was diagnosed with diabetes at about age forty-five, they retired him on full pay and benefits, but he maintained his connections and remained an asset to the firm.[25] His motto in life was to be "persistent" as both his younger son and his granddaughter readily avowed. It seems he employed this trait in his pursuit of Chelta McMurrin and passed it on to both his sons, or at least, the belief in its efficacy. There is no doubt that being persistent played a major role in Robert Horton's career, but his persistence was not the result of a fond father-son relationship. Rather it was a learned response to something held up to him as an ideal to follow. Robert Horton says nothing of "family time" shared in his recollections of home life, no ball games on the lawn, and no other activities in which father and son indulged, except the occasional horse ride in Griffith Park, and that was often a time when Mead Horton chose to upbraid or chastise Robert for some misbehavior. Mead Horton's granddaughter Joan described him as "sweeter" and "more approachable" than his wife, but Robert Horton never spoke of a warm, affectionate relationship with his father. In fact, what does exist in terms of comments refer more to his father's inability to relate to him in a way that made sense to Robert, even if later, as a grown man, he was able to better understand and appreciate his father's motives. That he longed for his mother's love is inarguable and evident in a handful of letters which he wrote to her in his late teens and early twenties, but it was a love he never seemed to attain, regardless of how hard he tried. No matter what was said or printed about his life and family relationships, his childhood left much to be desired. Materially, he wanted for nothing, but it seems that there was no joy or warmth in the family.[26] It undoubtedly affected his adult behavior, but what is not so easy to determine is how he might have fared as "the strange egg" had he had the unqualified love and affection of his parents and brother from the very beginning of his life.

# Chapter 3
## All My Success Came Because I Rebelled

Robert Horton called himself a rebel, and within the Horton family he certainly was. How much of that was his genetic make-up and how much was environmentally created is anyone's guess. He was a solitary little boy, and he very quickly learned that he was not the paragon his brother was. There must have come a time when he figured out that he was different from everyone in the family he belonged to and he either had to change and conform, or else march to the beat of his own drum. He chose to do the latter. Indeed, he persisted in doing so.[1] He was always being compared unfavorably to Creighton. No two brothers, it seems, could have been more different.[2] Creighton was at ease with his home, his surroundings, his family, but there was nothing about the stuffy, conventional home which agreed with Robert's taste, and nothing about the careers of his male relatives or their sober clothing and cars which he found appealing. The more he was compared unfavorably with Creighton, the more he rebelled against the expectations his family had of him. The fact that he had a short fuse did not help him. From an early age his temper got the better of him and from an early age he absolutely refused to toe the line. How much his temperament was his own, imbued within him by his genes, and how much the result of the concussion he suffered as a four-year-old is hard to say. It is an acknowledged fact today that concussion suffered in childhood, and even later, can produce symptoms such as uncontrollable temper fits, and throughout his life, Robert Horton was known for his short fuse.[3]

His middle teenage years found him without Mary Augustine's love and support, without the stimulation of his relationship with his brother and, undoubtedly, without any meaningful interaction with his parents. Much later he spoke of "his crazy mixed up years" and the fact that he felt "picked on" at home.[4] Whether or not it was the case, it was his perception and therefore his reality. Despite recovering reasonably well from the kidney ailment, his parents insisted on his avoiding physical exertion, which meant his exclusion from sport at school where he failed to live up to the reasonable expectations his intelligence warranted.

Meanwhile he was a youth experiencing all the turbulence of adolescence. Since his parents avoided discussing the facts of life with him, he found them out for himself. Despite being overweight he was nonetheless an extremely good-looking boy and had great charm when he chose to use it. He had girlfriends, though nothing which might be labeled serious. In a few articles of the late Fifties he refers to these friendships, and there was certainly one in particular which probably got him in to some trouble. He was, it seems, seldom out of trouble, during those "crazy, mixed-up years," and by the time he was sixteen he felt that he was the object of everyone's disapproval. So much so in fact, that, with the excuse that everyone at home was picking on him, at some point during his sixteenth year he decided he had had enough. He ran away. This was no tricycle run, to see what lurked around the corner.[5] He got in his brother's car and left home. He had on him a gasoline credit card, some candy and, for company, Jay Lawyer, a friend. He was fed up with life at home and perhaps he hoped that by leaving he might actually get his family's attention. In a way he did. Exactly how long he absented himself is up for grabs. This escapade was featured, in a sanitized version, on the *This Is Your Life* program which aired on NBC in 1961, as well as in an error-ridden article published in the late Fifties,[6] but at the heart of the article are truths which coincide with the television program sufficiently to bear out the thrust of the story. Robert himself recounted to *National Enquirer* journalist Mike Tomkies in May 1959 that his life at home was always unstable. There were conflicts within his home. "When I was sixteen, I just said 'To hell with it' and ran away." He made it all the way to Salt Lake City where he had a number of relatives, and where, for a time, he found sanctuary in a building owned by his father. He gained that sanctuary by breaking in.[7] Whether he was gone for just a few days, or longer is immaterial. He left home, stayed away for a period of time and finally returned. No matter what was written in the article, or said on television, there is no doubt that he disgraced himself and brought the wrath of his parents down on his head. He was threatened with military school, where strict discipline would be imposed and, unlike his brother, such an environment was not of his choosing. Given that he was already under threat of expulsion from John Burroughs Junior High for truancy and poor grades, no doubt his parents were ready to take a course of action in an effort to control his behavior. What exactly happened on his return is not documented, though it is certain that all was not forgiven.[8]

Other things were going on in his life which no doubt contributed to the welter of trouble in which he found himself when he got home to 333 South Kingsley Drive. When he spoke of sex being taboo in his family, he also talked about his early efforts to get to the nub of the matter of "the facts of life." In an article entitled "Alone in a Honeymoon Cottage" published in the April 1960 edition of *TV and Movie Screen*, he said, "The problem of *sex[sic]* in my family was treated like it happened back in the Middle Ages." He went on, "I was twelve years old when the arrival of a close relative's baby prompted me to approach my mother at her ironing board with the inevitable question of, 'Mother, where do babies come from?' After a long pause her answer was 'They just appear.' And then added, 'I'll tell you when you're older,' just for good measure.'" He was thus dismissed.

Sometime later, when Robert was between thirteen and fourteen and when he was out on a ride with his father in Griffith Park, the topic was raised once again. Mead Horton chose a venue and an activity which would help him explain "the birds and the bees" to his teenage son. He enjoyed riding and being on horseback would do away with the need to look his son straight in the face. Robert Horton may have been fine with a short trail ride with his father. No doubt it was his father who raised the subject, but in his retelling of the incident, Robert Horton does not say who started the conversation. What he does say is that his father was so poor at handling the topic that he more or less gave him permission to drop it. It was too uncomfortable for both of them, so he spared his parents the discomfort of spelling out the facts of life to him.[9] As he grew, however, the relationship between the sexes became fundamentally important to him. Discussing his adolescence with his first putative biographer, Toby Wolfe, he said that it was through an experience with an older girl, a household servant, that he was first introduced to the "facts of life."

When Mary Augustine retired from the Horton household, Robert Horton was thirteen years old. A younger woman replaced her, named Roberta. Her surname is unknown. She is simply "Roberta". In various stories of his early life, Robert Horton mentions her possibly twice, or she is referred to twice. It is hinted that she was only about three years his senior. When he became the object of endless adulation in the late Fifties and Sixties, and the subject of endless journalism, albeit much of it suspect, he referred to a day "which changed his life". It was when, he said, he was told by a young (but "older") lady that he was attractive, that despite his pudginess "there'll come a day when you won't be able to keep the girls away from you!"[10] He certainly entertained an affection for Roberta who was still employed by the Hortons when he joined the United States Coast Guard Reserve in March 1943. In a letter written to his mother from Eureka where he was stationed and dated August 26, 1943, he signs off with,

*"Give my best to our large family and of course to Rob."*

In a second letter, written at approximately the same time, he says, *"Give my love to Rob."*[11]

Meanwhile, growing up, his escapades ranging from running away to misbehaving with the maid and playing truant from school, it is hardly surprising that when, sometime following his Salt Lake City odyssey, he absented himself again, his father did not hesitate. On this occasion it was the result of a car accident. Robert crashed his new car. Nothing and no-one was hurt but the car. Robert, however, did not go home and "fess up". Instead, unable to deal with "all that talk" he telephoned his parents, told them what had happened and stayed away for a week.[12] Where he stayed he does not say, but it's possible it was with Mary Augustine or a friend. Whatever the fallout from this episode, the fact remains that he was enrolled at the Harvard School, a military academy for boys situated on Coldwater Canyon, not too far from Kingsley Drive in May 1941, at the age of sixteen years and ten months, two months before his seventeenth birthday. It is an interesting date to enroll in a new school, and all the more so because it was not the result of a family move. Robert himself said "It's a long story," when asked by his first biographer why he had been enrolled at Harvard School.[13] It was undoubtedly the result of disciplinary measures. A letter written to his mother on May 11, 1941, Mother's Day, seems to imply regret for something as well as assurances of his future good behavior and his deep love for his mother.

"*Dearest Mother,*" he wrote, "*The beauty of these flowers pass into insignificance when they are compared with my love for you. They are however, a small token expressing my endless love and devotion for you. They express seventeen years of love that grows greater as each day goes by. My only wish is that you will always remember this eleventh of May, 1941. For it is a day when your younger son explains that his real aim in life is to make happiness more abundant for you. I really only live for your happiness. Howard.*"

Perhaps that young boy hoped to ward off the inevitable through his letter. If so, he failed.

# PART II GROWING UP
## Chapter 4
### *The Sentinel*

Harvard School was established in 1900 as a military academy for boys by Grenville C. Emery who hailed from Boston. He wrote to Harvard University requesting permission to use its name for his school, and it was granted by the university's president, Charles W. Eliot. In 1911 the school received the endorsement of the Episcopal Church and became a non-profit organization. In 1937 it moved from its original location in Los Angeles to Coldwater Canyon in Studio City after receiving a loan from Donald Douglas of the Douglas Aviation Company.[1] Perhaps it was the military aspect of the school which attracted the attention of the Horton parents, perhaps it was its religious affiliation, perhaps it was simply its location and the fact that it was an all-boys' school, but whatever prompted its choice by them, it proved to be less of a punishment than they perhaps anticipated. Their second son seemed to thrive in its disciplined atmosphere. He joined the band and its conductor wrote in Horton's yearbook, "*To one of the best bass-drummers I've ever had*". He joined a number of the school's societies, The Harvard Club which involved debates, among other activities, and was formed the year he joined the school, and the H Club, a varsity letterman club. Best of all, and constantly referred to throughout his life as a notable achievement in it, was his selection as a member of the Harvard School football team. Despite all the admonitions and exhortations of his parents against participating, he went out for football and became left tackle on the team. He played every quarter of every game throughout the season. On graduation he was presented with a small gold charm in the shape of a football. He kept it all his life and said that it represented one of the most successful of his achievements. His pride in this is singular, and heart-warming, and throughout his life Robert Horton was a dedicated aficionado of football.[2]

Harvard School was divided into four sections: Red, Blue, White and Green. Howard Horton, red-headed Howard Horton, was put into "Red" and became known as "Red", and that is the name stamped in gold onto the front of his yearbook, *The Sentinel*, "Red" Horton. Produced in 1942, his graduation year, it is full of inscriptions from a plethora of friends, all of which are sincere, generous tributes from other boys who clearly liked "Red" a lot. *"A swell guy", "To the best of friends", "Lots of success to a super fellow and a future All American", "To A Swell Guy Who I Will Never Forget", "To one good red-haired monster and wonderful friend", "To one of the swellest fellows I have ever met at Harvard"*, and so on.[3]

In all, his time at Harvard lasted from May 1941 through June 1942, so when he graduated, he was not quite eighteen. In December 1941, the Japanese bombed Pearl Harbor and America was immediately caught up in the war which had raged in Europe since 1939. Young men like Robert Horton attending a military school were undoubtedly keen to join up although in 1942 it was "early days". However, in his yearbook are pasted a couple of notices of the deaths of some classmates, a poignant reminder of the realities these boys faced. His own comments as a member of the football team and graduating class are funny and tinged with pride. Pictures of him in his football uniform show a strong, healthy, handsome young man, and his graduation picture as a Private First Class in his dress uniform show his trim, athletic figure, squared shoulders, hands calmly folded in front of him as he smiles happily and confidently at the camera. Next to a cartoon sketch of himself on the Senior "legacy" page is printed what he wrote for *The Sentinel*. "I, Howard Horton, leave my honored position of "Best Apple Polisher" to Dick McMahan and to him also the hole I make in the right side".

How he fared academically is unknown, for sadly all the records of the boys who attended the school up until it became incorporated with Westlake Girl's Academy in 1982 were destroyed by a zealous janitor on behalf of the incumbent headmaster who was intent on creating more space when the school buildings were

*Graduation, Harvard School, June 1942.*
*Robert Horton, author's collection.*

enlarged and remodeled.[4] It's safe to presume, though, that his grades improved with his own improved self-image, a self-image which was helped tremendously when in January of 1942 he put himself on a strict diet and proceeded to lose thirty-five pounds in less than three months. He was sick of how he looked and with the football season over those extra pounds simply weighed on him. Having got himself down from the rotund 205 pounds to a fighting weight of about 170 pounds he was on his way to becoming the devastatingly handsome man who thrilled the hearts of millions, as well as those of numerous girlfriends, paramours and wives. The first photograph of him in his school dress uniform so upset him that he hid it, though not well enough that it escaped future publication.[5] The second photograph, taken upon graduation, demonstrates effectively just how successful his dieting and exercise regime was. He maintained that figure and weight for almost all his adult life.

Much of the impetus to lose those troublesome pounds in January 1942 was to be acceptable and attractive to the fair sex at a multitude of seasonal parties. He got the result he sought. In *The Sentinel* several inscriptions allude to his success with the ladies. "*To Red Wolf*", says one enigmatically, "*Be good!*" says another, "*Take it easy and try to be good*", "*Lots of luck to that silver tongued gentleman*", and "*Howard lots of luck with Sally, Mary, Helen, Pat, Virginia and all the other millions – seriously, luck to a swell friend*". On the page illustrating the Senior Dance, an annual event put on and hosted by the graduating class, is a picture of several couples on the dance floor. Easy to see, and accentuated by an arrow inked on the page, is "Red" Horton dancing with a young, attractive blond wearing a floor-length gown.[6]

He gained some self-confidence in his time at Harvard School. The teachers he asked to sign his yearbook taught him Mathematics, English, Latin and Spanish, History, Science and Music. Among his friends who signed his book was a Jewish boy who inked in the Star of David, and signed his name, and the football team's most valuable player who graduated with him. The captain of the school baseball team signed, as did the captain of the school gymnast team, as well as a member of the school choir. A member of the school color guard wrote "*To Red, one of the best guys I ever met*".

While details of his academic achievements are no longer known, he did graduate on June 12, 1942, six weeks before his eighteenth birthday. His diploma certifies that "Meade Howard Horton, Jr., has satisfactorily completed the prescribed Course of Study and is hereby granted this Diploma of Graduation". Perhaps more important and meaningful to him was the gold football charm which represented the part he played on the school's championship team.

Leaving the military school behind upon graduation, Robert Horton went straight to the University of Southern California, in Los Angeles, which he attended for one semester only. The course he undertook is listed as "general" on his Coast Guard application, and presumably was the result of family pressure to continue with his schooling. At the same time, he worked as a route supervisor for three months for Curtis Publishing, a job which paid him $24.00 a week and put him in charge of up to forty boys at a time.[7] The job ended in December, as did his attendance at USC. He applied for entry to the Coast Guard the following January, and it is tempting to think that between his dislike of the university life, and the sense of freedom brought about through earning his own pay packet, combined with parental pressures to decide on some kind of career, Robert Horton challenged authority and chose to enter the military.

Being six years older than Robert, Creighton was well ahead of him regarding his studies. Robert was twelve and struggling at John Rice Burroughs Junior High when his older brother left the military academy in Carlsbad and thirteen when Creighton went to the University of Utah for his freshman year. However, Creighton returned to Los Angeles when his first year at Utah ended and resumed his studies at UCLA as a sophomore. He gained his undergraduate degree there. He then went East to study medicine at the prestigious Jefferson Medical School in Philadelphia in 1941 but unfortunately, during his first semester there, he contracted amoebic dysentery which forced him to quit his studies and go home to recover.[8] Amoebic dysentery was then, and still is, often confused with a form of cancer. It did not, however, prevent Creighton from marrying upon his return. The young couple set up house in a basement apartment in the bride's family home, where Creighton struggled to recuperate. It must have been a desperate time for both families. Little is now known about this marriage, except that Creighton's recovery was slow and protracted and his young wife, unable to deal with the realities of his illness, finally left him after less than two years together, probably sometime in 1943.[9] There is no evidence that Creighton attempted to join up when America entered the war in December 1941. He was a full-time student at the time and when he became seriously ill he was deemed too sick and too weak to continue with his studies. At that point he was not military material, and in any case, when he was finally able to pursue his post-graduate medical studies at USC he was automatically ineligible for the draft.

Robert Horton graduated from Harvard School in June 1942. The atmosphere in the Horton household must have been tense. The favorite son, sick and unable to continue his studies, living the life of an invalid and dealing with a failing marriage while his sturdy younger brother gave up his education at USC after only one semester in 1942 and in January 1943 applied to join the service.

# Chapter 5

## *The Coast Guard*

Reading between the lines, it is evident that Robert Horton was not interested one little bit in furthering his academic studies immediately after graduating from Harvard School. He had other things on his mind. He had formed a very special friendship with one young lady who had attended a girl's school close to Harvard School, and who he had dated, along with others, while at Harvard.[1] While much of the relationship has to be subject to pure speculation, the eventual outcome, which is a matter of record, was such that it had to be serious. With his general studies at USC of no interest to him and earning the princely sum of twenty-four dollars a week with Curtis Publishing, he could easily play the role of young man about town. At eighteen he was well aware that he was extremely attractive to women, and no doubt any excuse was a good excuse to get out of the house. The girl he dated was sufficiently smitten to go along with him and his ideas.

The pressure to join up must have been compelling as well, and he is quoted as saying that he attempted to join the Army Air Corps, as well as other branches of the service, but his troublesome kidney condition worked against him. Service physicians saw the scar on his torso and turned him down until he applied to the United States Coast Guard in 1943.[2] His registrant's affidavit is dated January 13, 1943 and he underwent the medical examination in February. He lists as a physical defect his "kidney ailment," but under the examining physician's remarks are written the words "denies any disability".[3] He states that he is unmarried, unemployed and that his next of kin is his mother, Chelta Mary Horton. He signs himself Meade Howard Horton, Jr. His application for enlistment as an apprentice seaman in the Coast Guard Reserve is dated March 17, 1943. He was accepted by Local Board 230 in Los Angeles that day and was immediately given leave, unpaid, for one week, before being required to report for active duty on March 25, 1943.[4]

Exactly what happened in that week will probably never be known for certain. Whatever the truth of the matter, and according to Horton himself, he secretly entered in to "one of those war time marriages".[5] There are a number of stories in existence regarding the situation. In the first version, Joan Evans, Robert's niece, said that Horton, shortly before he went on active service, eloped to Las Vegas with the young lady, got married and returned home, where he intended to install his bride, the marriage a "fait accompli," perhaps in imitation of his brother's first marriage. He must have hoped that, having taken such an enormous step, his parents would be forced to accept the situation. They did not. His father gave him short shrift. There would be no support and there would certainly be no marriage![6] Another version of the story given was that, having married secretly, it was the couple's notion to return home, live as before, see each other on weekends, and, no doubt, announce the marriage at a time when both were of age, and perhaps, therefore force the issue so that a real wedding could take place.[7] Immediately after he went on active duty, Horton wrote to the girl and her mother from boot camp, but in the rush to make mail call he inadvertently put the wrong letters in the wrong envelopes, and was thus discovered.[8] This was the version that Robert Horton himself gave to inquisitive journalists at the height of his *Wagon Train* fame.[8] What Robert Horton felt about the outcome of this situation is unknown except that he subsequently spoke of it only in cursory terms, and he never mentioned the girl's name. In an article entitled "Don't Pin Him Down" written by Allene Case and published in the July 1960 edition of *Screen Spotlight*, he is quoted as saying, with regard to his three marriages, "The first really wasn't a marriage because immediately after the ceremony I left for military service and her mother had the marriage annulled." This quote, and a brief mention of it in the *Saturday Evening Post* article "Big Talent, Big Ego" of December 1961 are the only substantive references to his first foray into the world of matrimony. In his old-age, however, two latter-day friends of his said that he told each, independently, that the young woman's name was "Sally".[9] Indeed, in *The Sentinel* yearbook, there is that cryptic inscription from a schoolmate, *"Howard lots of luck with Sally"*. In fact, her name was Sally Heath. She is the girl in *The Sentinel* yearbook photo.

Robert Horton, then, somewhere between graduating from Harvard School in June 1942, attending the University of Southern California for a semester and applying to join the Coast Guard in January 1943, decided that he was going to marry Sally, and hatched the plan to do so in Las Vegas. He wanted someone to care for him, to come back to. It is clear that his family simply did not meet that need. He did not admit to being married when he completed the paperwork for the Coast Guard in January, but if he married Sally during his week's unpaid leave before he left for boot camp in March, he was telling the truth.

No doubt Robert Horton found life at home, after Harvard and after a semester at USC, too confining, and that by entering the service and by marrying he could escape from that influence. He lost the marriage bet, but on March 25, 1943 he made his way under orders to report to active duty at the Alameda Training Base on Coast Guard Island in the Oakland Estuary. That was boot camp, and that was where he earned the starting pay of fifty dollars per month, rather less than the $24.00 per week he earned with Curtis Publishing, and from where he undoubtedly mailed those incriminating letters. On April 8 he took out a national service life insurance policy in the amount of $10,000.00. The beneficiaries were his mother, Chelta, who was to receive the sum of $5,000.00 in the event of his death, then his father and brother in equal shares of $2,500.00 each. Thus, his marital status, such as it was, remained unknown to the Coast Guard.[10]

On April 22, 1943, he was interviewed at Alameda with a view to directing his progress with the Coast Guard. Some interesting facts came to light as a result of that interview. He lists as previous military experience time spent in the R.O.T.C. with a discharge date of 1942, which coincided with his graduation from Harvard School. He was a Private, First Class, and under "special training received" it is noted that he was in the band and commanded a platoon at Harvard Military School. Under "Service Schools Desired" with the Coast Guard he lists Seamanship School 15, and Specialist branches, though these are not specifically identified other than

*U.S. Coast Guard, 1943. Robert Horton, author's collection.*

by the letters "D" and "T". Under "Remarks" following on from his previous military experience, it is noted;

"Hobby – raises tropical birds.

This man is commanding a platoon in his company. Likes this job; would like to continue as platoon leader.

Played football. Was an average student in H.S.

Realizes he had too easy a time in school.

Was president of his English club.

Sang with popular band in H.S.

Had a lead in H.S. play."[11]

A number of letters which Robert Horton wrote to his mother during the first few months of his time in the Coast Guard paint a picture of a young man away from home for the first time in his life, dealing with homesickness, his kidney ailment and endeavoring, still, to convince his parent of his love and respect for her. While still at boot camp, he wrote to his mother on May 9, 1943, Mother's Day. On U.S. Coast Guard notepaper, at 10:00 am, he greeted her, saying,

*"Dearest Mother,*

*Happy Mother's Day Mom; I am very sorry that I can't conclude this greeting with a kiss, but I can't and so you will just have to try an[sic] realize that at this moment in my heart I am kissing you."*

He goes on,

*"In your letter to me you asked for a certain Mom's Day present and I want you to know that you will always have it. Mother darling you will always own my love and you never need to worry about my actions as they will never be anything that will cause you any anxiety or worry."*

It is easy to conclude that, in fact, his mother was worried about his actions and had said so. Perhaps she referred to his "marriage". Later in the letter he writes,

*"I am a little blue today as I think this is the longest we have ever been apart – seven weeks Thursday you know."*

He tells her that he has a 72-hour pass coming up which will have him home by midnight on Saturday. He closes with the following words,

*"Once again I say "Happy Mother's Day Mom", I love you very much and as you know, I always will. Howard."*

He went through boot camp successfully and on July 1 achieved the rank of Seaman Second Class. That was the rank he held when, on the day before his nineteenth birthday, he was assigned to the U.S. Coast Guard Cutter *Shawnee*. Built in 1922 in Oakland the *Shawnee* was accepted by the Coast Guard and commissioned on March 8, 1922. When Robert Horton joined her, she was stationed in Eureka where, in the summer of 1942, she underwent conversion and repair. The conversion included the addition of two 20mm/80 single barreled anti-aircraft cannon and four "single thrower projectors". She was just over 158 feet in length, had a beam of thirty feet, a draft of almost fourteen feet and displaced 900 tons. Her complement numbered 68. Her maximum speed was 12 knots. The *Shawnee* was a sleek little vessel with attractive lines and she patrolled as far north as the Barents Sea.[12] Robert Horton served on board her for just under two months before being forced to report sick. The rough seas irritated his kidney condition and he was in sufficient pain to seek help. In another letter to his mother dated August 26, 1943, he wrote,

*"My Dearest Mother,*

*I received your sweet letter when we came into Eureka and I did enjoy it a great deal. I was especially fond of the picture – the house looks lovely and it made me feel warm all over just looking at it.*

*We will be going out again tomorrow for a four day patrol. I certainly hope the weather is nice.*

*My kidney has been bothering me again and I believe I am going to be able to see the doctor again tomorrow. He will probably send me to San Francisco for a complete kidney study; cistoscopic[sic]treatment and all. I can't say I'm looking forward to it. . ."*

Then he writes,

*"I believe I will take in a movie tonight as I do need a little entertainment. I feel pretty good mentally although I do hope I will be able to attend seamanship school."*

Evidently he wanted to take his mind off his forthcoming appointment and he was clearly anxious that whatever came of the appointment, it would not hinder his chances to gain further experience within the service.

A third, undated letter written by Robert to his mother, but probably Monday, September 6. 1943, given where his Coast Guard records place him at the time, suggests that, despite everything, his relationship with Sally remained in place. It also makes clear that he was feeling unwell. Simply annotated "Monday 9:30" he began,

*"Dearest Mother,*

*Your welcome letter was awaiting me today when I returned from a six day patrol and I was surely glad to hear from you.*

*As you say, Mrs. Heath is exceptionally generous, but it is her nature and she enjoys giving. Why not send me a jar of jelly?"*

Evidently Mrs. Heath had presented Chelta Horton with some jars of preserves. He goes on to refer to a forthcoming visit from Sally and her family in October. He wrote,

*"As you probably know, the Heaths are planning to come up here in Oct and I am naturally counting the days. It will certainly be wonderful to see Sally – I love her and miss her so much."*

He tells his mother that he suffered pain and discomfort associated with his kidney problem while at sea.

*"I felt pretty well during the trip with the exception of Sunday and I don't feel well now. I took several aspirin Sun. but they didn't help at all and the pain finally wore off."*

He went on to reassure his mother yet again with regard to his behavior.

*"The opportunities are abundant here to meet both nice and cheap girls but I have kept a reasonable distance from both types. I have not dated at all even tho one girl, a waitress recently openly asked me to go to a dance. My vices so far are only an occasional beer so don't worry about my morals."*

There is evidence, too, in this letter which points to his emotional state engendered by the kidney situation.

*"I want to assure you that I will not come home unless authorized to do so so don't worry. I was gripped when I wrote that letter as I imagine you can understand. I am waiting now and may be transferred to the hospital at any time."*

If he was seeking help or reassurance from his mother, there is nothing to show that he got it. As for the visit from the Heath family, if it occurred there is no evidence of it. However, the existence of this letter and its content casts a different light on all the stories related to Robert Horton's first excursion into marriage. It seems that the Heaths and the Hortons were on friendly terms. Mrs. Heath made and gave preserves to Mrs. Horton. And, according to Horton's letter, she gave a watch to him, a watch which his father appropriated and which he demanded he send to him. In this same letter Robert also refers to the fact that his brother Creighton is taking Sally out.

*"I hope he and Sally will continue to go out – it makes it nice for both of them."*

A purely platonic arrangement, no doubt, as well as an indication of how the Horton parents felt about the young lady in question, Creighton being their "blue-eyed boy". It also indicates that Creighton's health was much improved, and that he was now single, and it illustrates Bob's own generous spirit in regard to sharing the girl he "loved so much" with his older brother. Exactly when his marriage was annulled is unknown, other than Robert Horton's own terse observation that "her mother had the marriage annulled" but Seaman Second Class Horton's clandestine marital status remained unknown to the Coast Guard, and reasonably unknown amongst the social community in Los Angeles to which his family, and hers, belonged. Sally was ultimately sent East. Both young people got over it, for there is no indication of any serious attempt to resume their relationship, although Robert Horton kept a picture of Sally in his den until the day he died, and, as an old man said that, in fact, he was more interested in Sally's mother than Sally. When he was discharged from the Coast Guard, that lady told him that she hoped he would not "camp on her doorstep."[13] Probably the mother was in her late thirties, and Horton was not shy when it came to friendships with older women, but it may explain why he did not pursue Sally herself in earnest, and it also gives pause for thought in regard to his need for acceptance by an older woman, specifically his mother.

The medical examination he underwent on August 27, 1943 proved unhelpful in furthering his hopes of a sea-going assignment for on September 11, 1943 he was detached from further duty on board the *Shawnee*. By September 19, 1943, he was at Loleta, California, assigned to beach patrol duties. Loleta, then Samoa, his next posting, were, and still are, remote little towns in Northern California clustered about the Humboldt Bay within a few miles of Eureka. It can only be imagined how the new duty sat with him. In October he underwent further examinations as an outpatient at the Eureka Relief Station over a period of two days. The medical certificate provided by the examining doctor is quite clear. "Apparent irritation of adhesions (scar tissue from previous operation, left kidney)." It goes on to state that the enlisted man could be passed fit for duty providing that "said duty did not involve exposure or over exertion." That was at the end of October 1943.[14]

This sequence of events is important. It shows very clearly that, through no fault of his own, Robert Horton was deprived of the opportunity to prove himself. He was assigned to further beach patrol duties and made Seaman First Class on January 18, 1944. Now stationed at Samoa, his service record shows that he maintained a good, steady 3.0 rating in proficiency, seamanship and mechanical abilities throughout his short service career, and that his conduct was consistently rated at 4.0. On September 16, 1943, between leaving the *Shawnee* and being stationed at Loleta, he is credited with achieving the "Special Qualification" of pistol sharpshooter. His kidney trouble did not clear up with the new duties at Samoa and by February, 1944 he was sufficiently unwell to be admitted to the Marine Hospital in San Francisco on Valentine's Day where he remained until March 9. All the hateful procedures which he had undergone as a child were repeated over the course of those three weeks. On his release a month's leave was recommended pending a board of survey.[15]

By this time Robert Horton must have been fairly depressed. His hopes of achieving some kind of success within the military were fading fast, but he made it clear at the time that he did not seek and did not want any kind of discharge. He speaks of enjoying the sense of independence which being in the Coast Guard brought him, of being his own man, in charge of himself. He grew up in those few months, and he resented the idea of having to give it up. Nevertheless, a month's leave had been ordered, and he had to take it. He went home to South Kingsley Drive and his family, his future uncertain and time heavy on his hands.

In a number of articles written about his life, there are several allusions to the importance of this month in his life. He had a brief encounter with the acting fraternity in Los Angeles and, otherwise at a loose end, without any real aim in life except to await the findings of the Board, he stumbled across something which intrigued him and held his attention. Real, grown-up acting.

This was anathema to his family. They had no time for the profession. Creighton Horton had been courted by Hollywood agents bowled over by his handsome features, even to the extent that these men knocked on the door at Kingsley Drive seeking his parents' consent to their requests to get him involved in the film world.[16] Creighton viewed them with utter disdain, as did his mother and father. The notion that their second son, whose looks could not possibly compare with Creighton's, would get involved in the theater or film world was definitely unacceptable, but Robert Horton declared that it was the first thing he had ever done which did not bore him.[17]

Nevertheless, he hoped for a positive outcome to the military review of his situation. In that he was to be bitterly disappointed. If indeed this exposure to the theater and acting took place within the month's enforced inactivity as he awaited the decision of the Coast Guard Medical Board, it could explain his desire to pick up the life again when the Coast Guard finally decreed him unfit for service. He had nowhere else to turn, he evidently was not interested in a university career of any kind at that time, and the pension of twenty dollars per week, for one year, which he received following his honorable discharge, allowed him to investigate an acting career without too much financial pressure.

# Chapter 6

## *The 52-20 Club*

There is something sad and fatalistic about the various papers which document his honorable discharge from the United States Coast Guard. Memos, certificates, reports, mustering-out pay chits, cancellation of life insurance are all straight forward, baldly stated, completely unemotional. One thing which is not left in any doubt whatsoever is the state of health which brought about this discharge. According to the military medical personnel, his condition was chronic, incurable and sufficiently serious to render him unfit for service. The Report of the Medical Survey dated March 9, 1944 details the diagnosis, briefly states its history, states that treatments administered were "without benefit" and states, "This trouble will persist indefinitely." Four endorsements dated through March 22 agree with the report so that on March 29 the HQ Medical Office recommended "Discharge for Physical Disability Existing Prior to Enlistment". On May 25, in a memo to DCGO, 12th Naval District, (Board of Survey) the recommendation is for "ordinary discharge under honorable conditions by reason of physical disability."

His actual discharge papers show that he rated a 3.5 overall during his tenure with the Coast Guard and that his conduct had been "Good". Whether or not he actually returned to any kind of active service after his leave was up and his date of discharge is unclear, but his Coast Guard papers show no sign that he did. On June 22, 1944 almost exactly sixteen months to the day he was called up for active duty, Robert Horton received an honorable discharge from the United States Coast Guard.[1]

Thus began an aimless period when he "bummed around," at a loss, without any purpose to his life. Almost twenty, he was a young, seemingly fit man in the midst of a world war in which he could take no part. He had been earning sixty dollars a month as a Seaman First Class, all found.[2] Now he was on a year's disability pay of twenty dollars a week, the "52-20" club, and was back in the place he had tried to escape from only a year before. He did not know what to do with himself. He loafed, went to the beach, did nothing of consequence.[3] His parents let him know of their displeasure. They wanted him to embark on a career, something steady and solid, medicine, law, the church. His father urged him to join him in the insurance business. Robert Horton recollected,

"I never understood my father. He was difficult. He wanted me to go into the insurance business, as he did. He was at me all the time. He was so disappointed that I didn't follow him into insurance."[4]

Horton, with his fiery temper, short fuse and rebellious nature no doubt told his parents just exactly what he thought about all that.

Creighton was, by now, studying medicine at USC, which did not help Robert's cause for once again his brother showed him up in the eyes of his family. Creighton's friendship with a young lady who he first met when they appeared together in a church play had blossomed into romance. Anne Richards, a Mormon girl, who could trace her ancestry back to the founding of the Church of Latter-day Saints, became his fiancée, but Creighton concentrated on his studies first, living at home and putting off thoughts of a second marriage.[5] The contrast between the studious son and his footloose brother must have been stark. There is no doubt that Robert was treated to endless sermons and exhortations to do something of a substantive nature. The "something" his family wanted for him was nothing he wanted for himself. He might have thought about returning to university, but he did not pursue it. Instead, he frittered around until he once again got caught up with the acting crowd. There is no doubt, too, that his parents and the rest of the Horton/McMurrin families disapproved. To them, in Robert's words, the stage was "the devil's playground." "My relatives refused to come and see me act."[6]

However, as he idled his time away, he also found friendships among the acting crowd he'd mingled with during his enforced leave from the Coast Guard. Among them was young Rory Calhoun (real name Francis McCown) who was under contract to 20th Century-Fox at the time. It may have been Calhoun who invited Bob to visit him while filming. Bob took him up on the offer. A photograph of Calhoun, sold out of Bob's Estate and inscribed to him was dated September 24, 1944. It read, *"To Bob, Your[sic] a swell guy, and it's a pleasure to know and have you for a friend. Your Pal, Frank McCown."*

The visit to the film set paid off because Bob landed a job as an extra in the movie *A Walk in the Sun*, which was being filmed at 20th Century-Fox's Auguro Ranch. It is interesting to note that Bob became a member of the Screen Actors Guild, under the name "Robert Horton" on October 23, 1944. [7] Filming of *A Walk in the Sun* began on October 24 of that year and wound up in January 1945.

*A Walk in the Sun* (1945) subsequently became acclaimed as one of the better war movies produced by Hollywood at the time. In fact, in 2016 it was deemed "culturally, historically, or aesthetically significant" by the U.S. Library of Congress and selected for preservation in its National Film Registry. Robert's participation in the film resulted in his being placed under contract with the David O. Selznick Studio for a period of time though it did not result in any other movie work. *A Walk in the Sun*, however, played a pivotal part in helping him on a career path, and though Robert Horton himself said his part in the movie was so brief as to pass unnoticed, it was extremely significant to him. In fact, he played scenes with both Dana Andrews and Richard Conte, the lead stars, and made an impression when he did so.[8] In Robert Horton's black loose-leaf binder, *Scrapbook IV*, recording his early career there is a photograph of a scene from the movie which includes him and there is an arrow inked in just above his head, no doubt by Bob himself. No matter how insignificant this part, for which he received no billing, the experience was enough to convince him that he had found what he wanted to do with his life. He wanted to become an actor. Having been given the part after meeting the movie's director Lewis Milestone, he vividly remembers rushing home, bursting with pride and running up the stairs to find his father and tell him the good news.

"I've got a part in a movie!" he exclaimed. His father's reaction must have stopped him in his tracks.

"That's probably the worst thing that has ever happened to you," Mead Horton said, once again firmly squashing his son's enthusiasm. It was a response that lived with Robert, was retold often by him and which surely scalded his heart, but it did not make him give up.[9] Speaking forthrightly in a March 1970 article published in the *Palm Beach Post*, he said,

"I'm from a background of professional people. My father was an insurance broker. When I indicated I was interested in the theater there were a good many upraised eyebrows in my God-fearing, Christian family." Despite those raised eyebrows, however, there can be little doubt that he found the atmosphere of the theater stimulating and exciting, and that it suited his nature in a way that other life pursuits did not.

There are numerous stories in numerous articles about just how Robert Horton decided on an acting career, and it's evident that some writers mixed and matched those stories as it suited their own convenience. However, there are two instances which come from Robert himself. The first resulted from a 1964 interview conducted by Rebecca Franklin, a New York free-lance correspondent writing for an unidentified publication. He told Franklin,

"I was walking along Sunset Boulevard one day when a man stopped me and asked me for a match. I didn't have one because I don't smoke." (It should be noted that at the time of the interview he was starring in *110 in the Shade* on Broadway. At the time of the incident he related, he was living with his parents in their Mormon home and was aged twenty-one. Both these circumstances explain the comment about smoking. Robert Horton certainly did smoke through the late Forties and throughout the Fifties until he took up serious voice lessons). The quote goes on, "He said I was a good type and should go into motion pictures. Then he told me his name, Everett Crosby (Bing's brother). He suggested I try out for a part in a play being done by an amateur company in Beverly Hills. He said they needed a red-headed boy. I got the part and liked acting so much it changed my life."

The second came about in 1998, when, as a panelist at the Memphis Film Festival, Robert Horton was asked by a member of the audience what inspired him to take up acting. He answered,

"I don't know that anything inspired me. I was with a friend one day when he was taking vocal lessons and a man came in with a very attractive red-headed woman who was considerably his junior, and he said, "We're doing a play at a little theater in Beverly Hills and we need somebody to play this woman's younger brother." And her hair was red thanks to L'Oreal or whatever cosmetic firm you want to speak of, and mine was red because that's the way they made me, and I had freckles and they thought if I could play the brother, it would lend credulity to the fact that her hair was dyed. And I got involved with this play in a little theater in Beverly Hills and at the time I had just gotten out of the service with a medical discharge and really wasn't sure what I wanted to do. I was going to go to college as soon as I – as the right semester arrived and I did this play for – we rehearsed it twelve weeks in a little theater called The Jewel Box Theater and it ran twelve weeks and I was never bored and I was always interested in what I was doing, and that made me think, I think I'm going to give this a shot!" He went on to say that if anything inspired him it was the fact that he was never bored while acting, a statement which appears repeatedly in articles covering his life throughout his career.[10] Certainly, elements of both these stories entered into the motivation behind Bob's induction into the world of acting and certainly his coloring played a fundamental part.

The Jewel Box Theater, run by a man named Bob du Roy in the 1940s and located at 856 Robertson Boulevard in Los Angeles had gained a reputation for putting on original plays which went on to bigger and better things either on Broadway or as the basis for movies. *I Give You My Husband*, a murder mystery, was one such production, which was re-staged in 1946 for a second year following its 1945 rave reviews. Catherine (Katie) Blondell, Joan Blondell's mother, had a lead part in it. Robert Horton auditioned for the part of the romantic leading lady's brother. It was a small part, and he got it, mainly due to his looks and coloring. This was the production of which Everett Crosby spoke. It opened on January 30, 1946 and got to be known as "the biggest show in town". Blondell took a fancy to Robert Horton and he said that she told him he was a "born actor".[11] Of course, he was also a very handsome, charming and engaging young man. This experience further convinced him that he had found his niche in life, for being on stage, before a live audience gave him immediate feedback, reinforcement and approval. As he said, he was never bored. There is an interesting little story attached to this event in his life, as it illustrates some of the dichotomy which existed between him and his family about his choice of career. At some point during the play's run, he felt unwell, unwell enough to stay home and miss a performance. His mother, according to him, told him off. "You go out there and be your sexy little self!" she said. Since Robert Horton told this story to two of his closest, latter-day friends, there is little reason to dispute it, although it casts a slightly different light on the "cold, proper" personality of his mother and hints, just a little, at the conflicting attitudes to which Robert Horton was subjected within his family relationships.[12]

His theatrical debut at The Jewel Box led to other opportunities. Two items carefully pasted into Robert Horton's *Red Book* of memorabilia attest to this. An article in the entertainment publication *Hollywood Nite Life* dated April 5, 1946 reports that "Bob Horton, formerly associated with the Selznick International Studios is being tested for a feature role in Sol Lesser's "The Red House," which co-stars Edward G. Robinson and Lou McCallister". Backing this up is an inter-office 20th Century-Fox memo from Delmer Daves to Jim Ryan dated October 20, 1949 which reads;

*"Dear Jim,*

*Bob Horton says he has been interviewed for a part in "CHEAPER BY THE DOZEN". I have followed this boy with interest for some time now. I made a test of him for "THE RED HOUSE" and he was excellent in it and would have played the role had it not been that Selznick made a deal for us to use some people under contract to him. Rory Calhoun played the role, did very well and thus got his start. I feel the same thing would have been true for Bob Horton had he played the role, but wisely, he completed his college education. I feel he is ripe now. Cordially, Del".*

So, though he was unsuccessful in getting the part in *The Red House* (1947), it had nothing to do with lack of talent. To be given a tryout for the legendary producer Sol Lesser was no mean feat and demonstrates Robert Horton's determination to succeed in his chosen profession. The article also demonstrates in print that he was using the name "Robert Horton" professionally.

The name change he adopted has been attributed to various sources, including David O. Selznick in an unidentified clipping in the *Burris Scrapbook*. Horton himself said that he changed his name to "Robert" to avoid embarrassing his family. It was, he said, the name of a good friend. Exactly who that friend was has not come to light. In his eighties he told his last good friend that it was suggested by someone he hired as a consultant because he hated the name Meade. "Robert," apparently, at that time within Hollywood circles, was deemed to represent success.[13] However, just how he could afford to pay a consultant in the mid-Forties is questionable. Another possible influence may have been his older brother's roommate at the Carlsbad military school. Robert Walker (not to be confused with Horton's friend of the same name whom he met at UCLA in 1948) became a supremely successful actor in the early Forties and his marriage to Jennifer Jones was the stuff of novels. Walker told Creighton Horton that he felt lucky to be rooming with "the best-looking guy in school."[14] Perhaps Walker's success in a series of movies between 1939 and 1944 persuaded Robert Horton that the name "Robert" was synonymous with success. One thing is certain; by the fall of 1944, when he joined the Screen Actors Guild, he joined as Robert Horton, he was calling himself "Robert," and despite his family's insistence on calling him "Howard," this same family who had a nickname for everyone, to his fans, to his wives, his girlfriends and most importantly, to himself, he was Robert, or Bob, for the rest of his life.

# PART III A YOUNG MAN'S FANCY
## Chapter 7
### *With Passion*

There exist few other details about this period of his life, except that it gave him some structure and an aim in life, albeit a structure and aim which clashed terribly with the aims and structures his family wished for him. He lived at home, for his 52-20 pension ran out around July of 1945. He also busied himself with night club gigs, appearing and singing with name bands at the Palladium, Avadon and Aragon ballrooms in Los Angeles.[1] Meanwhile, the exposure to the theater and film world persuaded him that he wanted to study acting, at which point the perfectionist within him kicked in. He decided to go back to university to study acting, to thoroughly learn the craft and all its aspects. This may have mollified his parents to an extent; getting a degree in acting probably engendered their disapproval.[2] Interestingly, with UCLA and Hollywood on his doorstep, he chose to apply to the University of Miami where he was duly enrolled in their theater arts school for the fall semester of 1946. Meanwhile, as he approached his twenty-second birthday that same year, he was on his way to the altar for the second time. Mary Catherine Jobe was a script reviewer or reader. Exactly how he met her is the subject of various tales, but the fact is that she lived only a couple of blocks from the Horton home. She was one year younger than Robert. Her father was a banker, so the family was well-to-do. One story says that they met when Bob had to read for a part, and if so it makes sense that it was possibly for the role in *The Red House* (1947) as reported in the April 5, 1946 edition of *Hollywood Nite Life*. Whatever the facts, once again he fell deeply in love, and because he was a young man who desperately needed the comfort of a woman's love, her physical companionship, he could not wait to marry her. According to the many stories sub-

*Bob marries Mary Jobe, June 27, 1946.*
*Courtesy of the Horton family.*

sequently printed about it, the romance was a three-month whirlwind affair leading up to marriage which certainly fits with the timing of Bob's audition. A clipping from an unidentified Los Angeles newspaper of the time, and tucked into a page of *Scrapbook II* stated,

"Plan To Wed ... Two Film Couples (applying for marriage licenses) ... Then came grinning, red-headed, freckle faced Robert Horton, 21 year old actor, with Mary Catherine Jobe, 20, an aspirant for stage honors. They plan to be married next Thursday at the Wee Kirk o' The Heather, Forest Lawn Memorial Park, and then honeymoon in Florida prior to going to New York for stage roles. She is a daughter of John H. Jobe, retired Los Angeles banker of 433 S. Harvard Blvd and Horton, also a native Angeleno, is a son of Meade*[sic]* H. Horton, former president of the Life Underwriters Association, of 333 S. Kingsley Street *[sic]*."

And so, on Thursday June 27, 1946 at the Wee Kirk o' The Heather, a non-denominational, rather secular little church modeled on a Scottish original, and favored by the entertainment industry, Mary Catherine Jobe became Mrs. Meade Howard Horton, Jr. A photograph taken in the formal drawing room at the Kingsley Drive home shows Robert standing slightly behind his bride, glowing with happiness and pride. Beside him stands his older brother, beaming. Both men are exceedingly handsome, but there is something emanating from Robert which sets him apart, elevates him, distinguishes him. His bride is lovely. Creighton, meanwhile, at twenty-eight, had yet to marry his fiancée, Anne. He did so on October 1st of that year, three months after his younger brother tied the knot for the second time in his young life.[3] Meanwhile, Robert and Mary had left for Coral Gables to set up home there, and Bob took up his course of study in theater arts at the University of Miami. There is no evidence that he and Mary made the trip from Florida to Salt Lake City to attend his brother's wedding. At all events, as a non-practicing Mormon, a man who had rejected the church and, in fact, never officially joined it, he would be denied entry to the Temple.[4] There was, therefore, no reason to disrupt a newly undertaken course of studies.

Creighton's marriage to Anne Richards took place in the magnificent Mormon cathedral in Salt Lake City as befitted his bride, a direct descendant of Dr. Willard Richards, who had been a power within the Mormon Church from its inception. It also befitted Creighton as grandson of the Church's great elder, Joseph McMurrin.[5] Much thought and planning must have gone into the occasion. The same cannot be said of Robert and Mary's marriage and much of it speaks of haste, decisions made in the heat of passion, perhaps even defiance. The brief courtship, the departure to Florida and his immediate embarkation upon several years' worth of undergraduate studies is hardly the stuff of a thoroughly thought-through enterprise. However, it is typical of the Robert Horton of the time. He was not prepared to wait until he graduated to marry Mary. The complexities of combining student life and married life did not occur to him, or if they did, he chose to ignore them. He was also eager to put some distance between himself and his family, a distance which the University of Miami effectively provided.[6]

He had to be thinking of applying to university either late in 1945 or sometime early in 1946, in order to gain admittance for the fall semester, and based on his own words, it seems that the "right" semester proved to be the fall of 1946, probably because he finally decided on the course of study he wished to follow, theater arts.[7] At any rate, over two years passed between his medical discharge from the Coast Guard and his embarkation on a university career. Mary's advent in his life did not sway his decision making. He wanted her and he wanted his studies, and he was determined to have both. He was driven by his need for love, for acceptance and approval and that drive was overpowering. Perhaps there was an underlying need to demonstrate his true independence, to get away from his family and its influence. Despite the burdens of having to earn a living as well as go to school and earn a degree, he wanted a legitimate relationship with a woman, so he married Mary only two months before embarking on his university studies. Whether or not he ran up against objections from his family is unknown, but if he did, he overcame them. Perhaps his parents thought the acquisition of a wife would calm their hot-tempered son, steady him, maybe even redirect is life into some kind of acceptable, "useful" direction. There is also the fact, repeated by Robert Horton in a number of interviews, that he was barely aware of the responsibilities and commitment involved in a marriage. In one article he refers to his perception of marriage as "a bit of a lark".[8] Mary was aware of his plans and was willing to give up her job (it could hardly be called a "career") to become his wife and travel with him to Florida. At twenty she left behind her family and all that was familiar to her to be with him. Robert said that for a time they were very happy and very much in love. They drove across country to get to Coral Gables, taking their time, honeymooning along the way. They took up residence in a small apartment on Granada Avenue, and then spent some time looking for employment before the start of school. The allusion to Mary being an aspirant for stage honors in the pre-wedding newspaper clipping was unfounded. She worked as a waitress and may have done some clothes modeling with Bob in Miami, but she had no desire at all to be before the footlights, or a movie camera. Hers was a shy and retiring personality, unlike her ebullient, dramatic husband. Bob quickly found work as a male model for Miami's Gibson's Department Store, wearing everything from sweaters to swimwear, and he sang in Miami nightclubs.[9]

His nascent career on the stage of the University of Miami, from *Streamliner* to *Golden Boy* is faithfully recorded via clippings of reviews, mostly unidentified, playbills and photographs in Robert's large brown, tooled leather scrapbook, *Scrapbook II.* It began at the end of October, when Bob, as a new member of the University of Miami Playmakers, appeared in his first production with them on October 28 and 29 in *Streamliner*, a one-act play by fellow student Barry Lipkin. It required only two actors, a man and a woman, who represent a couple who meet while traveling on board a train. Saralee Entin, also a student, was Bob's co-star. A review of his performance said, "Robert Horton was very good as Peter Drake. His voice is pleasant, he projects well, and he is undeniably handsome which lends good stage presence." *Accent on Youth* opened on December 4 and Bob had a starring role as Dickie Reynolds. A review states, "Bob Horton plays Dickie, the juvenile lead. Mr. Horton is a native of California, where, prior to his matriculation at the University of Miami he was under studio contract. He was last seen in the picturization*[sic]*of the best seller, "A Walk in the Sun." Evidence then, that Bob's prior work in Hollywood was known, even if only through a playbill profile. A second critique, dated December 13, reads:

"The last part, that of temporary husband, was played a little out of key by Robert Horton. Horton makes a fine stage appearance and seemed an excellent type for his part, but there was more of pathos than of comedy in his interpretation."

Christmas came and went and on January 22 and 23, 1947, he appeared in another one-act play written by student William Couch. *Mr. Mick Hangs a Moon* was a dud. A critic wrote,

"Bob Horton in the role of a third-rate song writer, is to be admired for bringing some life to Mr. Couch's banal lines, he projected a sustained tempo, which is even more admirable in view of the fact that he had no-one to play to."

A little over two months later he starred in the title role of *Golden Boy* which ran from April 8 through April 12, and he drew varying reviews in this story of a violin player turned boxer. One critic wrote,

"Dream Boy, Bob Horton, Gibson's versatile male model, gave a first-rate performance as lead in 'Golden Boy' at Miami University where he is a dramatics major. Six feet of red-headed dynamite headed for fame and fortune." It's interesting to note that

*As Joe Bonaparte in* Golden Boy, *April 1947. Robert Horton, author's collection.*

that description, "six feet of red-headed dynamite" followed Bob throughout his career. Another critic wrote,

"Most difficult portrayal is that of Joe Bonaparte, the "Golden Boy" who has to fight his own convictions as well as ring opponents. King size Robert Horton looks every inch the athlete and for most of the play he does a fine job. Now and then he overacts, but here's a lad with movie potentialities."

Yet another wrote, less appreciatively,

"Bob Horton as Joe Bonaparte, the "golden boy" was not convincing. He was wooden and showed animation only when he had lines or action, instead of playing up throughout. He looks good up there, but it is hard to believe that someone with Horton's physical attributes would have no social life. The ability to play a violin would just be dressing on the salad."

Photographs taken of Bob in the role of Joe Bonaparte show a slender but well-muscled youth whose face is earnest and sincere. Ten years later, posters advertising the play hung in his small Brentwood cottage. In *Scrapbook II*, which covered his college years, a telegram from his family in Los Angeles cabled to Robert Horton on April 7, with the instruction to deliver, not phone, read:

"DEAR HOWARD. WE ALL JOIN IN SENDING LOVE AND BEST WISHES FOR AN OUTSTANDING PERFORMANCE IN THE LEADING ROLE AS 'GOLDEN BOY' MAY SUCCESS AND HAPPINESS CROWN

YOU[*sic*] COURAGEOUS SINCERE EFFORTS. AS YOU APPROACH YOUR TASK IN HUMILITY AND CONFIDENCE BE ASSURED YOU HAVE OUR IMPLICIT FAITH THAT YOUR EFFORTS WILL BE ABUNDANTLY AND RICHLY REWARDED THIS END MAY GOD BLESS YOU   MOM DAD CREIGHTON ANNE EVERARD STEVE DREW AND LUCILLE"

Mother, father, brother, sister-in-law, three uncles and an aunt all came together to wish him well. The telegram comes across just a little sanctimoniously, but it does demonstrate the family's interest in Bob's efforts and their apparent affection for him. The rather enigmatic statement about efforts being rewarded "this end" does give pause for thought, however. Exactly what was meant by it is uncertain, but perhaps it refers to that very "affection," in some kind of way. Or it may simply be a misplacing of words, and the message should have read "implicit faith this end."

He did not let any grass grow under his feet. When school closed in Miami in June 1947, he returned to Los Angeles and attended summer school at UCLA. Playbills from the school demonstrate that he performed on July 23 and 24 at the Campus Theater at UCLA in a production of *Uncle Fred Flits By*, a P. G. Wodehouse play, and in *Lilacs and Ticker Tape* by O. Henry, undated. A letter written on March 8, 1948 by the Director of the Motion Picture Division at UCLA, John Ross Winnie, to the Chairman of the Yale University Drama Department substantiates his summer school attendance in 1947, as well as his interest in pursuing his studies at Yale.

Winnie wrote, "*He is an excellent student and an unusually promising actor. The chap has a serious interest in professional theater and particularly in legitimate acting. I give him the highest recommendation and know that Yale can do him a great deal of good.*"

This brief summer return to Los Angeles explains a change in address when he and Mary went back to Coral Gables in the fall. From Granada Avenue they moved to Castile Avenue and into a much smaller home. There, as a member of the Public Speaking class 155b, he appeared in *The Little Foxes* as Horace Giddens, on September 4. A couple of photographs of him in this performance are pasted into *Scrapbook II*, and there he is, young and vibrant, standing out in the group of players, a walking cane held in one hand, essaying the role of a man three times his age. Thus he began his sophomore year at the University of Miami.

Meanwhile Mary had to adjust to her husband's involvement in studies, acting and part-time jobs. There is no doubt that their life together must have been challenging. Mary had no ambition to be anything other than Robert's wife but she had to contribute to their household. Working as a waitress and keeping house was not easy, not to mention putting up with a young husband who was following his studies with his usual passionate dedication. There were no breaks from the pressure of school and it's clear that Robert Horton was dead set on graduating at the earliest possible opportunity, then going on to get a postgraduate degree. There were other things which contributed to a growing tide of unhappiness. Mary was shy, content to be at home, uninterested in the social demands of building a career in the acting profession. Robert felt it incumbent upon him to be out, to be "seen," to throw himself with energy into any and all opportunities which might result in some kind of successful exposure. In an article purportedly written by Robert Horton, though it is more likely that it was "ghost" written, and published in the May 1958 issue of *TV and Movie Screen* under the title "Why My Marriage Failed" he said, "I regard my first wife, Mary, as one of the finest girls I have ever met. She was and is a wonderful person. However, she was shy and retiring and didn't like mixing in crowds, and my career as an actor made it necessary for me to be in contact with all kinds of people. Socially we had a great deal of difficulty."

In another telling statement later in the same article, he said,

"The problems we had were far and above our abilities to cope with them. We got married and I started right off to college . . . taking a heavy course that demanded a great deal of my time and I went after my schooling, as I do most things, with a passion. Now, Mary had one wonderful quality . . . the ability to lead a quiet life in the home and at an easy pace. But in college, naturally, with the extra burden of rehearsals for a couple of school plays added to an already crowded class-and-study day, the quiet life wasn't to be. The adjustments for Mary weren't easy either. I remember her saying sometime after our separation, 'Bob, you'll never know how I felt, when I had to face the problem of cleaning our first little apartment's bathroom . . . it was almost the end of me.'"

Time passed and perhaps the happiness quotient in their relationship was sufficient to keep things on an even keel. There is no doubt that Robert Horton was not easy to live with. He was intense, impetuous, and had been starved of affection and approval all his life. Within the theater and modeling world he perhaps felt as if he got some of that positive reinforcement he craved. How that affected his relationship with Mary can only be pondered. Theirs was not a marriage upon which Robert had embarked with any real notion or concept of longevity. After the ceremony, and according to his own recollections, he observed flippantly to his young bride, "If we get through two years together we'll be doing pretty well."[10] In fact, the marriage lasted for almost seven years on paper. Nevertheless, at some point between their arrival in Coral Gables in 1946, and his award-winning appearance in the Miami University's production of Emlyn Williams' *Night Must Fall* in April 1948, something changed. This time the "good luck" telegram pasted into *Scrapbook II* from the Hortons in Los Angeles has an altogether different tone. Sent significantly to Howard Horton at the Castile Avenue address on April 15 it reads,

"DEAR HOWARD WISHING YOU GOOD LUCK GOOD SUPPORT GOOD PERFORMANCE MOM AND DAD."

What happened? No-one now knows, but perhaps, a few months shy of their second anniversary, either Mary or Robert decided that their marriage had no future. Perhaps Mary came to realize that she could not adequately handle her young husband. Perhaps Robert discovered that having a shy, retiring wife did not help him with his career aspirations. In a number of articles written about Robert in the late Fifties, there is reference to their separation "around the two-year mark". In an article published in 1959 in an ad hoc magazine bearing the title *Hollywood Life Stories* under the headline "Robert Horton – Little Devil," "quarrels and separations – reconciliations and more quarrels" are cited. That might explain the frosty nature of the April 15 telegram from Mom and Dad Horton. Possibly Mary let her family know of her unhappiness with the life she was leading. Once again, in the eyes of the Hortons, their red-headed son had let them and the family down. He did not, however, let himself or his audiences down. Sharing the lead role of "Danny" in *Night Must Fall*, he nevertheless came away with an award for his outstanding performance in the play. Staged by the University of Miami Players in the school's revolutionary Ring Theater, it drew critical acclaim, and Robert Horton's depiction stood out. In a preview of the play, an article headlines "Two Actors Share Role of Imaginative Murderer," and goes on, "According to drama department head Fred Koch, Jr., 'We feel an obligation to the paying students as well as the paying audience. Therefore, when two talented students appeared equally competent to play this coveted role, it seemed only fair to give them both the opportunity to perform." Horton and Rosner *(the alternative lead player)* are not strangers to theaterites*[sic]*of the University. Both are students here. About a year ago Bob Horton was in "Accent on Youth" (Ring Theater) and "Golden Boy" (Box Theater). Before coming to the University, Horton was under contract in Hollywood, Calif. and appeared in "Walk In The Sun".

In *Scrapbook II*, after several large black and white photographs of Bob in *Night Must Fall*, as well as newspaper clippings, advertisements of the production and some reviews, there is a photograph of Fred Koch, Jr., in shirt sleeves, cigarette in hand, looking up at a poster promoting, among other plays, *Night Must Fall*. Written in a bold hand at the bottom of the picture are the words,

"All best wishes for a rich theater adventure Bob. May your night never fall till the last great curtain. Fred Koch, Jr."

The play ran from April 14 through May 15, 1948. One critic wrote, not very enthusiastically,

"Robert Horton, A Sophomore Drama major from Los Angeles, appeared here last year in the title role of 'Golden Boy' and in 'Accent on Youth'. He is a member of Theta Alpha Phi, a national dramatic honorary society."

The *Miami Hurricane* critic of the day, Chuck deBEDTS, however, wrote on April 23,

"Mr. Horton, when I saw him, was stronger in the early... and in the final scenes. They both have plenty of charm, yet watching Mr.

Horton, I felt that here was a man of the world bellboy – here was charm. Here was justification for the line snapped by Olivia at him '. . .not half so bad as men who think they have charm'. Oh, one quick afterthought on a positive comparison between Mr. H. and Mr. R – Horton definitely sings better."

Finally, in a later, follow-up article, Chuck deBEDTS wrote more specifically,

"The other big job is by Mr. Horton as Danny, the psychopathic bellboy. Mr. Williams' play is actually built around the development of Danny's character. It is Danny's show. And it is perhaps a clue to the relative merits of Mr. Horton and Mr. Rosner (who shared the lead with Mr. Horton running on alternate weeks) that when Mr. Rosner is working one feels that he is good, but that it is definitely Miss Bailey's show. When Horton is on stage, though, it is every-one's show."

An eyewitness account of Bob's performance in *Night Must Fall* comes from an unexpected quarter, but it meant enough to him to preserve it in his *Red Book* scrapbook. Pasted in the early part of the book is a hand-written letter sent to his brother Creighton. Dated April 15, 1948, it reads in part,

*"Dear Crayt –*

*I just saw your kid brother in "Night Must Fall" at the local Ring Theatre and I thought you'd like to know what I think of him.*

*Well, he's got it. The only thing that will stop him is impatience to get there in a hurry. Your brother is a stand-out and he combines his natural gifts with hard work. He has intensity, devotion and that intangible something – the magic X of the artistic personality which so often spells the difference between success and failure."*

The letter is signed "Jerry," or possibly "Terry." It's interesting that Creighton gave the letter to Robert, but its contents must surely have encouraged him and it must have been meaningful to him that Jerry wrote in such glowing terms to his older brother. Robert Horton received an award for his performance, a small, elegant silver bowl engraved with the words "Outstanding Performance, ROBERT HORTON, "DANNY", NIGHT MUST FALL, UNIVERSITY OF MIAMI, 1948". He kept the bowl throughout his life. It is now in the author's possession.

*As Danny in* Night Must Fall, *April – May 1948. Robert Horton, author's collection.*

By the end of the play's run, it was the middle of May 1948, and closing in on the end of the school year, only a month or so off the young Hortons' second anniversary. There are a few clues as to what happened next. Contained in *Scrapbook II* a number of playbills and programs bear witness to the fact that Robert Horton appeared in several Summer Campus Theater productions at UCLA, beginning with *Footprints on the Ceiling* which played at Royce Hall 170 from June 28 through July 3. His appearance in the first play took place one day after that second anniversary. Horton's part was that of a dancer. Shortly after this he played "Al" in *Three Men and a Horse* in the Royce Hall Auditorium on July 14, 15 and 16. There are several other productions by the Summer Campus Theater in which he appeared, so he was home in Los Angeles in the summer of 1948. According to Robert Horton himself, he worked hard to get through school as quickly as possible, so he was once again enrolled in summer school at UCLA and by the time he appeared as the lead in *Thunder Rock* with Campus Theatre 170 (undated in the program) he was definitely enrolled as a full time undergraduate with UCLA.

A number of reasons are cited in more unreliable articles as to why he left the University of Miami and returned home to Los Angeles. As a private school, the University of Miami was expensive, and if his parents were footing the bill, pressure may have been brought to bear to make the young couple return to Los Angeles. There are references to his using the G.I. Bill to cover his living and tuition fees. Later in his life he claimed that he had always intended to graduate from UCLA and that, furthermore, UCLA was more of a challenge due to the much larger numbers of students attending its theater arts school.[11] These reasons are characteristic of Robert Horton, but it should be remembered that his foundering marriage also had a role to play. A return to Los Angeles would reunite Mary with her family. As for Robert Horton, he returned, but not, initially, to his family. His first putative biographer, Toby Wolfe, says that at first, as he took up studies at UCLA, he slept in his car.[12]

Whether or not Robert Horton exaggerated this state of affairs for effect is hard to say. However, at some time he did return to live at Kingsley Drive. Mary's home was a mere two blocks away. This arrangement would make sense if they separated for a period of time. There were a number of separations during the length of their marriage, but it is also possible that the couple returned to Los Angeles and took up residence in an apartment. Whatever the situation, Robert Horton had a heavy load of study again, as well as a very busy schedule in terms of stage work. UCLA may have been a less expensive school than the University of Miami, and it is more than likely that his parents contributed to that tuition bill, augmenting the G.I. funds, but he was no stranger to hard work, to picking up odd jobs to earn money, and there is no reason to believe that being back on home territory changed that. Two other credits which are documented in *Scrapbook II* are from his junior year at UCLA. *Twelfth Night* played at the Campus Theater 170 from November 28 through December 11, 1948, in which Bob played "Antonio," and the following spring he starred as "Yank" in *The Hasty Heart* from March 20 through April 2, 1949. On behalf of the UCLA *Daily Bruin*, critic Don Fanger wrote on March 23, 1949, "Robert Horton, the 'Yank' from Georgia slipped out of character several times, swapping the Southern drawl for a broad New York 'a' once, but strangely enough, the drawl was not missed and the characterization lost none of its strength." In what looks like a class critique an unidentified reviewer wrote, "Performances were generally excellent . . . Bob Horton stood out. Horton produced a fine and strong characterization of his Southern "Yank"." Further evidence of his involvement is a critique of a first reading of a new musical play entitled, *Clown*. Undated, it reflects students' observations of the first reading by the designated actors, but there is no direct reference to Horton.

Every indication, every piece of information still extant from those college days prove that he worked hard at his studies, he was dedicated and diligent and bent on success, even if his personal life was not so exemplary. He formed friendships and relationships, one in particular with a young woman named Betty Ebeling. Betty grew up in Washington State, the child of a larger-than-life father and a dysfunctional mother. The parents separated, and Mr. Ebeling became a used car salesman in Los Angeles. Betty, as an innocent teenager, all of sixteen years of age, traveled to California in June of 1945. In fact, she had run away to join her father. She found herself in the care of his live-in mistress, before ultimately taking up acting studies while she shared a dingy apartment with another young woman. Betty, who subsequently became the wife of Lee Marvin, wrote her own memoirs in a delightful book entitled *Tales of a Hollywood Housewife* published in 2011. Her first serious boyfriend during the early years of her adventure in Hollywood was Robert Horton. They met while they studied together at UCLA in 1948. Betty was one of the students who critiqued his reading for *Clown* which may explain its appearance in *Scrapbook II*.

In an interview he gave to Dwayne Epstein, Lee Marvin's biographer (*Point Blank*) on July 8, 1995, Bob spoke genuinely and warmly of Betty and his friendship with her. Referring to his friendship with Lee Marvin and why that lasted he said,

"Part of it was my affection for Betty, who I'm very fond of. I hold her in very high regard." He went on, "She is a very nice woman. When we were dating, I was very fond of her. That affection has never gone away . . .We started out as friends. As a matter of fact, the first time I went out with her, I really wanted to go out with her roommate. Her name was Beverly Dixon . . .I went over to see Beverly and she had this date . . .She was living with Betty. Betty and I had one evening that was the perfect date. Absolutely perfect date. I never would say that Betty was a particularly pretty woman but she's an attractive woman. That night she was pretty. We went to dinner and then, we drove out to the beach. Then we drove back to the apartment and she changed her clothes and I changed mine. We drove down to Newport Beach and we didn't come home until five in the morning. Everything we did was perfect and I've never forgotten it."

To Betty he gave a "friendship" ring as a token of commitment, but he was not committed in any way, shape or form. However, Betty "wanted him desperately," and knew that he was the object of a lot of girls' attention and desire. The ring "legitimized" their physical relationship and allowed the young, naive Betty to lose her virginity to him with a clear conscience, although there was also the pressure exerted by the knowledge that if she didn't "go all the way," he would get what he wanted from another. It was, however, an "on-again" and "off-again" relationship and throughout its existence he was still married to Mary. Indeed, Betty met Mary on at least one occasion. Whether or not Mary was aware of Betty's involvement with her husband is unknown, but given that their marriage suffered a series of separations and reconciliations over this period, it is possible. The "on-again, off-again" nature of his affair with Betty upset her to a degree, for she knew that he was not at all faithful to her despite the ring. It is an interesting sidelight on his nature that he felt the need to give her a ring. Perhaps it salved his conscience to a degree. It was more than merely a token and it is worth noting that he and Betty remained friends throughout their lifetimes. At the time of their affair, however, he held her in thrall; to this small-town girl from upstate Washington, he was "sophisticated, handsome and arrogant." But when he suggested she join him in New York City when he finally got there, she chose not to go, although she admitted to missing him when he finally left, and to waiting, longingly, for his telephone calls.[13]

There is no doubt that Betty lost her heart to Bob and subsequently cherished her friendship with him, but not long after he went East, she met Lee Marvin who she married in 1951. She lost the friendship ring. Eventually Robert Horton and Lee Marvin became good friends, meeting one another through Betty. Robert Horton never claimed to have a lot of "good" friends within the act-

*Graduation,
UCLA,
August 13,
1949. Robert
Horton,
author's
collection.*

ing fraternity, and certainly not many male friends, but he counted
Lee Marvin as one, and attended Marvin's memorial ceremony in
1987 following his death at the age of sixty-three. They were of an
age; Marvin was about five months older than Horton, and they
shared similar types of background, coming from good families
which each boasted some stellar ancestry. They also, to a degree,
shared conflict with those families and while Marvin's views on life
are much more widely disseminated through books and interviews,
it is clear that they shared, to a significant degree, a common view
of the world.[14]

When I met Betty Marvin in June 2017, she was in a home in
Santa Barbara, not fully compos mentis, but she became more
coherent and engaged as we talked about Bob. Her eyes lit up,

focused, and she spoke of him affectionately. Sadly, it was not possible to confirm some facts about her time with Bob before she married Marvin, and she died a year later, on March 9, the anniversary of Bob's death.[15]

The Horton family takes a back seat during these years. While Robert and Mary may have tried to reconcile several times following their return to Los Angeles, it's clear from what is known about him as he worked and studied at UCLA that he was leading a fairly independent existence though all the evidence available indicates that, as he pursued his studies, he lived, for the most part, at home with his parents.[16]

There were other friendships as well, notably with Bob Walker, a fellow student and a friend of Betty Ebeling's. Bob Walker subsequently played a pivotal role in Horton's selection by Revue Studios for the part of Flint McCullough in *Wagon Train*, but at UCLA they studied and worked together and Walker remained a friend of Horton's throughout his life. Meanwhile, Robert studied hard and received his Bachelor of Arts degree, graduating from UCLA with honors in Theater Arts on August 13, 1949. The entire course of study took him just under three years and inarguably demonstrated his dedication, passion and intelligence.[17]

He also undertook work on a post-graduate degree, and in the course of the *This Is Your Life* program reference is made to at least one semester's study, while one article on the subject states that he was within eight credits of achieving that goal.[18] In the *St. Louis Globe Democrat* of October 26, 1958, the headline reads, "What does this hard-riding "scout" do in his spare time? He's studying for his Master's degree at U.C.L.A. and his thesis is "The effect of the American Theatre Wing on the postwar theatre." Another reference to his work on a Master's degree is made around the time of his affair with Nina Foch in the late Fifties but there is no concrete evidence that he ever got it. That he had an earnest desire to gain his Master's degree is nevertheless evident. On September 12, 1949, the Assistant Professor of Theater Arts at UCLA, G. Edward Hearn, wrote to the Director of Admissions at Yale University recommending Bob as a candidate for their graduate college. He wrote, "*Mr. Horton is one of the most sincere students of acting that I have had the pleasure of directing. He is intelligent, earnest and capable. He is an excellent student in and out of theater and an extremely hard worker. He would be an invaluable addition to any department."*

In one of the so-called life stories about Robert, there is a short tale describing how he traveled across country to attend Yale, having been accepted by that institution. It claims that, after a month, he left, there being no classes of interest still available to him. In fact, he spent six days at Yale where he very quickly learned that its atmosphere and courses were not for him. He may well have taken this opportunity to visit the American Theatre Wing in New York. He returned to Los Angeles and embarked on a post-graduate course at UCLA but he had set his sights on pursuing his craft in New York, home of theatrical professionals and world-class stage productions as well as the Actors Studio and the American Theater Wing. At all events, the letters to Yale speak for themselves, and the evidence re: timing, and Robert Horton's definite location in Los Angeles during the last months of 1949 cannot be refuted, evidence so carefully preserved in his own memorabilia of the time. At some point early in 1950 he either called or wrote to two good friends, Nolan Harrigan and Barry Lundin, both in the business, seeking their advice as to how he should pursue his goal, when he clearly mentioned both these institutions.[19]

# Chapter 8

## *Life on the East Coast*

Robert Horton did not go to work and study in New York until the early spring of 1950, where he enrolled at the American Theatre Wing. "The Wing" concentrated on holding seminars on American theater as well as funding various acting scholarships and it is probably best known for founding the "Tony" awards, named for one of its World War II co-founders and chairperson, Antoinette Perry. He also auditioned for and secured a place with the Actors Studio, a workshop for professional actors, directors and writers where Lee Strasberg taught method acting. There he spent three months studying very hard and working nights in various jobs in order to earn the money needed to cover his day-to-day living expenses. He was acting on advice he received in two separate letters which came to Kingsley Drive days apart in mid-February in response to those contacts he made earlier that year. Both letters were saved in his *Scrapbook II*. The first, dated February 11, 1950, came from Nolan Harrigan, and is five pages long. Harrigan starts out bluntly naming a couple of hotels which might provide affordable accommodation, then goes on to say that a *"Miss So-and-So"* at Charm Equity *"is a great helper of singers."* He directs him to the man in charge of hiring for the Chicago production of "South Pacific" and recommends a couple of roles he should try out for. *"Failing that,"* he writes, *"why not see if they'll have you in the chorus. They have to be stripped to the waist and sing "Nothing Like a Dame."* He goes on to exhort Bob to keep trying things, and then writes *"I think the Wing's a great idea."* He tells Bob that his (Harrigan's) father might get him a night shift job earning about $40 a week, which he thought would work well for Bob if he took night classes at *"the Wing."* He does not mention the Actors Studio. He said his mother might help Bob find a furnished apartment. The next pages contain heartfelt advice to Bob on how to go about following his career, *"his art,"* and based on how his career developed, there is no doubt that he paid attention to the advice he was given. Harrigan finishes his letter with the words, *"You'll get there. In time. And you'll be happy."* The second letter, six pages in length and dated February 28, 1950, came from Barry Lundin, and begins:

*"Dear Bob, I would advise anyone else to stay in California, but of course I am going to make an exception in your case. New York is over-run with actors and people who want to be actors but as far as you are concerned this need not be competition. The points in your favor are: 1 – You're still the best looking person I've ever seen. 2 – Your physical type is uncommon in New York and consequently at a premium. 3 – You have talent and most important, self-assurance, emotional stability, and drive. 4 – You're capable of making a wonderful impression on people because of your innate charm. I feel you know me well enough to take the foregoing as rather self-evident factors. We both know they're true and accept them as a matter of course; this is not flattery."*

The letter talks about getting an Equity card, how to go about that through summer stock work, it stresses the accessibility of powerful people versus the closed-door community in Hollywood, and Lundin states, *"Another New York advantage is that people are constantly being spotted here, because big people do go to small things; Summer stock and off-Broadway groups."*

His final paragraph reads,

*"At any rate, I've tried to be as factual as possible concerning the most un-factual type of endeavor in life. Hope to hear from you soon. Love to Mary. Barry."*

It is interesting to read Barry Lundin's observation that Bob has "self-assurance" and "emotional stability," as well as "drive" and "innate charm". It is a description of Bob's character which is repeated time and again throughout his life. His "emotional stability," however, deserted him at crucial periods although his "self-assurance" counter-balanced that in many ways.

Robert Horton took much of the advice he was given by both Harrigan and Lundin. He made his way to New York City and rented an apartment on the upper West Side. The exact dates of his attendance at the Actors Studio and the American Theatre Wing are unknown, but based on a letter written to his parents in April 1950 and given that he went on to a highly successful summer season with the Atlantic City Players, it's logical to assume that it was through spring and early summer of 1950, probably the months of March, April and May. He returned to continue his studies with both in September 1950.

In the *Red Book*, a letter written by Bob to his parents dated Saturday, April 24, 1950, is illuminating in many ways. It is clear that he and his wife remained in touch. He tells them that Mary called him "*last Wednesday*," that she is happy in her new apartment in Hollywood, and also in her new job where she is "*learning a lot*," but which he does not enlarge upon, which implies that his parents were probably familiar with some of those details. What he does say is that Mary expressed her unhappiness at "*no longer being one.*" He goes on to say that he received a letter from her "*today*," and that she has been ill. He says that he referred her to his uncle, Drew, a doctor (married to his mother's sister Lucille) and expresses his hope that she will act on his advice. He makes no mention of his own feelings with regard to "*no longer being one.*"

While he speaks enthusiastically of his time in New York, there is a note of homesickness too. Yet again there is a sense that he is trying to convince his mother of his love and respect for her as he praises her letter-writing, as well as her cooking. He wrote,

"*Mom, you character, I love your letters. I thought I made that quite clear when I answered your last one. You must never underestimate your charm, Mother, a charm that permeates every sentence in every letter you have ever written. When I came to your comment about your "funny little letters" I did laugh, but only at your own evaluation of something I think is very fine. I could see your face, a face I treasure, saying the gravy was too dark just after someone had complimented your dinner. I haven't had as good a dinner since I left, by the way.*"

He is also clearly conscious of the fact that he has financial obligations to his parents.

"*I wish I could get some work that would enable me to lessen the burden on you, Dad, and at the same time not interfere with my work.*"

He refers to a California grant he can get, but only if he is in California. He notes a refund of an insurance policy, which they may have enclosed in their letter to him, all of ninety-three dollars, which he says he will use to have photographs done, photographs he says he needs, and which will help him in his efforts to get work. He says he "loves the Wing," is very happy, loves the weather and the city more and more. He talks of friends he has made and mentions people who his parents had to know but for whom there is no further provenance. It is a fascinating letter as it paints a picture of a family which is coming to terms with his dedication to his chosen profession, if not enthusiastically, but they are in touch even if Robert wishes that he would hear from them "more often." Robert even refers to his brother, his niece and his new nephew warmly and with real affection. He also mentions "Yucca". Yucca is a cat, living with his parents. He says,

*"About Yucca; if you like him and want to keep him, you keep him. I only thought that if you were tired of him I would like Betty to have him. Mainly because she likes cats, and because she lives in the Glenn."*

Here then is a tiny bit of light shed on his character, and it reflects back sweetly and poignantly. Betty is Betty Ebeling, Yucca is a cat which is his, but which he had to leave behind in his parents' care. He signs off,

*"Give my love to the family, and write as often as you can. I miss you all, and am glad that you miss me and my noise. Lovingly, H."*

At the time he wrote this letter, he had just finished an audition with the "Talent 50 Showcase," but had not been successful in getting on the show. Their letter of rejection was saved in his *Red Book*. He was very disappointed, but told his parents that the letter had also praised his work highly. Such were the realities of his chosen profession and which he had to learn to overcome.

He was also struggling to decide whether or not he should remain on the East Coast during the summer season or return to Los Angeles to work on his master's degree at UCLA summer school. He states, categorically, in the letter *"I want to finish my Masters."* It was a dilemma, for he had the opportunity to join the Westport Summer Theatre, owned by the Theatre Guild, as an apprentice. He also had the chance to avail himself of a thousand-dollar grant, which would help cover tuition fees at The Wing. In order to get the money, however, he was required to be a resident of California. He was pulled, therefore, in several directions. While he was contemplating his options, he was hard at work attending classes at the Actors Studio and The Wing, and earning money working odd jobs to augment whatever money his father sent him. He eventually succeeded, working as a short-order cook, a waiter and ultimately the host at a California themed restaurant.[1]

Much as he loved it, his time with the American Theatre Wing and the Actors Studio was not all sweetness and light. He said he "worked like a dog" but that his fellow actors never had any difficulty finding things about his work to criticize. He said,

"Then came a wonderful day. I did a scene from Steinbeck's "Burning Bright." When it was over – silence. Not a word. When the co-director (of the Actors' Studio) Paula Strasberg said, 'I have nothing to say' it was like somebody had given me an Academy Award!"[2]

At some point between his first stint with The Studio and The Wing and his tenure with the Atlantic City Players he returned to Los Angeles. Several telegrams from various individuals during the month of June hoping to engage his services were sent to his home. He undoubtedly returned there in order to qualify for the California state grant, but he did not enroll in summer school because he received offers of work from the East Coast. No doubt he chose to work with the Atlantic City Players in preference to the Westport Summer Theatre group because the roles he was offered were preferable to being a mere apprentice. His first engagement began with a role in the play *Harvey*. In a telegram dated June 13, 1950, he was asked by Bill Blood, one of the co-producers, to be available for rehearsals at the Playhouse on the Million Dollar Pier in Atlantic City on June 22, as well as attend a pre-rehearsal press party on June 16. He headed east without hesitation.[3]

Accommodations were provided at the Brighton Hotel, a couple of blocks down the boardwalk from the pier. It was a large, elegant hotel built in the 1870s, situated on Indiana Avenue. Its gardens stretched unhindered to the beach, and it let the world know that it "catered to the finest of clientele". Much, much later, it was razed to the ground and even later the Sands Hotel and Casino arose on the vacant lot in the 1970s, but when Robert Horton stayed there, through his summer season with the Atlantic City Players, it was a gracious home away from home, and gave the boy from California a beach to play on, and waves to play in.

*Harvey* opened on June 30 and starred Jean Stapleton, who was to go on to a storied career on Broadway and in television, most memorably as the long-suffering wife of Archie Bunker in the 1970s sitcom, *All in the Family*. Bob played the young doctor in *Harvey*, a substantial supporting role. A week later, on July 10, *Born Yesterday* opened, and this time Bob starred opposite leading lady Margie Hart as the young newspaperman who becomes the lady's love interest.[4] *Born Yesterday*, the story of a gangster's moll who ends up showing her boyfriend and his cronies that she is much smarter than all of them put together, was a smash hit on Broadway at the time, starring the inimitable Judy Holliday. Margie Hart deserved a lot of credit for taking on the role. Her show business background was colorful, to say the least. She had been a star of burlesque before giving that up to pursue a "serious" acting career. She had been "serious" for eight years when she found herself playing opposite twenty-six-year-old Robert Horton. She was thirty-seven. Press clippings of the time refer to Hart's "going straight" in theater for eight years but she had enjoyed a varied and vibrant career as a burlesque dancer and strip tease artist up until 1942.[5]

Within the pages of *Scrapbook II* is tucked a small photograph folder containing four black and white 3x3 pictures. Two, identical, are of Bob reclining on a blanket on the beach, clad in brightly patterned bathing trunks, cigarette in one hand as he grins up at the camera. Behind stretches an Atlantic City beach no-one would recognize today.

Written on the reverse are the words, "September 1950". The other two photos are of Margie Hart, his *Born Yesterday* leading lady. Demure in a short-sleeved sweater and straight skirt, she stands before a clapboard house, smiling quietly. The pictures were taken by a photographer named Van Williams who was busy on Broadway at the time, photographing actors and others involved in the theater of the day.

At the time Margie Hart was married to a comedy writer, Seaman Block Jacobs, who wrote for such notables as Bob Hope, Lucille Ball and George Burns. Various bios of Margie, written upon her death in January, 2000 refer to her intelligence and quick wit, and while she could not be said to be a conventional beauty, she was described variously as "voluptuous", "flame haired", and "statuesque". A contemporaneous dancer, Sherry Britten, said of her, "She had a very great stage presence, very sexy, gorgeous body." Mayor Richard Riordan of Los Angeles said, "Margaret was one of the funniest, most outrageous and loving women I ever met." [6]

Robert and Margie's performances in *Born Yesterday* drew excellent reviews. One critic wrote, "An extra bow (they're called back for several after the final scene) should go to. . .Bob Horton, the romantic lead." Others made hay with Margie's past. One column was headed, "Starring Margie Hart, the reformed strip-tease . . ." Another said, "Former Burlesque Queen a hit in "Born Yesterday." Miss Hart, as a former expert in the art of "bumps and grinds" was a natural for the role of "Billie Dawn," and received excellent support from Bob Horton." [7]

Conversely a note sent to Bob by well-known playwright and producer Vincent McConnor on the occasion of his having seen the play disses Margie Hart entirely while complimenting Bob on his performance. Vincent McConnor wrote on July 24,

*"Dear Bob:*

*I thought you were fine – the only one in the entire production who approached a professional performance. I thought you had real presence – you knew what your lines meant – and your acting was forthright and honest. You needed direction, obviously, but not quite as badly as most of the others in the cast. I was pleased with what I saw you do. And, God willing, you will be in my new play this coming season. When you get back to New York, I'll let you read at least the first act.*

*By the way, I thought Margie Hart was incredibly bad. Her performance had absolutely nothing. She walked through every scene like a somnambulist – except her two scenes with you in the second act.*

*I stayed, by the way, to see both of your scenes in Act Two. Almost missed my train. I thought it left at 11:00 but, instead, it was 10:45. Fortunately, the taxi driver knew this and got me there just in time.*

*It was good seeing you – in person and on-stage. Let me know when you'll be returning to New York. Best – Vincent"*

Robert Horton appreciated McConnor's informed assessment of both the play and his performance in it, enough to save the letter in his *Red Book*. McConnor played a part in assisting him with his career. If he agreed with McConnor's opinion of Margie Hart's abilities, there is no evidence for it. It is intriguing that he kept those tiny black and white pictures of Margie who looks, in them, like a perfectly unremarkable young woman. Perhaps they had a little fling. She was earthy, intelligent, and funny. She ticked all the boxes in terms of what he found attractive in women, and the age difference between them would have mattered not a jot. There is little doubt that she found her leading man irresistible. She would not have been the first. She certainly wasn't the last. It lends weight to Betty Ebeling's observations, although Betty, together with Bob Walker, cabled the following to Bob on July 11, the day after *Born Yesterday* opened:

FROM SANTA MONICA, CA JULY 11, 1950 6:26 AM. TO ROBERT HORTON BRIGHTON HOTEL ATLANTIC CITY.

"PROUD FRIENDS ANNOUNCE BIRTH OF A STAR – "BORN YESTERDAY" NAME BOB HORTON – SEX DEFINITELY – HEIGHT UNBOUNDED BY THE STARS WEIGHT – AND BEE. BETTY AND BOB."

It is a witty and loving message and the telegram was pasted into *Scrapbook II* where the photographs nestled along with a *Born Yesterday* playbill.

*Born Yesterday* was followed by *On the Town* and by the time he had starred in *The Respectful Prostitute*, which opened on July 31 and was held over twice for a total run of five weeks, Robert Horton had earned a fine reputation as one of Atlantic City Players' leading men. An article published in the *Atlantic City Reporter* on Saturday, August 12, in "Footlight Footnotes by Rick" and entitled "Playhouse Personality," said:

"This week it's Robert Horton, as impressive as an actor as he is handsome in appearance. This star of three or four shows presented at The Playhouse thus far this season, is that rare person: "a native Californian." Bob got his first taste of theater at the age of thirteen, and went on to M.C. shows in High School and college. He was awarded "Best Actor"honors at Miami U. and UCLA. After three years in the Coast Guard he returned to star in many plays for the American Theater Wing, and then a minor but key role in David Selznick's "A Walk In The Sun." The call of the footlights brought him east again to starring roles here at our own Atlantic City Playhouse and one hears (off the record) a leading role in a new play scheduled for Broadway this fall. With his theatrical background in mind, Producers William Robins and William Blood have entrusted him with the job of directing their new show "Angel Street" due to open Monday, August 21st. I'm betting my bucks that before long the name of Bob Horton will be marquee magic on both Broadway and the nation's Movie Theaters."

Putting aside several glaring errors in the piece – Robert was fifteen when he first had a part in a school play, and spent but sixteen months in the Coast Guard and the reference to him starring in plays with the American Theatre Wing is incorrect – it is a resoundingly positive assessment of young Robert Horton as well as a telling estimation of his gifts as an actor. It also helps to clarify a period in his life which was heavily glossed over when he came to prominence in the role of Flint McCullough, and paints a definitive picture of a young actor not just teetering on the edge of a great career, but of an actor who has established himself pretty strongly in the vaunted theater milieu of the East Coast. Another small, but significant achievement he gained at this time, as evidenced by his membership card contained in *Scrapbook II*, was to be given Deputy Credentials by the AEA within the Atlantic City Playhouse Company. The AEA is a branch of the Associated Actors and Artistes of America and represents actors and stage managers within the United States.

There is no further mention of *Angel Street*, perhaps because Bob, held over in *The Respectful Prostitute* through early September, was unable to take up the job of being its director, but there is no doubt that he remained on the East Coast. After the summer season in Atlantic City was over, he returned to Manhattan, to an apartment next door to the one he rented while studying at the Wing. He took up further studies at the Wing and the Actors Studio. While he attended both he took whatever opportunities came his way to practice his art. He secured a very small part on *The Danny Thomas Show* broadcast live on NBC on October 11, 1950, but it did nothing for his career. He was always seeking work, and a letter sent to him dated October 25, 1950 demonstrates this. It came from H-N Productions, Inc. on Sunset Boulevard and was written by Paul Henreid whose company it was. Paul Henreid was known better as an actor, most particularly for his iconic role of Victor Laszlo in the 1942 movie, *Casablanca*. Another letter saved by Bob in his *Red Book*, it reads,

*"Dear Mr. Horton:*

*Your work as an actor has been highly praised by professors at UCLA, in particular by Professor Henry Schnitzler. He advised me to get in touch with you when I reach New York on the 30th of October.*

*I am about to cast a motion picture which I will co-produce with Mr. Edward Nassour. There are several parts which should be cast with young talented actors who will have to play college students.*

*I would appreciate it if you would contact me at The Stanhope Hotel. The telephone number is Butterfield 8-5800. If I should not be in when you call, please leave your phone number so that I can return your call and we will arrange a meeting. With best regards,*

*Yours Sincerely, Paul Henreid."*

Sadly, it seems that nothing came of this contact, but it must have meant a great deal to Robert Horton as he worked ceaselessly at furthering his acting career in New York City. He also had a small part in an Ed Sullivan show on November 19, 1950, which was one of the first "remote" broadcasts of the time. It was beamed from the Boston Opera House, so clearly Robert was prepared to travel to get work and experience. In 1950 he took up fencing, studying under Olympic gold medalist Giorgio Santelli and also Edward Lucia. He became sufficiently proficient to fence competitively, and he did well. He saw fencing as an additional asset to his acting skills, as well as a means of keeping fit and trim. He described the sport as being a "more gentlemanly way of expressing aggression."[8]

Paula Strasberg of the Actors Studio was, however, instrumental in getting him a small part in *Suspense*, a weekly television drama series broadcast live from New York. The director, Robert Stevens, liked Bob well enough to give him two additional parts. Each succeeding part in *Suspense* was of more importance and if stories told by those who knew are to be believed, his final appearance was as the lead. Unfortunately, there is no record extant of those plays, their titles or his part in them. However, on December 1 of that year he appeared in the *CBS Ford Theater* series, in a presentation entitled "Another Darling". It was his first TV play, it brought him his first fan mail and paid him the princely sum of $240.00, as recorded by him on the reverse of a black and white photo of him on stage in the production contained in *Scrapbook II*.

His personal life at the time is a closed book, for while he remained married to Mary it is quite clear that it was a marriage in name only. Betty Marvin referred to him as having "girlfriends" and being "quite a womanizer,"[9] and undoubtedly as an exceptionally handsome young man imbued with charm and sophistication he must not have wanted for or denied himself the pleasure of feminine company. However, he also demonstrated his dedication to his chosen profession and in order to support himself he once again took on a series of mundane jobs outside the theater which allowed him to seek work within the acting world.

# Chapter 9

## *I Took the Big Money*

A number of stories written about Robert Horton's early career in movies when he was the star of *Wagon Train* refer to his making a choice between a leading role on the New York stage in an uniden- tified play for about a hundred dollars a week versus a movie con- tract in Hollywood. He is quoted as saying he "took the big (movie) money," and that it was a mistake. A mistake which he regretted.[1]

However, mistake or not, he returned to Hollywood in 1951, where he signed a single deal contract with Warner Brothers who put him in the un-credited role of a young tank commander in *The Tanks Are Coming*, initially released in October 1951. There is no information in regard to the film's budget; what it cost or what it ultimately made. The lead roles belonged to Steve Cochran and Philip Carey. Robert himself, remembering his part in his eighties during a radio interview conducted by Boyd Magers on KSAV on September 18, 2007, said it involved "about four lines," but he was probably referring to *Bright Road* (1953) in that instance, which would have been accurate. In fact, in *The Tanks Are Coming* (1951) he had a great many more than that, and his scenes were acted with conviction. His looks are undeniable and his un-credited appear- ance drew letters of enquiry as to his identity. One reviewer, who described the film as "rugged" wrote,

"Handsome newcomer Robert Horton playing Captain Horner looks like a find to us."[2]

One little personal note attached to the filming of the movie con- cerns Robert and his estranged wife. During filming at Fort Knox in Kentucky, their anniversary took place on June 27. Mary sent Bob a card and wrote to him, "*I'm glad we stretched the two years,*" i.e. the "two years" her young husband had so flippantly referred to on their wedding day. It is a touching display of lasting affection, an affection which endured through Mary's second marriage, up until her death, when her daughter telephoned Bob with the news, and told him, "My mother always loved you."[3]

Just how they "stretched the two years" is open to conjecture. They were certainly legally married at the time, but their actual status in terms of "living" is unclear. In a 1959 publication titled *Hollywood Life Stories*, the piece on Robert Horton bears the headline "Robert Horton – Little Devil". The writer is unidentified, but the meat of the article is fundamentally correct. Without being explicit, it hints at "other kinds of problems" when Bob took off to New York in the spring of 1950. "Quarrels, separations and reconciliations" are referred to, but it is probable that Mary knew that Bob was being unfaithful to her, and though this particular article carries a picture of Mary with Bob at a house warming party held for Barbara Ruick, a budding MGM starlet in 1952 with whom he had formed a close friendship while filming *Apache War Smoke* that year, it also refers to the fact that at that point, the Horton marriage was all but over.

Nevertheless, a letter from Bob's agent, Paul Small, in February 1952, enclosing confirmation of his being put under contract to Metro-Goldwyn-Mayer, was sent to an address in Hollywood, just off Sunset Boulevard, which may indicate that at that point he was once again with Mary.[4] Further confirmation of this comes in another article dated October 5, 1952 and published in the *Worcester Sunday Telegram* under the title, "Robert Horton – His Interest in TV Led to Film Contract" reads,

"I love the stage," said Bob, "and there is nothing that can take the place of an interested, enthusiastic audience. But television intrigued me. It's what brought me back here, and then," he laughed, "TV introduced me to Warner Brothers, and here I am, all sold on my new profession, the films." The piece continued,

"Robert Horton became a benedict (a newly married man) on June 27th, 1946. His wife is the former Mary Katherine Job*[sic]* and they live in an attractive apartment not more than a mile from the studio. They may have to give it up, however. "We have a dog you see," and Bob smiled a bit ruefully. "He's a beautiful Springer spaniel, and I went to the airport, actually to pick him up for my brother. But when I took him in my arms I knew I'd never be able to give him up. So, if we have to move, we'll move." That's the way he is. No wonder everyone at Metro loves Bob Horton."

By the time this article was published, there is no doubt that Robert or his wife had filed for divorce, but it serves to confirm, if ever so slightly, that for a time, when he came home from New York, he returned to Mary in an attempt to effect yet another reconciliation.

His contract with Warner Brothers ended when *The Tanks Are Coming* (1951) was completed. At the time he was represented by the Paul Small agency which was involved with getting a contract finalized with MGM. In January 1952, he signed the agreement with MGM, which resulted in his being employed under a "term agreement" which became effective on February 18, 1952. The details of the contract are unknown today, but there are several references to its being for a period of seven years. A sum of $7,000 is also referred to. In fact, he made seven films for MGM before the contract was cancelled in 1954. Later he said that he ultimately regretted that move, knowing, in hindsight, that had he stayed in New York and studied his craft there he could have had a more successful and personally satisfying career, but to a young man struggling to get started, there is no doubt that the money, as well as the lure of Hollywood, was hard to refuse.[5]

His first film for MGM was a black and white Western entitled *Apache War Smoke* which was released in September 1952. Starring Gilbert Roland, it featured Robert Horton as his co-star. He described it as a "B" budget movie, and "a nice little film" which gave him much greater exposure than *The Tanks Are Coming* (1951). The story of a group of people besieged at a stage relay station in the arid desert, it was filmed entirely on location, with the exception of interior shots. Horton's part, that of the relay station manager, and son of a devil-may-care outlaw, Gilbert Roland, is well acted, genuine and authentic, and he is quite clearly at ease in his surroundings and within the context of the movie. Altogether it is a pleasant film and it got his movie career, if not into high gear, at least moving well toward it. During filming he struck up a friendship with Gilbert Roland, and although not close friends, he respected the older actor, who subsequently appeared in an episode of *Wagon Train*. The feminine interest in *Apache War Smoke* (1952) was divided three ways amongst veteran actress Glenda Farrell, up-and-coming beauty Patricia Tiernan and newcomer Barbara Ruick, daughter of actress Lurene Tuttle. Barbara Ruick was Horton's chief love interest in the story and it was during filming that the relationship which led to his third marriage began.

How complicated and convoluted these "screen" relationships were at the time, under the all-powerful studio system which dictated so much in terms of actors' behavior, is hard for people today to comprehend. In 1952, in another article published this time in *Modern Screen* in October of that year, Mary is pictured with Bob attending the house-warming party at Barbara Ruick's new apartment. Given the lead-in time in publishing it's fair to assume that the party took place early in 1952, the year Horton starred with Ruick in *Apache War Smoke*. Mary, in this photograph, looks quiet, pensive and introspective. Bob radiates life. No doubt he was obliged by the studio to take his wife to the party which was probably a publicity stunt for Barbara Ruick as well as the other young, budding actors who were present. It was a small "party," not many people, but looking at the pictures it's easy to see that Bob was happy to be there, Mary was not.[6]

*Apache War Smoke* was initially released on September 25, 1952. It was filmed on the Iverson Ranch in Chatsworth, not far from Los Angeles, a popular shooting venue. Robert Horton's exposure in this movie was worthwhile. With a budget of $382,000 bringing in revenue of $797,000 at the box office, it was a decent investment for the movie moguls involved and its two young stars, Horton and Ruick, must have felt that their time was coming.[7] According to Robert, he met Barbara Ruick when both were attending lessons with MGM drama coach Lillian Burns about a year before they came together on the set of *Apache War Smoke*. When they embarked on their affair is unclear, but later, at the height of its passion, Barbara Ruick confidently asserted that her mother, Lurene, told her that every leading lady had to be "a little in love" with her leading man, and in love they certainly were, so much so that Robert Horton initiated divorce proceedings against Mary, or set in motion a divorce which was already in the works. Whatever the case, he was determined to marry Barbara, and he had to be free to do so. As the interlocutory divorce which was finally granted in 1953 required a twelve-month waiting period, and since Bob and Barbara married on August 22 in 1953, it's likely that he instigated divorce proceedings sometime in the first half of 1952, possibly during the filming of *Apache War Smoke*.[8]

Robert's niece Joan related the story that Bob came round to their home one night in 1952 seeking Creighton's advice on the matter. In an effort not to intrude on the young family, he threw pebbles at Creighton's window to attract his attention. His older brother dismissed him curtly. "Go home to your wife!" was his advice. The story was also substantiated by a close, later friend, who was told it by Bob himself. It is a sorry little tale, for once again it illustrates the gulf which existed between Robert and his family, between him and his brother. He sought help, and received none.[9]

1952 and 1953 were busy years professionally for Robert Horton. If Barbara's career was on the ascendancy, so too was his. Following *Apache War Smoke*, he was loaned out to 20th Century-Fox by MGM, and made two movies for them. *Return of the Texan*, a black and white movie set in modern times in which he co-starred with Dale Robertson, was first released on December 4, 1952. This preceded Robert's first color film, *Pony Soldier* (1952), in which Tyrone Power starred. Robert played "the baddie," his one and only role as a no-good in his film career, and he played it to perfection. He and Power became good friends on and off the set, and Bob later spoke of him as "a mentor". He credited Power with showing him how to behave on set, how to interact respectfully with others, from the lighting engineers to the actors involved.[10] *Pony Soldier* hit the movie theatres on December 19, 1952. However, neither movie made much of an impact although one critic wrote about Robert in *Return of the Texan*,

"Robert Horton, as the doctor who comes close to leading Joanne Dru to the altar is impressive," and another said, "Robert Horton comes a step closer to stardom."[11] Lukewarm reviews of *Pony Soldier* don't merit repetition. Even the great Tyrone Power could not draw positive acclaim.

Robert had a cameo role in the well-known movie, *The Story of Three Loves* (1953), appearing for a matter of a few minutes with

Leslie Caron. His part, that of a young passenger on an ocean liner, is minimal, confined to picking up a glove or handkerchief dropped by Caron, and fixing her with his captivating smile and one of "those looks". *The Story of Three Loves* was released in March of 1953, so it is likely that his part in it was filmed sometime in 1952, possibly after *Apache War Smoke* and somewhere in amongst the filming of both the December releases.

*Bright Road* (1953), initially known as *See How They Run* came next, and in it he played a young doctor dealing with discrimination amongst poor blacks. He co-starred with Dorothy Dandridge and Harry Belafonte. He called the movie a "missed opportunity" to make a cogent and meaningful point about racism and education. His was the only white face in the movie. Instead of making a serious statement about discrimination (and Robert Horton's early life and relationship with Mary Augustine gave him a unique point of view as a young white man from a well-to-do family), it focused on Harry Belafonte's singing. Horton felt that that insulted Belafonte, the actor, and furthermore, demeaned the story itself.[12] The movie came out to poor reviews and lost $152,000 at the box office, almost half what it cost to make. Initially released by MGM on April 17, 1953, *Bright Road* was quickly followed by *Code Two* (1953), released on April 24. Bob may have had reason to be grateful for the closeness of those release dates. A movie about handsome young motorcycle cops in Los Angeles was likely to attract a great deal more positive attention, possibly burying *Bright Road* swiftly and thankfully for all concerned. *Code Two*, starring Ralph Meeker, Keenan Wynn and Sally Forrest, almost doubled its cost in box office sales and possibly helped the Hollywood moguls get over their chagrin at the failure of *Bright Road*.

In June 1953, MGM released *Arena*, a highly touted movie employing the daring new 3D cinematography which, it was claimed, would revolutionize movie making and become the rage. It was undoubtedly an attempt by the studios to stave off the encroaching influence of television. Filmed in glorious Technicolor, it was the biggest budget movie Robert Horton had been in to date, and it was very successful, bringing in $1.2 million revenue. It also placed him in a starring role with Gig Young, Polly Bergen,

Barbara Lawrence and Harry Morgan. Lee Van Cleef had a small role. The movie was filmed on location at a real rodeo in Arizona and relied heavily on its 3D gimmick.[13] Robert's part, that of the up-and-coming young rodeo star, literally bucking for supremacy, and with a young man's eye for a pretty girl, is solidly acted and for anyone paying attention to him, he impresses with his authenticity and believability. Barbara Ruick was with him on location and their relationship was firmly established. By the time *Code Two* and *Arena* were released, their affair was public knowledge and, indeed, it was recorded in a plethora of publicity shots for both movies, though the *Code Two* photographs also included most of the other stars, while *Arena* shots began to concentrate on Horton and Ruick alone. There is no doubt that Bob gained experience in both movies, though he was less than enamored with the motorcycle riding required for *Code Two*. Nevertheless, it's obvious in the movie that he went about learning the skill to ride a bike with the same dedication he brought to anything to do with his craft. By contrast, in *Arena*, the shots of him driving fast down a California highway show a young man in his element behind the wheel, and he was. All his life he carried on a love affair with the automobile, and all his life he preferred an open top car to the closed-in sedans driven by his family. He drove convertibles because he loved them, and he began by driving them in defiance of his family. Throughout his life he was a keen collector of automobiles, although he seldom owned more than a dozen at a time. He bought them to drive, not to show. Most of them were convertibles and most of them were unique. All of them were sleek, beautiful examples of their kind.[14]

*Arena* was also an exposure to concentrated horse riding and many of the photographs taken on the set with Ruick had them riding together. He was no stranger to the back of a horse. He had spent enough hours riding the trails of Griffith Park with his father to have better than a passing knowledge of horses. However, it was the first movie which required him to ride competently. *Apache War Smoke* did not.

# Chapter 10

## *Emotionally Naked*

At this point in his career, Robert Horton must have felt pretty assured of success, although his later comments about the films he was allocated are less than complimentary. By the time mid-1953 rolled around, he was twenty-nine, twice-divorced and looking for something a great deal better both professionally and personally. Professionally he kept up his fencing, taking lessons with the great Aldo Nadi at his Los Angeles school, and he also began taking singing and dancing lessons.[1] Personally, he embarked on his third marriage. Barbara Ruick was a very different kettle of fish from Mary. She was a career girl and she hailed from a show-business family. She knew the ropes. She too had been married briefly, in 1949, but that marriage had been annulled.[2] She was eight and a half years younger than Horton, and her parents, Lurene Tuttle and Melville Ruick, were both well-known in the entertainment world; Lurene was an actress and star of screen and radio, Melville was an actor and radio personality. They divorced in 1945 and Barbara grew up with her mother in California, close to the entertainment world.[3] Considering their relationship, there is an argument for Horton being attracted to someone with such a background, given his own staid, prosaic pedigree. Perhaps he thought that Ruick's world would rub off on his; at all events, there is no doubt that the affair started out based on a deep attraction, a need for one another, and possibly Robert Horton's own need to once again prove himself, at least to himself, in the matter of personal relationships.

His romance with Barbara Ruick culminated in their marriage in Las Vegas on August 22, 1953. While the media of the day, mostly magazines, played up its romantic aspect, the realities were harsher. Barbara's mother, Lurene Tuttle, was against the marriage from the start, deeming it a threat to her daughter's burgeoning career. Barbara's agent, too, objected, for the same reasons. If the Horton parents had anything to say about it, perhaps their views were the same as his brother's – "Go home to your wife!" Horton and his bride eloped against family wishes on both sides and returned to Hollywood to announce their marriage as a fait accompli. It was yet another rebellion by Bob. He said, "There was pressure put on us against the marriage and this merely made us more determined to marry." There was little anyone could do about it. Both were of age, both had been married before and both were legally divorced. Everyone got on with it.[4]

There was no time for a proper honeymoon. Bob was once again making a picture, *Men of the Fighting Lady* (1954), a story of fighter pilots flying from an aircraft carrier in the Korean War. Van Johnson, Walter Pidgeon, Keenan Wynn and Dewey Martin were his co-stars.[5] His part was that of a young married officer, and one gets the impression, certainly from yet more publicity photographs featuring him and his bride, that his part may have been larger initially, but that much of it was cut. Photographed in full flying kit with Barbara, he is never seen in it in the film. Released shortly after the end of the Korean War, the movie was well-received by the theater going public. Unfortunately, Horton's role was scarcely big enough to gain him notoriety. What he does, he does well. He is nothing if not a consummate professional, but this was hardly a vehicle which would promote him, and in the company of the wildly popular Van Johnson, it's not surprising that *Men of the Fighting Lady* did little to move his career forward. The *USS Oriskany* served as *The Fighting Lady*. She was engaged in readiness training along the coast of California from May through mid-September, before heading back to Japan and Korea, where she served until April 1954.[6] A great many publicity shots were taken on board the *USS Princeton* in San Diego, many of them featuring Bob Horton and his brand-new bride, and mention is made in at least one news clipping that Bob got his part in the movie as a "wedding gift".[7] *Men of the Fighting Lady* was initially released by MGM on May 7, 1954. It received good reviews and made approximately $1.8 million at the box office.

Only three days before, *Prisoner of War* (1954), a black-and-white movie based on the true stories of American POW's experiences in Korea, was released. Horton's co-stars in *Prisoner of War* were Ronald Reagan, Steve Forrest, Dewey Martin and Oskar Homolka.

It was an honest effort to disclose the truth about prisoner-of-war camps during the Korean War, based in part on the real-life experiences of at least two of the movie's consultants, and the torture inflicted on American prisoners by the Koreans, with the complicity of their Soviet masters. Horton's performance is powerful, when he appears, but again, he is not given the chance to fully exploit the material. The leading man was Ronald Reagan and once again Bob was acting with Dewey Martin and Steve Forrest. It was during the filming of this movie that Bob first formed his friendship with Ronald and Nancy Reagan, a friendship which, while not close, lasted down through the years. *Prisoner of War* was successful, earning $1.7 million, and like *Men of the Fighting Lady* was a timely commentary on recent and current events. Though credited with giving "good support" in both films, Horton does not earn much more recognition from reviewers. *Prisoner of War* drew cool responses from some critics who felt that the movie was "brutal".[8]

These two pictures marked the culmination of Robert Horton's movie career, his "hot" period. They were both box office successes, the former bringing in $2.64 million against an expenditure of $829,000.00. They came out in the spring of 1954, and it was in 1954 that matters within the major studios of Hollywood began to have a negative effect. Television, the new entertainment medium, was making itself felt. Bob was no stranger to television. He had done live appearances and made his first TV film in 1950 while still in New York which had resulted in his being "spotted" and signed by Warner Bros. He subsequently appeared again in 1952 when he had a part in "From Such a Seed," broadcast on May 16, 1952 as a *Chevron Theatre* presentation but the demands of his movie career appear to have kept him off the small screen through 1953.

Despite the intensity of emotion which brought about their marriage in 1953, or perhaps because of it, Robert Horton and Barbara Ruick were experiencing real difficulties by the spring of 1954. Bob's career, in particular, had gone "cold." MGM, after seven movies, dropped him and he was an out-of-work actor desperately seeking employment.

Early in 1954 he tried out for a part in the film production of *Oklahoma!* which was to be directed by the famed Frederick

Zinneman. There is evidence to support this. In May 1954, Robert Horton wrote a letter to Zinneman, who had *The Men* (1950), *High Noon* (1952) and *From Here to Eternity* (1953) to his credit at the time. This letter, a carbon copy, was pasted into Bob's *Red Book*. It is a telling piece of writing from a young, troubled Robert Horton. On May 25, 1954, he typed this letter:

*"Dear Mr. Zinneman:*

*Putting off this letter hasn't made it any easier to write, and if your character were not as it is, or at any rate as I evaluated it to be, I doubt if I would have had the courage to compose it. It is a rather frightening thought to realize that you have stood emotionally naked in front of another man, particularly when that man is to all accounts a stranger. But, as I picked a stranger to burden with my problems, I'm happy that it was you. I'm deeply grateful to[sic] for your attitude of compassion, in an hour of need, and also for your advice. I regret, naturally, that such a critical point in my life should be associated with an attempt to impress you with my craftsmanship; I wanted so much for you to believe in my work. I did appreciate the opportunity of working with you and hope that the test was successful for Gene.*

*May I extend my best wishes to you that OKLAHOMA may be an even bigger success than "Eternity", and thank you for your understanding, and patience and help from here to eternity. I'm not very religious, but God Bless you. bob horton"*

He no doubt signed the original he sent, but it is interesting that he typed his name minus capitals.

Undoubtedly this letter refers to Horton's taking a screen test with Zinneman, and it was for the movie version of *Oklahoma!* which came out in 1955. He is on record as stating categorically, later in his life, that he tried out for the part of Curly in *Oklahoma!* (1955).[9] The reference to "Eternity" is, of course, *From Here to Eternity*, released in 1953. What happened within the test is unknown, but perhaps, under stress, Robert Horton lost his temper, or, perhaps, on failing the test, he broke down. His reference to being "emotionally naked" is compelling. He wanted, and needed his abilities to be recognized, but how critical the point in his life was may only be guessed. His marriage was certainly under threat at the time and he felt that his career was as well. His movie career was going nowhere in 1954, and the chance to be in a film such as *Oklahoma!* must have meant a great deal to him. As it was, he failed the test and felt compelled to write this heart-felt letter to the great director.

Television was a fallback position for a lot of young hopefuls in the mid-Fifties, none more so than Robert Horton. However, 1954 brought him only two "small screen" appearances. He was "The Tenderfoot" on a *Lone Ranger* episode of that name that year, and much more significantly, *Ford Television Theatre* gave him the lead role with Donna Reed in "Portrait of Lydia," aired on December 16, 1954, and which he remembered fondly in later years. Writing to a fan in December 1993, he said, *"My favorite leading lady was the late Donna Reed. We did a television film together in the early fifties called a Portrait of Lydia. We played young lovers in Paris and for a few days we were in love. It was wonderful. Robert Horton."*[10] It is worth noting that Donna Reed had starred in a supporting role in *From Here to Eternity* and won an Oscar as Best Supporting Actress for her work in it. The idea that Zinneman may have had a hand in the "Portrait of Lydia" assignments gives pause for thought. Regardless, "Portrait of Lydia" brought Bob positive acclaim. The *Red Book* contains this letter written by Donna Reed from her home on Coldwater Canyon to Robert on October 5, 1954,

*"Dear Bob,*

*Your get-well card was very much appreciated – thank you so much and I am happy to say I feel fine once more.*

*I took a look at "Portrait" this week, only a rough cut and I couldn't begin to tell really, but the production values seemed good, and I think the scenes played, especially those of the last day's work. I hope you will be pleased.*

*Again, I want to thank you for a finely turned out performance – actually, I can't think of anyone else who could have done as well – and "Greg" was a tough one to cast as well as play.*

*My very best wishes to you for the big success your talent deserves. Sincerely,*

*Donna R. Owen."*

Obviously, Bob had sought her opinion of the film. Perhaps, for those few days he mentions, they were "in love," though of course

Donna Reed Owen was a married woman and a mother at the time. Robert Horton was married too, but by 1954 had already come up against difficulties with his wife. "Portrait of Lydia" was broadcast on the *Ford Television Theatre* on December 17, 1954. Another letter saved in his *Red Book* came from Bob Raison, of the Nat C. Goldstone Agency, who wrote to him the next day:

"*Dear Robert,*

*You were nothing less than wonderful last night on FORD and I thoroughly enjoyed the show. . ."*

"*I thought you looked very handsome and that you matched very well with Miss Reed. This should end any opinions that you are too young to play opposite the screen's aging leading ladies."*

"*All in all, I'm sure this will do you a lot of good and I trust you will speak to us when you are a big fat star this time next year.*

*Have a wonderful Christmas, Robert.*

*Most sincerely,*

*Bob."*

It was a sincere compliment to a young man whose career was still very much in its early stages but it took more than "Portrait of Lydia," good as it was, to raise Robert Horton's profile above other actors plying their trade within television.

His turbulent marriage to Barbara Ruick, meanwhile, was taking its toll on both partners. From all the contemporary writings it's clear that a passionate romance did not translate into a successful marriage and during their less than three-year partnership events and circumstances combined to make for a very rocky road indeed. Both were career orientated; both wanted to make it to the top. It seemed to both, in August 1953, that that was where they each were headed. Robert Horton had been exposed to the movie-going public in ten films, discounting his small part in *A Walk in the Sun*, and though touted at one time as "the new Clark Gable" the truth is that by the release dates of his final two movies for MGM in the first half of 1954, things had taken a distinct downturn for him. The other hard fact which had to be faced, and about which Horton was ruthlessly honest, was that none of the movies he worked in were of any great caliber. None gave him a chance to shine, to make an impression, to stamp his persona on them and only four of them gave him anything like a solid role. At best, they were grade B movies, but the studio system of the day gave very few the opportunity to rise, unhindered, to the top. Talent and ability had nothing to do with stardom. An actor was a commodity, used by the studio system and then simply discarded. Robert Horton spoke of one day being "hot" – the next, "cold".[11]

Bob and Barbara had been married less than a year when they first separated. Divorce papers were filed, then they reconciled and the action was dropped. By the close of 1954, with "Portrait of Lydia" behind him and his wife back with him, Bob may have felt more optimistic about life. There were five television shows between January and early June, then he landed the part of Drake McHugh in Warner Brothers' new trilogy series, *King's Row* in mid-June of that year. The other two shows which made up the trilogy were *Cheyenne* and *Casablanca*. Although friends were full of compliments for his acting in *King's Row,* Robert Horton himself disliked the role. He knew he had taken it without giving it much consideration. He was an actor who was no longer under contract, he needed work and he accepted the assignment. He was also under pressure from Ruick's parents to find work. They accused him of not supporting her, and this was a contributing factor to his taking the role.[12] The series was short-lived and did very little for his career. Jack Kelly and Nan Leslie were his co-stars and his thick head of auburn hair was dyed blond for the role. He said of *King's Row,*

"I was never so glad to see anything come to an end. Actually, Kelly got hurt much worse than I did. He was "hot", and I wasn't." He came to the conclusion that, despite its being a failure, *King's Row* saved his professional life. "They told me it was going to be the big hit of the three – *Casablanca* and *Cheyenne* were the other two – and I believed every word of it. It taught me to be a lot more selective about what I do."

From that point on Robert Horton took greater control of his career. He had learned a sobering lesson: that he had to take command of his career and future, not meekly accept roles handed out by the studio. It helped him establish within his own mind the need to be in charge of his own destiny, and this was later reflected in his determination, throughout his career, to be associated with quality work.[13]

It's easy to think that between his years as a contract actor with MGM and a freelancer following the cancellation of his MGM contract, Robert Horton slipped into obscurity, but this is not so. He had work, his interest in a singing career grew and he was a known face. However, without a contract of any kind, he had to find his own work. He had an agent, but with the movie industry in a state of flux and television still something of an unknown quantity, it was a hand-to-mouth existence. Nevertheless, he studied voice, he acted on stage and he was seen on television. In 1955, he appeared on television half-a-dozen times, not including *King's Row*, and in 1956 he doubled that number, including the memorable "Tongue of Silver" in which he sang and which won for *Matinee Theater* and NBC the coveted Sylvania Award.[14] His depiction of a roguish young troubadour in Ireland had elements of the singing Starbuck he would portray seven years later on Broadway, and was a fully rounded, professional, heart-warming piece of acting. Three leading roles in three *Alfred Hitchcock Presents* shows brought him added recognition.

He had fans too, though not in the numbers which followed him later as a result of his portrayal of Flint McCullough. One in particular, Beverly Linet, was a writer for *TV Star Parade*, one of the scores of movie and television magazines which proliferated at the time. She met Horton at a cocktail party given by the actress Barbara Britton in September 1951, and wrote about the experience on a number of subsequent occasions, when it was clear that she had, inevitably, lost her heart to him, although she denied that in print at the time.[15] Much, much later, a good friend of hers in the business said that she had always carried a torch for Horton, and loved him until the day she died. He was certainly her friend. He may have encouraged a friendship in the beginning, because he was smart enough to know that her literary and publishing contacts could only help him in the publicity game, but in the end there is no doubt that they were friends, friendly enough to "double date" at the time Horton was married to Barbara Ruick. It is interesting to note here that Beverly, while quite attractive, was no beauty, and she

*First appearance in* Picnic, *with Felicia Farr, Los Angeles, June 1955. Robert Horton, author's collection.*

had a withered left hand.[16] It reflects well on Robert Horton who often said that a woman's looks were not what principally interested him. A bright, engaging personality and an inquiring mind were more important to him, as was honesty and sincerity.

It was Linet who, in June 1955, while he was working in *King's Row*, pushed him to read for the lead part of Hal Carter in William Inge's hit play *Picnic*. The play was put on by the Player's Ring Theater in Hollywood and ran for a two-week engagement early in July 1955. Exasperated by his apparent inability to make time to try out for the part, she left the *Picnic* script in his car on the final day

of tryouts. Discovering it a short time later, he took the hint, went to the theater and tried out for the part. He got it and subsequently earned rave reviews for his performance.[17] Under the title "'Picnic' Earthy Emotional Play at Ring Theater" Margaret Harford of the *LA Mirror-News* wrote in a July review,
"Horton makes this blond tiger of a man a brash extrovert, vulnerable because of hidden hurts, yet appealing in a rawboned way. He gives a strong physical performance and a promising dramatic one in his initial appearance at the Ring."
The reference to his being blond is, of course, because he was, as he continued to shoot episodes for *King's Row*. The description of his performance could have been of Robert Horton himself.
Robert Horton was clear that his performance as Hal in June 1955 at the Player's Ring Theater was pivotal in his career, a turn-around point which brought him critical acclaim as well as the attention of key people in the industry. He essayed the part of Hal for over two decades in various theaters and locations, from his late twenties through his early forties. It says much for his physical looks that he did so, but various critiques of his performance over the years remain consistently high. He followed *Picnic* with another Player's Ring Theater performance early in 1956, this time as Starbuck in *The Rainmaker*. That too produced a torrent of top reviews and that too was a part he undertook throughout his acting career.
In the midst of his see-sawing fortunes career-wise, his private life was no better off. By mid-1955 the Horton marriage was very firmly on the rocks, although Barbara sent him a telegram on the opening night of *Picnic*, June 22, which read,
"MAMA JOINS ME IN WISHING YOU GOOD LUCK TONIGHT LOVE AND KISSES = SOLDIER ="
Another treasure saved in his *Red Book*. Soldier was, of course, their dog, but the sending of the telegram illustrates the turmoil of their feelings for one another. He and Barbara separated on June 13 of that year and while it was not their first separation, it proved to be their last. Barbara, chosen by 20th Century-Fox to co-star in their new musical, Rodgers and Hammerstein's *Carousel* (1956), was kept busy on the lot and in New England, where much of the movie was filmed between August and November. The volatile rela-

tionship had been subject to several episodes of parting and reconciling, but following this one Barbara Ruick, Mrs. Robert Horton, filed suit for divorce on August 10, twelve days prior to what would have been their second anniversary.[18] The break-up came at what Robert called a very low point in his life. Nothing seemed to be going right for him, either professionally or personally.

There is no doubt that their careers played a major part in their inability to get along. Barbara had had a busy career up to this point. She came from an entertainment background and was confident of her ability to succeed. When Robert Horton met her, in 1952, she had chalked up successes in radio and in the nascent television business. She also had several movies under her belt and was already under a long-term contract with MGM. In 1953, the year she married Robert, she had a lead role in *The Affairs of Dobie Gillis* (1953), but after that success and for no apparent reason, she was relegated by the studio to bit parts. So, while each of them was intent on carving out a successful career, neither of them seemed able to do so. In a number of brief "on-line" bios of Ruick, reference is made to her going to New York in the early Fifties to help boost her career, and indeed, it's conceivable that that was one of the separation periods the pair went through. She was certainly very much busier than her husband through 1954 and in New York she made regular appearances in various television shows. Then, in 1955, she was lured back to Hollywood to star as Carrie Pipperidge in *Carousel* (1956), her biggest role to date.[19]

Other things rankled between them. He was a young, proud man. Throughout his life he held that it was a man's job to provide for his wife and family, and his wife's job was to take care of her husband and the home. Finding himself unemployed and left to take care of household chores while his wife went out to work did not sit well with him. Nevertheless, he did it. He knew that part of his responsibility was to help as and where he could. A careless jibe from her to the effect that it was a shame he could not also make a fist of doing the ironing brought his efforts in the house to a screeching halt. This incident, related by Robert Horton much later, was one of many, but it effectively illustrates how things went wrong between them. When Barbara Ruick filed the divorce suit she charged her husband with "cruelty". She accused him of causing her great "humiliation and embarrassment" which, she claimed, resulted in "the deterioration" of her health. Exactly what the "cruelty" amounted to was not specified, but it is true that he often left her to her own devices when attending parties where he was determined to be seen and noticed. He was also known to bluntly speak his mind, without thought for the feelings of those on the receiving end, a trait he carried with him throughout his life. Regarding his divorces, he was perfectly at ease to go into print with the words:

"I have been divorced twice. This is something I'm neither proud of nor ashamed to relate..."

Being cited for cruelty did not appear to upset him. Later in the article he spoke honestly about some of the things which made life difficult for each of them. Her career in the ascendency, his being dropped by the studio, being an "out of work" actor, her family castigating him for "not supporting" Barbara, for relying on her. In fact, they did not have money trouble, according to him. He said, "As it turned out, the money I earned was of no importance. We had enough money to live on and live well, and at the time it was too late to do anything to help the marriage anyway."[20]

In a number of other articles printed on the subject, he said that he and Barbara should never have married, "We should just have been friends," but in everything he ever said about the marriage he blamed himself for its failure. With his quick temper and lack of patience it is easy to understand, but no-one in a marriage is absolutely blameless. There is no doubt that Barbara Ruick contributed in her own way to its lack of success. She must have had a sense, throughout their relationship, throughout the separations and reconciliations, of Robert Horton's character, of what drove him, of what he had come from, of what he was striving to achieve. They continued to struggle with their feelings for one another, and even while the divorce action was underway, Robert Horton escorted his estranged wife to the premier of *Carousel* in February 1956.

By this time, Robert Horton was at a low ebb. A career in movies had come to nothing. One picture for Warner Brothers, two for 20th Century-Fox and seven with MGM. As the bean counters in the movie industry sought to stem losses being encountered by the studios, television was the only alternative. He had failed to make good on the "new Clark Gable" label. "Clark Gable was still around," he observed, "What did they need me for?" He was overlooked for people like Rock Hudson, Tab Hunter and even Troy Donahue. Was there a reason for that? Robert Horton certainly had the looks, not to mention the talent, but he did not attract the kind of attention which was given to some of his contemporaries. Was it something to do with his personality? Perhaps. He was never a compliant employee. He knew what he wanted, he had standards he lived by and demanded of himself. It is easy to suppose that he might have locked horns with those in charge above him. When he spoke of this period in his life, however, he simply says that perhaps his face did not fit, or that he was surplus to requirements. Even that the movies in question weren't filmed in glorious Cinemascope.[21] He is quite clear that none of the movies he had a substantial role in was memorable. After 1954 he made no more movies, bad or otherwise, for MGM, until, in 1956, he took a part in a movie produced by Republic Pictures, *The Man Is Armed* (1956). It was yet another flop. Dane Clark and May Wynn co-starred with him. It was a small budget piece and did nothing at the box office. It was released in the United States on October 19, 1956. Republic Pictures itself, a venerable institution of the film world since 1935 and keeper of a veritable lifetime's library of movies, was also heading for oblivion. In 1958 it was announced that it would cease feature film production. In 1959 it closed its doors. [22]

Robert Horton had long since moved out of the home he and Barbara shared and had been renting a little house in Brentwood since 1955. It was a home he loved and which he made entirely his own. It had four rooms on two floors and a wildly unkempt yard behind it on the side of a hill. He spent long hours clearing the yard, though not entirely. Its privacy attracted him. He liked the wooden paling fence which stood shoulder high and reminded him of his home on Kingsley Drive, and he liked the mature trees and shrubbery which surrounded the house. He liked the quiet street situated well away from busy highways and thoroughfares. His only companion was Soldier, the Springer spaniel he had shared briefly with Mary in 1952 and which had been meant for his brother

Creighton. Robert kept Soldier when he finally split with Barbara. His nephew remembers a visit to Brentwood, and the excitement of being allowed to keep the dog for a weekend.[23] When Soldier died, Robert acquired Beau James, "Jamie," a standard dark brown poodle which went everywhere with him, and which was his boon companion well into the Sixties.

In 1955, a year of heartache and trouble on all fronts as far as he was concerned, he met and fell in love with a young, rising star named Inger Stevens. Just how he met Inger Stevens is unknown, but in the interview he gave to Dwayne Epstein he said that he met her in 1955, and dated her through 1957. At the time of his association with her, and for years afterward, he never named her publicly. Throughout their affair, she was married to her agent, Antony Soglio. In fact, they were married in July of 1955 and remained married until August of 1958. Horton said that she told him she was divorced. The fact is that Robert Horton fell in love with her. Once again he gave his love unwisely. Inger Stevens was beautiful, intelligent and different, hailing originally from Sweden. He thought, for a time, that she returned his love honestly, but it wasn't the case. He took her home to meet his parents, who did not like her. They found her entirely self-centered.[24]

Inger Stevens was, beneath her very beautiful exterior, a pretty hard case. Born in October 1934, she came from a troubled background, and when her mother walked out on the family and her father went to the United States, she and her sister were left with an aunt near Stockholm. They joined their father and his new wife in New York City in 1944. She was thirteen when they moved again, this time to Manhattan, Kansas, and by age sixteen she was working burlesque shows in Kansas City. Within a couple of years she had returned to New York City where she got work as a chorus girl as well as less glamorous stuff in the Garment District, and took up classes at the Actors Studio. A career in various television series, commercials and plays followed.[25] By the time she met Robert Horton, she was busy enough to require the services of an agent, which is how she met and married Antony Soglio. Being married to Soglio did not seem to be a deterrent to embarking on the affair with Horton. Indeed, being married did not deter her from engaging in liaisons with a lot of men, especially if being associated with them might prove useful to her career.

In the *Red Book* there is a letter written to both Bob and Inger on November 26, 1956, addressed to the house in Brentwood by Edina and "Gar", expressing great fondness for both. Bob is praised for a recent performance, praised for being handsome (with graying hair and a mustache) in an unidentified television play which was, in fact, the *Alfred Hitchcock Presents* play, "Crack of Doom". Inger is exhorted to slow down and say "no" to more film work, but "not to Bob, of course!" Unfortunately, there is nothing in Bob's memorabilia to identify who Edina and Gar were, nor has research produced any information, but Robert Horton was sufficiently at ease with them to take Inger to visit them.

He thought that he had found his perfect woman and his grief and disappointment when she turned him over for a more promising relationship with a much bigger, and older star, was profound. It did not matter to him that his parents did not like her. He loved her. He thought she was, finally, the woman who would fulfill all his dreams. When he found her out, his world came crashing down around him. To discover that he had been used by her hurt him desperately. Throughout his career he never named Inger Stevens publicly, but there is one reference to her by him in a July 1960 article under the title "Don't Pin Him Down!" Allene Case interviewed him for *Screen Spotlight*. Talking about his marriages to that point, he said,

"I've only said 'I love you' to four women in my life and I married three of them. The fourth time I told a woman I loved her I didn't get married but it was not my fault. This time I got the short end of the stick. One day she was my girl and the next day, without any warning, she was the girl of one of the giant stars of America. I gather she thought he could further her career more than I could. I would have done anything for this girl including giving up my own career had she asked me to. When we blew up I found myself very preoccupied and embittered and suspicious of women for a long time."

In the end, Robert Horton proved to be no more important to Stevens than a rung on a ladder as she single-mindedly pursued her movie career. Her big break came in 1957 when the "giant star of America," Bing Crosby, wanted her to star with him in the movie *Man on Fire* (1957). He invited her to Palm Springs. Horton knew what that meant, as did she. "If you go, don't bother coming back," he said. She went. She got the part and moved on. She conducted affairs with James Mason (1958) and Harry Belafonte (1959 – 1960) among others, divorcing Soglio in 1958. Of course, Robert was totally cast aside but there is little doubt that Inger Stevens had what it took to attract him and hold him in sway as he dealt with his divorce, stumbling career fortunes and general inability to make an impact in his chosen profession. She certainly blinded him to the realities of their relationship.

However, during the course of 1956, his fortunes took a slightly upward turn. He starred as Starbuck in the J. Richard Naish play *The Rainmaker* at the Player's Ring Theater for seven highly successful weeks that summer, following up his previously acclaimed performance of Hal Carter in *Picnic* the year before. He appeared in eleven individual television shows that year, records of all of which still exist. All dramas. Three of the eleven were part of the *Alfred Hitchcock Presents* series. The second in which he starred, "Crack of Doom," aired on November 25, 1956. It was this episode which Horton's old university friend, Bob Walker, now in the television business himself, showed to the decision makers at Revue Studios, NBC's distribution arm, in order to persuade the powers that be to give Bob a screen test for the new Western series they planned entitled *Wagon Train*. Robert Horton also cited "Tongue of Silver" as having played a part in his selection.

On April 28, 1956, his divorce from Barbara Ruick became final. She very swiftly married an old school friend, John Williams, who would go on to become the fabulously renowned screen composer. They had three children. She died in March 1974 as a result of a cerebral hemorrhage.

It was a turbulent time for Robert. His career was alternating madly between highly successful roles and much work which was not. His emotional life was a case of swings and roundabouts too, and he decided he had to do something about it. He started to undergo a course in psychoanalysis. Whether or not he did this because he felt it might help him adjust his personality, or because it was "the thing" in Hollywood at the time he never said. What is a fact is that his brother, Dr. Creighton Horton, had nothing to do with it, despite what was written in the press of the day. Creighton had no time for psychotherapy, or psychoanalysis. He did not believe in it. His daughter Joan has been quite clear about this. She says that it is possible that her father might have yelled at Robert, sarcastically, in the course of one of the many arguments between the two brothers, that "you should go and see a shrink!"

Whatever brought it about, Robert Horton began to see a psychiatrist, or psychologist, about this time, and he maintained a course of psychotherapy for a little over three years. He was quite open about it at the time, although he did not discuss it in any great detail. How intense and regular were the sessions? Did they help him come to terms with himself, with his upbringing and the conflict he surely felt about it all? One article written by Paul Denis and published in *TV Illustrated* in June 1958 did refer to his psychoanalysis. Under the headline "Bob Horton: Still Learning The Facts Of Life" it covered a number of issues which troubled him, and Horton himself is quoted thus:

"In my work, I have become less eager but more confident. I am not overdrawn anymore. I work hard and I am as enthusiastic as ever. I have learned to get along with people better than before. I am no longer a man who has to be right all the time. I know that's not realistic. I know I have to be wrong some of the time. I used to suffer when I disagreed with somebody because I did not know how to present my view. Now I believe I've learned to present my ideas."

Just a little over a year later, in the September issue of *TV and Movie Screen* which went on sale at the end of August an unidentified reporter wrote,

"That Bob had talent as an actor no-one, including himself, ever doubted. But he had to overcome one handicap to be successful: tensions. The deeper he got into theatrics, the more tense and easily upset he became, the less able to take direction. After several extensive sessions (of psychoanalysis) the analyst credited his feelings to a resentment of authority."

This hardly seems to be a revelation, but smacks more of the obvious. Robert Horton's life up to that time demonstrated his innate rebelliousness, his determination to be himself no matter the cost.

Within all those statements, however, are several key points which shed light on Robert Horton's nature and the things which troubled him. If he gained maturity through his psychoanalysis, he nevertheless remained a complicated, diverse personality. He referred to his "strong feelings about his family." "I never understood my father. He was difficult. He wanted me to go into the insurance business, as he did. He was at me all the time. He was so disappointed that I didn't follow him into insurance. Now I've learned to understand the intention of his comment, but not the comment itself. I have learned that he wanted me to benefit from his mistakes. Thank God for my being analyzed; I appreciate now his good intentions." [26]

He is quoted as saying that there came a day when his doctor sent him on his way with the admonition that he could do no more for him. He had reached the point where he was "cured". Cured of what? His anger, his frustration, his sense of rejection? His need to rebel against anything which was contradictory to his own desires? His resentment of authority? Given the way his life evolved, the answer to these questions is undoubtedly, "no," although at the time the article was written he clearly felt that he had learned to be more relaxed and mature in his life. Much, much later, as a man in his sixties, he told a close friend that psychotherapy had done very little for him. [27] It is a perfectly reasonable observation. He was a highly intelligent man, clever, articulate and gifted. He did not need to be told what he was feeling, or why. However, it is more than likely that he gained some sense of justification as a result of the sessions, that his own thoughts and feelings were confirmed and validated as he talked them through with a disinterested party. What is also certain is that the therapy did not cause him to change or modify his behavior significantly. His five years working on *Wagon Train* probably did more for him, in that way, than any psychotherapy.

# PART IV WAGON TRAIN
## Chapter 11
### *The Rise of Flint McCullough*

When Robert Horton contemplated writing his biography in his late eighties, he was adamant that he would write the part about his tenure with *Wagon Train* himself. He even came up with its title, "The Rise and Demise of Flint McCullough".[1] Sadly, it came to nothing, but his title for this singular, stellar period says a lot about his own perceptions of this particular time in his career. When he landed the role of the scout in *Wagon Train* he was emerging from a low period in his life, both professionally and personally. Divorced from Barbara Ruick in April 1956, he had gone through the painful love affair with Inger Stevens and although he made a few appearances on television, notably "Tongue of Silver" and "Crack of Doom," he described himself as akin to a beaten boxer, flat on the ropes, gazing up, dazed, at a blue sky. Blue as in mood.[2]

Although, at first, he did not want to, he was persuaded by his old college friend Bob Walker, now a casting agent with Revue Studios, to take the screen test for *Wagon Train* in April 1957, after turning down two other offers to star in two different television series. He turned them down, he said, because the first offer required him to be the single lead and he did not wish to be identified only as the star of that particular show. He turned down the second offer because the material did not appeal to him. *Wagon Train* meant a co-starring role with established Western actor Ward Bond, and as such reduced the possibility of his being typecast. He was already quite clear in his mind that he was an actor, capable of undertaking diverse roles, and that was what he wanted from his career.[3]

He felt he handled the tests well, particularly when it came to holding his own on camera with Ward Bond, though he admitted that his riding ability was merely "sufficient" at the time. Uncertain as to his success in the tryouts (he was up against a slew of young, eager, wanna-be TV stars and he said he was, at just over six feet, "the runtiest guy of the lot") and still badly bruised by the failed relationship with Inger Stevens, he did something which was typical of him. He went on an unscheduled trip, first to New Orleans, then Miami, and finally, Cuba. He needed to be alone, he needed to think, and he needed to get to grips with his life. Despite the screen test for *Wagon Train* and the other offers, he felt his career was going nowhere, and maybe he thought the same of his life.[4]

As with so many of the stories attached to Robert Horton's life, how he heard that he had landed the part of Flint McCullough, scout to Major Seth Adams' wagon train, comes in at least two versions. The first version had him taking off by car, driving to New Orleans and then to Miami, where he visited with friends from his days at the University of Miami. He had good memories of his time there and he may have sought reassurance from those friends. It is certain that being alone, driving, was something he did when he needed to think things through, when he needed to deal with the complexities of his life. Always attracted to that which was different and exciting, he then flew to Cuba and stayed there for a few days. It was in Cuba that he received the message from his agent which would change his life irrevocably; he had won the part he had tried out for in the new Western television series, *Wagon Train*.[5]

The second version of the story is that he flew to New York on vacation, then went on to Cuba. Indeed Beverly Linet, who lived in New York, claimed to have been with him when he received the news, and she also wrote about being in Cuba with him, but whether or not that was on the same occasion it is impossible to say. In all likelihood, the first version of this story is the true one, but this serves as an example of how writers were quite willing to bend stories about Robert Horton after he reached stardom to suit their own needs. However, both versions of the story were agreed on the fact that he did not return directly to Los Angeles. In typical Robert Horton fashion, he drove home via the old wagon train routes to see for himself the country over which hundreds of thousands had once upon a time, within the last hundred years, toiled to reach their lands of milk and honey. Always curious when it came to things which intrigued him, he saw for himself some of the terrain that his character, Flint McCullough, would have traversed and it helped build in his mind the basis for the part he would play. As he traveled, he thought of his own ancestors trekking West with Brigham Young to Utah to build their city about the shores of its great Salt Lake, though he later described that area as unbelievably barren, causing him to question why so many hundreds of thousands risked their lives to make the journey out West.[6] Arriving home in Los Angeles he was immediately caught up in May in filming, and *Wagon Train* premiered on NBC on September 18, 1957.

So, at the ripe old age of thirty-three, living reasonably content-edly in a four-room rented cottage shared only with his dog, Robert Horton embarked on a five-year contract with NBC-TV and Revue Studios, a subsidiary of MCA, the Music Corporation of America, at whose head presided the legendary Lew Wasserman. MCA was a huge power in the American entertainment business. Lew Wasserman wielded that power in a singularly autocratic fash-ion. Everyone who came under his aegis knew it.[7] *Wagon Train* had an initial period of five years to run, specifically the airing seasons: 1957-1958, 1958-1959, 1959-1960, 1960-1961 and 1961-1962. There was no guarantee of each season following on automatically from the last, although Robert Horton was initially guaranteed at least eighteen episodes at the outset. Much depended on sponsor-ship, and when it was first broadcast, *Wagon Train* was sadly lacking in heavy-duty backers. Meanwhile, Robert had already made three appearances in the suspense series, *Alfred Hitchcock Presents*, he was keenly interested in expanding his singing capabilities in musi-cal theater and he had no interest in being typecast. He therefore negotiated a contract for himself which allowed him to take other roles in other productions from time to time as long as these did not interfere with the series' schedule, although this arrangement became a bone of contention at times between him and Revue.[8]

*Wagon Train* proved to be more than a sturdy vehicle for his suc-cess. Within months of its first showing, it was climbing up the popularity ratings at record speed, and much of this was simply due to Robert Horton and his portrayal of the scout, Flint McCullough. It was, however, a long and winding trail which brought him to the immense fame and adulation which *Wagon Train* engendered.

He was a serious actor. He wanted the show, and his role in it, to be taken seriously. His relationship with some of the cast members, notably his co-star Ward Bond and Bond's friends Terry Wilson and Frank McGrath, was never totally harmonious. Though the chemistry between them on screen was undeniable, off-screen Horton kept himself to himself. He had very little in common with any of them and his main alliances were with some of the stunt men and wranglers who worked the set. He admired these men and said often that they were some of the best, most decent, honest men he had ever encountered.[9]

From the first day on the set, however, it was clear to Robert Horton that he had a lot to learn about the intricacies of being part of a recorded television series. In the first place he found himself up against one of filmdom's most well-known actors, a close friend of John Wayne and John Ford, who went about the business of acting in his own blunt, straightforward fashion. Ward Bond, although he had been seen in over 150 movies by this time, was now, finally, "the star" in his own right. The young co-star he had to share the screen with was nothing very special in his opinion. They were two very different men. Bond was established, powerful in his own way, with connections within the movie industry which were not to be ignored. He owned a share in the series and therefore had a financial stake in it. He brought other friends with him onto the set of *Wagon Train* because he could. He wanted McGrath and Wilson as part of the show, and he got them. His politics were right wing conservative and he undoubtedly exhibited the same prejudices as many others of his time and generation. If you were part of his clique, you were okay. If you weren't, you didn't matter. Robert Horton, liberal in politics, always ready to be identified with those of a different color or persuasion, a product of the method school of acting, was never going to be accepted in that clique. Moreover, he was half Bond's age, in the full bloom of life, handsome, virile and as determined to be recognized for his talent as Bond.[10]

Although Ward Bond said on a number of occasions that he himself wanted Robert Horton to play the role of his scout, it is doubtful that he made any great effort to get Horton hired. A lot of people were consulted, including a number of support staff within the Revue Studios' offices, all ladies, who vehemently voted for the auburn-haired actor. In the end it was undoubtedly his acting prowess in "Crack of Doom" which sealed the matter for him. Nevertheless, when he got on the set of *Wagon Train* he initially described feeling as if he was "the cowpoke who snored and was voted out of the bunkhouse."[11]

The series was filmed throughout the spring and summer of 1957, so that by the time the first episode aired in mid-September, there were about eight stories "in the can". Throughout this time Robert Horton realized that very little attention was being paid to the story or background of the scout, and that indeed, it did not seem to matter to the various writers just exactly how, or why, he fit in to any given episode. Furthermore, he got the distinct impression that his only role in the series was to act as a kind of "traffic cop," appearing to deliver a line which might direct the story, then disappearing. His actual job as scout, or his personality, were simply ignored. His character was one-dimensional and as an actor accustomed to developing a character's personality, this irked him enormously, as did the writers' seeming inability to keep his character consistent.[12]

True to his commitment to his acting craft, he sat down and wrote a profile of Flint McCullough and requested that it be distributed to all writers who worked on a *Wagon Train* script. The profile itself was detailed, thorough, and described Flint McCullough in such a fashion that he came to life in a way that the script writers seemed incapable of portraying. The "Flint McCullough Story" created by Robert Horton caught the imagination of many TV critics and entertainment industry writers, and was reproduced often, but it is Robert Horton's letter to Allan Miller, Vice-President of Revue Productions, enclosing and requesting that his profile be distributed to and used by the script writers which is even more telling. Robert Horton, on September 23, 1957, five days after the first *Wagon Train* story was telecast, wrote:

*"Dear Allan,*

*Here is the outline of the character of "Flint McCullough" as created by me in an attempt to trace his life before he joins the Wagon Train in St. Joseph. This outline is designed to explain how Flint became the man he is, why he has turned to the Frontier as a livelihood, why he isn't mar-*

*ried, and is in complete accord with every word said about him in the series thus far, both by other characters and by himself, and always keeping in mind that Flint exists in the physical state of an actor named Robert Horton, possessing his voice, physique, emotional flexibility, physical dexterity and limitations. In general "Flint McCullough" as created thus far has no personality but mine. He has been given nothing to do that would directly invite understanding of him as a character, no light has been turned on to illuminate his past. Most of the time he is a convenient prop to be used in a heroic way to get other people out of trouble. It is unfortunate, but true, that the average audience watching <u>Wagon Train</u> knows more about "Chuck Wooster" as played by Frank McGrath than they do about Flint. It is also important to realize that the entire characterization was based on material in the <u>Jean Lebec</u> story that was first submitted to me as the test scene in April and was later completely edited out of the finished film that was screened last Wednesday. This continued treatment of Flint has made my job of making the character believable infinitely more difficult. This is the main reason I have insisted on doing as many of the physical things connected with the character as possible, because if <u>you see</u> the character, that is me, spin off a horse on a dead run, jump off of places that are as high as eighteen feet from the ground as in the Rossiter story, then the audience has to gradually believe that regardless of whether they feel Flint is, to use John Brahm's\* description, "elegant", or George Waggoner's,\*[sic]"educated", or Robert Florey's\* "refined", he is capable of doing the things that a man of the frontier is expected to be able to do. However, the problem is to get something into the scripts to explain <u>why</u> Flint is refined, <u>how</u> he became educated, etc.*

*If either Mr. Ingster\* or Mr. Lewis\* had a point of view about "Flint" based on what they had seen on the screen as I portray him, then they would be able to give some insight to the various writers who create our scripts; but they don't, or don't seem to if you judge by their efforts thus far.*

*On the next page is my background for "Flint" based on the Lebec story, and what I have said, or has been said about me so far in the series. It is historically accurate, and, if now and then improbable, still within the range of possibility."*

\*Boris Ingster – Associate Producer, 1958 – 1965
\*Richard Lewis – Executive Producer, 1957 – 1958

*John Brahm, George Waggner, Robert Florey – Directors, 1957
Robert Horton's profile of the scout Flint McCullough reads as follows:

"WAGON TRAIN  <u>FLINT MCCULLOUGH BIOGRAPHY</u>

Flint was born in 1839, in Virginia (the son of a middle-class family). His mother was a native of Virginia, his father an immigrant from Scotland who earned his living as a teacher at Virginia's College of William and Mary.

By selecting the teaching profession as his father's occupation, and by choosing Virginia as his mother's home, I feel that a certain grace in his everyday living habits can (easily) be explained, as the old South was certainly the home of graciousness in early America, and also his early contact with education would not be too difficult to understand.

In 1850 his family moved from Virginia and headed West to Salt Lake City. I chose this year as this was the year the University of Utah was founded. This would give a logical reason for the move from the father's standpoint economically, and if you chose to have him interested or converted to the Mormon faith you would only double the motivation. This would also give young "Flint", now eleven, his first contact with the problems of crossing the plains, acquaint him with the Oregon Trail as far as the South Pass, and then through the pass to Fort Bridger, and on to Salt Lake. As you know, this route was the route of the Donner Party, the Mormons, and the great majority of those pushing on to California.

While at Fort Bridger, where the wagon trains were accustomed to stopping for repairs and supplies, "Flint" meets Jim Bridger. By 1850, Bridger was already a legend, had been spoken of most generously in Fremont's book, published in 1842, <u>Reports on Expeditions exploring The Rocky Mountains</u>. It stands to reason that a person who could read and who planned to make the trek west would certainly have read this book within the eight years after it was published, especially in an academic environment. Therefore Flint knows about Bridger and can have a kind of hero worship for the scout, and Bridger, who took up the study of Shakespeare when he was in his later years, could be flattered and more than casually interested in a young boy who could read, and had read about him.

This friendship could be developed in imagination as Bridger often went through Salt Lake City.

In the Winter of 1852, the Mormons had a particularly bad cold season, and during this winter, in my story, I choose to have Flint's father pass away with pneumonia. This, I feel, would aid in Flint's rather rapid maturation, as now he, in essence, would be the head of the family. This would also serve in motivating an even closer relationship between him and Jim Bridger, the latter becoming a kind of father. This relationship now opens up and explains Flint's understanding of Indians. The Mormon people were on friendly terms with the Ute tribe, and this tribe spoke a dialect of Siouan language, one of the great linguistic families of the North American Indians, engulfing nearly all the tribes which lived between the Mississippi River and the Rocky Mountains. Add to this the fact that Bridger had two wives, both squaws, picturesquely named Blast Your Hide, a Cheyenne, and Dang Your Eyes, an Arapahoe, and you further explain Flint's understanding and acceptance of Indians and their customs, and as he was Jim Bridger's friend, the Indians accepted him. Bridger was celebrated across the frontier as a scout, trapper, hunter and fur trader and by linking Flint's life with his, from 1850 through 1857, the <u>how</u> in my characterization can be gradually explained.

To continue, in 1855 Bridger returned east and ultimately was hired as a scout by General Albert Sydney Johnston. In my story, Flint goes with him and crosses the plains for the second time, and with the advent of the Civil War, why shouldn't Flint cast his lot with the South? After all, his mother was from Virginia.

At the end of the Civil War, with the South in ruins, Flint returns to the thing he knows the best; the frontier. The last I heard of him he was scouting for Major Seth Adams."

Both of these documents, in carbon copy form, were carefully preserved in Robert Horton's *Red Book* of memorabilia. Thus was the Flint McCullough who millions came to know, love and admire, born. There is much in this short piece of writing which contains echoes of Robert Horton's own life, and indeed, he also said, memorably, of his characterization of the scout, in an interview given to Robert Johnson of the *Saturday Evening Post* in 1961,

"As it was left for me to develop the character, I naturally created a character that would be easiest for me to play."

In doing so, he (Horton) endowed Flint with traits which he personally admires and practices – among them honesty, forthrightness, courtesy and an aversion to religious, racial and social discrimination." The title Johnson gave the piece, "Big Ego, Big Talent" did not go down well with Robert Horton but it reflects, in part, some of the impressions he gave to others at the time as he stood up for himself in the superficial world of show business. By the time this article was published in December 1961, much had taken place in terms of Horton's relationships with his co-stars, directors and producers, but it all began in the early days of his signing with Revue, MCA and NBC.

So, only a few months into his contract with Revue Productions, he was encountering obstruction and pitfalls, and was making his stand in his own true fashion. None of which endeared him either to the studios or to his fellow actors, particularly Bond. Still, Robert Horton was listened to, the "McCullough history" distributed, and with few subsequent exceptions, and there were, glaring exceptions, his profile was accepted and used by the writers and directors of *Wagon Train*. It is, however, interesting to note that the original first episode of *Wagon Train* due to be aired was, in fact, "The Jean LeBec Story," but instead the producers chose to air "The Willy Moran Story" first. Starring Ernest Borgnine as Willy Moran, this episode also gave Ward Bond a bigger part than the one he had in "The Jean LeBec Story," starring Ricardo Montalban. Robert Horton played a significantly more important role in this than he did in "The Willy Moran Story". A careful viewer will note dialog in the Borgnine show which clearly states that the wagon train is already on its way into Kansas, while the LeBec story is set in St. Jo, Missouri, before the train has even begun its trek. The disdain the producers had for their viewers' knowledge of history is obvious, as is the fact that Bond played a much more emphatic part in the Moran story. Horton is barely seen in it. Perhaps Ward Bond saw this, too, and demanded the switch. Whatever drove the decision, it undoubtedly served to irritate Robert Horton.

At the time, many stories and rumors circulated about Robert Horton's less-than-comfortable relationships with his *Wagon Train* co-stars. He certainly admired Ward Bond and respected him as an actor. He acknowledged the man's experience and his straight-forward approach to his art. He often said, when asked about his relationship with Bond, that he worked hard, always knew his lines, delivered them accurately and on cue and that you always knew where you were with him. That he differed from this modus operandi did not, he felt, make him less of an actor. His involvement with and interpretation of his character required him to "feel" who his character was, from the way he glanced at something, picked something up, walked and spoke. His letter to Allan Miller reflects that dedication to his craft, and he did not accept any ridicule shown him for his methods any more than he indulged in ridicule of others' methods.[13]

Throughout his contract with *Wagon Train* he questioned anything which he felt compromised the validity and believability of his character, or his part in a story. He wasn't being difficult. He was being true to his art. In a press release dated March 2, 1958, subsequently published in *TV Illustrated* and saved by him in his *Red Book*, he is quoted as follows;

"I create a lot of enemies because I ask questions," Horton concedes with no visible demonstration of regret. "Not only with directors, either. Other people in the company hear me and say, 'That's disrespectful. Who does he think he is? What does he know about it?'

"Well, I think I know quite a bit about it!" says Horton, an adherent of the same school of acting which produced Marlon Brando and James Dean. "I'm not exactly a kid in this business. I've studied, and I've worked. I'm thirty-three, although most people think I'm younger. Authority alone means nothing to me. Talent and ability within authority, that's the thing. I simply won't read lines like a puppet. An actor should never forget that the viewer doesn't look at that screen and say the show's badly directed or badly produced. He just looks at the star and says, 'Boy, is he lousy!'"

He was determined to be seen as an actor, and a good one, and his efforts to maintain a high quality in terms of his depiction of Flint McCullough paid off handsomely. Within a very few weeks of *Wagon Train* appearing each Wednesday night on NBC, fan mail for Flint started coming in, and how it came in! Letters by the hundreds, far outstripping that of any of the other main protagonists on the show, soon brought Revue Studios to the conclusion that their young, feisty, intelligent star should indeed be given bigger parts, and a great many more close-ups. This undoubtedly went down badly with Ward Bond, who finally had a part which billed him as the star, but who was not on the receiving end of anything like the fan mail which poured in to Robert Horton. Furthermore, entertainment press writers were noting Robert Horton's abilities. In a piece headlined "What Makes *Wagon Train* Go?" in *TV Views* on March 1, 1958 Edward Nitram wrote,

"He's brought a solid impact to "Wagon Master" (as the show was first billed, thus giving Bond's role more prominence) that strong men envy and ALL women lap up. He's a perfect contrast to the ageless wisdom of Bond . . .young, incredibly handsome, reckless and not above playing footsie with any beautiful babe."

In *The American Weekly* of March 15, 1959, under the banner "Husbands Hate Robert Horton," his effect on and contribution to the show was noted.

"*Wagon Train* started rolling across the plains – and the TV sets – with Ward Bond as its boss and star performer. Since Flint McCullough, a young scout who is Horton in the flesh, began to take an increasingly prominent part in the proceedings, it has risen to be the nation's top-rated TV show. The 2,000 letters that Horton receives each month are mostly from young married women and some of the passages are a lot purpler than those Elvis Presley used to be exposed to by his teenage fans."

If there had been some animosity on the set at first between the "method" actor from New York, and the "good old boys" of Bond's set, the fan mail business did not help.

However, the show which had started life without sponsorship now received support in the form of the Ford Motor Company, which came on board before the end of the first season, by which time *Wagon Train* was challenging the perennially successful *Gunsmoke* for a spot at the top of the rankings board. Indeed, so pleased was Ford by this achievement that it gave both Horton and Bond a car early in 1958, and *Wagon Train* topped the television ratings by early 1959.[14]

The professional animosity which developed between Robert Horton and Ward Bond first surfaced publicly in early 1958. A letter from an irate Bond fan regarding Horton's insistence on equal billing was published in a January 1958 edition of the *Los Angeles Mirror News*, and began with the words, "Who the hell does he think he is?" Word of Horton's fight to gain acknowledgment for the part he played in *Wagon Train*'s success was out. The fan ripped into the newcomer for wanting, too soon, the rewards which Bond had labored for over decades. The newspaper responded with the words, "Horton apparently sees no point in waiting twenty years if he can get these things in his contract, which he did, and now he just wants the contract executed properly."

By this time, Robert Horton was firmly established as a star in his own right with *Wagon Train* and his personal appearance calendar, at rodeos, on summer stage and television far out-stripped that of Ward Bond, although they did make a few such appearances together late in 1957. In April 1958, the *Los Angeles Mirror News* once again wrote of reports of a "real life dissension between Ward Bond and Robert Horton." Then, on May 7, they wrote that "word is out that Ward Bond got real tough with producers and told them that they would have to can Robert Horton." Studio representatives played down the situation and told the press that Horton would be required to report for the start of shooting the 1958-1959 season on May 22. Horton was aware of the demand made by the older actor of *Wagon Train*'s producers, but it was just one more example of the rift which had grown between them from early in the program's production when Robert Horton complained that he was being upstaged by Bond on all fronts.

By the time shooting of the 1958-1959 season began, and in response to pleas, requests and demands from legions of women viewers, the show's producers agreed that Robert Horton's character should get larger parts, more close-ups, more romantic involvements and much more attention than had thus far been the case. Certainly, his personal appearances and the honorary positions awarded him by various organizations and associations warranted it. In order to maintain some semblance of harmony on the set, an agreement was reached whereby Bond and Horton would star in alternate episodes of *Wagon Train*, with the sub-title to each such episode reading "Tonight Starring Ward Bond" and "Tonight Starring Robert Horton." This state of affairs was further aggravated when Robert Horton decided that, no matter what the script called for, he would not appear in any of Bond's episodes and he asked that the arrangement be reciprocated.[15]

Meanwhile Ward Bond was unable to comprehend Horton's lack of total dedication to *Wagon Train*. He was of the opinion that Horton did not take the show seriously but used it to make more money elsewhere. Robert Horton, meanwhile, stuck to his contractual obligations, but also took advantage of those contractual terms which allowed him to appear elsewhere, and it is true that he earned extremely good money appearing as the star of rodeo shows around the West where he refused to wear his Flint McCullough garb, but rode into an arena, dismounted and proceeded to sing, to the surprise and delight of the gathered crowds. These appearances brought him fees in the tens of thousands, whereas his *Wagon Train* earnings in the early days were relatively modest. In fact, in order to retain the flexibility of his contract, he never received any increase in his earnings over and above the initial agreement, throughout the five years of his tenure, so while the extracurricular appearances he made met his need to act and sing and avoid being typecast, they also put substantial amounts into his bank account.[16]

By mid-1959, Robert Horton was an established star of the small screen and his fans were legion the world over. His worth to Revue Studios and its parent company were indisputable and while matters within the world of *Wagon Train* and on its sets were at times tense, Robert Horton understood clearly that he was an integral, vital component of the show. He was also very clear that he was an actor, playing a cowboy, not a cowboy in a Western. He demanded respect for that, and he demanded high standards of the scripts he was asked to work with.

Nevertheless, when Bond and Horton were on the screen together, a certain magic chemistry took over. They played off each other, the grumpy, irascible but steady and kind-hearted wagon master who had to deal with his young, independent, clever, romantically inclined scout. It was a chemistry which lit up the screen and which may have had something to do, in part, with the fact that the characteristics each portrayed were, in fact, part of their real-life personalities. Though polar opposites in so many ways, they fitted together on the screen and people loved them for it. The formula they created of old, world weary, experienced man versus young, enthusiastic, somewhat reckless man was one which was copied again and again in numerous other shows. Bond was much more a cowboy playing in a Western, but he had come by his fame and reputation honestly. He was a bluff, down-to-earth character who felt a certain antipathy toward the young Horton who was handsome, virile, talented and who did not fall down and worship at his feet. Bond ridiculed Horton for wearing make-up on the set, completely overlooking the desire of directors to cover up the young man's heavily freckled face.[17] They disagreed about acting styles. Bond read his lines and got on with them. Horton queried his lines, especially if they did not hold true to the character he was playing. Bond had his friends employed by the studio. Terry Wilson, who Robert Horton described as "a sycophant," started out with an undefined role as a mere passenger on the wagon train but soon became a wagon train wrangler at Bond's side, and lost his TV wife in the process. She simply disappeared from the scripts. Frank McGrath, too, came on board as the scruffy, wiry little cook, constantly put upon by the wagon master. McGrath was known to drink a bottle of whisky a day, so his scenes were shot early in order to avoid any drunken mishaps later. Both men were gifted stuntmen and earned Horton's admiration for those skills, but they were never friends. When Bond, Wilson and McGrath retired to Bond's dressing room a locked fridge was opened and beer ran freely.[18] That did not interest Robert Horton. Besides, he was never invited to join them. As he said succinctly,

"I don't believe in horsing around on the set. I'm not trying to win a popularity contest. I'm there to work. I want to be good, not just fair."[19] The people he did admire on the set were the wranglers and horse trainers. His observations on them are telling. He said, repeatedly,

"I've learned so much from men who ride and take care of horses. They're a fine bunch of men. They're on the level. If they have nothing to say they keep quiet. If somebody else talks, they listen."[20]

When it came to shooting an episode of *Wagon Train*, he had his own ideas about quality and believability. If a script was questionable, Robert Horton questioned it. If a director's direction was questionable, Robert Horton questioned it. He was acutely aware of the fact that the viewing public were not fools and he resented them being treated as such by the studio. He resented being associated with anything less than the best, and if he felt standards in production were below par, he questioned it. He is on record as saying that the first two seasons of *Wagon Train* were the best. After that, he said, the studio cut corners, used too much stock footage, indoor sets and accepted poor quality writing. To a man who cared deeply about the quality of his work, things such as splicing in scenes of him riding a completely different horse half way through an episode from the one he was first seen on galled him, not to mention showing the same campsites incessantly in clearly different stories.[21]

The business of producing an episode of *Wagon Train* every week for thirty-nine weeks each season was exhausting. Scripts had to be read, agreed, then filmed. Early morning rises, long grueling days and nights spent studying scripts and any revisions meant that there was very little time for anything else, especially when shooting on location. It was hard work, draining work and not in the least bit glamorous. Robert Horton, always something of a perfectionist, worked hard at his role, at perfecting his character. He was not prepared to hand over all the action scenes to a double. He was young and fit and he demanded that he be allowed to perform as many of his own stunts as was within reason. He took lessons in stunt riding from the highly acclaimed Lennie P. Gear. There are several dozen photographs of these training sessions which may have taken place at the now extinct Hudkins Stable Ranch in the Valley. He worked with the horse trainer-wrangler on a regular basis, until he was comfortable with handling any horse in any situation. He became a highly proficient rider, loved to ride fast as much as he loved to drive fast, and by 1958 decided that he would acquire his own special horse to ride in the series.[22]

Several horses have been associated with Robert Horton's role as the scout; a horse named Two Spot was his ride in the first season of *Wagon Train*, a horse he chose himself and which was "fast". He liked that speed. When the second season rolled around he was given Little Buck, a buckskin with a broad white blaze. It may have been Ward Bond's influence which brought about the change, but Robert Horton disliked Little Buck because, he said, "you couldn't get that horse to move!" Then there was Trophy, a dark bay with a star and narrow blaze below it. He owned Trophy, although he had not actually purchased him, and retired him in 1959.[23] Horton loaned Trophy to Barbara Stanwyck to ride in the 19th Annual Palm Springs Mounted Police Rodeo, which took place on February 7 and 8, 1959. He was Grand Marshal to Stanwyck's Queen of the Rodeo.[24] By that time he had acquired an Appaloosa during an engagement as star of the Lewiston Roundup in Idaho the previous September following a serious, lengthy search for his own horse.

He had clearly put the word out that he was looking for a horse when he starred in the Caldwell Rodeo in August, 1958, just about a month prior to the Lewiston date. In the *Lewiston Morning Tribune*, it was reported that Eddie Cole, Executive Secretary of the International Rodeo Association advised that "the actor is in search for a movie horse and wants an Appaloosa. He has been to Texas and many other places in his search. Horton, Cole said yesterday, feels the Appaloosa would best lend to his role of a scout in Indian country. Cole said the actor wants to build this horse into a character with which Horton can also be identified." The lead-in to the article stated,

"He (Horton) plans to take a look this morning at a gelding Appaloosa at Roundup Park." It went on:

"An extensive search for a horse may end at Lewiston for Robert Horton, the television star of *Wagon Train*. The thirty-four-year old actor wants an Appaloosa horse to supplement the character of Flint McCullough, a scout whom Horton portrays on the television set. And waiting for Horton here Thursday upon his arrival from California will be a seven year old registered Appaloosa gelding picked out for his inspection by the Lewiston Roundup Association. The horse is owned by Clark Mason of Lewiston, one time contestant at Lewiston Roundups. The gelding is out of Stormy Knight, one of the top Appaloosa stud horses in the country and has unusual markings on its flanks. Even if Horton does not select the Lewiston horse he will become familiar with it. It is the horse he will ride at the Roundup."

In fact, Robert Horton bought the Appaloosa, which he named Stormy Night, and he rode him throughout the next three seasons on *Wagon Train,* and in the *Shenandoah* series. In the March 1960 edition of *The Appaloosa Journal* his enthusiasm for Stormy and his pride of ownership is evident.

"As far as I am concerned, I'm having a love affair with him. This is the first horse I ever purchased. He has a wonderful disposition and is extremely smooth in all gaits."

At first, however, in Lewiston, he rejected the animal as his mane was clipped. Then he determined that a "wig" might be fashioned for the horse until such time as his mane grew in. He named the horse as he did because he finalized the deal on a stormy night in Idaho, having ridden him twice in the Roundup.[25] It was a delightful play on words. A horse named "Topaz" was also associated with Robert Horton, but that was, in fact, Stormy Night. A British newspaper held a contest amongst its readers to name Horton's new Indian pony, and "Topaz" was chosen. Whether or not the British viewers understood that this name was never applied to the horse is immaterial; it was a publicity exercise. In several scenes throughout the series Horton quite clearly calls his horse "Stormy" and that was how he was known throughout his life. One of the things which infuriated Bob after he acquired Stormy Night and rode him in *Wagon Train* was the slip-shod editing which cut in clips of him astride his earlier horses rather than filming him correctly astride the Appaloosa. He may have thought that Stormy's unique markings would force the producers to avoid such situations. He was, unfortunately, wrong.

# Chapter 12
## *Sophisticated Lady*

A major facet of *Wagon Train* which set it aside from its competition, established or otherwise, was its format. One hour in length, each episode was tantamount to a short film, and the additional draw of a "star" name meant that viewers, not necessarily Western fans, would watch to see the likes of Ernest Borgnine, Ricardo Montalban, Edgar Buchanan, Michael Rennie, Nina Foch and Shelley Winters, all of whom appeared in the first season. This had the added effect of keeping the "regulars" in supporting roles and added a dimension to each week's story which was lacking in the competition. Throughout the five seasons in which Robert Horton played Flint McCullough, other famous names appeared – Dan Duryea, Bette Davis, George Montgomery, Virginia Mayo, Raymond Massey, Rhonda Fleming, Dean Stockwell, Claude Rains, Charles Laughton, Peter Lorre, Mickey Rooney, Dame Judith Anderson, Farley Granger, Anne Blyth, Angie Dickinson, and even Lou Costello, to name a very, very few. A whole raft of the current young television stars of the time appeared as well; Susan Oliver, Robert Fuller, Debra Paget, Tommy Sands and James Drury were among that group, as well as child actors Patty McCormack, Evelyn Rudie, Michael Burns and Roger Mobley. Some of these stars appeared more than once.[1]

Nina Foch starred in "The Clara Beauchamp Story" which was the thirteenth episode of *Wagon Train*'s first season. It was filmed during the summer of 1957, and it was aired on December 11 that year. It brought Nina Foch and Robert Horton together in a relationship which lasted for eighteen months. In fact, Robert Horton admitted, much later, that Nina lived with him, off and on during that time, though he was careful not to say so then.[2] Contemporary entertainment publications hinted at the closeness of their friendship but were never forthright about its status.

*With Nina Foch in* Much Ado About Nothing, *May 1958. Robert Horton, author's collection.*

Nina Foch was a few months older than Horton, having been born in April 1924. Her father was a Dutch musician, her mother an American actress. They divorced when she was just a toddler, and her mother returned to New York where Nina grew up. Tall and blond, she was intelligent, gifted and attractive. She had many attributes which held Horton's interest, and it was she who encouraged him to consider becoming involved in a Shakespeare production. Both were exceedingly busy in their respective careers, but they ultimately appeared together in "Much Ado About Nothing" on NBC's *Matinee Theater*. Robert Horton told the story.

"I met Al McCleery, one of the producers, on his set one day, and he asked when I could come over and do a show. I said I'd like to very much, especially if it could be in a Shakespeare role. You see, Shakespeare is a sort of a challenge to an actor, and it's a lot of fun." In *Matinee Theater*'s 637 performances, there had never been an attempt to enact any of Shakespeare's work. Within a month McCleery called Horton wondering if he would still be interested in a part in "Much Ado About Nothing." The actor said "I grabbed at the chance," and the play was broadcast in color in two parts on May 21 and 22, 1958.[3]

Much was written about the Horton-Foch friendship at the time, much conjectured. Nina Foch was married throughout that period, though not happily. She and her husband, actor James Lipton, were married in June 1954. She separated from Lipton early in 1958, perhaps because of her affair with Horton.[4] Rumors about plans between the two to marry were publicly scotched by Horton. Foch was quoted as saying, "We're either madly in love or not speaking to each other."[5] Another volatile relationship. Another case of unwise love. Whatever the truth of it, they were a twosome for some time, pictured together at the house in Brentwood and clearly happy in each another's company during their work together. There is no doubt that they complemented one another in certain ways, and no doubt that Robert Horton enjoyed Nina's intelligence as well as all she was able to teach him about the profession they shared. When they met, she had already made a name for herself in the movie industry and had established herself as something of a star, appearing frequently in movies, television and theater since 1943. Her European background intrigued him as well as her sophistication and cosmopolitan ways.[6]

Sometime during their relationship, Robert Horton's friendship with writer Beverly Linet suffered a change for the worse. They had known one another since 1951 and Horton had shared a great deal with Linet, much of which he allowed her to publish in the magazines for which she wrote, which included *TV Star Parade* and *TV*

*Movie Life*. Linet was based for the most part in New York City, and the bulk of what she wrote about him was published in the years 1957 and 1958. In particular, in an article published in the December 1958 edition of her magazine she wrote about dating Bob over a period of seven years, describing the experience in a headline which read, "Perfectly Wonderful, Miserably Awful – What it's like to date Bob Horton." She claimed that theirs was an "unromantic, true friendship" but it was not so for her. In reality, she was desperately in love with Robert, and he described her to a latter-day friend as being "besotted" with him, although he valued her as a friend.[7] Press tidbits of the time refer to his "dating" Linet when he visited New York, as well as stating outright that Linet bitterly resented his involvement with Foch. Indeed, gossip columnist Walter Winchell on his Feature Page of the *Herald-Express* declared on October 17, 1958, "Don't invite Nina Foch and screen mag writer Beverly Linet to the same party. The feud isn't over anything Beverly wrote, but an actor named Bob Horton. (Girlz)…" Linet's work called for her to travel to Los Angeles periodically, and during one of these visits, she overstepped the line of what, to him, had been an acceptable friendship. After she dogged his footsteps one day during the visit, he finally lost patience with her, put her in a cab and told her to go home. He returned to his Brentwood cottage only to discover that she had broken in and was waiting for him in his bedroom. When she refused to leave, he called the police.

"I don't want her arrested or hurt," he told them, "I just want her out of my home."[8] Just how this episode affected their friendship is hard to say, but there is nothing by way of publicity material on him written under her name after 1959. However, she appeared to be back on friendly terms with him when he finally got to Broadway in 1963, and by her own admission much later in life she carried a torch for him until the day she died.[9]

Nina Foch, meanwhile, obtained a divorce from her husband James Lipton on February 2, 1959. When asked if the divorce meant that she would soon marry Horton, she replied that she thought it "tacky" to discuss such issues so soon after the event. There were reports of expensive gifts which Robert Horton gave her in February 1959, to mark the occasion. There were other reports saying that Nina Foch was "sharing" Horton with a young pre-med UCLA student named Ellen Dorn, with whom he had been linked over a period of several months. Another name which made the press at the time was that of Cindy Robbins, referred to as Robert Horton's "new romance". He was seen on numerous occasions in the spring of 1959 wining and dining Barbara Stanwyck as well as Rhonda Fleming following her appearance in "The Jennifer Churchill Story" which was shot sometime in 1958 and aired in October that year. These and other liaisons Robert Horton was reputed to have had probably brought about the numerous break-ups which he and Nina Foch had in their relationship, but when he finally split with Nina in 1959, it was undoubtedly because he had fallen in love with a young singer-actress named Marilynn Bradley. They met in June, in Warren, Ohio, in a summer stock production of *Guys and Dolls*. He played Sky Masterson to her Sarah Brown in his first lead role in a musical. She was extremely pretty and blessed with a wonderful voice and he said that they "fell madly in love."[10] Marilynn Bradley ultimately played the most significant role in his life. However, as he took up his new role in *Wagon Train* in 1957, still nursing a wounded heart, Nina was struggling with her own marital difficulties and they found solace in one another's company. Nina had attributes which may have reminded him of Inger Stevens. What they did not find was a perfect relationship. Nina Foch, however, was reportedly devastated and angry when Bob put an end to their relationship. She moved on to establish a partnership with her second husband, psychiatrist Dennis DeBrito, who she married in December 1959, and with whom she had one child before divorcing him in 1963.[11] Though some said that Foch never spoke to Robert Horton after the break-up, in fact she starred with him in an episode of *Shenandoah* in 1966, "Marlie," in which both seem perfectly at ease with one another.

Robert Horton's name was constantly linked with beautiful women of the stage and screen from the moment he attained real "star" status through his portrayal of Flint McCullough on *Wagon Train*. His affair with Inger Stevens never saw the light of day while it was happening, but at the time, he was of little account in Hollywood and her liaisons made it politic for him to keep quiet about their association. Besides, she rejected him in favor of the older but far more powerful man, Bing Crosby, so there was nothing for him to gain at the time by making it public. Most of the women who appeared in the entertainment press with him, touted as "dates", "romances", "affairs" were no more than publicity material, with the exception of Nina Foch and possibly the student Ellen Dorn, who he candidly admitted he liked because she was not interested in his actor status.[12] However, Marilynn Bradley's appearance heralded something different in terms of his relationships, although the media of the day continued to make much of various women who were seen with him at restaurants or receptions, premiers and social functions.

# Chapter 13

## *Behind the Scenes*

As if he were not busy enough with *Wagon Train*, ad hoc act-ing assignments and personal appearances, he took up voice les-sons again. Then, through an encounter with a friend, he decided he would try his hand at flying. At first, he said, he did not think he would succeed, but typically he persevered and "suddenly it all made sense." He wrote enthusiastically about his accomplishments and the pleasure of flying, as well as its usefulness in his career in a one-page letter to his British Fan Club in March 1960. Of course, interest in flight was not new to him. The aviary he kept as a boy in the back yard of the Kingsley Drive home, and the model aircraft he built when confined to the house or his bed during his kidney-induced illnesses attest to that. There were references to his attempt to join the Army Air Corps before he was finally accepted by the Coast Guard in 1943. His first flying lesson took place in February 1959. His first solo flight, according to his handwritten note in his Pilot's Flight Log, took place on February 24, 1959. His own description of his first flying lessons reported by columnist Sheilah Graham in the *Citizen News* of March 12, 1959 was,

"It reminded me of live television. You're on your own and no-one can help you."

He qualified as a student pilot in April that year and wasted no time in buying his own aircraft. He took delivery of his first, and only plane, a Piper Comanche PA-24, on May 15, 1959 in Cincin-nati where he was beginning a series of summer engagements.[1] The Comanche had a single 250 hp engine and cruised at a top speed of 190 miles per hour. A Piper company pilot, Don Hart, ferried the aircraft to him from the Piper factory in Lockhaven, Pennsylvania, and then flew with him to Craterville, Oklahoma, before accom-panying him to other personal appearances. However, by this time, early June, Bob was doing most of the flying himself as he became familiar with his new aircraft.[2]

His second solo flight, identified as "cross-country" and also entered as a handwritten note in the back inside cover of his Pilot's Log, took him from Detroit to Lansing, then to Battle Creek and back to Detroit. He had two major theatrical engagements to undertake; he was scheduled to play the role of Hal Carter for the second time in *Picnic* in Detroit, and then appear in the lead role of Sky Masterson in *Guys and Dolls* with the well-known Kenley Players of Warren, Ohio.

On June 29, 1959, following his engagement in *Guys and Dolls*, he flew his first solo trans-continental flight between Youngstown, Ohio and Van Nuys, California when he logged twenty hours, twenty-five minutes solo time. Once again, this flight's particulars were noted on the inside back cover of his Pilots Log, which spanned the dates between February 1961 and October 1993. He was proud of these achievements. Unfortunately, all that exists of a previous log book are the words entered on Page 1 of this Log in Bob's handwriting "From Book #1 145.55" (flying hours logged). The second Log contained two photographs of the Piper Comanche he bought in May 1959, and owned for forty years, as well as the telegram regarding its delivery to him. Horton kept the plane on the east coast until he had met his theatrical commitments in the region, then flew it home to what would be its base at the Van Nuys airport in the San Fernando Valley.

*Bob's Piper Comanche at Van Nuys Airport, 1959. Author's collection.*

To gain his full license, he was required to complete a solo, transcontinental flight so in typical, Horton-ish pragmatical style he achieved this by picking up the aircraft as and when he did. Exactly when he qualified as a full pilot is unknown; there is no reference to a specific date, although there exists a replica license confirming him as a qualified Private Pilot with ratings for Single Engine and Multi-engine (Land) aircraft bearing an issue date of September 17, 1966 and this is supported by an entry on Page 11 of the Log which reads "Multi Engine Land Flight Test Passed" dated September 17, 1966. The aircraft flown was a Piper Aztec. According to several news items dated in the early part of 1961, Bob was telling curious reporters that he was a fully licensed pilot, and he had no reason to mislead them. Syndicated columnist Sheilah Graham reported on March 2, 1961 that "Robert, who has flown all over America as a student pilot, tells me he now has his pilot's license." In *The Des Moines Sunday Register* on June 18, 1961, a captioned photo of Bob as Flint McCullough standing on the driver's seat of a wagon reads in part, "Flying Scout – An excellent horseman . . . he's also a qualified airplane pilot."

He became a member of the Aircraft Owners and Pilots Association (AOPA) at some point, although the exact date of his joining isn't recorded anywhere. There are, however, several entries in the log which record his attendance at various training sessions in Pennsylvania at the AOPA's headquarters during the 1970s.

On May 22, 1962, Bob's good friend and Hollywood gossip columnist Hedda Hopper wrote in the *Los Angeles Times*,

"He flies his single engine Piper Comanche on his tour and his wife flies with him. "She was my first passenger. I fly only by daylight." I wondered if he might not be safer in a two engine plane. "That's a matter of theory; you have to be a better pilot for a two engine plane because if one goes out you have to balance the plane. With a single engine you can prove to passengers it's not going into a spin immediately by taking them up, shutting off the power and letting them see it will glide and doesn't fall straight down. That gets rid of the fear. I took my father up the first time a year ago. When we landed he said, 'This is a day I won't forget in a hurry, flying in a plane piloted by my own son!'"

There are no other mentions of family members flying with him, other than his wife, Marilynn. His niece Joan alluded to the fact that she herself (a nervous flier anyway) was afraid that, if she went aloft with him he might do just as described – shut off the engine and frighten her to death.[3] In various articles, whose validity is always suspect, Marilynn was portrayed as equally confident in the air as her husband. In fact she was not. She was sufficiently nervous about flying that she persuaded him to drive her to Las Vegas for their December wedding. He complied and was rear-ended in a multiple collision enroute. No-one was hurt, but as he pointed out succinctly, flying takes about five minutes hard concentration on take-off and landing. Lose your concentration on a freeway for half a second, and you are liable to end up in an accident.[4]

Reporters of the Hollywood press and other publications latched on to his new "hobby" and much was written about his flying adventures. How much of this was accurate reporting or embellished stories is hard to say now. Did he really have to crash land on a freeway? So said one item which went on to say that the moguls of Revue Studios placed a restraint on his flying during the *Wagon Train* filming season. According to Bob, they weren't too fond of his hobby when he took it up. In an unidentified, undated article pasted in a *Burris Scrapbook* page annotated "November 1960," under the headline, "Horton's Flying – More Dangerous Than Dean's Driving?" the story went, "In the feuding department, Bob Horton and his studio are having words. Bob loves to fly his own private plane. It is a little job, and the studio worries that it is a more dangerous hobby than the late Jimmy Dean's sports-car racing. Bob is under pledge to take all weather precautions but there is still a lot of concern about his casual dating. Often Bob will pick up his fiancée Marilynn Bradley, drive to the airport, fly to Palm Springs or Vegas for an evening, then fly back the same eve. Only recently Bob had a near tragedy when something went wrong with his landing gear and he had to put down without it. It is real worry material for everyone but Bob, who thinks it is fun." Jack O'Brian, writing for the *New York Journal-American* on January 24, 1961 said, "Wagon Train's Bob Horton was ordered not to fly his plane – get a horse! – until the current series is in the can." Given what's known about Robert's personality, it is hard to believe that he would pay much attention to such an order. As for the forced landing, there is nothing in the Horton memorabilia about it, and nothing in his Pilot's Flight Log, although it is true to say that the log's first entry is dated February 1961. However, in a profile of Bob in a latter-day playbill, alluding to his hobby of flying, there's a mention of his having to put down on a Los Angeles freeway in the course of a flight as a student pilot, due to engine failure. Happily, it says, he landed safely.[5]

"Terror in The Skies" was the attention-grabbing headline involving the Hortons which purported to be about a landing in a commercial flight which originated in Paris on June 18, 1961. This was about the time that Bob and Marilynn returned from their six-week sojourn in Britain and Europe. Paul Denis wrote for *Movieland and TV Times* in a 1962 issue. It reads like a rather bad "true-life" story, all about a brakeless landing at New York's Idlewilde Airport (subsequently John F. Kennedy Airport), although there is a brief reference to the incident in an unidentified 1966 magazine article entitled "Bob Horton's Wife Tells How She Succeeded Where Three Others Failed." There are no other references to the incident, either in Robert Horton's memorabilia (where it was not found) or in the listings of "crashes and incidents" at Idlewilde in that year. A rather colorful description in this article of Marilynn Bradley's experience of crash landing prior to meeting Robert Horton is also difficult to credit, since there are no references to it associated with other, later articles describing her as a "nervous flier". There may be a nub of truth in the story, but with no other substantiating evidence it's hard to give it much credence. There was a fair amount written about the fact that any "serious" woman in Horton's life would have to take an active interest in his flying otherwise his active interest in her would be short-lived. Marilynn may have given it her best shot in the beginning, but with the best will in the world, once a nervous flyer, always a nervous flyer. His much-loved dog, Jamie, was, however, an enthusiastic passenger according to Bob, and accompanied him on most of his flights during his lifetime, as did later dogs in the Horton family.

Taking up flying at the time he did seems logical. He could afford to do it. It was something to get him away from the long grueling hours of work on the *Wagon Train* set, something to take his mind off his emotional problems. Pragmatically, it allowed him to travel freely to make the personal appearances which were more and more in demand of him, as well as the theatrical roles he took up in the off-season.[6] It was also a tax write-off. Owning a personal airplane may appear, at first, to be extravagant, but Robert Horton was fiscally conservative, and throughout his life owned just one aircraft. The Piper Comanche he bought new in 1959 was repainted in February 1973, according to his Pilot's Log by which time he had acquired a personal aircraft ID number, changing from N5919P to N59RH. That was his one and only aircraft until he gave up flying in the mid-Nineties.

Nineteen-fifty-nine was filled with high points in his career, bringing with them a realization of the success which had so eluded him throughout the early 1950s. *Wagon Train* was at its zenith, in no small part due to Robert Horton's portrayal of the scout, Flint McCullough, and his was a household name. His fan mail from around the globe was legendary. Meanwhile, true to his own aspirations, he continued taking voice lessons. Interviewed by Earl Wilson of the *New York Post* in 1963, as he prepared to appear on Broadway, he said,

"I've studied voice three years very hard. Literally on my lunch hour . . . while I was doing the TV Series. I was the terror of the freeways, driving between the studio and my voice teacher on my lunchtime."

Indeed, by this time, 1959, Horton was gaining attention for his singing, although he did nothing at all to promote this talent within the scope of *Wagon Train*. He did sing briefly, with Rhonda Fleming, in the "Jennifer Churchill Story," aired on October 15, 1958, and in the "Mary Ellen Thomas Story," aired on December 23, 1958 he led the assembled pioneers in the first two phrases of "Silent Night," but he refused to have anything to do with singing in the "St. Nicholas Story" in Season Three. He argued, justifiably, that the script called for the wagon train to be attacked by Indians and that his singing Christmas carols at such a time was ludicrous.

As a result, he bowed out of the entire episode. Viewing "The St. Nicholas Story," one can only marvel at its puerile content (Ward Bond scrambling about in a 1950s Santa suit) and agree whole-heartedly with Robert Horton's decision.[7] He was adamant that his singing abilities would not be predicated on his role as Flint McCullough. Late in 1958, while explaining his experiences as a rodeo star attraction earlier that summer to Bob Hull of the *Los Angeles Herald and Express*, he said,

"It was a new experience for me and I loved it. It gave me a chance to practice my singing. Sure, I sing. Records? Not now. I know if I decided to make an album, some wit would label it "Flint McCullough Sings Songs of the *Wagon Train*" and I just don't feel like playing that game."

He had other singing appearances to his credit beyond his summer stock work, for he guest starred on *The Tennessee Ernie Ford Show* as a singer on March 19, 1958 and March 17, 1959. He also sang on *The Lux Show*, hosted by Rosemary Clooney on April 10, 1958. On July 17, 1959 he sang at The Hollywood Bowl, and on November 13 he appeared on the Andy Williams special, "Music from Shubert Alley". His first appearance in a stage musical alluded to previously also took place in 1959 when he starred as Sky Masterson in *Guys and Dolls* in Warren, Ohio and Detroit, Michigan respectively.

His popularity was immense, not just in the United States. In Britain,*Wagon Train* became the top-rated show in television, mainly due to Robert Horton. Ward Bond could claim some notoriety there, but compared to the adulation demonstrated for Flint McCullough, old Major Adams stood little chance. One of the leading impresarios and theater managers in the United Kingdom was a man named Val Parnell.[8] He had been foremost in the business since the 1940's, and in 1955 had established a highly successful and reputable variety show which aired every Sunday night on Independent Television (ITV). Known as *Sunday Night at the London Palladium* it showcased stars from all walks of entertainment and often featured big names from the world of singing, dancing and cabaret. It especially featured big names of the day. It was, for anyone in Britain who owned a TV set, a "must see" date at the end of the weekend.

Parnell and Lew Grade were leading board members of one of Britain's first commercial television stations, Associated TeleVision, ATV. The Grade Agency represented hundreds of actors in Britain and duly agreed to work on behalf of Robert Horton when Parnell, who spent fabulous sums of money bringing top entertainers to appear in his Palladium Theatre as well as on television, saw the chance to cash in on Horton's huge popularity in Britain. He invited him to sing at the London Palladium, and offered him the highest fee ever to an overseas performer at that time.[9] He knew that in the British Isles the man who played Flint McCullough on *Wagon Train* was a huge draw, "A sex symbol," Horton said of himself a little disparagingly,[10] but the truth was he pulled crowds in by the thousands when he finally traveled to the land from whence his family had originated and where his mother had been born. Indeed, when it was announced that he would head the bill at the London Palladium in December 1959, over 15,000 requests for tickets were received within hours. The theatre's capacity was 2,000.[11] Robert Horton was overwhelmed by the greeting he received when he arrived in London, and the papers were full of the fact that his fans turned out in their thousands. His appearance on the London Palladium stage on December 27, 1959 practically brought the house down, and critics were enthusiastic about his performance. One wrote, in the December 28 edition of the *Daily Herald*,

"Flint McCullough, '*Wagon Train's*' daring scout, made the most fearless foray of all his intrepid career last night when he starred in ITV's Palladium show – as a singer. Horton's obviously trained voice and his relaxed romantic singing of 'They Say That Falling In Love Is Wonderful' put in the shade Eddie Fisher's version, sung on BBC earlier in the night."

So great was his success at the Palladium that the PYE recording company issued a disk of his appearance cut from a tape made of the show and it quickly became a runaway best seller on its release in the spring of 1960. On December 29, two days after the Palladium, he appeared in his own show, taped at the ATV theatre in London and named simply *The Robert Horton Show*. Agents swiftly

*On stage at the London Palladium, December 17, 1959. Robert Horton's collection. Courtesy of Boyd Magers.*

recognized the irresistible attraction of the man who played Flint McCullough and he was signed to return to Britain the following year to do a series of live performances around the country. He also, then, made several more 45 EP recordings for PYE. That was the year he received the invitation to appear before Her Majesty Queen Elizabeth II at the *Royal Command Performance* held at the Victoria Theatre, London, on May 16, 1960. In 1961 he returned, as a married man, and starred in yet another *Robert Horton Show* which he then took on tour around the country for two weeks. Marilynn participated in these shows.

When he returned to Hollywood for New Year immediately after his first conquest of Great Britain, he went straight back to work on *Wagon Train*, taking a few days off to appear on the fabulously popular television variety show *The Perry Como Show. Boston Herald* writer Authur E. Fortridge reported on January 21, 1960 that,

"Perry Como offered one of his more entertaining colorcasts last night on Channel 4 when he presented the lovely Lena Horne, Robert Horton of *Wagon Train*; comedian Corbett Monica, a newcomer, and the Ray Clarke Singers. My guess is that the men chose Lena and the women picked Robert Horton as the star of the show. Frankly we loved them both but we must say we can't blame the women for choosing Robert. He was very handsome in tails as he sang, "They Say It's Wonderful" in a very pleasant voice. He displayed a nice sense of humor, too, as he and Perry took turns calling a square dance. Perry chose the old-fashioned tunes and Robert the current popular bits. It was a very cute number and extremely well done."

The American recording business, however, took little notice of him and his talents until he appeared on Broadway in *110 in the Shade*. That produced a cast recording of the musical in its final form in 1964, and in the same year Robert Horton cut his first LP entitled *The Very Thought Of You*. He followed it in 1965 with the album *The Man Called Shenandoah*. Sadly, there were no more, although he did record the song, "They Came to Cordura" for the Gary Cooper movie of the same name in 1959, which also featured on the Shenandoah album.

Mentions of his family throughout this period are few and far between. One gossip columnist of those days referred to the fact that Horton took his parents to dinner on a weekly basis. The favored haunt was Stiers (spelled variously as "Steers" and "Stears" in other articles), a steakhouse situated on the famed Restaurant Row on La Cienega Boulevard in West Hollywood. Another wrote that Bob's mother was pleased to be asked for her autograph when she attended one of his rodeo appearances.[12] His parents accompanied him to England in 1959 for his first appearance there, and again when he appeared before Queen Elizabeth II in 1960. He did visit his brother's family from time to time and appeared to enjoy interacting with his two nieces and two nephews.[13] His eldest nephew, Creighton Horton II, recalled that, at the height of his uncle's fame as Flint McCullough, he reveled in the kudos this brought him as a young boy among his peers. He spoke of having "the coolest uncle" in school. When Robert Horton came to visit he would get his pals together in the driveway of the Creighton Horton home in San Marino to await his arrival. Lined up as if on parade, the boys greeted the Thunderbird convertible, which he described as "a really cool car," as it pulled into the driveway. They were, as often as not, treated to a meeting with whichever pretty young starlet accompanied their hero at the time. All of Creight's friends knew Horton as "Uncle Howard," just as did his nieces and nephews, not as "Bob" or "Mr. Horton", or even "Flint", which did not seem to trouble Bob, if indeed, he ever took notice of it.

# PART V ROLLING, CREAKING WHEELS
## Chapter 14
### *We Didn't Get Along at All*

The May 1958 *Matinee Theater* production of "Much Ado About Nothing" was only one of many, many opportunities which were put Horton's way as his popularity soared and he became the most idolized star of the small screen on three continents.[1] The vast majority of the offers which came his way he had to decline. *Wagon Train*'s shooting schedule simply did not permit him to take up the myriad of roles he was offered. Some he turned down without hesitation, particularly any which were Westerns, but he deeply regretted the many offers for Broadway appearances which came his way, for that was where he wanted to go. Nevertheless, he honored his commitments to Revue Studios throughout the tenure of his contract, albeit he took a number of stands in its course when he felt that the studio failed to honor its side of the deal. Robert Horton's name, popularity and ability to draw audiences was proven repeatedly. Indeed, the list of his appearances outside *Wagon Train* which he was able to take up is formidable and never wavered throughout his tenure with the show. If this grated with his aging co-star, Bond never specifically said so. He simply alluded to Robert Horton's "lack of dedication" to the show.[2] Amusingly, however, on December 24, 1959, under the title, "Presents Never Presented" a *Los Angeles Examiner* columnist wrote, "To Ward Bond – Bob Horton's Fan Mail!"

Robert Horton, however, never made any secret of his ultimate desire to move on to other challenges within the acting profession, and his determination not to be typecast as a "television Western actor." From the beginning of his tenure with the show, he refused to appear in the buckskins he wore as Flint McCullough when he made personal appearances, and before the end of the first season he quietly changed this costume for a less gimmicky (and more comfortable) look. He did so several times throughout his contract. Furthermore, he was absolutely clear that he would not remain with the show for an indeterminate length of time, and each season brought the question from anxious fans as well as his employers, "Will Robert Horton stay on as Flint McCullough?" To which the answer was invariably "Yes" although as far as Horton was concerned that "yes" only remained in place until his five-year contract came to an end.[3]

As his fame and popularity grew, he must have felt empowered to dictate terms to those with whom he worked, and he wasn't wrong. If *Wagon Train* lost Flint McCullough, there is no doubt that it would have tumbled down the ratings table, so the studio was prepared to listen to his demands and meet them. Early in 1960, there was a rumor that Ward Bond might "roll out" of the program the following season, and that Robert Horton insisted that if that came about, he wanted guest stars only to join the train, not a regular "star". By the end of January of that year, *Variety* reported that Horton's "pact" was being adjusted to eliminate his appearance in segments which required him to make only minor showings. In February he had a "big argument" with director Allen H. Miner.[4] An article written that same month by Charles Denton, a regular columnist for *The Los Angeles Examiner* entitled "Horton Fights, On and Off the TV Screen" put forward Robert Horton's case in these matters as follows:

"Anyone looking for evidence to support the theory that a man must fight for what he gets in our competitive society could get a couple of volumes of it from Robert Horton.

In his going on three years of scouting for *Wagon Train*, the tall, square-jawed Horton has found his way out of the bog of obscurity and into the intoxicating upper altitudes of the popularity polls, won the mystical, magical title of "star" and, of course, acquired a favorable bank balance.

The correlation between these achievements is obvious, and Horton, whose directness occasionally has caused his employers some embarrassment, would be the last to conceal or depreciate*[sic]* it.

He candidly admits that he has warred with his bosses over roles and billing, with directors over character interpretations, with writers over scripts and with sundry other personnel when the events seemed to him to warrant a show-down.

But he insists with the firmness of deeply-rooted conviction that his motives in these disputes, if not always correct, were at least pure and selfless, entirely disconnected from either ego or mammon.

"I fight when I think I'm right, sure," he explained evenly. "But I'm not money hungry. I've been around money all my life, and I know it isn't that important. I've lived in the same house for five years. I pay $100 a month rent for it, and I love it. I'm not interested in money, but I am interested in acting."

That is most of where Horton's troubles have started. It ignited his first major conflict with his employers – the one that led to his much-publicized "feud" with co-star Ward Bond.

The basis of the battle was inherent in the nature of TV. When Horton signed on for the series, he was promised starring roles in half the shows. But in the first year, the producers, understandably, focused on Bond, who had "name value".

Horton waged an implacable campaign for equal time with his elder colleague and eventually won.

"The way they designate major and minor roles in this business is on the basis of who's getting the most money," he said. "Well, that's okay. I don't care, but in the early setup I couldn't do anything as an actor and I said so."

The triumph was not without some bitterness. Relations between him and Bond began being reported as severely strained. The "feud" became one of those legendary Hollywood affairs, but Horton denies that it ever actually reached that point.

"Ward and I get along as well as any two people have to get along to work together," he shrugged. "We don't associate much with each other off the lot, no. But that's not really so strange. After all, there's quite a disparity in our ages. Ward's been in the business a long time and has his own circle of friends. I have mine. But we work together marvelously, I think. I'm a great foil for him, and he's a great foil for me. There haven't been a half-dozen angry words between us in three years."

While this conflict, if any, occupied the gossip columnists, Horton quietly marched forward to new ones. Early this season (3rd season) he notified *Wagon Train* masters that he was losing interest in continuing the trek along the uppermost regions of the ratings because they were neglecting to give him top billing in the episodes in which he starred.

"This isn't a matter of ego," he protested, "It's business in this town, billing is important. Maybe it should not be, but it is. If you want better parts, you've got to have the name. In this case it turned out to be merely an oversight, though. The producers admitted they'd been wrong and asked me what they could do to make up for it. I said they could give me more spare time to do other things."

As a result, Horton has been able to go guest starring around happily in recent months. He just returned from a smash-hit personal appearance at the London Palladium, and has a Tennessee Ernie Ford Show and a Startime drama, "Last Day of Glory" on his agenda. He also did a stint for Perry Como and has hit the rodeo circuit occasionally.

Horton's latest explosion involved a director on *Wagon Train*, a gentleman he insists never will have the chance to stoke up his temper again.

"I suppose this sounds like a matter of ego to many people, but it isn't with me at all," he insisted. "I'll argue about lines, you're darned right. But solely over whether they will play or not. It isn't a question of whether they make me look good. If a show comes off, everyone in it comes off. If it doesn't, and I'm the star, then it's my failure. So I have a big stake in seeing that it does, and to me that doesn't mean only that I show up well."

This lengthy quote, in fact the entire article written by Charles Denton in February 1960, goes a long way to explaining Robert Horton's view of his relationship with Bond, Revue Studios and his career.

However, it cannot be denied that, by the start of Season Three, Robert Horton was tiring of the series, and of his role. He must have been enormously frustrated by the fact that he was the recipient of so many exciting offers both in the United States and abroad, very few of which he was able to take up due to his *Wagon Train* commitments. He was growing bored with the whole thing, he saw corners being cut by the studio but he was locked into a five-year commitment which, without costly legal assistance, he could not break. Perhaps he also viewed the remaining two years of his obligation as a continuing opportunity to put his stamp on the entertainment world and establish himself fully within its ranks. There is no doubt that he wielded a very great deal of power in terms of name draw by the start of 1960, which undoubtedly gave him the confidence to negotiate with the studio for the things he wanted most; the chance to do anything other than appear in *Wagon Train*.

Nineteen-sixty was a year of change in his life, as well as a manifestly successful one. Instead of living alone, he had Marilynn Bradley with him, and her name first appears, if incorrectly, in print on January 10, 1960, in the *Minneapolis Sunday Tribune*, under the headline, "Horton's Girl Sulks." "Horton, who came to St. Paul to be The Grand Marshal of the Winter Carnival Torchlite Parade, said his girlfriend (Marilyn Bradford,*[sic]*a singer) 'got a little mad' because he came to the carnival instead of spending time with her."

Despite his personal living arrangements, the Hollywood press continued to print articles linking his name with all sorts of starlets, in particular Cindy Robbins, who had appeared on a couple of *Wagon Train* episodes with him. It was claimed by the *Los Angeles Herald Examiner* that he took her to dinner on February 3, "his first night home after a month in London." This was nonsense, as he had returned to California in time for New Year's Eve and his Perry Como Show appearance in January, as well as resuming work on *Wagon Train*. Cindy Robbins herself, in the March issue of *TV Star Parade* stated unequivocally that, despite having been photographed many times with Bob Horton, these "dates" were strictly for publicity purposes. "I date a boy who isn't in the business, and I'm sure that Bob's REAL dates are with girls who are NOT actresses." To back up this information, Cindy Robbins wrote the following email to me in May 2016, when I contacted her regarding her friendship with Robert.

*"Dear Aileen,*

*I'm sorry that I don't have much to offer on your RH book. We dated a few times and I thought he was a really nice guy. And that's about it. Not much excitement I'm afraid.*

*Good Luck,*
*Cindy"*
His extra-curricular acting stints also kept him busy, and in an article published in the *Detroit Free Press* on March 13, 1960 he is quoted as follows:

"Actually, because I'm tied to the show, I have to plan all my outside work around its shooting schedule. I can't do everything I'd like. I've had to turn down two invitations for Broadway plays. I haven't done any movies because, frankly, the ones that have been offered to me have been too much like *Wagon Train* and I don't feel they offered any challenge. There was a chance for me to do *The Misfits,* the movie Arthur Miller has written for his wife, Marilyn Monroe. But I found that he and I were a long way from each other in how we saw what would have been my role. Instead, next summer I will tour with *Pal Joey.* I may also go to England again to do *The Rainmaker* for the BBC."

He did return to England that spring for one of the biggest performances of his life in May 1960. He accepted an invitation to

*In rehearsals for* The Royal Variety Show, *with Sammy Davis, Jr. and Liberace, May 1960. Robert Horton's collection. Courtesy of Boyd Magers.*

appear in London on *The Royal Variety Show*, which was held annually to benefit the Variety Artistes' Benevolent Fund and Institution of which both Her Majesty The Queen and His Royal Highness The Duke of Edinburgh were patrons. It was a "royal command" performance, scheduled to take place on May 16, 1960, at the Victoria Palace Theatre. Robert Horton, Nat King Cole, Sammy Davis, Jr. and pianist Liberace were among the American artists along with a staggering list of British stars of stage and screen. Robert recalled later, in a speech he gave at the Wild West Film Festival in Sonora in 1993, that he and Nat King Cole were so nervous they could scarcely, at first, find their voices and, indeed, Nat Cole forgot the words to "Unforgettable"! At the end of the show, all the performers were presented to the royal couple. Robert told Hedda Hopper, who subsequently printed the story in her "Entertainment" column in the *Los Angeles Times*, that,

"I was presented to Her Majesty and Prince Philip. They complimented me on how becoming my tails were. I explained *(that the)* only other time I wore them was for the Queen of Greece in Beverly Hills." Queen Elizabeth also told him that *Wagon Train* was her favorite television show. It is fun to think that, only two years younger than Bob, and a highly accomplished horsewoman, the Queen was a fan of *Wagon Train*. Perhaps she, like so many of her female subjects, had fallen under the spell of the handsome wagon train scout and may have decided that he should sing for her following his smash hit performance at the Palladium. All of that is pure speculation, of course, but it is a delightful thought. His parents joined him for the Royal Command Performance. He said that rather than revel in his obvious success, they grew annoyed and agitated when the limousine taking them and their son to the theater was held up by legions of fans who impeded its movement by their huge numbers.[5]

Afterwards, Robert Horton always referred to this Royal Command Performance as one of the highlights of his career. The Leslie Grade Agency of London, so impressed with his U.K. appearances in December 1959, set up a series of performances around England, and Marilynn Bradley accompanied him. The press of the day knew very well the status of their relationship, though one writer rather

*Being presented to Queen Elizabeth II, May 16, 1960. Robert Horton,*
*author's collection.*

primly referred to the risqué nature of her traveling abroad with
Horton.[6] In all he was out of the country for several weeks, taking
time to tour Europe with Marilynn before returning to London to
tape a television performance of *The Man*, a serious drama about a
psychotic killer by playwright Mel Dinelli, which was aired by ITV.
Horton's performance as the killer drew excellent reviews from
British critics which were subsequently printed about ten days later
under "Foreign Television Reviews" in *Variety*, America's leading
entertainment publication.

His return to Hollywood and *Wagon Train* filming brought
various observations from the entertainment press, but most of it
expressed relief that Flint McCullough still rode scout for Major
Seth Adams. The rancor which existed between the two actors,
however, had not dissipated. The rumors which went around Hollywood about the Horton – Bond feud were rife from the moment

they started in 1958 and in an unpublished press release dated April 29, 1960, *UPI Hollywood* writer Rick Du Brow typed up an interview with Robert Horton which states very clearly Horton's view of matters:

"Three years together on TV's *Wagon Train* have failed to breach the personal coolness between co-stars Ward Bond and Robert Horton.

"We hardly see each other on the show because of a new arrangement so we get along fine," the thirty-five-year-old Horton said cryptically of his relationship with his gruff, tough older partner.

"At the beginning of the series," Horton explained, "we agreed to alternate starring roles – and whoever wasn't starring would appear briefly in a minor way. This year, if it's not my show, I don't want to be on it. But for some reason, Ward wants to be on mine. I'm not so interested in the exposure. I like to do other things, such as appearing at the London Palladium, and singing."

An album of songs by the 6ft 1inch actor is the third best seller in England although he has yet to record one here.

Why did the coolness develop between Bond and Horton? Horton thinks it may be because he got equal billing from the start with the veteran actor – even though he didn't have as big a name as Bond.

"I went in to *Wagon Train* with the concept of it as our show," Horton said. "It could be that Ward may think of it as his show. I'm not taking credit, but I get much, much more fan mail than he does. And he can't take the blame if people identify with me – I'm the hero."

Bond plays a crusty old wagon-master with a heart of gold, and Horton is his sensitive young scout. The characters are pretty close to their true natures – and the on-screen conflict of the generations they represent is reflected in their off-screen relationship.

"The best thing we do together is work together," Horton said. "We have a wonderful rapport before the camera – much more than we do behind it. He's a real professional. He says his words to you and they're right on the button. The time we got along best was when we had a few drinks together. Usually, when you have a few drinks, you release your antagonisms, but you wouldn't believe how close we got and how many personal things we discussed. I thought it would give us a closer relationship, but when I saw him a few days later it was the same old story. It's pretty obvious from articles where Ward Bond discusses the show that he hardly considers me in the series. He doesn't mention me from what I've seen. But it's hard for me to discuss *Wagon Train* without mentioning Ward Bond."

Will *Wagon Train* continue into next season despite their personal coolness?

"Yeah," said Horton. "Sometimes I think it's type-casting."

Fuel was often added to the fire by the journalists of the day. On May 24, 1960 *The Hollywood Reporter* said, "Did you know that Robert Horton hates Westerns, teevee serials and buckskins damn near as much as he hates Ward Bond?" This was undoubtedly a piece of yellow journalism, but even if it were true, it did not serve to help the situation. In July, it was noted that *Wagon Train* topped the charts and according to *Screen World and TV* "that's due to Robert Horton's 'derring-do'!"

In mid-August he went to Connecticut to star in *Brigadoon* with Marilynn. It was their first show together since appearing in *Guys and Dolls* the previous September. It was a two-week engagement and it was a roaring success. By this time, the press was full of references to Horton's "pretty girlfriend" as well as alluding to the probability that they would "soon marry". Horton's work schedule continued to be punishing; *Alfred Hitchcock Presents*, *The Steel Hour*, variety shows and state fairs and rodeos, as well as a continual stream of offers from Broadway producers, including David Merrick.

In September he picked up a cool $20,000 for topping the bill at the New Mexico State Fair in Albuquerque and followed that up by appearing at the Arkansas Livestock Exposition in Little Rock which ran from October 3 through October 8. Three weeks prior to this an incident occurred on the *Wagon Train* set which brought about one of the biggest rifts between him and Revue Studios, and it involved his crusty co-star, Bond. While filming a short scene involving both, Bond decided that his lines made him look ridiculous. He demanded that the lines be cut. Horton said that if the lines were taken out, it would leave him with nothing to do. His solution to the situation was that he not be in the scene at all. He described the scene as "ludicrous" and "low comedy". The producer, Howard Christie, refused to have the script changed and thus created an impasse. Ward Bond would not play the scene as written, and when he skipped the offending lines, Bob simply exited the scene. When the situation reached a critical level, the director called for Christie again who demanded to know what was going on. Bob said,

"I just want to know who's producing the show. If you're producing it, then produce it, and we'll do the scene the way you O.K.'d it. If Mr. Bond's producing it, then I shouldn't be in the show. It's that simple."[7]

The producer spoke with Ward Bond, persuaded him to accept the script and the scene was finally shot as written. However, Bond, infuriated by the outcome, confronted Christie in his office and told him that he would not work with Robert Horton again. Bob was un-phased. He said he'd had enough and it suited him very well not to work with Bond again. Three weeks passed before another episode involving both actors came up. By that time Bond had backed down, but Horton had not.

"I had taken a stand," he declared, "and I meant what I said." His friend Hedda Hopper duly reported his words. To underscore his stance he absented himself from the studio for a week, which retaliated by suspending him until he reported for work the following week. The situation naturally made the press. *Variety*, one of the most read and possibly most reliable of the entertainment industry publications printed on October 5, 1960,

"MCA To Suspend Robert Horton Unless He's Back On '*Wagon Train*' by tomorrow.

Robert Horton, co-star with Ward Bond of Revue-NBC's top rated *Wagon Train* will be placed on suspension if he fails to report tomorrow morning (i.e. October 6) for the start of a new episode. He is now playing a fair date in Little Rock (Oct 3 – 8) which reportedly takes him through remainder of the week. MCA spokesman said yesterday Horton was notified by wire to report Thursday but that no reply had been received from him. Milt Rosner, agent for Horton, declined to affirm or deny that Horton would be suspended if he didn't report to work Thursday. Understood that under clauses in his contract his failure to report would constitute a breach of contract and that he would be held responsible for any losses to MCA in production delay."

On October 7, *Variety* reported, "Bob Horton Suspended for Missing 'Train'; Ward Bond Denies Feud.' Robert Horton went on suspension for failing to report for the start of a new episode of NBC's top-rated *Wagon Train*. He is due back Sunday from Little Rock, Arkansas where he has been appearing at the livestock show. Contacted on the phone by Milt Rosner, his agent, Horton said, "Revue knows why I didn't report." This could be interpreted to confirm reports that he and Ward Bond, his co-star on the hour Western, have been feuding for weeks. Bond, contacted last night, retorted to the 'feud' thus:

"I wouldn't say we've been precisely feuding, but I feel Horton was never particularly interested in the show. He seemed more interested doing work where he could make more money once the series established him. I would feel more loyalty to the series than that."

Indeed, Ward Bond made very few appearances elsewhere during his time with *Wagon Train*. A handful of roles between 1957 and 1958 included his brief appearance in the movie *Rio Bravo* which starred his old buddy John Wayne. Filmed between May 1 and July 23, 1958, it was put on general release in April 1959. No doubt his young co-star's popularity elsewhere, as well as on *Wagon Train* irked him. The *Variety* article went on,

"Horton told Rosner, the agent says, that he would look at a script of the next episode if it is offered to him by Revue but it is considered doubtful he will accept it if Bond is in the opposite starring role. Terry Wilson, a cast regular playing the role of 'Hawks' was given the part originally written for Horton in the segment now being shot."

There is little doubt that this was the suspension when Horton, finished with his engagement in Arkansas, returned to Hollywood and went to ground at Lee Marvin's Malibu beach home. On October 15, Hedda Hopper wrote in the *Los Angeles Times*,

"Bob Horton tells me: 'I'm not trying to break my contract with *Wagon Train* nor am I asking for more money. Ward Bond and I haven't been seeing eye to eye for a long time. I'm fighting for a moral principle and will continue doing so, but I believe things will be worked out in the next few days.'"

By October 21 it seemed that matters had been resolved to Horton's satisfaction, for the *Los Angeles Examiner* published,

"Cow-rousing...All's quiet on the western front – for the moment. Bob Horton rejoined the *Wagon Train* under a flag of truce. No details on the peace pact yet, but one paragraph could be that Horton and Bond refrain from drawling dirty about each other. At least, they're working together and neither's said a cuss word so far. . ."

However, it is more than likely that when the studio got wind of the fact that Horton was cooling his heels with Marvin, panic set in. Marvin's reputation by that time was well known, and Revue did not want their property sullied. They extended an olive branch and Bob returned to work getting pretty much what he had wanted in the first place. Much later, in his interview with Lee Marvin's biographer, Dwayne Epstein, he said,

"I remember one day, Lee said to me on the set . . . it was the first time we ever worked together. He said, 'You'll fight for what you believe in, won't you? You don't care if it takes a little while.' I said, 'You bet your ass, I'll fight for what I believe in.'" In that instance, with his lawyers and his agent on his side, Robert Horton fought and won the day.

This rift and Robert Horton's determination not to be cowed by MCA or Revue-NBC was the most public of all the upsets which occurred in the relationship between the two men. When Horton's Revue bosses learned that he was lying low with Lee Marvin, their anxiety zipped off the Richter scale. Marvin's reputation was sufficiently negative for them to make every move to get their boy, Flint McCullough, out of Marvin's influence before it rubbed off indelibly. As Horton told Epstein,

"I had a problem at the studio. The studio suspended me. I said, 'Okay, suspend me.' I spoke to my business manager and my attorney and they all felt that I had been suspended in a way that the studio was at fault. I went down to the beach, at the Marvins' invitation, with Marilynn. The studio finally tracked me down. They said, 'Holy Christ! You're with Lee Marvin? All is forgiven. Come home.'"

When Robert Horton reported for work, and was placed back on the Revue payroll, Ward Bond went to the same bosses and requested a month's vacation. It was granted. Bond was tired, must have looked it, and the studio was determined to pin Horton down for an extended period. A television guide shortly afterwards stated,

"The day Robert Horton returned to *Wagon Train* after his one week*[sic]* rebellion, no-one in the cast or crew said one extra word. Just went around, doing their jobs, silent as snow. Too bad not one person tried to patch up those hostilities between hot-headed, dedicated Bob and cool-headed, cagey Ward Bond."[8]

Some civility must have been restored for, just before Bond left to begin his vacation, Horton, according to several articles relating the incident, was bothered yet again by another poor script and visited the older star in his dressing room. They both agreed that the script was "lousy," and they were each having difficulties with it. Robert Horton said to Ward Bond,

"Well, we may have our differences about some things but at least we agree on this script."

As he started to leave, and just as he got to the door, Bond called to him,

"Bobby, we don't really have any damn differences." Horton said that 'it was the only time he ever called me Bobby'."[9]

It was the last time Robert Horton saw Ward Bond. Two days later the veteran actor collapsed and died, felled by a massive heart attack while he was taking a shower in his motel room in Dallas, just before attending the Cotton Bowl college football game. He was 58 years old. Bond's unexpected and shocking death on November 5, 1960 came hard on the heels of Robert Horton's October rebellion. How Horton actually felt about that he never said explicitly, although a brief comment in the *Los Angeles Examiner* on November 11 stated,

"They weren't exactly close pals, but Bob Horton was badly shaken by the death of his *Wagon Train* master, Ward Bond." Horton told the dressing room story repeatedly whenever he was asked about his relationship with Bond. Thirty-eight years later, however, at the Memphis Film Festival in 1998, Robert Horton, as a panelist, talked about his relationship with Ward Bond more candidly. In response to a question from the floor, he replied,

"Well, Ward Bond and I didn't get along very well, but we worked together marvelously." He went on to elaborate on the relationship he had with Bond on screen, saying, "Our chemistry was about as good as anything that's ever been on the screen. It really set a precedent about a younger man and an older man working together in an area of conflict with the same objective. Ward was a terrific man, very charming, *(but)* as I said we didn't get along at all from the very beginning!"

The fact that they did not enjoy a positive relationship off the screen he also put down to chemistry as well as the disparity in their ages and backgrounds. Ward Bond's belief that *Wagon Train* was primarily his show, and the initial disregard of the writers for the Flint McCullough character all played a part, not to mention Robert's method acting training and his willingness to question scripts and directors. He made the point that as his character developed the series became more related to the scout and that became a bone of contention with Bond. In an early episode which gave Horton the primary role, Bond walked off the set with an apology to the director that he was leaving as well as implying that the show would encounter problems because he wasn't there. Horton's feeling was that they would do fine, and they did. He further noted that at the time of Bond's death in November 1960, the show was second in the ratings, but that in the following two seasons, 1961 and 1962, it became the top show in the country. Perhaps, at age seventy-four, his memory was not as keen as it might be, for *Wagon Train*, in fact, achieved the number one ranking with the Nielsen ratings in 1959, or perhaps he referred to other ratings' systems. No matter what, it cannot be denied that the show was a top performer from early in its first season throughout Robert Horton's tenure as Flint McCullough.

He spoke frankly about Bond's efforts to get rid of him, which culminated in a "big meeting" with the heads of Universal Studio. In the course of the meeting it became abundantly clear that nobody was going to get him off the show regardless of their feelings, and that the success of the show was predicated on the contribution of both actors. He also referred to their last meeting which took place shortly before Bond took off on vacation. A contentious article, purporting to speak for Robert Horton and telling of the differences which existed between them angered Bob because it was fundamentally untrue. He went to Bond's dressing room to apologize for the situation and said,

"I'm sorry about this article and I'm sorry we have our differences."

Ward Bond's response was to bark: "We don't have any goddam differences!"

Horton finished by saying unemotionally, "The next day Ward Bond went to Texas and dropped dead."[10]

So, at the age of seventy-four, Robert Horton bluntly set forth his feelings about Ward Bond, their relationship and the program which sky-rocketed him to fame. He also scotched the story about the troublesome script and never mentioned Bond's calling him "Bobby".

Ward Bond's funeral service took place on Monday, November 7, 1960, a mere two days after his death in Dallas. John Wayne, Bond's close friend and all-round great buddy, gave the eulogy to a congregation of about three hundred, which included Robert Horton. Halfway through shooting Season Three, the wagon train was minus its wagon master, and with no-one to replace Bond, the onus fell on Horton's shoulders to pick up and go forward until the matter of Bond's replacement was resolved. As a result, Horton's plans to head to England for yet another series of personal appearances, recordings and shows had to be cancelled.

Robert Horton, in November 1960, was closing out a year of immense personal achievement and professional greatness and was halfway through his five-year commitment to *Wagon Train*, MCA and Revue Studios. He must have felt trapped as a result of Bond's untimely death, but he was not a man to renege on his commitments and so he made the necessary adjustments to his working life while still holding fast to his determination to move on from the television series as soon as he could. He made adjustments in his personal life as well. Plans to travel to London in December for a television special and enjoy a honeymoon with Marilynn Bradley in Europe were cancelled. So was the wedding, if in fact a specific date for the ceremony had been determined. Finally, in what seemed to be a last-minute decision, Robert Horton married Marilynn Bradley on New Year's Eve, a Saturday, December 31, 1960, in a brief ceremony in Las Vegas. One day later, on Monday, January 2, he rode in The Rose Bowl Parade and on January 4 he was back at work on *Wagon Train.*

# Chapter 15
## *His Wonderful Wife*

An un-named writer said of Robert Horton in the June 1959 issue of *Screen Stars,*

"The gal who gets Bob, however, will find herself with a quiet, intelligent and considerate man, a far cry from the actory type of characters so common in these Hollywoods."

It was in June 1959, that Robert Horton met and fell in love with Marilynn Bradley, but it took almost a year and a half for him to commit himself to her by marrying her. It was a pivotal move in his life. It came halfway through his five-year contract with MCA and Revue Studios and at a time when he was at the height of his career. He was thirty-six years old and had been quoted in the press over and over again that he wanted marriage but was extremely wary of it. He had established a reputation as one of Hollywood and filmdom's most eligible bachelors. He had made a very bold and unequivocal point of the fact that if he ever married again, it would not be to a woman who was an actress, or within the entertainment industry.[1]

One thing he seemed to want, if the many articles published in Hollywood's magazines of the time are to be believed, was a companion, a woman with whom he could share his life, a friend, someone to love and be loved by.[2] Nevertheless, through the years between his divorce from Barbara Ruick and his *Wagon Train* contract, he lived the life of a confirmed bachelor, squiring scores of pretty women and girls to various Hollywood functions and on dates, being photographed for the benefit of the legions of his fans who undoubtedly believed wholeheartedly in the veracity of what they read. Ninety percent, perhaps more, of these occasions were nothing more than publicity vehicles, but there is no doubt that he had a number of serious affairs at the same time which included his romances with Inger Stevens and Nina Foch and the young UCLA student Ellen Dorn.

Although he had negotiated a contract which gave him a certain amount of flexibility and the right and opportunity to take other parts in the off-season, or even within the production season when his services weren't required, his appearances in other television shows or on stage were necessarily limited by the demands of *Wagon Train*, especially over the first three seasons it ran. Nevertheless, he got away. His interest in music, singing and studying voice had always existed, witness those letters in the early Fifties with advice on how to pursue a theatrical career on Broadway. He was good enough to get parts in musicals on the summer circuit, and his fame as the ruggedly handsome Flint McCullough on *Wagon Train* only served to help him, for summer stock theater producers also understood what a draw his name on a billboard would be.

By June 1959, his was pretty much a household name, he was at the peak of his career and his horizons, like those he saw as he flew his Piper Comanche from one gig to another, were limitless. Later that month he appeared once again as Hal Carter in *Picnic* at Detroit's Northland Playhouse for a week, earning $2,500 a week versus the $25 a week he had earned in Los Angeles when he first undertook the role, as well as resoundingly fine reviews and setting a house record in terms of receipts.[3] From there he moved on to Warren, Ohio, where he had accepted an invitation from John Kenley of The Kenley Players to play the part of Sky Masterson in their production of *Guys and Dolls*. It was his debut in musical comedy.

When he got to Warren, he met his leading lady, a young woman whose stage name was Marilynn Bradley. Born Marilynn Elayne Bladd on March 5, 1934, her family lived in West Roxbury in Boston. She graduated from the Jeremiah E. Burke High School and the New England Conservatory of Music, where she trained as an operatic singer. She claimed a "white Russian" ancestry, that is, Russians of good birth who supported the Russian royal family. Her father, Harry Bladd, was born in 1909, exactly where is unknown, but her mother Fae (Fanny – nee Kaplan) was born in Russia in 1911. Several different references exist to Marilynn Bradley's heritage but she was certainly born into a Jewish family.[4]

Marilynn Bradley was undoubtedly deeply smitten with her handsome, sophisticated, exceedingly famous suitor. She was a married woman when she first met Bob in June 1959 but that marriage was in trouble at the time. Her husband, Norwood Smith, was nineteen years older than she, and was a well-known actor in summer and winter theater stock, radio and television as well as being a leading man in Broadway musicals.[5] They married in August 1956, but divorce proceedings were underway when Marilynn met Robert Horton. Aged twenty-five, she had enjoyed a reasonably good career as a singer up until the time she got the lead female role in the Kenley Players' summer stock production of *Guys and Dolls* in the summer of 1959. Although she majored in opera at the Conservatory, she opted for musical theater and did some work on Broadway, mainly in the chorus. Nevertheless, throughout their lives together, Robert Horton was always quick to say that his wife's voice was superior to his. He always praised her singing talent and described her voice as rich as that of the great lirico-spinti soprano, Renata Tibaldi.[6]

Articles of the time referring to their meeting said that Bradley and Horton got along well on a business-like basis. The truth is somewhat different. Marilynn Bradley claimed, at that time, to be

*On stage in* Guys and Dolls, *Marilynn Bradley at the footlights, June 1959. Robert Horton's collection. Courtesy of Boyd Magers.*

too busy with her own career to know much about the man who was the leading television star of the day. She did say that when she learned who her leading man was to be in *Guys and Dolls* she made a point of watching a *Wagon Train* episode. "That's how I found myself saying to myself, 'What a guy!'"[7] Although it was said that Horton and Bradley's initial relationship was conducted on the basis of colleagues working together, in later years he admitted that he took Marilynn out to dinner because he was attracted to her. Furthermore, he knew that she was a married woman, but was not aware of the status of her marriage. Nevertheless, there is little doubt that it was a very strong attraction between the pair which launched their love affair. It is naïve to think otherwise. They met and they fell in love.

*Guys and Dolls* ran for its scheduled week, then Horton flew home to California in his brand-new Piper Comanche, clocking up his first solo transcontinental flight, and resumed his *Wagon Train* work, as well as making an appearance at the Hollywood Bowl Family Night on July 17. Then, in September, he and Marilynn were re-united for a second run of *Guys and Dolls* at the Cass Theatre in Detroit, and it was then that the affair became more than an attraction between two beautiful people. For Marilynn certainly was beautiful. Robert Horton, roguishly, said that he was first attracted to her when he saw her bending over a water fountain during rehearsals in Warren. He thought, as well, that she had "the most beautiful hair I had ever seen."[8]

There is a telling critique of their performance in Detroit, written for the *Windsor Daily Star* by its critic, John Gardiner and published on September 9, 1959.

"Robert Horton of television and stage fame was the star, playing the part of the ace gambler, Sky Masterson. Horton is indeed an able trouper. Moreover, he astonished his audience by projecting a very fine singing voice. A good actor, a good singer, a good lead. Horton was the artistic pivot of the show. He did nobly. As for the show in its entirety, it got seven curtain calls – which may indicate just how much the audience liked it. Horton – excellent – a real, rugged Sky Masterson. Marilynn Bradley as Sarah Brown, the "save a soul mission" gal – tops. Good voice, pulchritudinous personality, versatile actress and songstress. She twinkled like a star."

There is no doubt that these two people were mesmerized by one another, and the attraction between them seems to have permeated their performance in the show. A dark-eyed brunette, Marilynn differed radically from the many blondes Robert Horton had favored, but she was, without doubt, strikingly lovely and indeed on one occasion during their courtship she was mistaken by a stalking journalist for Elizabeth Taylor.[9]

There are quite a large number of articles of the time which talk ingenuously about the affair. Begun in June 1959, in Ohio, it went on until the pair married in December 1960. Shortly after the Detroit *Guys and Dolls* engagement, Marilynn Bradley came to California, at Bob's invitation, and lived with him in the little four-room cottage in Brentwood, the home he had rented since 1955. One article said primly that Marilynn boarded with friends of Horton's, and acted as his secretary, but there was no such arrangement.[10] Marilynn Bradley happily gave up her acting and singing career and lived with Robert Horton for an extended period of time before marrying him. Although he was quoted often enough on the subject of marriage, and what a successful marriage entailed, he had been unsuccessful on three notable occasions, had been a bachelor since his divorce from Barbara Ruick in April 1956, and seemed perfectly at ease with that status through 1960, the year he did, finally, commit to Marilynn.

His life as a bachelor suited him. In his prime, between the age of thirty-two and thirty-six, he was his own man, managing his own business affairs, living comfortably but not extravagantly, growing in popularity and with a handful of friendships which meant a great deal to him. Yet he hankered for more. He is often described as being "lonely," and though his family background had never provided him with much in the way of comfort, fun and firm relationships, it's true to say that he was surrounded by a large family – grandparents on his mother's side, uncles and aunts as well as a considerable number of cousins. He said on several occasions during this time that he envied his brother his family life. Creighton was a successful and highly respected doctor with a devoted wife and four children by the time Robert Horton was attaining his phenomenal status as Flint McCullough in *Wagon Train*. [11]

Loneliness was an emotion, a feeling, a sensation with which Robert Horton was deeply familiar. He grew up with it, he went in to the U.S. Coast Guard with it, he battled it in two marriages and perhaps only overcame it periodically as a result of his career. He found acting and everything to do with it endlessly stimulating but when he went home at night, to an apartment in New York, or a hotel room in Atlantic City, or wherever he was appearing; home to his delightful little cottage in Brentwood after a long slog on the *Wagon Train* sets, he went home to an empty house. He went home as a man alone. Even his beloved dog Jamie was insufficient to fill what was undoubtedly an aching void and a burning need. Marilynn Bradley arrived in the City of Angels and, with her own divorce underway, lived with Bob as his wife. The family viewed the situation with a certain amount of horror. As his niece Joan said forcefully,

"That is something we Mormons don't do!"

There is little doubt either that the beautiful Jewish woman and the Mormon Hortons did not hit it off. When Bob introduced Marilynn to his parents, he did so on neutral ground at one of Los Angeles' finer restaurants, possibly Stiers on La Cienega. The atmosphere was frosty and it was clear that Chelta Horton, in particular, was not happy with her son's choice. [12] It did not auger well for future happy family relationships.

On the other side of the continent, and the other side of just about everything the Hortons represented, was Marilynn's family. How Bob fared with his in-laws is difficult to assess for very little has been written about them, though he candidly told his last close friend, Eugenia Fredricksen, that he disliked his mother-in-law and merely tolerated what he described as her hen-pecked husband. Marilynn's younger brother and only sibling, Stephen Jo Bladd, was eight years younger than she, and also an accomplished musician. He was a founding member of the well-known 1980s J. Geils Band and it is said that Bob admired his talents, although it is debatable as to whether or not he thought much of his style of music. [13] Robert's relationship with his parents-in-law got off to a rocky start. He and Marilynn flew from Los Angeles to Boston for their first meeting. He was nervous, so he had a couple of cocktails on the flight. Smelling liquor on him put the Bladds off their future son-in-law at once. Besides, hadn't he been married at least seven times before? They believed Hollywood's rumors and its yellow press. In the article published in 1966 entitled "Bob Horton's Wife Tells How She Succeeded Where Three Others Failed" Marilynn referred to her mother's concern over Bob's marriage record. She said, "But I think my mother was a little frightened. She had read that Bob had been married seven times (a lie) and told me about it." However, neither the Horton family negativity, nor that of the Bladds, swayed the two principal players, who got on with their lives and accommodated, as best they could, each other's families.

Throughout 1960, once it was clear to the voracious entertainment press that Robert Horton was serious about his relationship with Marilynn Bradley, articles sprang up speculating on its exact status. When he took her to London, and then on a European trip, some of the press made snide remarks about Marilynn's self-respect. One wrote,

"Marilynn has not been the epitome of restraint and decorum since she met Bob. She followed him to California, went to England and Europe with him. She has certainly sacrificed propriety for love of Bob. So far Bob seems to appreciate her impulsive gestures born of an overwhelming emotion."[14]

That was hypocritical, coming from Hollywood. Both were adults and both appeared unimpressed by sanctimonious observations from a jaded medium. In a second unidentified clipping pasted into the *Burris Scrapbook*, and dated in Burris's hand "Nov 1960," a Hollywood journalist wrote,

"Bob Horton didn't think it at all improper that his fiancé, Marilynn Bradley, travel through Europe with him before their wedding date was set. After three marriages and an active bachelor life, it was inevitable that Bob would be sophisticated. Strangely enough, he is also the little boy in many ways, quite capable of absurd temper tantrums, fearful of being "trapped" by any woman. Fortunately he doesn't feel that Marilynn has trapped him, thinks he can find lasting happiness in marriage."

Sometime in the early spring of 1960, he moved out of his much-loved Brentwood home to take up residence in a rambling, two-storey Cape Cod-style house on a smart but secluded street off Laurel Canyon Boulevard in Studio City. He rented the home from Norman Luboff, the famous choir director, music arranger and music publisher, who was in Europe. Bob was happy enough in Brentwood, but perhaps he felt the constraints of his little home once he began to share it with Marilynn. The ever-attentive press pondered in print as to whether or not the move came about due to "femme influence".[15] The new house, which was home to the Hortons for at least two years, boasted a pool, patio, gazebo, tennis courts, and a double garage on a spacious, attractive corner lot. It also reflected, resoundingly, Bob's status as a leading star of television and gave them both a place in which they could entertain in more fitting surroundings.

If any of the entertainment writers of the day were aware of Bob and Marilynn's actual living arrangements, it's to their credit that they said nothing about it in print, other than to hint at it obliquely by saying that "Bob and Marilynn may be secretly wed!"[16]

Hedda Hopper, by this time a confidante and friend to Bob, wrote in her syndicated Los Angeles column on August 1, 1960 that "Bob Horton introduced me to his beautiful fiancé Marilynn Bradley. No date has been set for the wedding. They've both been married before."

The November edition of *Movie Life* heralded the news of Marilynn's divorce from Norwood Smith becoming final, but more time passed before anything definitive in the couple's status came to pass. When Ward Bond died early in November 1960, the entertainment press was full of the news, as well as hinting that the "imminent" Horton marriage was postponed by Bob as a mark of respect for his late co-star.

After Ward Bond's death, Robert Horton, amidst the pressure of his *Wagon Train* obligations, said,

"The possibility that Marilynn Bradley and I will be married by the first of the year is not impossible."[17] Additionally, he was quoted in regard to Marilynn's desire to be married in Boston, her family's home, but the demands of *Wagon Train* minus Bond were all encompassing. He said, "We don't want to fly there and back the next day. We are in the process of trying to make plans but I guess the marriage will have to wait until I can get time off from work."[18] His actions, in this regard, speak of a man who had made a decision; he would marry Marilynn – and a determination to carry them out as best he could under the altered circumstances occasioned by Bond's death.

In an article entitled "I Never Thought He'd Marry Me," in the September 1961 edition of *Movie Mirror*, written "as told by Mrs. Bob Horton," Marilynn spoke of the immediate events which led up to her marriage. Despite all the press ponderings throughout 1960, and most especially in the months preceding the event, she said that the proposal and wedding came as a complete surprise to her, even though she had lived with Bob for almost sixteen months, a fact which she, naturally, at the time, did not allude to. She also, understandably, did not mention the fact that Bob had told her repeatedly that he was not marriage material, and he had no intention of marrying again.

Much later Bob himself was quite forthright about the situation. He told freelance writer Micki Siegel in 1983 that when he and Marilynn first met they fell madly in love with each other. He said,

"I was still doing "Wagon Train," and I had to get back to the studio when the run ended, and I invited her to come out. I told her, 'I'm not interested in getting married. I don't think it's a constructive institution. I have to tell you that out front. However, it seems to me that we have a wonderful relationship.' Marilynn moved to California and they lived together from September 1959 to New Year's Eve, 1960. Then he decided it was time they got married."

So, after sixteen months living together, and on the heels of heated press speculation, he knew he could not go on introducing Marilynn as his fiancée without doing something about it. He decided to turn their living arrangements into something legal and official. He did it in typical Robert Horton fashion. He said nothing to Marilynn but set about planning the surprise of her life. He did tell her that they would go to Las Vegas to celebrate New Year's Eve. He then arranged for a special party to take place at their home on Wednesday, December 21, 1960 and Hedda Hopper wrote in her column in the *Los Angeles Times* on that very day that "Bob Horton's introducing his fiancé Marilynn Bradley to friends at his home tonight." Hopper must have done so with his knowledge.

Marilynn claims not to have known anything, though, when, in a short article in *TV Picture Life* she said, referring to the party, "I had no inkling of what was really going on . . . when I arrived to find all the book matches and cocktail napkins designed with "Bob & Marilyn"*[sic]* inscribed through a heart design. Confused and slightly resentful, I asked if he wasn't taking too much for granted. And all he did was smile and say 'Just wait.' I had little choice, and when his party was in full swing, he publicly announced to the gathering that he was in love with me . . . and right here and now was asking me to marry him. In fact he stated in no uncertain terms that we were going to get married, then turned to me and said, 'Right honey?' I was speechless and could only whisper back a very weak 'Right.'" For propriety's sake, she implied in the article that she only arrived to assist Bob with the preparations as they had been "steady dating" for a while. Of course, that was nonsense, but undoubtedly Bob kept his plans and arrangements a secret from her as he was determined to surprise her. He succeeded.

A December 30, 1960 piece in the *Los Angeles Examiner* penned by Louella Parsons stated, "This wedding isn't too surprising since Bob announced his coming marriage to the very pretty Miss Bradley at a buffet dinner he gave at his home Wednesday night. Marilynn was wearing a new engagement ring, a bouquet of gold leaves and diamonds. The young couple, however, gave no inkling at that time, however, of when the ceremony would be performed since they wished to keep the date of their marriage secret even from their closest friends."

And, it would seem, from both their families. It was this article which forced Bob to tell Marilynn that day that the New Year's weekend trip to Las Vegas would, in fact, be the occasion of their wedding.

Between announcing his engagement on December 21, and the marriage in Las Vegas on December 31, ten days passed. Christmas took place. On December 30, a Friday, and respectful of his fiancée's wishes, Bob drove Marilynn to Las Vegas rather than flying there

*Bob and Marilynn after their marriage in Las Vegas, December 31, 1960.*
*Author's collection.*

in his own plane. Near Barstow, two cars collided in front of them. He slammed on his brakes, skidded, and wound up with a dented fender, only to be rammed from the rear by another car. Fortunately, no-one was hurt. Later he remarked ruefully that the six-hour drive held more potential for accidents than the flight would have, but Marilynn's fear of flying won out.[19]

They were married on Saturday, December 31, 1960 at the Sands Hotel in a short ceremony in the Emerald Room, the private suite of its president, Jack Entratter, who handled all the arrangements. Judge David Zenoff officiated. It was New Year's Eve and Robert Horton said, romantically, that from then on, the whole world would join them in celebrating their anniversary.[20] Pictures taken at the brief civil ceremony show two people transported by love. Marilynn looked lovely in a beautiful dress of French lace, the bodice aqua, the full skirt avocado in color. It was Bob's choice, bought by him and presented to her at Christmas. He wore a dark lounge suit. There was no honeymoon. On New Year's Day they drove back to Los Angeles so that he could ride in the Pasadena Tournament of Roses Parade the next day.

The last-minute wedding date may have been prompted in the main by Ward Bond's unexpected death, and the subsequent crush of work which fell on Horton's shoulders. The reference to keeping the date a secret from "even their closest friends" is interesting but it certainly aided Bob in his plans to surprise Marilynn. Her wish to be married in Boston was probably given very little serious consideration. To be married in Boston, in the midst of the Jewish community, would demand a great deal more planning and lead time, time which Bob definitely did not have under the prevailing circumstances. As for the Horton family, it is unlikely that their presence at the wedding would mean a great deal to either Bob or Marilynn. A quick flit to Las Vegas over the New Year weekend made a great deal more sense. Thus, to quote Bob, he gave up his carefree life.[21]

Whatever ultimately prompted his marrying Marilynn Bradley, it is hard to deny the fact that, at first, they were deeply in love, besotted with one another. Marilynn seemed more than content to settle into the role of housewife and homemaker. Robert Horton thought he had found his perfect companion and the end to a lifetime of loneliness. Over the following years a great deal was written about their marriage in the entertainment press and the theme never wavered. Robert and Marilynn Horton were deeply in love with one another to the exclusion, almost, of all else. Robert Horton spoke lovingly and glowingly of what Marilynn meant to him, what she had brought to him and what she had done for him – the difference she had made to his life. She was, he said, "My wife, my love, my friend".[22]

Indeed, within days of their marriage, Marilynn's devotion to her new husband was demonstrated in a rather unique fashion. During the late Fifties and on in to the Sixties, NBC Television produced a half hour program which told the story of its weekly subject, subjects who ranged from actors, to politicians, to celebrities of all kinds as well as some very humble but special individuals – people from all walks of life, but people who had lived lives worthy of note.

It was entitled *This Is Your Life*. The program followed a specific format. The subject was always surprised by the presenter and host, Ralph Edwards, in some location where they would suspect nothing, then they were whisked off to the NBC Studios where the show was taped for later broadcasting. It became immensely popular and was obligatory weekly viewing for millions while it lasted.

On Wednesday, January 18, 1961, Robert Horton was the subject of *This Is Your Life*. Aged thirty-six and a half, eighteen days into his fourth marriage, halfway through his *Wagon Train* contract with Revue Studios and NBC, he was caught out at the door of his home in Studio City by Ralph Edwards, and told,

"Robert Horton, this is your life."

These programs seldom revealed anything negative about the subjects, concentrating instead on various highlights of its subject's life. Robert Horton's story was no different, except that the producers determined to link his life story with that of his fictional *Wagon Train* character, Flint McCullough. It was, perhaps, a necessary gimmick. Horton himself had written his character's profile which incorporated aspects of his own family history. Meanwhile, it had taken the producers of *This Is Your Life* a fair amount of time and effort to get the necessary co-operation from his parents, who at first refused to assist because they felt that their world-famous son had done nothing to merit such attention. Only after he sang before Her Majesty Queen Elizabeth II, at her command, were they persuaded that he deserved such an honor.[23]

Marilynn Horton played a key part in the planning of the program, which had to be done in secret in order to avoid the element of surprise being ruined. Later, she spoke of the difficulties created by the need for secrecy in the first days of their marriage but she coped and their "surprise" wedding in Las Vegas on December 31, 1960 was followed very quickly by the surprise on their doorstep on January 18.[24] Robert Horton, made to answer the doorbell by his brand-new bride, found himself facing Ralph Edwards, a battery of television cameras and a television truck, and, hastily tucking his shirt into his trousers with one hand while pulling on a shoe with the other, heard the famous words which opened every show.

Meanwhile, Jamie tore out of the door past him into the darkness as Bob, laughing, could only say,

"That's my dog!"

The show aired the following Sunday night at 10:30 pm on January 22, 1961. Various people from Bob's life came on stage to talk about him; Alan Miller, Vice-President of Revue Studios, his parents, Mary Augustine, Jay Taylor, a boyhood friend, Robert Walker, his friend from his days at UCLA and the man who got him his audition for *Wagon Train*, Alan Livingston, Vice-President in charge of programs for the Pacific division of NBC, Peter Pritchard of the Leslie Grade Agency of Great Britain and finally, Marilynn. Throughout the program Bob seems genuinely pleased if a little nonplussed by the event. His parents, particularly his father, appear somewhat uneasy or possibly just ill-at-ease in unfamiliar surroundings as well as dealing with the slick narrative, but it is

*This Is Your Life, January 1961. Standing L to R: Ralph Edwards, Bob Walker, Mead Horton, Alan Livingstone, Peter Pritchard, Jay Lawyer, Alan Miller. Seated: Chelta Horton, Bob, Mary Augustine. Robert Horton's collection. Courtesy of Boyd Magers..*

Mary Augustine who steals the show and strikes the most genuine note, mainly due to Bob's effusively loving greeting, and her own evident delight at being re-united with "her boy".

One discordant note was struck, however. In part of the narrative, Ralph Edwards tells Bob that, had it not been for two critically ill patients, his brother would have been on stage, too. The fact of the matter is that Creighton Horton, according to Joan, his daughter, "flat out refused" to appear on the program, much to the disappointment of his four children, who had been very excited at the prospect of appearing on television with their Uncle Howard. There were no "critically ill patients" and Robert Horton undoubtedly knew that. He knew it because a violent row had erupted at Creighton's home on New Year's Day when he and his new bride visited to break the news of their marriage to everyone there. No doubt taken aback by this turn of events, Anne Horton inadvertently, and understandably, referred to her sister-in-law as Marilynn Bradley. Marilynn, expecting to be received and referred to as Mrs. Horton, or Marilynn Horton, was offended. There was a terrible row as each brother defended his wife's position and the newlyweds were sent packing with the admonition from Creighton Horton "never to darken their doorstep again!"[25] This unhappy episode established another barricade between the brothers which was never fully overcome. Robert Horton could say whatever he liked to Marilynn, but no-one else was to be allowed that freedom. If her feelings were hurt, the perpetrator would suffer the consequences, and the devil take the hindmost. It began an estrangement of sorts which was never fully overcome on either side. Creighton refused to appear on the program honoring his younger brother and he barred his wife and children from appearing as well. Nevertheless, Robert pasted in to the front of the leather-bound script of the program, which he received from NBC, the telegram Creighton found time to send to him at 6:12 pm on Wednesday, January 18. "Deliver personally 8:30 pm, Hollywood Roosevelt Hotel Care Redwood Room" the cable read. Its message said,

"WISH WE COULD HAVE BEEN WITH YOU TONIGHT. HOPE YOU HAVE A WONDERFUL TIME. LOVE. CRATE AND ANNE".

Perhaps it was Anne, his sister-in-law, who actually sent the telegram. There is evidence that she and Robert got along, corresponded occasionally and indeed, she kept a number of press cuttings about Robert which ultimately went to her daughter, Joan.[26]

The script for the program, held in Ralph Edwards' hands throughout the show, was presented to Robert Horton at its end. Each of the people appearing had to be coached in their responses, for it was a scripted show. The only person without lines was, of course, Horton himself. When compared with the taped show, a number of Edwards' lines have been changed, or simply deleted. Heavy pencil is scored through several references pertaining to the Horton parents and it is interesting to speculate whether or not this was something which Edwards did at their behest during a run through, or, indeed, if Robert Horton had a hand in it just prior to the show being recorded. Did he ask to see the script, or was he kept completely ignorant as to its contents until the show took place? At one point in the script, Edwards was to introduce Mr. Horton again, who was to say,

"Bob's mother and I were against his following an acting career unless he could be top dog tops in the profession. Not mediocre – but the best."

These words are heavily scored through in black pencil.

Also scored out late in the show are the words,

"You certainly did follow your parents' advice about becoming 'the best'."

No-one now knows about these script changes with the exception of Robert Horton's widow, and they could just as easily have been her recommendations, as she was the prime contact in the preparation of the show. Whatever the case, the changes are interesting in terms of shedding further light on the complicated relationship which existed between the parents, their son and his fourth wife. Together with the Royal Command Performance and his first solo trans-continental flight, Robert Horton spoke of his *This Is Your Life* appearance as one of the supreme moments of his life.

# Chapter 16
## *End of The Trail*

With hindsight, Robert Horton's years with *Wagon Train* may be seen as the high point of his overall career, and there is absolutely no doubt that, throughout the run of his five-year contract with Revue, he was riding as high as he possibly could and he was one of the biggest stars of the small screen, if not the biggest. His fan mail was legendary, he was known across the world and he could have anything he wanted. However, the death of Ward Bond ushered in a period of uncertainty, underscored by Horton's uncompromising attitude to his future and his association with the show. He felt keenly that the quality of *Wagon Train* was being compromised, that the scripts were becoming weaker and repetitive, that more and more stock footage was being used, along with more and more indoor sets. Attention to detail in the contexts of the stories was suspect. He particularly objected to being touted as the man who would take over Bond's role as wagon master.

He said, "I thought it (the role of the wagon master) should be played by an older man . . . part of Flint McCullough's appeal was that he accepted responsibility when he chose to. He had never gotten into a situation where he was tied down. He was independent and very much a loner." He did fill in for Bond in four episodes in Season Four, one in particular titled "The Prairie Story," co-starring Beulah Bondi, aired in February 1961. The story entailed an Indian attack on the wagon train which resulted in the abduction of a woman and which depicted McCullough completely out of character.

Horton commented derisively, "The story involved a woman being dragged off by the Indians. By the time it was cut and edited, it looked as if I stood by and made no effort to prevent it. Now with an older man in that situation, his physical limitations would prevent him from doing anything. Or with Ward in the role, with his knowledge and maturity, he'd say, "There's nothing to be done" and you'd believe it. But when Flint stood by in the prime of his life and did nothing, it invalidated his image."[1]

His friend Lee Marvin, making his second appearance as a co-star on *Wagon Train*, starred in another "transitional" episode, "The Christopher Hale Story," aired in March 1961. He played a ruthless type whose only concern was making time, and to hell with the general condition of the pioneers. This episode introduced John McIntire as Chris Hale, who ultimately became the replacement for Ward Bond. It is interesting to watch from the point of view of Horton and Marvin's off-screen friendship but there is nothing to see of any relationship whatsoever. They were both consummate actors in their own ways and remained in character throughout the story.

Rumors were thick and heavy in the press of the day about what would happen to *Wagon Train*, including much speculation as to whether or not Robert Horton would take over the role of the train's wagon master. There were feverish articles naming possible successors to Bond, including Dan Duryea, Ernest Borgnine and Broderick Crawford.[2] The fact of the matter was that Robert Horton had no interest whatsoever in stepping into Bond's role. On February 3, 1961, *The Hollywood Reporter*, under the headline "Star Bright Wants It Light" said,

"Printed innuendo to the contrary, Bob Horton makes it plain he doesn't want (nor has ever wanted) to continue as sole star of *Wagon Train*. In fact, he's probably more anxious than anyone connected with the series that a wagon master to replace the late Ward Bond is found pronto and he'll plump for same when he meets with MCA and Revue execs this week in Palm Springs, where next season's plans for *Wagon Train* will be thrashed out."

And thrashed out they were. Robert Horton flew to Palm Springs to participate in negotiations with Revue. His friend and current agent, Edward Traubner, went with him. Entries in Horton's flight log for February 1961 state:

"Feb 18, 1961 – Van Nuys to Palm Springs – Eddie Traubner Conference Regarding Revue Negotiations.

Feb 20, 1961 – Palm Springs to Van Nuys.

Feb 25, 1961 – Van Nuys to Palm Springs – Meeting with Lou [*sic*] Wasserman regarding Revue.

Feb 27, 1961 – Palm Springs to Van Nuys."

Among other things, the negotiations included discussions on what to do about replacing Ward Bond in Season Four of *Wagon Train* and Robert Horton lobbied for more time off to do other work outside the series. Meanwhile, *Wagon Train* rolled on, with Horton growing increasingly bored with his involvement in it. He appeared less and less, with seventeen shows in Season Four versus twenty-eight in Season One. Revue Productions began to look for someone who might take his place on the train as it was growing increasingly clear that his avowals to move on at the end of his contractual period were not idle threats. The outside demands for his work went on unabated although he was always at the mercy of the series' shooting schedule and continued to be unable to take up many of the offers which really appealed to him. He had two years to fulfill and had to do so without the company of the irascible Ward Bond. Finally, the studio selected John McIntire to replace Ward Bond as wagon master, a decision which pleased Horton. In the book, *Wagon Train – The Television Series* by James Rosin (2008), he told Rosin, "I was delighted when they picked John McIntire to be the new wagon master. In fact, I had suggested him for two guest roles that season. John was a versatile actor and my kind of performer."[3] He liked McIntire, who was a seasoned veteran of both film and television, and had worked with him, notably in a previous *Wagon Train* episode titled "The Andrew Hale Story". McIntire was duly hired and came on board as wagon master Chris Hale. Their relationship on screen, however, was very different from the relationship which had existed between Flint McCullough and Seth Adams. It was a cozier, more collegial, more supportive relationship, and while it worked, it lacked the magic and spark of the one which had existed between Horton and Bond.

Horton continued to lock horns with MCA and Revue, although there were no reports of disagreements or suspensions until September 15, 1961 when he was suspended for "not learning his lines."[4] The young "replacement", Denny (Scott) Miller, took over his role. By September 18 reports said that all was resolved between Horton and the studio and that he was due back on set on October 2. This suspension came fast on the heels of a letter Horton received from the US State Department's anti-trust division in August, requesting that he make available all documents which might assist the department with its investigation into alleged anti-trust violations which had taken place within the entertainment industry. The letter itself was pasted into Horton's *Red Book* together with two newspaper clippings referring to his October 1960 suspension, so it is reasonable to assume that the two were related.

Nevertheless, on September 27, 1961, he received a cablegram from Robert Kintner, President of NBC, stating,

"IT IS REASSURING FOR US TO KNOW THAT YOU WILL AGAIN BE WITH US FOR ANOTHER SEASON OF WAGON TRAIN CONGRATULATIONS ON THE DEBUT OF WHAT I KNOW WILL BE ANOTHER SUCCESSFUL YEAR = BEST WISHES ROBERT E. KINTNER PRESIDENT NBC"

This, then, represented the beginning of Robert Horton's fifth and final season with Revue Studios. At the time he was besieged with offers of films, television appearances, plays and Broadway deals, and the frustration he felt at having to turn down so many plum roles must have been enormous. However, NBC knew in October 1961, with Horton's fifth and final season about to get underway, that MCA and Revue Productions had sold *Wagon Train* to ABC for the heart-stopping amount of twenty million dollars. Ten million dollars were to cover the cost of new *Wagon Train* episodes, and the balance was to cover 189 repeats, which represented Season One through Season Five, the seasons which involved Robert Horton. Whether or not they were gambling on Horton remaining with the show can only be conjectured. What Robert Horton knew of the negotiations and sale initially is also unknown, but ABC must have thought that they were buying the entire property, stars included.[5]

*Wagon Train* retained its popularity throughout the Flint McCullough years because Robert Horton kept the viewing public glued to their TV sets. His disappearance from the series would render, if not a fatal blow to its success, at least a crippling one, and to the careful viewer watching the putative replacements for McCullough being put through their paces, mostly when Horton was off doing another gig, it's obvious that there was no way for any of them to fill Horton's boots – not Denny (Scott) Miller and not Robert Fuller. Denny Miller was a genial young giant with practically no acting experience and no real charisma on screen, and Robert Fuller was a nice guy who had made a name for himself as Jess Harper of *Laramie*, but who, despite claims that he resembled Horton physically and shared the same birthday (whatever that had to do with it) was scarcely the overwhelmingly handsome and magnetic personality Horton was.

In the background, administratively, the studio heads were intent on keeping Robert Horton in the traces. The early Sixties was a time of change and unrest within the studios and networks and the tried-and-true formulas for successful television were being challenged. Westerns still dominated the rankings, along with variety shows, quiz shows (largely populated by celebrities of the day), homespun comedies – but newer stuff was slowly breaking through, and in a world where ratings were everything, hanging on to a top placing meant life or death to a program. In its first season *Wagon Train* entered the Nielsen Top 30 at number 23, but shot to the number 2 slot in its second year, a dizzying feat, all things considered. It stayed at that spot until Season 5, when it finally displaced the much loved *Gunsmoke* despite the loss of Ward Bond in Season 4 (1960 – 1961). That Robert Horton had a great deal to do with the show's popularity is inarguable and it's significant that, in the last year of his contract *Wagon Train* secured the number one spot in the Nielsen ratings.[6] This was not lost on MCA, NBC and Revue Studios, and when rumors, then substantiated stories of Horton's intent to move on became impossible to ignore, the television moguls moved in and put the full-court press on the actor.

"I was promised the state of Georgia," Robert Horton said of the negotiations which took place with Lew Wasserman, "King of Hollywood," who made the unprecedented concession of traveling over "to the wrong side of the hill" to meet Horton in his Studio City home to negotiate a deal with him. How that deal actually translated in terms of real money is anyone's guess now. The rewards to stay in harness for a further five years have been described variously as "Ten thousand dollars a week and twenty-percent of Wagon Train", "Two million dollars over five years", "Ten million dollars over five years", and "The State of Georgia".[7] Only Robert Horton, and possibly Marilynn Horton could say for sure. One story, shared by Robert Horton as he contemplated having his biography written, refers to a moment over a dinner when Robert Horton left the table, and the room. Wasserman and his cohorts immediately grasped the opportunity to pressure his wife into persuading her husband to renew his contract.

"You will have everything you ever wanted! Furs, limousines, homes, vacations, the very best of life!"

"You'll never want for anything again!"[8]

They desperately wanted her to make Bob see sense and renew with them. They desperately needed him to sign up for another five years. None of the pressure worked. Marilynn stood by Bob's decision to move on and he did not renew his contract. As it turned out, Marilynn never wanted for anything materially, anyway. Her husband took care of that through his talent and his own sound fiscal management and they lived very comfortably throughout their lives together.

What the studio and Wasserman failed to understand was the fact that Robert Horton, all along, made it clear that *Wagon Train* was not forever. He had his sights set on higher things. Indeed, on the reverse of a promotional picture of him in the role of Flint McCullough, dated December 5, 1958, the snipe reads,

"Robert Horton portrays the scout, Flint McCullough on *Wagon Train* (NBC-TV Network, Mondays 8 – 9pm NYT). "Someday," he says, "I'll want to break away and try something completely different."

He took regular voice training lessons, he took roles in non-Western television productions and he made no secret of the fact that he wanted to establish himself as a musical theater star, on Broadway. When faced with the inducements offered to stay on as Flint McCullough, Robert Horton simply said, "No." Marilynn Horton backed him up. Lew Wasserman was livid. He was unaccustomed to failure, unaccustomed to having anyone stand up to him, accustomed to getting his own way. The fact that Robert Horton stood up to him, did not bend his knee to him or bow to his wishes infuriated him. It mattered little that Horton was within his rights to put Wagon Train behind him, to call it quits and walk away from the glittering prizes dangled before him. Wasserman could not accept that someone he expected to dance to his tune refused to do so. His vindictiveness was legendary. When Robert Horton refused to renew his contract, he became a marked man. Wasserman determined that he should never work in Hollywood again and he attempted to carry out that vendetta until the end of his life. When he died in June 2002, his widow Edie carried it on. Robert Horton, much later, stated flatly that his departure from *Wagon Train* was "legal, but not amicable".[9]

Exactly when the negotiations regarding his future with Revue Studios and MCA took place is uncertain. They certainly began in February 1961, in Palm Springs, at which time Robert Horton was committed to at least one more year with *Wagon Train*, although it is clear from Robert Kintner's cable to him in September of that year that it was not necessarily a "fait accompli." The emergence of his contract with NBC following the sale of *Wagon Train* to ABC that fall must have given Wasserman apoplexy. If Robert Horton, having secured a year's exclusivity with NBC following the end of his contract with MCA – Revue, felt he was in a position to walk away from the latter, he may well have done so, but there is no doubt that his career was at its zenith, he was the subject of constant demands for his work and he probably felt very secure in doing what he did. Besides, he was determined to forge a career which would be far more important. Money was not a motivating factor for him, his art was.[10] Marilynn, in several contemporary articles, is credited with supporting her husband's career move, credited with encouraging him to follow the dictates of his own heart. He was weary of the Flint McCullough character and said openly that he was bored with the entire production. Unlike James Arness of *Gunsmoke* he was not in the slightest interested in being safe and secure in a familiar role. He alluded to the danger of mixing up his own identity with that of the scout as early as May 1959, when Charles Denton wrote for the *Detroit Free Press* that "Horton Says TV Stardom Can Bury An Actor's Name." Horton's words on that occasion were, "I'm happy to do constructive publicity for the show, but not identifying myself indelibly with one character." In 1962, in an unidentified clipping he observed, "I've been playing one show for more than five years. Sometimes I even confuse Flint McCullough with Bob Horton. Such total identification can be dangerous for an actor."

During the last two seasons of his contract with *Wagon Train*, Bob's appearances became less and less frequent. He continued to exercise his right to appear on stage and in other television productions, particularly as a singer, and it's clear that Marilynn encouraged him in this. He made no secret of his ambition to develop a career in musical theater. As the time drew near for him to renew his contract with Revue, more and more appeared in the entertainment press of the time that he was determined not to do so.

One article, written by Jack Hellman and published in the April 24, 1961 edition of *Variety*, quoted Horton at length, and goes a long way to stating his point of view regarding his obligations to Revue. It began,

"Robert Horton is throwing away an opportunity that most actors, in and out of tv,*[sic]* would give their right arm for, as the saying goes. Revue hankers him for another five years as costar of *Wagon Train* but he has bluntly told them "forget it." It's such a flattering deal," says Horton, "what I'm getting now would be nothing to what they offered me for another five years on a participation deal, which means keeping money." Horton doesn't believe he will be penalized by MCA (Revue) for refusing to re-sign, like having his part played down in the last 26 he does with an option on an additional 13. "I don't see why I should be spanked for wanting to graduate from Westerns and broaden my career," says Horton. "If they play me down because the show is losing me and start grooming Scott Miller (also a UCLA grad) for my part it won't go too hard with me. My contract calls for a major role in one half plus one of the 26 'Trains' I owe them. I believe I've amply repaid Revue for what they've paid me."

Horton is not without gratitude to Revue for giving him his big break after years of minor parts in pictures. "But I don't want to always be a Western star. I want to branch out like MCA did in Tokyo and Australia. I could have had my own Western series last year but I've had it in tv*[sic]* and want to spread my thespic wings while I'm still young. My immediate passion is a Broadway musical, which may be coming along under the aegis of Richard Rodgers and Alan Lerner. I would also like to do a big Western for theatres. But, frankly, I'm tired of playing traffic cop to direct guest stars through the 'Train.' . . . If Revue wants to censor me for reaching into other areas of my acting profession that's their privilege."

Even if he had continued to have the freedom to go outside *Wagon Train* as he had done, doing other work, it simply wasn't enough, but the thing he utterly refused to submit to was being typecast. He also utterly refused to be dictated to by Wasserman. In the final analysis, his decision may have been the wrong one. Wasserman lived to a ripe old age and wielded a huge amount of power until his death, and he made quite sure that he kept his promise that, having rejected all the offers made to him by Revue, MCA and Wasserman, Robert Horton would never work in Hollywood again. That went for making records as well.

The last two seasons of *Wagon Train* saw less and less of Robert Horton as Flint McCullough. In April 1961, he participated in a lecture series entitled "The Living Stage" at UCLA, his Alma Mater, appearing on April 26 with Eva-Marie Saint, Ralph Freud, Jeffrey Hayden, Sanford Meisner and John Houseman to discuss "The Actor, Director and Ensemble." William W. Melnitz, acting dean of the College of Fine Arts wrote him this thank-you letter on April 27:

*"Dear Bob,*

*You were absolutely delightful and so charming that I felt I should have paid you the compliment that you so generously directed to me. I thought you found just the right words to spark the discussion, and I am really most thankful for your contribution.*

*It was very good to see you again and to make the acquaintance of your lovely wife. I hope both of you will have a wonderful time in England, and it will be most interesting for you to compare once more the different climate in the theater.*

*With very best wishes and warmest regards,*

*Affectionately yours,*

*William W. Melnitz."*

If this letter, and Robert's participation in the lecture series says nothing else, it demonstrates the fact that he was a highly respected member of the acting fraternity as well as within the halls of his Alma Mater and lends weight to Horton's confidence in himself and his decisions.

Despite the reduction in his appearances on *Wagon Train*, Robert Horton was extremely busy otherwise in 1961. He made a third trip to England and Europe in May 1961 which lasted a month. In England he appeared in a television special, *The Robert Horton Show* and took it on tour for two weeks, appearing in a series of variety theaters around the country each night. Despite all the fuss made about his wife being only that, a wife, he introduced her on stage at the Hammersmith Gaumont, in London, where they sang together, charming both audiences and critics alike. A critic for the *Musical Express* wrote in the May 19 edition of the paper, "Bob Horton took a chance. *Wagon Train* star Robert Horton certainly chanced his luck when he introduced his glamorous wife, singer Marilyn*[sic]* Bradley, into his opening night act at the Hammersmith Gaumont on Saturday. At first, I thought that the fans, most of them teenage girls, would resent her intrusion into the rugged Mr. Horton's performance. But happily, I was wrong – they loved every minute of it, and Bob's gamble paid handsome dividends.

"What do I do with myself when I'm not working on "*Wagon Train*," Bob asked his audience. "Well, I have a wonderful hobby – and I'd like you to meet her." He went on, waving a hand at the advancing figure (and what a figure!) of dark-haired, curvaceous Marilyn.

After a bit of cross-talk, we found that Marilyn has more than beauty – she can really sing, too!

Mr. and Mrs. Horton duetted*[sic]* nicely in "So In Love With You," then turned in a pleasantly humorous, tongue-in-cheek version of "Let's Do It" before closing with "Long Before I knew You."

The on-stage romantic touch (they hardly stopped looking in each other's eyes throughout the three songs) was somewhat overdone, I feel, but otherwise the short routine was extremely effective."

Marilynn appeared with her husband on-stage at all the venues on the tour, in a clearly well-rehearsed program designed to appeal to the British audiences around the country. It may have been during this trip that Marilynn Horton grew more aware of the realities of her handsome husband's fan following. In the United Kingdom, it was huge. Appearing beside him on stage may have mollified her to a degree, giving her the status of "adored wife," but how she truly felt about his fans never came to light for at least four decades. In the Sixties and Seventies she involved herself by communicating directly, on his behalf, with fan club presidents, and those fans who met her spoke highly of her kindness, willingness to share Bob with them and tolerance of their invasion in his life, and, ergo, hers. Her participation in his career on stage and behind the scenes drew great admiration and veneration for her from "his" fans.

While in England, Robert Horton took another major step in his determination to be independent of *Wagon Train*, Revue Studios, MCA and NBC. He formed his own production company. Named "Bronze, Ltd.," after the Great Dane he had acquired in England the year before, the entity was established so that the Leslie Grade Organization of London, acting for Horton, could complete the purchase of "The Morning" by William Fay Glenn before its publication as a novel. Horton planned to produce the piece as a movie on the completion of his contract with Revue, but it did not come to fruition.[11] The Leslie Grade Organization also closed on a contract with Pye Record Company of England for an album, *Robert Horton Sings For Britain*. No such album was ever produced, sadly.

The newly married couple took a second trip to Europe that spring, after the British tour, to make up for the lack of a honeymoon in January, and Horton was back at work on the *Wagon Train* set in early June. His lack of interest in the Western which had launched his meteoric rise to fame began to show. He took less time to question script quality and though some of his later performances are exceptional and notable, among them "The Traitor," "Ft. Anderson" and "The Trials of Flint McCullough," there is a sense in some episodes that he has shown up, done his job and left. He was fashioning a future for himself in musical theater and Marilynn seems to have been behind him every step of the way.

Still within the first years of their love affair, Bob and Marilynn were still within that magic time when the object of one's desire is

*The long-delayed honeymoon, May 1961. Robert Horton, author's collection.*

also one's total obsession. Because he was the man he was, Robert Horton also deeply respected his new wife's knowledge of music, her classical training, her opinion of his abilities as a singer and how those abilities were enhanced by his acting prowess. He was confident that he could bring to any role he played not just a very fine, true voice, but the skill to enhance that voice with acting prowess matched by his exceptional looks. Under any other circumstances it was a winning combination, but he was up against powers he could not begin to reckon with. Neither he nor his wife really understood what their joint refusal to Wasserman meant. Both demonstrated a level of naiveté in this, but Bob was the ultimate decision maker. He was the man in the family, the head of the family, the one who dictated the way things would be and had Marilynn been swayed by the temptations – bribes – offered by Wasserman, Robert Horton would nevertheless have stood his ground. Two very good friends of his in his later years agreed that, if he took anything from his Mormon background, it was that the man is head of the household. Discussions may take place, but when a decision had to be made it was the man's place to make it. Then others, in this case, his wife, had to fall in with it. If the decision turned out to be wrong, he was absolutely prepared to accept full responsibility for it, but no matter what, he was the decision maker, full stop.[12]

The final episode of *Wagon Train* in which Flint McCullough appeared was poorly thought through and a shameless make-over of the "Flint McCullough Story" episode aired in Season 3. Robert Horton's lack of interest in its relationship to his character outline, written five years before, is evident in his lack of protest against what was obviously a slipshod approach to the demise of Flint McCullough. All that said, his acting in it is irreproachable. He takes on the story and somehow makes it work. He refused to be "killed off," he simply wanted to be "written out," so he was. There were a couple of powerful moments within the story, which included a fine performance from Cloris Leachman, his co-star, but in the end the similarities to the "Flint McCullough Story" are undeniable, as is his clear relief to be done with *Wagon Train* and the persona of Flint McCullough.

Meanwhile, by the time Robert Horton had filmed his final segment of *Wagon Train* in February 1962, he and Robert Kintner had worked out a contract which would keep Horton with NBC as its exclusive property for a year. Revue Productions was in the midst of producing a new, ninety-minute color Western based on the book *The Virginian* which it planned to broadcast each week in the same time slot which *Wagon Train* had occupied for five years. Robert Horton was touted as a possible guest star for *The Virginian*. The details of Horton's new contract with NBC were simple and clearly based on the star's requirements. He would have full approval of any material of any show he was asked to appear on. The number of appearances within the twelve-month period of the contract would be limited to ten, unless Horton chose to do more. NBC would provide funds to enable Horton's own production company, Bronze Ltd., to buy and produce its own programs. Robert Horton would appear exclusively on NBC network programs.[13]

All sorts of articles were written about these two developments; the moving of *Wagon Train* to ABC and the exclusive contract between Horton and NBC. One journalist wrote that ABC executives must have been swallowing aspirin by the cart load as they viewed the prospect of Robert Horton possibly making a guest appearance on *The Virginian* directly opposite his old show *Wagon Train*. In fact, it never happened. Revue Productions, who owned *The Virginian*, said baldly that they didn't want Robert Horton, and Robert Horton, although quite amenable to appearing on the show, probably did not want to do so, although he said at the time that if he was offered a good script, he would do it. He did, after all, have the last say when it came to the shows he might agree to appear on. While the contract with NBC offered him a great deal of flexibility it still tied him down for a year, and his sights were very firmly set on a Broadway gig.[14]

The end of his five-year contract with Revue Studios and MCA came with a good deal of acrimony and ill-feeling. He noted that the last two years of his association with the show were not particularly happy and that his relationship with the studio was marred by a steady decline in their treatment of him. He spoke of phone calls not being put through to him, many of which were about work he was being offered, or other engagements he was involved with – in other words, business calls. He couldn't help noticing that his portable dressing room was situated more and more inconveniently. His appearances in the final season were cut to a total of twelve, "which isn't much for a series," he observed. When the day came for him to leave the set forever, there was no farewell party, despite the wishes of his fellow actors, directors and producers. His co-workers were told not to make a fuss. In other words, the studio did not want any kind of publicity associated with his departure. Nevertheless, he was given a huge card, signed by a great many of his fellow workers, wishing him luck and declaring that he would be missed. That was a small gesture, but the parting of the ways demonstrated in no uncertain fashion that the might of the studios prevailed. Robert Horton's dedication and contribution over five years was dismissed. Thus came the demise of Flint McCullough, and while millions of fans across the world rued it mightily, and Lew Wasserman, head of MCA vowed that Horton would also rue the day he refused to co-operate and stay with the show, Robert Horton himself could not have been happier. He was ready to move on, ready to take his career in another direction, and he had high hopes for his success and his future.[15]

By the time he rode off into the sunset, never to be referred to again in the series, he was already involved in negotiations to appear in a Broadway musical, *I Picked a Daisy* by Richard Rodgers and Alan Jay Lerner. It was Rodgers and Lerner's first collaboration and was, therefore, a much sought-after role within the musical theater world, despite both its title and storyline being unknown at the time. A handwritten letter to Marilynn from a woman signing herself "Bernice," and part of the *Red Book* collection exclaimed, "*I think it's just wonderful that Bob's doing the new Rodgers[sic] show. You must be very happy. Everyone in the world wanted it.*" Within six months of leaving *Wagon Train* he had signed on as the musical's male lead. The congratulatory telegram from his agent, saved in his *Red Book*, is dated October 11, 1962. About this time, with certainty ahead of him in the shape of his much longed-for Broadway musical, and its opening slated for April 1963, Robert Horton pulled out of his exclusive contract with NBC. It was terminated by mutual consent for he had made certain that a clause was written into the contract in anticipation of just such a situation arising.[16] He felt secure and at ease in terms of his future, for he was at the peak of his career, in huge demand; in fact, one of Hollywood's hottest properties. The Hortons themselves were favorites of the press and a great deal was written about them, their marriage, their devotion to one another, their support of one another, and particularly, of Marilynn's commitment to her husband and to playing the role of faithful and supportive wife.

# PART VI SPREADING HIS WINGS
## Chapter 17
### Broadway, Here I Come

The time period between Robert Horton's departure from *Wagon Train* in spring, 1962 and his arrival on the Broadway stage in October 1963 was nevertheless busy. He spent the summer of 1962 on the road, mostly on the East Coast and in the mid-west. In May and June he starred in the chilling thriller play *The Man* at the Drury Lane Theatre in Chicago, which ran for six weeks. He had had a marked success with this play in England, where it was televised, but some critics felt that the "in-the-round" Drury Lane Theatre did not lend itself to creating the right atmosphere for the material performed.[1] However, he did receive a letter from a woman who saw the play, a nurse who had worked in the field of mental illness. It was dated "6 – 21 – 62"and came from a Mrs. Pat Bergstrom, who wrote,

*"I am writing this letter to tell you how much I enjoyed your performance as Howard in "The Man" this evening. I am sure that this particular role was a challenge and I certainly appreciated your portrayal. The illness that this character had is very hard to understand if not completely impossible to do so.*

*I myself happen to be a nurse and I have seen some very much like Howard. You were so believable that I kept thinking – if only he could get some professional help. Your portrayal of the quick mood swings were wonderful.*

*I had the impression at the end of the performance that you were not happy with the audience and if this is true I can't say that I blame you. Some of them I thought were very impolite. At this time I missed your smile.*

*This part may not have made you popular but to me it made you a better actor than I had thought. On "Wagon Train" I liked you but from now I think I will appreciate your work more.*

*Sincerely, Mrs. Pat Bergstrom"*

In an undated letter save for the heading, *"Tuesday PM"* Robert wrote to his father,

*"Dear Dad,*

*Just a note to say hi! and let you know all is well. Hope you had a nice "Dad's Day" and naturally, are pleased you liked your shirt. The show went well tonight – and the audience was particularly receptive – it makes a difference! Two more weeks and then – Boston!*

*Yesterday we drove all through the northern side of Chicago, and it is as beautiful as the south side is ugly. We visited some beautiful homes on the lake that would credit any block in Bel Air.*

*Enclosed is a fan letter I thought you would enjoy reading – I believe it is one of the sweetest I have ever received.*

*Say hello to all –"*

These letters form part of Bob's memorabilia. There is every reason for his pride in the fan letter which he shares with his father. It demonstrates again his need for his parents' approval.

He went on to Charlotte where, between July 16 and 22, he and Marilynn co-starred in *The Pajama Game*. Both received outstanding reviews, and it was clear that Marilynn's talents were not only a surprise to their audiences, but a delight, too. They received a similar response when they did the same show in Atlanta the following week.[2] Then, appearing for the first time in his career as Curly in *Oklahoma!* at the Pittsburgh Civic Light Opera, he played to sell-out crowds from August 16 to 19, where the managing director of the CLO, William Wymetal, said, "Horton was one of the most conscientious, disciplined and co-operative performers who has worked here." Following this success, he then went to Columbus, Ohio, where he again undertook the lead male role in *Oklahoma!* The show opened on August 21 and it received universally outstanding reviews. Of his performance there Columbus music and theatre critic Ron Pataky wrote:

"Let's get off the ground fast. Horton is a surprise. He is a surprise when he first opens his mouth to sing. Each succeeding effort becomes even more of a surprise. WHY? The man is a most capable vocalist with a rich natural vocal quality, result of which is very easy listening.

Generally, we expect a name such as this to travel mostly on the merits of the name, and less on whatever talent he may or may not possess. Not so with Horton. HE'S FINE. Just fine."

And Sam Wilson, Stage, Screen and Music editor for the *Columbus Dispatch* went into print on August 22 with the words, "Robert Horton Proves Himself an Arresting Singer and Actor in '*Oklahoma!*'" Marilynn Horton did not appear in the *Oklahoma!* productions, claiming that the role of Laurie did not suit her voice.[3] Later in their performing lives together, she changed her tune and undertook the role a number of times with great success.

Meanwhile, work continued on the development of *I Picked a Daisy*. Gower Champion, the man who would direct the musical, flew to Columbus from California to see Horton perform in *Oklahoma!*, saying that the magic of performers takes place on stage, and that was why he wanted to see Bob in person. Afterwards he said about Bob's performance, "He sings like a singer – is Catnip on a stage!" Gower Champion was an icon in the entertainment world, famous for acting, directing, choreography and producing. He had successful shows running on Broadway at the time and was looking for more. His appraisal of Robert Horton and his desire to have him begin his musical theater career in his brand-new undertaking speaks volumes in terms of Bob's talents.[4]

*I Picked a Daisy* combined the redoubtable talents of Richard Rodgers and Alan Jay Lerner, both of whom were without their original collaborators, Oscar Hammerstein and Fritz Loewe respectively. Indeed, it was Richard Rodgers who insisted on signing Robert Horton for the lead male role, though Alan Lerner had wanted Louis Jourdan. Lerner said that Rodgers wanted someone in the role who had a more legitimate voice, and at the time that meant Robert Horton.[5] It may be that Gower Champion sided with Rodgers in this matter and that issue may have been one of the things which niggled with Lerner as they worked together on the music and words. At all events, Robert Horton was certainly committed to the show by the time he appeared once more in *Picnic* that August in Columbus, when Gardner McKay, originally meant to play the part of Hal, went "missing". Now represented by the Ashley-Steiner Agency, it must have been a wonderful moment when Horton, in Jackson, Mississippi at the time, received a telegram on October 11, 1962 from Ray Smith, his agent, stating the following:

"1:21PM CST OCT 1162.
CONGRATULATIONS. I HAVE YOUR SIGNED CONTRACTS FROM ROGERS AND LERNER. LOOK FORWARD TO SEEING YOU SUNDAY SO WE CAN CELEBRATE." (*Red Book*).

On his return to Los Angeles a party must have taken place, although there was nothing specific in terms of arrangements beyond the confirmation of the contract. With nothing definite to go on, then, the couple remained in California, though around the turn of the year the Studio City home they rented was sold before they could renew their lease, and they moved to another rental home in Encino, on Balboa Avenue, not too far distant from Andasol Avenue, the place they eventually called home in the 1970s.[6]

Having concluded the business of bowing out of the exclusive contract with NBC, Bob lost no time in signing for a series of leading roles in summer stock, although rehearsals for *I Picked a Daisy* were scheduled to begin in New York the following spring. It's possible that he had an idea that matters were not going to move along as smoothly as he hoped, and he wanted something to fall back on, or he decided that he would gain as much stage experience as possible in the interim. At all events it was reported in the press on February 26, 1963,that he was engaged by The St. Louis Municipal Light Opera Company to star in *Showboat* in Kansas City from June 10 – 30, and in *Brigadoon* from July 1 – 14. From there he would go to Pittsburgh to star in *Carousel* with the Pittsburgh Light Opera Company between July 16 – 19, with a repeat performance in Indianapolis at the end of July, followed by *Kiss Me Kate* at the Dallas State Fair between August 12 and 26. Marilynn was to star opposite him in the first four productions.[7]

As it turned out, the path to Broadway itself proved to be strewn with obstacles. Though the script of *I Picked a Daisy* was written and completed (Robert Horton's personal copy was sold for a considerable sum following his death), the partnership between Richard Rodgers and Alan Jay Lerner came to a rancorous end in the midst of the musical's production. Rodgers was an organized individual who wrote copiously and easily. Lerner was not so disciplined and furthermore found Rodgers' preoccupation with agreements, contracts and all their minutiae a huge distraction.[8] Although Robert Horton was due to go to New York early in 1963, with tryouts to take place in Detroit, Toronto and Boston, and a New York opening scheduled at the Majestic Theatre for April 4, none of it happened. The show was postponed early in the year and Robert Horton received a payment of $4,000 as a result. It was sent to him on March 18, 1963 in a letter from the New York arm of the Ashley-Steiner Agency which also cited a letter amendment dated March 1 between him and Richard Rodgers. (*Red Book*)

Nine days later he received a memo from Richard Rodgers' secretary reminding him of a luncheon meeting scheduled for April 4, which had been the putative opening date of the show in New York. Lerner, Champion and Rodgers were the other participants, and after lunch all were to adjourn to the Broadhurst Theatre. (*Red Book*). Under the title, "New Rodgers-Lerner Musical Rescheduled," the *New York Herald Tribune* reported that Lerner had delivered the completed book only a few weeks earlier. Rehearsals were planned for early October, meaning that the show would open on Broadway by mid-winter. Meanwhile, Richard Rodgers, putting aside his final work on the score, left on a six-week European tour. What went on subsequently is not entirely clear, but a telegram addressed to Lerner from Horton's agent, Ray Smith, of Ashley-Steiner, sadly undated, read:

"FROM THE FIRST TIME YOU ASKED ROBERT HORTON TO STAR IN YOUR NEW SHOW IT HAS BEEN DIFFICULT TO UNDERSTAND YOUR ATTITUDE AND ACTIONS REGARDING THE NEGOTIATIONS. WE CAN ONLY SURMISE THAT YOU ARE NO LONGER INTERESTED. THEREFORE WE MUST AGAIN WITHDRAW OUR COUNTER PROPOSAL. WE ARE SURE THAT YOU ARE NOT UNAWARE OF HOW DIFFICULT THESE PAST FEW WEEKS HAVE BEEN FOR OUR CLIENT. AS A RESULT MR. HORTON KINDLY REQUESTS THAT SHOULD YOU WISH TO REOPEN NEGOTIA-

TIONS YOU DO SO ONLY WITH THE INTENTION OF COMPLETING THEM." (*Red Book*)

On July 10, 1963 the production was called off and the partnership between Rodgers and Lerner was dissolved on July 25.[9] It never saw the light of day as written but morphed into *On a Clear Day.* On August 1, 1963, Hedda Hopper of the *Los Angeles Times* trumpeted,

"Horton Gets New Broadway Musical – Daisy Cancellation Puts Him Into Merrick's '110 in Shade'. Robert Horton, caught in that swinging door between Alan Jay Lerner and Richard Rodgers which ended in the cancellation of "Daisy" didn't wait long to realize his ambition to do a Broadway musical. On his birthday (July 29), Bob signed to play in a musical version of *The Rainmaker,* titled "110 in the Shade." He will play opposite Inga Swenson, Pat Neal's replacement in "Miracle Worker" on Broadway." She finished by saying, "Lerner wanted Bob to wait for "Daisy" but Bob's a guy who likes to keep busy."

# Chapter 18
## *110 in the Shade*

When he received news of the new musical signing, Robert Horton was in Indianapolis with Marilynn, appearing in *Carousel* for Starlight Musicals, having just completed its run in Pittsburgh with the Pittsburgh Civic Light Opera where he drew rave reviews. Carl Apone, writing for *The Pittsburgh Press* on Wednesday, July 24, said, "To Robert Horton *(Billy Bigelow)* go the bows. His performance not only measured up to the requirements for Bigelow, it went beyond. Horton's 'Soliloquy' was loaded with emotional substance. In fact, the song not only carried the intended conviction, for me it was more impressive than Robert Goulet's version of the same song in the Carousel opener. (Horton's) "If I Loved You" in the second act was a thing of beauty. Horton's brilliant bombardment of the role from every direction brought power and poignancy to the part. . ." Apone also spoke glowingly of Marilynn's performance as Julie. "Horton's wife, Marilynn, was totally good as the innocent, starry-eyed, naïve Julie. This black-haired beauty had eloquently conceived ideas on how to sing the role, and the New England Conservatory graduate brought the songs forth in a manner that was graceful, simple, silken and always a delight." He went on to observe,

"In the final scene, at the graduation of Billy's daughter, there was more weeping than I have seen at a stage play in a long time. And one woman remarked that she had seen "Carousel" five times but had never seen anything to equal Horton's conception."

So, with less than twenty-four hours to prepare for the Indianapolis production, Robert Horton knew that he was about to head for New York and Broadway. *Kiss Me Kate* in Dallas went by the wayside. The local papers were full of the story. Interviewed by Louise Durham of *The Indianapolis News*, and in an article published on Thursday August 1, 1963, Marilynn said,

"It has been chaos these past few weeks. Long distance phone calls have been coming to the motel constantly."

Marilynn was starring as Julie Jones opposite Robert's Billy Big-elow, as she had in Pittsburgh. Durham wrote,"The couple arrived here Monday afternoon before opening in the show the same evening. They had finished the Pittsburgh production of "Carousel" only Sunday evening.

"It's been like that all summer. We have had no day off. Mr. Horton thrives on it. I do to a point, then I have to sit back and collect myself," Mrs. Horton said. "Carousel" is her favorite show, and the Indianapolis production is only the second time they've done it. This is their fourth season together in summer stock, however. One summer they took their own vaudeville-type show to England for a series of one-night stands."

Durham quoted Marilynn, "I'm just a housewife in the winter months. I'm a good cook. I love to paint. I took art lessons. I still take voice lessons."

This is one of very few articles amongst all the clippings and newspaper articles saved in various albums and scrapbooks which directly quotes Marilynn Horton. It certainly helps to clarify how they organized their lives at the time and is supported, six years later, by a clipping in the *Burris Scrapbook*, sadly unidentified, referring to a run of *There's a Girl in My Soup* at the Pheasant Run Playhouse in St. Charles, Illinois, in October, 1969. Over lunch with a reporter, Marilynn said with regard to her limiting her professional appearances with her husband,

"In fact, I do not seek a career for myself. I am quite content just to be with Bob while he is doing his work in the theater. However, when a part comes along in the same show, it is sometimes fun to be a part of the production."

This, then, was the modus operandi which they developed from their first meeting in 1959 and which they followed through to the early Eighties. Robert Horton was the attraction. He secured the work. Marilynn joined him on the stage as and when it suited either him, or her, or both of them.

*110 in the Shade*, the musical version of *The Rainmaker*, put Horton in the familiar role of Starbuck which he had played on a number of occasions. It was a collaboration between playwright N. Richard Nash, lyricist Tom Jones and composer Harvey Schmidt.

David Merrick, the legendary Broadway producer, wasted no time in offering Bob the lead male role as soon as *I Picked a Daisy* was canceled. He did it partly to annoy Richard Rodgers, with whom he was feuding at the time.[1] Bob naturally accepted. He said,

"I was offered a large guarantee to stand by until Lerner worked out a score with Burton Lane. But David Merrick came after me to do his show, the musical of "The Rainmaker" and David is a very convincing man."[2]

Of course, Robert Horton had had experience playing Starbuck in several productions of *The Rainmaker* by this time, and a musical version of the play undoubtedly appealed to him. The story of the rainmaker is well known – was well known – the handsome charlatan rolling into a small Western town in his "rain wagon," intent on fleecing the drought-stricken inhabitants of as much of their money as possible by persuading them of his ability to bring rain to their parched fields. The main theme of the story is that of the transformation of the "plain" farmer's daughter, Lizzie, into a lovely young woman secure in the knowledge of her own worth, a transformation brought about by Starbuck's romancing of her.

David Merrick had tried several times to pry Horton loose from his *Wagon Train* obligations in previous years, so this was no chance approach. One obstacle in the way had to be removed, however. Hal Holbrook had been signed for the role, had undertaken singing lessons and was ready to play it. Once again the issue of a legitimate voice came up, and while that was certainly a major consideration, Merrick also understood very clearly the kind of appeal Robert Horton's presence on stage would have to audiences. Merrick bought up Holbrook's contract and Holbrook was paid off with five weeks' salary. While a spokesman for Merrick refused to make any comment on the "sudden switch" Holbrook said,

"I wanted the part. I liked it and was looking forward to it but I got kicked out. Period."

He also said that Merrick had originally offered the part to Robert Horton the prior September, at which time Horton was tied up with *I Picked a Daisy*.[3]

Later Robert Horton would say that of the two Broadway scripts offered him, *I Picked a Daisy* was superior in all its parts, but in the end, a Broadway musical of some description was better than none at all. His co-stars were Inga Swenson and actor-singer Stephen Douglass. Swenson had a solid resume which included Shakespeare, television appearances on the *Hallmark Hall of Fame, U.S. Steel Hour, Playhouse 90* and summer stock appearances in musicals, and at the time she was named to *110* she was in a straight role on Broadway in *The Miracle Worker*. Like Horton, *110 in the Shade* brought Swenson her first Broadway musical role.[4] Stephen Douglass, however, boasted a strong Broadway background, including a lead role in *Damn Yankees, The Pajama Game* and *Carousel*, amongst others.[5] Will Geer, veteran of theater and film and to be known later as "Grandpa" in the television hit series *The Waltons*, also starred. The choreography was handled by the great Agnes De Mille, who had revolutionized the use of dance within musicals in the mid-Forties when she incorporated dance routines into the narrative of *Oklahoma!*[6]

There was no stinting in terms of the production and David Merrick's unmistakable stamp of quality and thoroughness was demonstrated in his selection of all the players, from director Joseph Anthony, set designer Oliver Smith, costume designer Motley, lighting expert John Harvey to the less well-known actors and music arrangers, who nevertheless held a number of notable awards amongst them. However, Merrick was also known to be mercurial and difficult, and he lived up to that reputation throughout the production of *110*. Nevertheless, he was a huge power on the Broadway theatrical stage of the time and that power was not to be trifled with.[7]

While the cancellation of *I Picked a Daisy* was undoubtedly a great disappointment, to be placed under contract to David Merrick so swiftly must have been not just a huge consolation but tremendously encouraging. Tom Jones and Harvey Schmidt were certainly no Rodgers and Hammersteins, but they were well known within the musical theater world and had penned the hit musical *The Fantasticks* together, which enjoyed a record-breaking run on Broadway, from 1960 through the 1963 season when *110 in the Shade* opened. *The Fantasticks* played in over 25 countries at one time, and to this day remains a favorite of the summer stock theaters around the world. [8]

As with all shows scheduled for Broadway, *110* ran off-Broadway for a number of weeks. Three-week tryouts in both Boston and Philadelphia at the Shubert Theatres located in each city were staged in order to iron out the kinks and tighten up the entire production. Gower Champion, who had scouted Bob for the lead role in the ill-fated *I Picked a Daisy*, cabled Horton on the September opening of *110* in Boston,

"DEAR BOB WE ARE IN A PERFECT SWEAT OF VICARIOUS EXCITEMENT AND ANTICIPATION. WE KNOW YOU WILL BE TREMENDOUS PERSONAL SUCCESS AND HOPE THE SHOW IS A SMASH. OUR LOVE TO MARILYNN. MARGE AND GOWER."[9]

David Merrick, too, sent Robert Horton a telegram when the musical opened first in Boston.

"DEAR BOB I FEEL PROUD THAT I HAVE STARTED A NEW GREAT AMERICAN MUSICAL STAR GOOD LUCK TONIGHT"

Merrick, though, who had other big productions on the go at the time, such as *Hello Dolly* and *Funny Girl*, continued to be difficult about the musical's length and direction. At one point, Lew Wasserman tried to intervene in the production, but David Merrick was not going to be dictated to by the West Coast Hollywood mogul and Wasserman's efforts to prevent Bob from appearing in the musical were to no avail.[10]

The cast was called together for the initial run-throughs early in August. Rehearsals followed and then the try-outs took place in Boston and Philadelphia in September and October 1963, so Robert Horton had been separated from *Wagon Train* and Hollywood for over a year by the time opening night took place on October 24 at the Broadhurst. He received a deluge of good luck telegrams, including ones from Alan Jay Lerner, Richard Rodgers, Agnes de Mille, Lee and Paula Strasberg and Hedda Hopper. Rodgers' message read,

"MY DEEPMOST THANKS AND WARMEST THOUGHTS FOR YOU TONIGHT".

Agnes de Mille said: "GREAT GOOD LUCK TONIGHT AFFECTIONATELY AGNES".

The Strasbergs' message read, "ITS GOOD TO HAVE YOU ON THIS COAST BEST WISHES TONIGHT AND ALWAYS", and Hedda Hopper's genuine affection shone through with,"DON'T THINK YOUR HOLLYWOOD FRIENDS HAVE FORGOTTEN YOU. WE ARE ALL ROOTING FOR YOU TOMORROW NIGHT AND I AM SURE YOU WILL NOT ONLY LIVE UP TO OUR EXPECTATIONS BUT EXCEL THEM WITH LOVE ALWAYS HEDDA HOPPER".

There were also cables from Gig and Elaine Young, Gordon and Sheila MacRae, Leland Heyward, celebrated Hollywood and Broadway agent and theatrical producer, and, one day late, from Robert Goulet. Interestingly there is no record of a cable from any of his family, nor is it clear if any of them attended his Broadway debut, although it is reasonable to assume that, at the very least, his parents may have been present.

There can be little doubt now that part of the musical's success was ultimately due to its leading man, Robert Horton, but Inga Swenson thought otherwise. In answer to a letter I wrote her asking for her recollections of the show and of Robert Horton she wrote that while she and Robert Horton got along well enough, she thought him miscast in the role of Starbuck. In her opinion, he could neither sing nor move well and was the least successful of the half-dozen Starbucks she subsequently acted with. That certainly flies in the face of the many reviews and critiques of his work elsewhere, but there is little doubt that her opinion is – was –negatively influenced. She said that David Merrick had fought to cast Robert Horton as Starbuck, lending credence to the articles concerning Hal Holbrook. She said she liked Robert, but they did not have any kind of a social relationship off-stage. She felt that he had an attitude of entitlement and observed that he insisted on top billing.[11]

There is just a hint of sour grapes in her note though perhaps she was justified, a little, in her feelings. It was her first starring role on Broadway as well, and the story itself is centered on her character, Lizzie. With Hal Holbrook in the role of Starbuck, Lizzie would have undoubtedly shone. The story was hers. The show was hers.

But Robert Horton stole the limelight, simply by being Robert Horton. The fact that the musical score produced nothing by way of memorable songs and lyrics cannot be disputed. It was no Rodgers and Hammerstein production, certainly, but it ran for 330 performances, from the tryout sessions in Boston and Philadelphia starting in September 1963 through the final show which took place in August 1964.

Reviews of the show's pre-Broadway tour in Boston and Philadelphia were mixed. Critics in both cities thought that it was top-heavy and required at least thirty minutes' cutting, tightening and pacing. No-one raved about the music, and while some termed it "eminently listenable" and "pleasant" it was clear to all that the show contained no "real big swinging number" and none of its music would ever become juke-box favorites. Both Swenson and Horton's voices were praised, however, as was their acting. At least one critic found nothing to praise in Robert Horton's characterization of Starbuck and Kevin Kelly, writing for *The Boston Globe* on September 22, 1963, felt that Swenson, a lovely blonde, was just too pretty to be believable as "plain" Lizzie. He too complained about the show's length, and wound up his review with these words,

"Under the direction of Joseph Anthony, the performances are excellent, but I wonder whether Anthony or Nash is responsible for doting on Inga Swenson, who plays Lizzie. Miss Swenson, despite the dialogue, is a beauty, a large Henry Moore figure with a lovely face. She sings well, if not with complete control, and acts with fierce conviction. As I've said before, however, she's on too long.

Robert Horton is fine as Starbuck, with a robust singing voice and magnetic presence. While he has a tendency to force his lines, as though he were always on the edge of a speech, this is perhaps his method of reprisal at Anthony, and/or Nash."

By the time the show got to Philadelphia, it had been cut to two acts, and several songs had been dropped. Henry T. Murdock writing for the *Philadelphia Inquirer* following the show's debut there said,

"When it's "110 in the Shade" things are bound to be easygoing and the musical comedy of that title at the Shubert manages to beguile its audience without working itself into a tizzy or going in for much of the tune show razzle-dazzle. It is pleasant, as pretty as it needs to be, it has likeable people with good voices and it has a score by Harvey Schmidt (music) and Tom Jones (lyrics) which is sentimental without being sticky."

Calling it, despite the involvement of famed choreographer Agnes De Mille, "not precisely a dancing show" he praises the acting.

"Very much on the plus side, however, is the fact that this story with music has principals who can act with sympathy and sing with vigor and leading this department are Inga Swenson, Robert (Wagon Train) Horton and Stephen Douglass."

If Miss Swenson's note is to be believed, critics in New York were harsher in terms of Robert Horton's performance than those in Boston and Philadelphia, and the few examples which Robert Horton kept bear that out. It is also proof that he was not averse to saving poor reviews he received and it's fair to say that he was always prepared to learn from adverse criticism. Did he feel, in the end, that the Broadway show he had longed for for years was not the huge hit he had hoped it might be? In an article written by Glenn Lovell of *Knight News Service* when he interviewed Robert Horton in 1979, Horton acknowledged that the show was not a critical success. "It was a modest success," he remembered, "but it really wasn't a good show. The music was very nice but never really elevated the action. The dances (by Agnes de Mille) didn't elevate the show either and were later cut."

Yes, it was up against other mega-hits of the day, but the material he had to work with simply was not of the caliber of those other shows. There was little he could do to change that and facts are facts. *110 in the Shade* ran for less than a year on Broadway and was never revived there. It managed an off-Broadway run for a few months, but it was not until 1992 that it was revived in New York by The New York City Opera. Even then its reviews were mild. Critic Clive Barnes said of the musical that it was "luke-warm" and that its music and lyrics never rose above B-plus. Of the original Broadway production he wrote this:

"On Broadway "110 in the Shade" survived an unnecessarily blistering review from the New York Times to last more than 300 performances, and obviously gave a lot of pleasure to a lot of people –

110 in the Shade, *New York, 1963. Backstage, with co-stars Inga Swenson and Stephen Douglass. Author's collection.*

some doubtless then attracted by the charismatic presence of super star Robert (Wagon Train) Horton in the cast."

Most critics of the day were reasonably fair in their praise of the performances and sets, though not so ready when it came to the substance of the musical. Listening to the original soundtrack of it now, it is hard to be enthusiastic or carried away by the songs, their music or their lyrics, but everyone involved did the best they could. Swenson's voice, a good lyric soprano, is a little strident at times; Stephen Douglass's is pleasant but unremarkable, while Robert Horton's performance is notable for his unmistakable voice and his pairing of his singing with his equally unmistakable interpretation of the lyrics.

Though some on the East Coast may have been surprised, startled even, to find their television favorite starring in a Broadway musical, it is hard to deny that his name alone was enough to draw the crowds, fill the theater and keep the play running for almost a year. When the critics wrote kindly and enthusiastically of his performances, attendances were guaranteed. Nevertheless, it is hard not to contemplate what might have happened had the first musical come to fruition. Once again, bad luck and poor timing got in the way of Robert Horton's undoubted ability to create a resounding success for himself and others on Broadway. A letter written to Bob in December 1963 by Richard Rodgers, however, says a little about how the play was received. Dated December 12, and handwritten on his personal notepaper, Rodgers said,

"*Dear Bob,*

*I shouldn't have been out of bed at all last[sic]tonight, which is why I didn't get back to see you and tell you how great Dorothy and I thought you were. It all happens for the best, you see. You are fine in a fine show and you and Marilynn should be very proud and happy. I am for you.*

*Fondly,*

*Dick.*"

It also speaks to some of the emotions which were undoubtedly engendered when *I Picked a Daisy* was canceled.

Toby Wolfe, who became a friend of Robert Horton's much later in life, and whose interest in his career was mainly focused on his theatrical life, saw *110 in the Shade* on five different occasions. She attended two of the try-out shows in Philadelphia, saw it again shortly after opening night in New York in October 1963, then again in July and August 1964, just before it closed. Her opinion, as a member of the audience, was that the show was very good, but that it got lost surrounded by such hits as *Hello Dolly, Camelot* and *Funny Girl.* She also noted that "Every time I saw it the house was full and there were long lines at the box office. Of course, most of the audience were women who were there to drool over Bob, but they were enthusiastic for all the performances."[12]

All that said, there is one clipping regarding his New York critics which was saved by his sister-in-law, Anne Horton. Under the by-line, "Point Of View" and headlined "Bob Horton Hits Back At Critics," an article written by Donald Freeman, the TV-Radio Editor of *The San Diego Union* states,

"Robert Horton, sitting in his dressing room flanked by his French poodle, wore a heavy white terry-cloth robe and a white towel draped over his head and white socks and in no way did he resemble the intrepid scout on "Wagon Train," a role he essayed on television for five years.

Now Mr. Horton, who has a New York-based CBS series forthcoming, is starring on Broadway in the musical "110 in the Shade," adapted from "The Rainmaker." He sings and dances and cavorts onstage with proper skill and bravado and this, too, is a far remove from "Wagon Train."

"The critics," Horton was saying as he drew the robe closer around his throat, "have not been overwhelmingly kind to me here. In fact, I'd say they've gone out of their way to take potshots. Directors come to my door after a performance and they say, 'Bob, the musical theater needs somebody like you.' Alan Lerner wants me to do his next show.

But the New York critics – that's a different story. Try to figure them out. One critic didn't like anything about me. Another critic didn't like anything about the show. Go fight it.

You can't please everybody all the time," Horton said, "and it's a good thing if you don't please everybody. Why should you? Not everybody likes John Wayne. Not everybody likes Cagney or Peck or Jimmy Stewart. To be a star – a real star – an actor has to be different; he has to have distinctive elements that are not duplicable and are easy to caricature as Cagney is easy to caricature. If you're bland, everybody will like you – but whoever heard of a star that was bland? Besides, as my father used to tell me, 'The higher you climb up the hill, the bigger target you become."

**A Royal Command Performance**

It was three years ago that Mr. Horton guest-starred as a singer on the Perry Como Show and then he popped up in his first musical. Then he sang at the Hollywood Bowl and he starred at the London Palladium and later sang for Queen Elizabeth at a Royal Command Performance. The hard riding scout of "Wagon Train" can, in short, belt out a tune. How, then, did he account for dissenting notices by the New York critics?

"A 'Hollywood actor' has one strike against him right off the bat," Horton said, "The critics sit back and say, 'OK, prove to us that you can function in a medium without gadgets or gimmicks.' And then, if you're known best from a TV Western – to a New York critic that's the lowest barrel of all, artistically. So there I was – from Hollywood, from TV and from a Western! I was a sitting duck!"

The red-haired actor paused. "Maybe they think of me as a cowboy actor, which is what you'd more rightfully call Jim Arness or Clint Walker. But I'm an actor who happened to make it in a Western show. And I say if you can succeed as an actor in a Western you can succeed in anything. Errol Flynn, Ty Power, Gable – they acted in Westerns and nobody ever sneered, 'Cowboy actor.'

And they say about this show, 'Horton waters down the role.' Look, I did 'Rainmaker' as a straight play."

This piece forcefully states Robert Horton's point of view regarding his New York critics and it is hard to fault his observations.

*110 in the Shade* ran on Broadway from October 1963 for 330 performances, not quite a year. However, the show received a bad blow in April. Chosen to headline an all-star revue at the annual Banshees Luncheon at the Waldorf-Astoria Hotel on April 21 before hundreds of publishers, editors and distinguished guests, Horton and Swenson performed "Is It Really Me?" and "The Rain Song" finale with the show's full company from what was described by a *New York Journal-American* reporter on March 31st as "David Merrick's hit Broadway musical comedy." Swenson, taking a final bow before the assembly, slipped on the stage which had been soaked by the rain effect of the finale's downpour and broke her ankle.[13] Her understudy Joan Fagan stepped in until Swenson returned in July, by which time the show had already suffered by being pitted against *Hello Dolly*, starring Carol Channing, *Camelot* starring Richard Burton and *Funny Girl* starring Barbra Streisand. Just before the show ended on Broadway, Bob received the following telegrams from David Merrick and Tom Jones and Harvey Schmidt respectively:

Merrick wrote, "THANK YOU FOR A WONDERFUL JOB I HAVE ENJOYED OUR ASSOCIATION AND HOPE WE CAN DO IT SOON AGAIN".

Schmidt and Jones wrote, "DEAR BOB WE ARE GOING TO MISS YOU BEST OF LUCK AND THANK YOU SINCERELY HARVEY AND TOM".

*110* closed on August 8, 1964.

# PART VII WHAT HAPPENED NEXT
## Chapter 19
### *Ringing Down the Curtain on Broadway*

During his eleven months with *110 in the Shade*, Robert Horton was busy with other projects. One in particular proves that he was looking to the future, beyond whatever the Broadway musical might bring him. By the time he left *Wagon Train*, Robert Horton was probably one of television's hottest properties. In the months following his departure, up to the opening of *110 in the Shade*, he had rejected nearly one hundred pilots offered to him, but in the Fall of 1963 he was approached by CBS in the form of its head, James Aubrey, and Dick Dorso, head of United Artists-TV, along with producer Robert Alan Aurthur to shoot a pilot, provisionally titled *Mark Dolphin*, for either their 1964-1965 season, or the 1965-1966 season, depending on the possible length of *110 in the Shade's* run.

Robert Horton said,

"They gave me a script to read, and it was very good. It was written by Richard Nash, who had done *110 in the Shade* and also *The Rainmaker*, on which the musical was based. It was just the kind of role I had been looking for after years in Westerns. The hero, Mark Dolphin, was a suave New York multimillionaire living in a Park Avenue penthouse. He involved himself in people's problems and solved them for them. Dolphin had a charming off-beat personality, so I signed to do the pilot. It was a great deal. I would have had thirty-three-and-one-third percent of the profits plus a big weekly salary."

Unfortunately, the entire production turned into a fiasco of miscommunication and mis-management at the highest level of television and came to nothing except to establish a low watermark in television planning and production. Robert Horton tried to withdraw from his agreement but was unable to do so. The pilot was eventually filmed in 1964 but bore no resemblance to the original script. By the time it was tested before an audience it drew some of the worst reviews ever given, and the title *Mark Dolphin* became synonymous with total disaster in the show-business idiom: "For God's sake, let's not have a *Mark Dolphin* on our hands!"[1]

There were other calls on his talents, including appearances on *The Ed Sullivan Show*, but much more successful for Robert Horton was the release of his first album which he recorded in 1964, following the release of the *110 in the Shade* Broadway production LP. *The Very Thought of You* was on the record store shelves in August 1964 and is a complete joy to listen to, beautifully sung and interpreted by Horton on every level. A letter written to Bob by Loonis McGlohon who was Music Director of the Jefferson Standard Broadcasting Company in Charlotte, North Carolina on August 25, 1964, waxes lyrical on the subject.

*"Dear Robert:*

*Damn! You rang down the curtain before I could get to New York to catch your performance."(110 in the Shade).*

He continued:

*"But this letter is mainly to deliver congratulations on your Columbia LP. Frankly (as a jazz pianist), I always have a moment of apprehension before auditioning a pop album turned out by a legit Broadway singer. In your case, there should have been no worry from the beginning, since I had heard your pop-legit style in "Pajama Game". Still I didn't expect to be overwhelmed. I was.*

*I have issued orders that the album is to be exposed until the balls show, so be assured that singer Robert Horton is getting air play up and down the east coast.*

*A very tasty package."*

McGlohon then addressed the album content; scores, material and so forth.

He finishes,

*"But after all the accolades, it is the Horton performance which says the most. You achieved a great deal of intimacy with such a big voice and yet reserved the power until it was needed. And what a joy to hear someone from outside the idiom (and let's face it, you didn't come up through the*

*Count Basie ranks) who can SWING! Robert Goulet, John Gary, Jerry
Vale and a whole raft of them can start learning from you.*

*I'm very pleased about your record debut, and I hope another package
is in the making."*

McGlohon had previously written to Bob about the *110* recording on December 3, 1963.

*"Congratulations! Few people have the ability to make a character
come alive on the typical cast album of a show. Usually, it is the association with remembrance of a performance that makes the record seem
personal. But since I haven't seen your show, I can say that your record
performance transmits the character of "Starbuck" immediately. Well
done. Too, your 'pop' style makes the songs much more believable."*

With his Broadway efforts scarcely a stellar success, and having
made it clear to Merrick that he would not take *110 in the Shade*
on the road, Robert Horton, in 1964, was forced to assess his career
and where it was going. He had come up against Lew Wasserman's vindictiveness by this time and was fully aware of all that that
meant. While many of his contemporaries – Lee Marvin, Charles
Bronson, James Coburn, Jim Garner, Steve McQueen and the like,
all perfectly good actors, were getting work and making big names
for themselves in Hollywood, Robert Horton was relegated to the
summer stock circuit and nightclub appearances. It's hard to say
now whether or not this was actually his choice, but there are clues
along the way. He referred once to being approached to star with
Debbie Reynolds in *The Unsinkable Molly Brown* (1964), but he was
involved with *I Picked A Daisy* at the time, and besides, he would
not go under contract again to MGM. "That would be regress-
ing," he said.[2] If there were other calls from Hollywood for him to
return and star in a major motion picture, there is no mention of
them within his memorabilia. He had as much, and probably more
to offer than many of those aforementioned actors, but instead he
played a number of summer stock theaters, often with Marilynn
appearing as well. Indeed, it is a fact that he made it a requirement
of his contracts throughout his theater life that his wife would be
included in the productions wherever possible, and thus he made
sure that Marilynn enjoyed a ready-made career beside him, without having to work at making things happen herself, or having to

engage her own agent.[3] It kept them traveling together, performing together – being together, but it went against his declaration that he would never marry an actress, and her avowal to always be simply, "Mrs. Robert Horton".

There was a decision made to continue calling New York home. On their arrival in the city to begin work on *110* Robert Horton had sublet an apartment on Fifth Avenue, overlooking Central Park. Sometime later he bought a duplex apartment on Park Avenue. That home served them until they moved back to California permanently, in 1975. He was of two minds when it came to staying in New York, and though he had reservations about it, he admitted that New York had things to offer which his hometown of Los Angeles did not. His mixed feelings were partly due to the restrictions imposed by theater work schedules. He spoke of New York's atmosphere being "interesting," and for a man who had studied with the American Theatre Wing and the Actors Studio the opportunities in New York were certainly attractive.[4] As an East Coast person, Marilynn was just as happy to remain there. New York was as good a base as any for summer circuit work.

Always determined to push himself and expand his horizons, he turned to the nightclub stage, and clippings of the time testify to his success as a nightclub singer. He did it for a purpose, he said. "There's no greater training ground than the nightclub. Why? Because if you stand up there and deal with the lyrics, you're dealing with thoughts which are put to music. If you can stand on your own and maintain audience attention you gain a great deal of respect for yourself."[5] Perhaps it was important to him to take on those audiences in a more intimate setting than the Broadway stage. He appeared at the Elmwood Casino in Windsor, Michigan in November of 1964, about two and a half months after *110* closed. *The Detroit Emergency Press* critic wrote on November 17,

"Robert Horton, star of television, radio and legitimate theatre opened as the headline star at Elmwood Casino, in Windsor before an enthusiastic crowd, making his cabaret singing debut in this area."

On November 25 Shirley Eder of *The Downtown Monitor* wrote,

"Robert Horton Dashing." "Robert Horton at the Elmwood is very handsome and dashing…and the gals love the way he sings… Matter of fact…his act is a huge success."

Jack Meredith in an unidentified publication wrote,

"Horton opened at The Elmwood, Monday night, in a role that he is less known in, that of nightclub singer, but one in which he is a stellar performer." Meredith went on to mention that Bob had flown himself to the venue. He said, however, that "His wife Marilynn travels by more certain transport." This is one of the first comments on Marilynn's growing reluctance to fly with Bob in his single engine Comanche, following praise lavished on her in their first days of marriage as his willing co-pilot and navigator.

From the Elmwood Casino he went on to appear at Tommy Henrich's Diamond Room in Columbus, Ohio, in February 1965. Tommy Henrich, a Yankee's baseball star of the 1930s and '40s and successful Ohioan businessman, founded the Diamond Room and spent many a night there regaling fans with stories of his days in the game. His nightclub was just as famous as he was.[6] It is worth reproducing a lengthy critique of Bob's performances there, written by Gail Lucas and published in the *Citizen Journal* of February 17, for it represents so much of what was said about Robert Horton in his appearances as a singer, either in the nightclub milieu or on stage in a musical.

"Robert Horton has an image. He wears a buckskin jacket, dirty hat, rides a horse and talks in a drawl. To know how distorted this image is, you must see him in person. He sings, he talks – and he puts across a song far better than he ever rode the range.

Horton is appearing this week in Tommy Henrich's Diamond Room, and this man is a wonderful surprise. His singing voice is magnificent: It's strong and resonant… and he not only sings a song, he acts.

(Horton) deserves an encore for choosing his material with care and discretion. Some singers have tried these songs, but with disaster the end product. Not Robert – they were written for voices like his. The rest of his program was chosen with equal discrimination. "Call Me Irresponsible" is done just exactly the way the composer meant it to be – warm, dreamy, appealing and absolutely over-whelming.

Then comes "Once Upon A Time" – and if ever a beautiful song was written, this is it. It takes great feeling and depth to put this song across. Horton does it.

Horton's delivery is excellent, his arrangements flawless, the orchestration is superb. And never let it be overlooked that the man is extremely good looking. An evening with Robert Horton is most enjoyable indeed."

Over and over again, critics and reviewers were surprised, nay, astonished by Robert Horton's singing talent, his stage presence, his ability to connect with his audience and many express apprecia-tion for his physical looks, so much richer and exciting in real life than on a small black and white television screen.

From Columbus in February, he moved on to a slot at La Fiesta Theatre Restaurant in El Paso, New Mexico. There Joan Quarm of the *El Paso Herald Post* reported on March 1, 1963, that "Wagon Train Scouts Sings Love Songs". She went on, "His voice is a very special combination of that vibrant Johnny Mathis quality in the lower register, and a fine masculine upper register which recalls sunlight and trekking West. Robert Horton is a relaxed performer with the trained actor's ability to play to his audience... He is never afraid to experiment ... His musical score is extremely difficult but well-handled ..."

So, with the Broadway period over, nightclub gigs in sway, Rob-ert Horton was seen by a very much restricted audience. Never-theless, he received rave reviews for his performances, and thor-oughly enjoyed being in front of a live audience and it is true to say that his magnetic appeal, that appeal he had engendered as Flint McCullough on *Wagon Train*, helped to pack the venues where he appeared.

It was during these nightclub appearances that he was contacted by Jack Neuman, who was a well-known script writer with cred-its which included *Gunsmoke, Climax!* and *Wagon Train*. Neumann had had an idea about creating a Western whose premise centered on the story of a man who, due to a violent and seemingly unpro-voked attack, suffers a complete loss of memory. On his recovery he is driven to go in search of his identity. Neuman knew it would take a special actor to handle the demands of the lead character and he thought of Robert Horton. He had written the *Wagon Train* scripts for "The Flint McCullough Story," "The Dora Gray Story" and "The John Cameron Story," all featuring Robert Horton in his role of Flint McCullough, and all were strong, well-written stories which respected Horton's characterization of the wagon train scout. When he first got in touch however, Horton, busy with his series of nightclub engagements, said "No thank you." Neuman persisted. After being approached yet again, this time by Alan Courtney who was head of MGM's television production department at the time,Robert Horton reconsidered the concept, and finally agreed to go ahead with it.

His respect for Jack Neuman and Alan Courtney played a part in his decision, but he was also very clear about the fact that the concept behind *A Man Called Shenandoah* intrigued him. Here was a character who did not know who he was, a character which would require careful and considered interpretation. A character who, as Horton himself said, bore a certain likeness to himself. [7]

Robert Horton is on record as having said that, following his departure from *Wagon Train*, he had no interest in appearing in another Western. He is also on record as saying that he recognized the power of television as a medium for acting success and that, given the right vehicle for his talents, he would never rule out a return to the small screen. In the end it was the storyline, the "hook" of the *Shenandoah* series which finally persuaded him to return to Hollywood. Horton also involved himself in the production of the series through his company, "Bronze Ltd." which may explain why he was able to circumvent, to a degree, any influence which Lew Wasserman may have tried to wield against him, as well as the fact that ABC Television, the broadcasting arm of the new series, an MGM affiliate, was not associated with MCA, Wasserman's company. However, it should be noted that, at that particular time, Wasserman was giving more and more time to, and gaining more and more power in the world of politics.[8] At all events, the role of Shenandoah returned Horton to the small screen and Hollywood. Despite the changes taking place within the world of television,

*As Shenandoah, in* A Man Called Shenandoah, *1965. Author's collection.*

he once again took up the part of a Westerner in the 1870s, a man called Shenandoah.

There was a great deal of pragmatism which accompanied Robert Horton's return to television. As long as he was unable to break back into movies due to the Wasserman vendetta, he could, using his own investment, attempt to return to the medium which made him. His production company, Bronze Ltd., was the very vehicle which would allow him to go ahead. When presented with the concept of *A Man Called Shenandoah*, he acted upon it and in collaboration with Courtney and Neuman, Shenandoah was born. At the time that this show was proposed, the series *The Fugitive*, starring David Jansen, was running. It was hugely popular among the viewing millions and it has been suggested that, in a way, *A Man Called Shenandoah* used the same type of premise. There are similarities,for sure, but *The Fugitive* relied on the tension created by the need for the lead player to avoid capture while attempting to bring the real culprit to justice. *A Man Called Shenandoah* had to rely on the viewers to be as eager as the man himself to find out who he was and why he had been so savagely dealt with.

Once again Robert Horton found himself in the position of demanding solid, imaginative, logical writing which would capture the viewer's imagination and keep them hooked on the story. Instead, despite Neuman's involvement, he found himself fighting a losing battle in terms of sameness, and the program, while hitting the top ten ratings consistently early in its existence, fell victim to the very things which had tried his patience in the closing years of his tenure with *Wagon Train*. Inevitably, he lost interest. However, during the making of the series, Horton cut an LP titled *The Man Called Shenandoah*. It was released on February 21, 1966. It featured his version of the famous folk song, "Shenandoah" which was used as the theme for the series, and for which, at Neuman and other's requests, he wrote new words. At first, he did that under protest as well, pointing out that MGM had lyric writers like Alan Lerner and Sammy Cahn under contract. It seems that the business of getting such lyricists to undertake the project was too much trouble for MGM, so Bob duly settled down one Sunday and produced new lines for the song which encapsulated, in verse, the premise behind the story of *A Man Called Shenandoah*, thus neatly avoiding having to repeat it tediously in each episode.[9]

Adverse scheduling did not help the series' cause, being pitted against such huge favorites as *The Andy Williams Show*, and the ever-popular *Andy Griffith Show*, not to mention a threatened lawsuit over the use of the name "Shenandoah". A movie using that name and starring Jimmy Stewart, was released by Universal Studios, on June 3, 1965, just three months before *A Man Called Shenandoah* hit the small screen. It helped put an end to the television series, which ran for only thirty-four episodes and was cancelled before the start of the 1966 season. How much influence Lew Wassermen had with regard to the *Shenandoah* lawsuit may only be pondered, but it is more than likely that he had a hand in some of it. The record certainly figured in legal wrangling related to the show. In an interview for the publication *Traildust* in the spring of 1994, Robert Horton said,

"Universal (Revue Studios, MCA) was never very kind to me after I left "Wagon Train". They offered me $2,000,000 to stay. I never worked for them again! They sued Columbia Records related to "The Man Called Shenandoah" because they'd made a picture with Jimmy Stewart called "Shenandoah". And Columbia pulled the record off the racks!"

Horton was not quite seventy at the time this interview was published, and this is only one of two references to the legal problems he encountered amongst a vast collection of articles, clippings and other records of the time. It came straight from Horton's mouth. Universal was, of course, Wasserman's company, and had been Revue Studios. MCA, the Music Corporation of America, was also Wasserman's. The other reference was in an article written by a James A. Perry for a New Orleans publication, unidentified, and published on June 16, 1967. It was on the occasion of Horton's appearing with the New Orleans Pops Concert. Perry wrote,

"There's still speculation about why the show was dropped by the network, but Horton believes that one reason is because of an entanglement involving the creators of the show.

"The last I heard there were four lawsuits to determine who created "Shenandoah," he said." He also spoke of the reorganization which was taking place throughout ABC. A complete change within the upper echelons of the company resulted in a clean sweep of programming, including *A Man Called Shenandoah*, which was cancelled on the last day of the production of the final episode, to everyone's astonishment.[10]

Robert Horton took a lot of heat when he returned to television in the role of Shenandoah. There is a particularly critical article written by one Dwight Whitney, a regular journalist with *TV Guides* various, entitled "Ride 'Em Sigmund Freud". Published in *TV Guide* covering the week of March 5 – 11, 1966, Whitney has very little positive or pleasant to say about Horton, and derides him for just about everything he did as an actor, most especially his departure from *Wagon Train*, his avowal to do no more Westerns, and his subsequent return to the medium. The truth is, Robert Horton was always acutely aware of what his career owed to television, and he never wrote it off entirely. In the 1960s, any clear headed, intelligent actor would have been a fool to say "no" to television, and Robert Horton was nothing if not clear-headed and intelligent. He had the talent, he had the ability and he had the looks. He also had Wasserman, and no matter how good he was, or how strong his friends and colleagues were, he could not confront the Hollywood mogul and win. Perhaps Whitney, by the time he wrote this piece, had fallen foul of Robert Horton. He had written, four years earlier, in a *TV Guide* on May 27, 1961,

"Robert Horton, for all the criticism fired his way and for whatever personality problems have been brought on by his quick success, is an actor – and a good one."

On consideration, timing – bad timing – played a part in his destiny. The clash of the Shenandoahs should not have happened. The movie was a huge box-office success months before the television show hit the air, and there was absolutely no similarity between the story content of either. While it ran, despite the scheduling conflicts, *A Man Called Shenandoah* drew excellent reviews, some good ratings and a substantial audience share.[11]

*Shenandoah* was filmed in California, so Robert and Marilynn moved out of their penthouse apartment on Park Avenue, Manhattan, leasing it to Peter Falk, and returned to Hollywood where they rented a Malibu apartment on the beach front from actor Jack Ging. That was to be home until a new direction was found, a successful series, or something else. Indeed, in December 1965, it was reported that Robert Horton bought a plot of land in Malibu which he gave to Marilynn as a fifth wedding anniversary present, and if this was so, they undoubtedly hoped for great things from the new television series. There is, however, no record of any home built in Malibu for the Hortons, nor of their occupying such a home.[12]

By the time the first half-hour episode of *A Man Called Shenandoah* aired on September 13, 1965 there were about eight "in the can."

Horton continued to do other work, undoubtedly because he made sure that he could on a contractual basis, but it was shortly before the new series premiered that he injured himself badly enough to be out of commission for several weeks. He and Marilynn returned to New York in August 1965 so that he could appear in the famed Persian Room of the Plaza Hotel, but it never came about. Leaning over to pick up a bag of groceries at their apartment door, Horton's back went out and he was effectively crippled. The nightclub show at The Persian Room was cancelled and Robert Horton found himself flat on his back, unable to move for five weeks. Doctors ultimately put the injury down to what had seemed to be a trivial accident while filming an early episode of Shenandoah, possibly the first. He had been hauled off a horse in an awkward fashion by two other actors. He was rendered helpless and in considerable pain for a lengthy period of time, threatening the future of the show. When he finally returned to California to resume filming, he was in considerable discomfort. It took a quartet of doubles and some clever camera work to enable the series to continue.[13]

Family relations continued to be strained as well, and the return of the Robert Hortons to Los Angeles did not seem to bring about much in the way of family intercourse. His niece Joan said candidly that her parents held Horton at arm's length and, when he took up with Marilynn Bradley, actively discouraged any close relationships being formed. Much of that animosity stemmed from the blow-up which had occurred between the brothers on New Year's Day, 1961. She said, furthermore, that her family never attended any of his performances, an admission which requires no further explanation, although her older brother Creighton recollects attending, as a teenager with his class, a performance of *Brigadoon* in the mid-Sixties in which his aunt also appeared.[14] In such an atmosphere it was difficult to cultivate a more integrated family. A further contribution to the coolness which existed between Robert and Marilynn and the rest of the Hortons was an incident which took place while Chelta and Mead Horton were visiting their younger son in New York. According to Joan, a "blazing row" erupted between them which caused the senior Hortons to cut short their visit and return to Los Angeles ahead of schedule. Chelta Horton vowed she would never return and she kept her word, even when Bob was hospitalized in New York and asked her to come and see him. She would not, and did not.

Exactly when this incident took place in the Sixties is unclear but take place it did. Neither Robert's niece or his nephew could be specific about it, but they did remember it. If matters could be rendered difficult with such an occurrence a continent away, expecting them to improve with Bob and Marilynn's return to the West Coast would be more than doubtful.

Other family matters to do with them were remarked upon. Now in their fifth year of marriage, the couple remained childless. Marilynn's avowal to have "a wagon train of children" was not fulfilled. The years passed, and there were no babies. Horton's niece stated categorically that it was her uncle and Marilynn's choice not to have a family, but the truth was far more fundamental. The damage he suffered as a child, as a result of the lengthy and painful treatments administered to alleviate his kidney ailment rendered him infertile.

While it is true to say that neither of his previous marriages produced children, it is also reasonable to assume that neither union allowed for embarking on parenthood. With Mary Jobe, Horton was a student at university, working hard at his studies and laying the foundation for a career in the theater. Marriage to Barbara Ruick came at a time when both of them were totally dedicated to their respective careers. However, both women went on to subsequent marriages which included children.

Nevertheless, in a variety of personal, contemporary articles, Bob spoke honestly of his desire to be a father. He even referred to a sense of envy of his brother's family of four.[15] He often said how much he liked children, and on numerous episodes of *Wagon Train* his appearances with children show his interest and empathy for them, and them for him. Particularly memorable is "The Millie Davis Story" which starred Evelyn Rudie, then aged eight. This episode aired on November 26, 1958, Season Two. "The Jess MacAbee Story" in Season Three also featured a pair of younger girls with whom Flint McCullough interacts very sweetly. "The Allison Justis Story" called for a sensitive relationship with a little boy, and Season Four's "The Odyssey of Flint McCullough" involves the need for Flint McCullough to care for several orphaned children. He spoke of this episode in James Rosin's *Wagon Train* in the course of the author's interview with him. He said,

""The Odyssey of Flint McCullough" was basically a story about five children and the effect they have on Flint. I enjoyed it because it called on all the relationships a man can have with children when he wants to trust them as equals and get them to feel a part of something and their responsibility as people. I got the chance to advocate for an Indian youth and express my feelings about minority problems and other things I felt strongly about."[16]

He might have said much the same in regard to "The Ben Courtney Story," a Season Two episode which aired on January 28, 1959. The story concerned a southern couple with two adopted boys, one white, one black. When the boys run away in order to avoid being separated, Flint McCullough goes in search of them. Finding them at last, tired, hungry and thirsty, he offers both children a drink from his water bottle. When the little black boy has quenched his thirst, Flint McCullough, without wiping the neck of the bottle, drinks from it. That gesture must have shocked a good many of *Wagon Train's* vast audience. Throughout his five years with the show, his feelings about life are ably demonstrated through his characterization of Flint McCullough, and no less so when it came to children.

Yet there were no children. In an article titled "Must A Childless Marriage Be Lonely?" published in the *TV Radio Mirror* edition dated September 1966, Horton is courageously candid. After two years of marriage and no babies, doctors were consulted and the diagnosis was handed down that there would be no babies. Horton proclaimed that, in the end, their lifestyle would make raising a family difficult, they were truly happy with one another's company and their dogs, and that adoption, as an option, would, for them (and probably particularly for him) not be an ideal solution.

"We talked about adopting during our first two years of marriage, when we discovered we might not have our own children," he is quoted as saying, and as the final quote of the piece he said,

"Marilynn and I have decided that our responsibility is to *each other[sic]*. We have such a wonderful relationship, what could adopting children add to it?"

That, then, was that. The couple remained childless throughout their long marriage, but they were never without dogs, Beau James (Jamie), John Smith, Jean Harlow and Mr. Gable, to name a few of the standard poodles they favored, and Bronze, the Great Dane Bob acquired in England, and Teddy B. the last dog Bob knew. In his interview with Dwayne Epstein, Lee Marvin's biographer, he related a little anecdote which says something about his own knowledge of his situation. While attending a party at James Sangster's, who wrote and co-produced his two spy movies for ABC in 1969, he was waylaid by the infamous Marvin mistress, Michelle Triola, who asked him outright if he was the father of one of Betty's daughters. Bob recalled that he answered, "That is the goddamnest *[sic]* question I ever heard. In the first place, if I were, do you think I would tell you? Secondly, I've been married four times and I don't have any children so I think it's very doubtful that that child could be mine under any circumstance." He went on,

"That's a true story. I later mentioned it to…I told my wife of course and she said, 'My god, what a thing to ask you at a party and out of left field.' I almost strangled on my martini."[17]

As a final postscript to this aspect of Robert and Marilynn's life, Bob said, very much later in life, that his brother Creighton, at some time following the infertility diagnosis, offered them the opportunity to adopt twin boys of whom he was aware. They rejected it. Or Robert did.[18] Perhaps his infertility suited them and the statement noted earlier, i.e. "Marilynn and I have decided that our responsibility is to each other. We have such a wonderful relationship, what could adopting children add to it?" explains everything. There is a great deal of evidence, too, that at that time the pair were deeply in love with one another and felt no need to bring children into their lives.

# Chapter 20

## *Uphill Diversity*

With *Shenandoah* disappearing from television screens upon the airing of the final episode, "Macauley's Cure," episode 34, on May 16, 1966, Robert Horton was already at work for MGM Television making *The Dangerous Days of Kiowa Jones* as the lead in the first Western movie made specifically for television and worldwide distribution. *The Dangerous Days of Kiowa Jones*, however, was not a standard Western. Typically, Horton took a role which was off-beat, out of the norm, different. Based on a book written by the well-known Western author Clifton Adams, and first published by ACE Books in 1963, the story centered on a drifting cowboy who encounters a U.S. Marshal who is taking two condemned prisoners to Fort Smith to be hanged. The twist in the tale is that the marshal is near death with fever. Knowing this, he deputizes the cowboy, Kiowa Jones, to carry out the task. Jones is a decent man faced with a tough dilemma. He has no interest in taking on this responsibility but he cannot refuse. His reluctance is cemented when he is forced to kill to keep his word to the dead marshal. Co-stars Sal Mineo, Diane Baker and Nehemiah Persoff round out the cast. Despite some hokey indoor sets, the movie is a well shot, interesting study of character, personalities and situations. The conflict which Jones experiences throughout are thoughtfully rendered by Robert Horton as this atypical cowboy but real human-being. He said of the character,

"I was given a chance to create a 'character', a man who is not a take-charge guy, and I liked making it."[1]

*The Dangerous Days of Kiowa Jones* was not without its own production problems. Producers Max Youngstein and David Karr originally hired director John Sturges, known for several fine movies, amongst them, *Bad Day At Black Rock* (1955). It was said that Sturges did not feel that Horton was right for the role of Kiowa Jones and so turned the job down. Alex March, whose directing

*As Kiowa Jones in* The Dangerous Days of Kiowa Jones, *1966. Robert Horton, author's collection*

record was principally television-based was then hired, and while his reputation was excellent he had had very little experience working on Westerns, and therefore, with horses. He saw no need for experienced wranglers, but after a nasty accident with some horses on the set was narrowly avoided, Bob refused to continue until the director hired men who could handle horses. The episode no doubt contributed to Horton's reputation for being difficult. In fact, he was being professional, and careful.[2]

The "made for television" Western was aired on ABC on December 25, 1966 and was distributed worldwide over the next few months. ABC had decided to test the concept of airing television movies without much promotion, thus *Kiowa Jones* got no more than the usual previews allocated to any television program, and showing it on Christmas Day night meant that the viewer percentages were lower than normal. More bad timing, and while it was meant to be a pilot for another series for Robert Horton, it was not picked up by any of the networks. Perhaps the Wasserman effect played into that lack of interest.

Following the completion of eight weeks' filming *Kiowa Jones* Bob and Marilynn forsook Los Angeles and returned to their penthouse apartment in New York before embarking on a series of summer stock engagements. In June and July 1966, he and Marilynn co-starred in productions of Rodgers and Hammerstein's *Oklahoma!* at the St. Louis Municipal Light Opera, as it was then known, and back in Warren, Ohio, where they had first met. The production ran for seven performances in St. Louis to fantastic reviews and full houses and grossed a record $143,320.75, which, it was claimed at the time, had never been surpassed. The Warren performances at the W. D. Packard Music Hall were sold out before the musical was staged there by the Kenley Players and grossed $53,000 over eight performances. Of the Warren *Oklahoma!* performance the following appeared in *The Tribune* under the headline "Hortons Make "Oklahoma!" Beautiful Evening Here."

"Oh What A Beautiful Evening" it turned out to be when handsome Robert Horton appeared on stage singing "Oh What A Beautiful Morning". Horton's voice registers depth and power as he sings his way through the two acts with never-to-be-forgotten melodies. Having proved his proficiency as an actor over the years, he took this opportunity in the role of Curly to display a melodious voice which is indicative of much training since his 1959 appearance on the Music Hall stage in Guys and Dolls. An unforgettable evening at the theatre."

The critic of *The Plain Dealer* wrote,

"Both Hortons have the quality of fresh, radiant youth. He has a rich baritone voice. Her operatically trained and throbbing voice has great warmth. He plays the cowboy Curly in love with flirtatious Laurie and as a couple truly in love they add an extra tenderness to their singing of "People Will Say We're In Love"."

And that oh-so evident love for one another, combined with their acting and singing talents is a recurrent theme in the many clippings and articles about Bob's and Marilynn's appearances together in their early years on stage.

With summer stock over, there followed a period of rest before Robert Horton undertook a series of nightclub gigs. In February 1967 the couple traveled to Houston, Texas where he appeared at the International Club between February 19 and 29. Interviewed by the *Houston Chronicle*, he said, on February 20, 1967,

"I'm breaking in a brand new nightery act at the International Club and it's the first time I've played a club in over two years."

The new act was a great success for in March 1967, again in Houston, he received wildly enthusiastic reviews following a run at the Continental Room, when *The Houston Post* proclaimed him "A Smash". In its March 1, 1967 edition, Bill Roberts wrote,

"Robert Horton is a pleasure in the Continental Room and a true rarity: he is a TV acting star who actually has a fine singing voice and a good nightclub show. His audience demanded an encore and he deserved it".

That same month Bob returned to *The Ed Sullivan Show* for yet another appearance. Between April 17 and 23 he and Marilynn appeared together in the lead roles in *Brigadoon* at the St. Paul Civic Light Opera. John Harvey of the *St. Paul Pioneer Press* reported on Tuesday, April 18, that "Robert and Marilynn Horton are an attractive and talented pair of young lovers reaching across the centuries, he the 20th Century New Yorker, and she a lass of 18th Century Brigadoon. You couldn't want a finer looking couple and both are equally able in the vocal department."

Robert Horton then made his first concert appearance at the New Orleans Municipal Auditorium during its 14th Summer Pops season in mid-June, when once again he received outstanding reviews. Critics wrote on June 16 and 17,

"He has a warm voice with a built-in echo chamber when he croons and a knack for staying in tune when he belts."

"Obvious from the start that he definitely has the makings of a top-notch performing vocalist."

"...since the only bone to pick with last night's performance was which song Horton sang best."[3]

He followed this success by flying to Australia with Marilynn and the pair took enough time to stop over for brief breaks in Hawaii and Fiji en route, which they reported in a letter to Robert's American fan club, subsequently reproduced in the September – October edition of *The Robert Horton Friend Club* newsletter. In Sydney, Bob was the star turn for a month at Australia's legendary nightclub, Chequers. The show ran from June 24 through July 26 and resulted in a taped version televised throughout Australia on their ABC (Australian Broadcasting Company) network. Rave reviews accompanied his appearances and once again it was the public's and critics' ignorance of his singing talents which caught them all off guard. In a leading Sydney newspaper the following appeared:

"It is all very hush-hush but Robert Horton, who is appearing at Chequers, is being wooed into doing a television special. Nobody thought of asking him to do this before he got to Sydney because nobody realized he had such a fine voice. If the special gets made I am sure a lot of viewers, who remember him only as the scout in *Wagon Train*, will be staggered by the power of this horse-opera hero's voice."

*The Sunday Mirror* of Sydney ran a full-page advertisement on July 9 trumpeting,

"HE'S SENSATIONAL – AND HOW HE CAN SING!" then went on,

"A fine voice with a polished style – Robert Horton surprises with a beautiful performance at Chequers." Bob Roger – 20t." The advertisement carried other enthusiastic reviews of Robert at Chequers, while in the *Entertainment Review of Sydney*, their critic wrote,

"I was both surprised and delighted with this TV and outdoor star turned singer. The man from *Wagon Train* and *A Man Called Shenandoah* projects an excellent image, voice and personality. This

*Performing at Chequers Nightclub, Sydney, Australia, July 1967. Author's collection.*

is undoubtedly due to his training as an actor. His diction throughout his forty five*[sic]*minutes on stage was crystal clear and never faltered. Such popular numbers with excellent arrangements as "Cockeyed Optimist", "Who Shall I Turn To", "People" (from 'Funny Girl'), "There's Nothing Like A Dame" (from 'South Pacific') and "I've Got You Under My Skin" were smooth and effortless. With an easy smile, Horton interprets his songs well and particularly *Shenandoah* which he sang six *[sic]* years ago at a Royal Command Performance and which he delivered with particular sensitivity. No doubt about it, Horton, who went on Broadway after TV-ing in *Wagon Train* has found two places in the world of entertainment – acting and now singing."

All of these reviews were saved by Robert Horton in a white binder he dedicated to his nightclub appearances. (*Scrapbook VI*).

At the end of his Chequers run, Bob and Marilynn returned to the States via Singapore, where they celebrated Bob's forty-third birthday. He was scheduled to appear at the famous Flamingo Hotel in Las Vegas in mid-August. This engagement followed the successful lawsuit which he had brought against the hotel for breach of contract when it cancelled his appearance there in 1966. He sued The Flamingo Hotel for $48,500 as reported in the *Los Angeles Herald Examiner* on September 19, 1966, charging the hotel with breach of contract, a contract which the hotel claimed had only been "oral," and therefore unenforceable. The suit was settled in Horton's favor, and a new date set for his appearance there. Between August 10 and August 31 he headed the bill at The Flamingo, appearing twice nightly at 8 pm and midnight over a three week period. The *Las Vegas Sun* said,

"Robert Horton, as crowd pleasing on a showroom stage as he is in the saddle, swings into the second half of his highly successful Las Vegas debut in the main showroom of the fabulous Flamingo. Horton. . . is quickly collecting an entirely new following with his fine singing voice. The rugged red-head projects an excellent image on stage, both charming and manly, as he works his way through such velvety offerings as "Who Can I Turn To", "People", "Shenandoah" and "The Impossible Dream".[4]

John L. Scott, writing for the *Los Angeles Times* in its Las Vegas review on August 16 said,

"Robert Horton makes his Vegas debut at the Flamingo with a voice of considerable range and pleasant stage manner."

The *Las Vegas Review Journal*'s Forrest Duke reported on August 13 that,

"Handsome Horton may surprise a lot of his fans who know him only as a cowpoke on TV. The red-haired vocalist has flexibility in range and versatility as he baritones such numbers as "Cockeyed Optimist", "There Is Nothing Like A Dame" . . . and the difficult to sing "Impossible Dream". Horton has a pleasing personality and probably would improve his session by tossing in a few more bits of chatter."

In fact, Robert Horton's reluctance to be over-chatty with his nightclub audiences is a true reflection of his personality. His interest was in singing, in putting over each song as if it was a mini-play set to music. He avoided chat, and he certainly avoided relying on his past fame as a Western television star. That was not him. He strove for excellence in all his stage appearances, and he strove to be accepted for who he was on stage, a highly accomplished and talented actor and singer. As successful as this engagement was, he did not repeat it. It seems that he did not gamble at The Flamingo and thus forfeited the possibility of a return invitation.[5]

Having completed his stint at The Flamingo, he went to Japan to honor another contract obligation. Earlier in 1967 Horton's agent had contacted him with the offer of a part in a movie which was provisionally entitled *Battle Beyond the Stars*. In a lengthy interview with Brett Homenick, a writer for the Japanese-English publication *G-Fan*, and published in the Winter 2009 edition, Horton explained that he was initially unsure about participating. At a meeting in New York with his agent and the scriptwriter, Horton was blunt. Over cocktails, having read the script, he disagreed that the movie was about "the agony of command". He recalled that he said,

"If you think that's what this script is about, then I have nothing to say about it."

Nevertheless, he agreed to take the part of Jack Rankin, a space commander faced with asteroid-alien trouble in space. It seems that there was little further discussion and he flew to Tokyo with Marilynn for a ten week stay, eight weeks of which involved filming. He knew the movie would not be "a masterpiece," but it offered him the opportunity to spend time in a part of the world which had always held a fascination for him, and in his pragmatic fashion, he seized it. The earnings were excellent, he and his wife were accommodated at the very fancy Okura Hotel in downtown Tokyo, and Marilynn passed her time taking cooking and flower arranging classes.

In the same interview he also observed,

"The name of the movie, when we were in production, was "The Battle Beyond The Stars". And that made it sound pretty good."

Indeed, throughout filming, everyone involved worked under the original title. Horton's comment might lead one to think that, had he been offered a part in a film called *The Green Slime* he would probably have turned it down. When asked by Homenick about preproduction, he replied,

"Well, we didn't really have any. We met in Tokyo, and we went to a little supper that the director arranged, who spoke no English. And of course, I do not speak Japanese. And we had a very pleasant evening, and I had different foods from Japan that I had never had before. And then we met on the set and started shooting."

The movie was a Japanese production in its entirety, and, while language may have been a barrier, Horton claimed that it did not hinder the film's direction, or its production. The film was made. Whether or not Robert Horton accepted the assignment in part to re-establish a cinematic career, or whether he took it for its earnings and an all-expenses paid trip to Japan is hard to say. Filming took place in September and October of 1967 and according to the records it was released over a year later by MGM under the title *The Green Slime* on December 1, 1968 in Los Angeles and December 19, 1968 in Tokyo. His co-stars were Richard Jaeckel and Italian beauty Luciana Paluzzi. The vast majority of the remaining cast were American servicemen recruited from nearby American bases around Tokyo.[6]

There were no opening night galas, although on July 10, 1968, *Variety* reported that the seven-day Trieste Festival of Science Fiction Films would open with *Battle Beyond the Stars*. Nothing of any note came of that introduction, and the title disappeared by the time the film made its American debut. Recollecting the opening of the picture, Horton told Homenick,

"When they changed it *(the title)* to 'The Green Slime,' they did a publicity thing. The way they dealt with that was that, all over Manhattan, when you walked from one block to the other, and you stopped for the signal and everything, on the pavement below you was just the name 'The Green Slime'. And my wife came in one day or one evening, and she'd been looking at *Variety* and she said, 'I think they've changed the name of your picture to "The Green Slim-ee."'And I said, "'Slim-ee"'?! And I looked at it, and I said, 'That's 'Slime'. She said, 'For some reason, I've never seen it written out like that. I thought it was 'Slim-ee'.' And then we went to see it, we went down on 34th Street, just off 5th Avenue, as I remember, and when I knew the film was coming to a close, I said, 'Let's get out of here! I don't want to meet anybody!'"

He also commented,

"I know that it's a cult film, but it's still a terrible picture."[7]

*The Green Slime* went on general release in the spring of 1969, and the *New York Times* critic Howard Thompson wrote his review, published on May 22, as follows;

"THE GREEN SLIME", a new science-fiction thriller that arrived yesterday, opens promisingly, keeps it up for about half an hour but then fades badly." He says later,

"Good science-fiction movies have hinged on less. This one simply runs downhill like a tedious game of hide-and-seek. The dialogue is wooden, so is most of the acting by a cast including Robert Horton, Richard Jaeckel and Luciana Pulazzi... This picture, opening yesterday at the De Mille and Murray Hill, could have mattered. Rather curiously, it was made in a Tokyo studio then scooped up for release by Metro-Goldwyn-Mayer... And it is the smoothly unobtrusive pacing of Mr. Fukasaku in the earlier portion and the clever use of miniature settings that make it count. But the picture falls to pieces when the green menace becomes an army of rubbery-looking goblins. From then on it's green corn."

However, like it or not, *The Green Slime* (1969) did indeed become something of a cult movie and on watching it, it's fair to say that, despite some of the creaky sets and awful aliens, the movie was better than described. Robert Horton was, as always, highly professional and totally believable, despite Mr. Thompson's observations.

He and Marilynn spent almost three months in Japan, lodged at the Okura Hotel, and were visited there by Lee Marvin who was in Tokyo for the October 6, 1967 promotion and Japanese opening of his latest film, *The Dirty Dozen*. They managed a number of evenings together over dinner before Marvin flew back to California.[8] Another evening Horton mentioned in his interview with Homenick was when he and Marilynn dined with an American cast member who had married a Japanese woman. The man in question was an ex-US Marine with whom Horton became friendly on the set. He was, said Horton, an attractive man and pleasant to be with. He came from an affluent New England family, but had settled in Japan. Horton thought his wife might be attractive, commenting that few Japanese women were, to him, particularly pretty. Not only did he find the wife less than attractive, he was surprised when she, in true Japanese fashion, did not dine with them. It was an interesting experience, he said, but rather strange.

The Hortons returned home to New York on completion of filming. There was a great deal to catch up on and some of it involved correspondence with the various Robert Horton fan clubs across the country. Bob and Marilynn were both quite responsible in their interaction with these clubs, sending out press cuttings and photographs, but being abroad for extended periods meant that their communications lagged. Marilynn undertook to write to the various secretaries of the clubs and it is obvious that both she and Bob recognized the clubs' importance to their careers, although the emphasis within the clubs' newsletters was invariably on Bob's work. There is nothing extant regarding work undertaken in the latter months of 1967, or early 1968, but in March of that year Marilynn Horton wrote to Pearl Wolf, secretary of the Robert Horton Friends Club. Dated March 13, eight days following her birthday, she wrote,

*"Dear Pearl and All,*

*A note of thanks for the many birthday cards I received from our friends here and abroad. It's lovely to be remembered, and I appreciate all the warm wishes.*

*I came across a note, that I obviously misplaced, regarding the lovely anniversary gift Bob and I received. It was signed by Hazel Lugg and listed the names of our friends who contributed.*

*We are offering a late but very sincere "thank you" to them all, and an apology for being so tardy. Sometimes I think we'll never straighten out our correspondence...having been gone such a long while, it's difficult to get into "the swing of things" once again.*

*Again, our warmest "thank you".*

The note is hand-signed, *"Marilynn and Bob."*

By June 1968, they were on the road again, Robert appearing as Hal Carter in *Picnic* at The Little Theatre in Sullivan, Kansas. Critic Bob Best observed of Horton's performance that the Little Theatre's producer, Guy S. Little, Jr. had booked an exceptional cast headed by Robert Horton. He went on,

"Horton's performance can make or break the show, and he does, indeed, make it. It was in *"Picnic"* that he received his first critical recognition, which led to a Warner Brothers contract. So the character of Hal Carter is an old and dear friend of Horton's. It shows every minute . . . Big booming, good looking (and as a little gray-haired lady said going out of the theatre, "Ain't he built!") Robert Horton will be causing commotion at the Little Theatre through June 18."[9]

As an interesting aside to this, a young Robert Osborne, who would later make his mark in the movie industry as host of *Turner Classic Movies* and who became a good friend of both Bob and Marilynn's, played the part of Hal Carter's old roommate in this production.[10] It should be noted that the writer of this piece got his facts wrong in regard to *Picnic* and Robert Horton's Warner Brothers contract. The play was premiered on Broadway at the Music Box Theatre on February 19, 1953 and starred a young Ralph Meeker. Robert Horton first played Hal in 1955 at the Ring Theater in Los Angeles. His one-year contract with Warner Brothers was firmed up in 1951 when he made *The Tanks Are Coming* (1951).

From Sullivan they went to Texas, appearing together as Curly and Laurie in *Oklahoma!* at the Houston Music Theatre from June 25 through July 7. Once again, they received enthusiastic reviews. One D. J. Hobdy, whose publication is unidentified, said,

"First, there's Robert Horton, who wears his blue jeans authentically faded and suitably tight and his Stetson on the back of his head. Visually he's a rugged, reasonable Curly with a sturdy tenor and a pleasing easy presence in mid-song or mid-action. From the moment he walks on singing about his "Beautiful Mornin'" until he rides away with his bride in a surrey, it's Curly's show. The role is strong enough to withstand an overdose of actor interference, but flexible enough to challenge for individual interpretation. Horton's offstage wife Marilynn is a sassy Laurey, less fragile than most. Her academic concert stage training is evident and her voice several cuts above the Houston Music Theatre average."[11]

Robert Horton wrote to his club members shortly afterwards that they had two very good weeks in Houston doing the best business the theater had seen that year. In a brief précis of their activities he said,

"*Monday AM we are off to LA for a conference on a picture. After summer is over we head for London for three months to make a new picture, "Private I." It is a very good script and I'm excited about the project. The film will be seen here on ABC television in the future.*"

*(Robert Horton Friend Club,* August – September Newsletter).

The negotiations between Robert Horton and ABC for two movies to be filmed in England that fall began in July. *The Holly-*

*wood Reporter* broke the news on July 23, 1968, under the headline, "Horton "Eye" Star – Robert Horton has been signed by producer James Sangster to star in "Private Eye" rolling in London September 23. The mystery – drama, written by Sangster will be directed by Roy Baker for Halcyon Productions, and distributed by ABC Films. Harold Cohen is executive producer."

Meanwhile, two weeks after the Houston triumph, Robert and Marilynn went on to Indianapolis where Horton starred in a production of *The Pajama Game* for Starlight Musicals at the open-air Hilton U. Brown Theatre in Indianapolis. The play ran for a week from July 22 and opened under grey skies and constant drizzle throughout the first act. Despite the weather, the audience remained in place throughout, and Charles Staff, writing for an unidentified Indianapolis publication, said,

"Robert Horton stars and one can only observe that it is curious he is not a bigger theatre personality than he already is. His success in New York in "110 in the Shade" and on television in "Wagon Train" is impressive but not relative to his gifts and talents. With his face, figure, voice and acting ability, he should be a matinee idol in the Broadway sense of that now probably passé term. As superintendent of the factory, he is actually convincing, and no-one attends the musical theatre with the idea that he is going to be convinced of anything by anybody."

Having completed the Indianapolis run, the couple traveled to Maine where Horton was once again featured as Hal Carter in *Picnic* in Kennebunkport at "Maine's Famous Theatre of Stars". The reviews he received were resoundingly positive. He was frequently quoted as saying that *Picnic* was his favorite play of all. Dated "8/21" in Bob's unmistakable handwriting is a write-up from the Kennebunkport's *The News* which is worth reproducing in part simply because it says so much about Robert Horton, the actor. S. Carleton Guptill wrote:

"Sometimes the theatre rises above entertaining and soars with its audience to a memorable dramatic experience. The Kennebunkport Country Playhouse scales these heights this week with William Inge's Pulitzer Prize play, "Picnic".

He goes on,

"Many are familiar with the characters and story of this Kansas backyard. This company is perfectly cast and must be described as excellent. The star is Robert Horton who plays Hal Carter, the handsome intruder who upsets the humdrum picnic plans. Here is one TV star who can really act. He will make you forget "Wagon Train", which by the way was a pretty good Western, by the end of the first act. I don't remember who originally created the role, but it should have been Mr. Horton."

Guptill wrote enthusiastically about the rest of the cast, about the sets, lighting and direction. He finished up with,

"The lights dimmed. We all clapped and went home feeling better because we, the audience, had been part of something good. This is a team effort that blends into an experience that made us all a little nearer to each other and gave us a little more understanding of the other person. That's been one of the main reasons for theatre since the Greeks, and if you think this is a rave review, you're right. It is."

The Drama Critic for WCSH-TV of Portland, Maine, Fritzi Cohn said,

"Robert Horton is the catalyst who takes the stage with his first dynamic entrance and never relinquishes it. Entirely believable in every mood...swaggering, tender, belligerent, boyish...the complete man and the complete actor. Moving with a lion's grace, he is a captivating performer."

Robert Horton's own opinion of the play was recorded by Charlotte Phelan, who interviewed the actor for the *Houston Post*. Her article appeared on Sunday, June 22, 1968 and she quoted him thus: "'Picnic' is my favorite play. William Inge didn't win the Pulitzer Prize for nothing. It's a very true play with characters a lot of people can identify with. I obviously found things about Hal Carter I could identify with. I really like him." Indeed, there is a lot about Hal Carter's character which is echoed in Robert Horton's personality and the rave reviews he consistently got for his performances in that role are proof of it.

In the meantime, matters with ABC-TV and their new anthology series which they called *ABC Movie of the Week* were coming to fruition. The series was to comprise twenty-five, ninety-minute original scripts which would be aired at weekly intervals. The cost of this enterprise was projected to be $16 million. Two of the proposed scripts were written and produced by English writer James Sangster, famous for his work with Hammer Studios, and in order to cut costs it was decided that they would be filmed back-to-back in London, the setting for the stories. Robert Horton was signed to play the main character, an ex-British secret agent named John Smith, the protagonist in Sangster's novel *Private I*. His two co-stars were Sebastian Cabot and Jill St. John. These were the three Americans who appeared in an otherwise entirely British production, directed by Roy Baker, who brought both movies in at a total cost of $850,000.00. The episodes were edited down to seventy-three minutes each to allow for commercials, and the first, "The Spy Killer" was aired on November 11, 1969, and its sequel, "Foreign Exchange" aired in January 1970.[12]

The Hortons, according to Bob's letter to his fan club earlier that summer, arrived in London on September 22, exactly one day before filming was due to start on "The Spy Killer". Because of Britain's strict animal quarantine laws which required pets to be incarcerated for a minimum of six months, they left behind their beloved dog, Jamie, and settled in for what was to be a ten week stay where Horton clearly enjoyed the experience of working in London with a British cast and crew. The frantic fan adoration he had experienced in 1959, 1960 and 1961 had subsided, and he savored the anonymity he experienced and the willingness of the British people to respect his privacy. He struck up a friendship with James Sangster which lasted over the following years. Unfortunately, although he and Sangster hoped to build on the success of the two John Smith spy movies, once again, nothing came of it. Both these made-for-television movies were entertaining, with sound acting from all concerned, and stories which demanded attention from the viewer. They were of their time and of the genre, but there was, and still is, an element of subtlety about the scripts, direction and acting which, when viewed today, puts other examples of the kind such as the James Coburn "spy" movies into a cruder category. Had Horton and Sangster been successful in promoting the John Smith character of "The Spy Killer" and "Foreign Exchange" the entertainment world might have been richly rewarded.

A "Television Review" (publication unknown) of *Movie of the Week*, "The Spy Killer", written by one Joe Bingham, went thus:

"Thrust in as it was as a bridge between two high-ranking other programs, "Mod Squad" and "Marcus Welby M.D." this ABC-TV Movie of the Week proved to be a sturdy structure. Written and produced by Jimmy Sangster, directed by Roy Baker with Harold Cohen the executive producer, "The Spy Killer" was filmed in and around London, dressing it up with an authenticity that increased its credibility. Robert Horton, whom we haven't seen since several "Wagon Trains" ago, was effective as a cold, calculating ex-British secret agent, now earning a meager living as a private investigator. Arthur Grant's photography of London and its suburban countryside is excellent, aided beautifully by the mod music of Johnny Pearson to move the story along at a fast pace." Bob Hull of *The Hollywood Reporter* critiqued the second movie "Foreign Exchange" on January 15, 1970. He headlined it,

"ABC's "Foreign Exchange" First Class Spy Thriller.

". . . Sangster's story is much more involved, as a good spy yarn should be, and his production deserves praise for making it believable and understandable. The involutions of the plot were carefully drawn and the action uncomplicated by side issues. Thriller fans could recognize echoes of "The Spy Who Came In From The Cold," which is not an odious comparison to make.

"Robert Horton, who wavered between querous*[sic]* anger and positive virility in his role played the ex-spy forced to do one more mission. . ."

"Director Roy Baker kept his eye on the script while megging*[sic]* this, never allowing the camera nor the actors to stray from the story. For the fan at home, the program offered a no-brainer session of pure divertissement, *[sic]* which isn't to the bad."

In between completing *The Green Slime* in 1967, and the ABC-TV spy movies in 1969, Robert Horton was kept busy appearing on stage, often with Marilynn beside him. By this time it was an accepted fact that Horton made sure that Marilynn had a part in many of the productions in which he appeared, and the idea that she would only appear once a year with him in summer stock was rapidly overtaken, as was the idea that her appearances were purely a hobby to her. She was involved in a fully professional capacity. The month prior to their departure for England, in August 1969, they appeared together in *There's a Girl in My Soup* presented as part of the Charlotte Summer Theatre at Ovens Auditorium in Charlotte, NC. One critic for *The Charlotte News* wrote on August 20,

"Girl In My Soup" opens as Naughty, Witty Stageshow*[sic]*." "Mrs. Horton is positively delicious in her few lines as a French maid."

"Horton accounts for himself handsomely."

Returning home from their movie-making stint in England, they appeared in the same play in October 1969 at The Pheasant Run Dinner Theatre in St Charles, Illinois. A review stated,

"Robert Horton, familiar to TV viewers of "Wagon Train" . . . is star of the current Pheasant Run Theatre production of "There's A Girl In My Soup." Mr. Horton has played the part before in summer stock and as a consequence the show is smooth, funny and enjoyable." A separate piece, written by critic Phyllis Warner for an unidentified publication focused more on Marilynn's attributes. Under the headline, "Current PRP Show Features The Hortons" it went on,

"Marilynn Horton plays her husband's mistress in the Pheasant Run Playhouse production of "There's A Girl In My Soup." A singer as well as actress, Marilynn met her husband while appearing with him in "Guys and Dolls." A native of Boston, she majored in opera at The New England Conservatory of Music. She was a soloist with the Minneapolis Symphony and sang in concert in New England. She appeared in several Broadway musicals and in summer theatres throughout the United States. Since their marriage in 1960, Mrs. Horton limits her professional appearances to working with her husband."

These post-Broadway years were busy, if not so high-profile as the *Wagon Train* years. Robert Horton's name was a constant and successful draw on the stage as he crisscrossed the country in his Piper Comanche for his theatrical engagements. Personally, he and Marilynn moved several times, both in Los Angeles and New York, only establishing a permanent home base in New York in the mid-Sixties in their penthouse apartment on Park Avenue. Towards the end of the decade, however, in January 1969, a significant family event took place. Robert Horton's mother, Chelta McMurrin Horton, died on January 3, aged eighty-one. The state of their relationship at this time is unknown, though there seems to have been a certain, almost reluctant, acceptance of Horton's career choice on the part of both his parents. There was no change, however, in terms of their acceptance of his fourth marriage. Nevertheless, the son who so resembled Chelta, but who she consistently rejected, flew to Los Angeles to be present when her body was interred at Forest Lawn Cemetery. He spent a day on the West Coast. Of his feelings or emotions on this occasion, nothing is known, or at least, nothing went in to print.

His younger niece Joan said that "Uncle Howard flew out for a day for the funeral."[13] There was clearly nothing to be gained by lingering. He returned to New York and got on with his life.

There is, however, one little vignette from this time which was related by Bob's older nephew, Creighton. He spoke of a family gathering on the West Coast when an incident occurred which shook him a great deal and helps to illustrate the state of the relations which existed between Robert Horton and his family. During a visit with their family, Robert was short with Anne, Creighton's mother. No longer a hero-worshipping "kid," Creighton told his uncle not to be rude to her. His uncle, he said, looked taken aback. He said to his nephew,

"Can we talk – outside?" They went outside and Creighton was staggered to see tears in his uncle's eyes. In a voice which trembled, Robert Horton said, "I have never been accepted in this family."

Creighton was astonished. Before him stood "this mega star," adored by millions, but who had never been accepted by his own parents or brother. It was a profound moment which Creighton found difficult to believe. It was, however, a truth and a fact which Robert Horton lived with throughout his entire life.[14]

# Chapter 21
## *Comfortable Obscurity*

By the time 1970 arrived, Robert and Marilynn Horton had established a way of life which, though not garnering the kind of adulation and fame which had attended him through his time as Flint McCullough, nevertheless provided them with an outlet to their creative and artistic skills, primarily on the stage and as a couple. It was not what Robert Horton had envisaged, but they were comfortable and seemed content with the arrangement. Or as content as they were prepared to demonstrate or admit to. It is, however, inarguable that with the advent of the Seventies, Robert Horton's fame was dwindling nationally and internationally, despite active fan clubs on both sides of the Atlantic.

Nevertheless, it is true to say that Robert Horton thrived on the demands and rewards of live theater. The fact that he was able to involve Marilynn in many of his stage appearances only enhanced the experiences and there is no doubt that he was able to earn a very comfortable living from the theater world. Indeed, when it came to his career over this period, Robert Horton often referred to the fact that the "dinner theater world" provided him with a richly rewarding life, both monetarily and artistically.[1] The couple developed a "modus operandi" which suited them. Summer stock in summer, time at home or to travel during the winter months. Sometimes he worked in the winter months. The schedule was entirely flexible.

1970 found Robert Horton starring in *Showboat* at the Memorial Auditorium in Burlington, VT, in February, and in runs of *Under the Yum Yum Tree* in June at the Playhouse on the Mall in Paramus, NJ, where Marilynn starred opposite him, and in July at the Cherry County Playhouse in Traverse City (where in 1968 he appeared in *Picnic*). An interesting review of this production said,

"Personally I have been a Robert Horton fan for lo these many years and have thrilled as he whupped Indians, bad men and foreign spies with dexterity and ease. Consequently I found myself fidgeting in my chair as my hero came on as an over-the-hill play-boy with a tiger in his tank, and just one thing on his mind – sex. I suppose the transition was quite a challenge for Mr. Horton and probably quite well done. . ." However, the writer finished up with these words,

"It is always a pleasure to see Robert Horton perform."[2]

The first observation that Horton's performance as the playboy being "quite a transition" is either naïve or simply ignorant. Robert Horton's ability to portray a man with sex on his mind was easy. To a degree, he was that man, and not for nothing was he called "the sexiest man alive," or referred to as "still sexy at sixty".

He was, none-the-less, multi-faceted. The outlooks, opinions and beliefs he formed throughout a lifetime and which certainly created major schisms between him and his family remained with him, and indeed, grew and matured with him. In February 1971, he toured in Vietnam for a month, entertaining the troops there. In the early Eighties he was featured in an article and he spoke of the time he spent in Vietnam.

"I went over there to form an opinion, and came back knowing little more than I did before I went over. The war seemed to be so remote, except when the helicopters came in with the dead and wounded. One night, after the show, we had dinner in a hotel south of Saigon, and we could see the fighters strafing the city less than 1,000 yards away.

"There was no official policy of segregation, but the black and white troops were seated completely apart. At one point in the show, I sang "Abraham, Martin and John" which created quite an effect. Then they asked me to sing "God Bless America". I said that I didn't know if I remembered it. So, we all sang it together. That was the only time I really felt that what I was doing over there was important."

He was awarded a Certificate of Appreciation by the Department of Defense for his "outstanding contribution to the morale and welfare of the United States and other free world military assis-tance forces," dated March 18, 1971, together with a medal struck for "Vietnam Service." He kept these.[3] It is not possible to credit the publication in which these words appeared, but the nameless clipping was saved by Betty Burris in her scrapbook, and it is very interesting to note that his early boyhood experiences being raised by a black woman and its resultant influences had not deserted him almost half a century later.

He returned from Vietnam to yet more stage work and between July 26 and August 1, 1971 he and Marilynn appeared in *Kismet* as part of the Sacramento Light Opera Association's summer season. In *The Sacramento Bee*, on July 27 under Arts in Review, their critic wrote,

"Over all "Kismet" would seem to be the clear leader quality-wise among the stage musicals presented this year. And it has, in Robert Horton and Linda Michelle, absolutely glowing performers. That the Music Circus production has that elusive thing called spark is on display nearly from the beginning, when Horton, as the poet, virtually leaps into the tune, "Rhymes Have I". The "Wagon Train" television performer never lets up through the show's duration.

His singing voice continues to gain in intonation and momentum, and those who saw his "Don Quixote" in "Man of La Mancha" last year at the Music Circus may recognize a new maturity."

Marilynn Horton's review is a little less enthusiastic, but it is worth reproducing because it comments on the couple's respective talents at the time.

"Mrs. Horton is the police chief's wife who has a penchant for extra-marital sexual action. She is as curvy as a freshly launched boat and she is all over the poet Hajj (Horton). Her singing voice has quite a bit of tremolo, as if she may be struggling somewhat with some of the songs' demands."

Between *Kismet* in late summer 1971 and May of 1972 there is little material which helps in fleshing out the lives of either Robert or Marilynn. A *Burris Scrapbook* clipping, however, records, in an interesting interview he gave in 1984, when he recalled with pride, his performance as Zorba in *Zorba*. He said,

"I did Zorba in 1970, and I never had a richer experience. I never had a role where I did so much to hide me. . .I mean, actually hiding the qualities that had helped me along the way in my career. Marilynn would say, 'I don't believe that this Anglo Saxon Wasp walks into the theater, and then comes out on stage as this Middle

Zorba. *"An amazing transformation from Anglo Saxon WASP to middle European." 1970. Robert Horton, author's collection.*

European.' The demands of the theater are infinitely greater than television. The communication with the audience is so thrilling – when you've got them, you know it!"

This quote from an article prompted by his participation in the television soap *As the World Turns* in New York is sadly unidentified, but it eloquently expresses Robert Horton's feelings about being on stage and further illustrates his relationship with Marilynn, a relationship which thrived on their joint love of musical theater. Robert kept at his work, individually, with Marilynn as his constant companion and sometime cohort on stage. Robert Horton was quite clear about his need to work. He worked to meet his own personal requirements, to fulfill his need to act and to sing, indeed, to perform before a live audience for the specific gratification which that supplies. Financially he was well off. He had trusted business managers and he was careful with his assets. He was financially secure enough to purchase expensive gifts for his wife, to maintain a collection of cars, to operate his own airplane and to own a penthouse on Park Avenue in New York. Living in New York kept him apart from his Los Angeles-based family and there appears to have been very little substantive interaction between either side of the Horton clan.

Various other appearances recorded within the pages of the *Burris Scrapbook* chronicle his activities in the early Seventies. For the first time the Neil Simon comedy, *The Odd Couple* was added to Horton's repertoire, and it is typical of Horton that he struck a new note within the context of the play's title, by playing opposite a black man. His role was that of Oscar, the "slob". A local black actor, Junior Waters, played Felix. The play involved a six-week engagement in Valparaiso, Indiana at the Bridgeview (BridgeVU) Dinner Theatre, in May and June 1972, and Horton not only starred as Oscar, but also produced and directed the show. It was a demonstration of so much of what made up Horton's character. Reviews were enthusiastic. One said, with regard to this particular production,

"First time we know that a black man will share the lead with a white man." It went on,

"Horton directs the comedy which has already earned a reputation of being the best so far on local stage. A professional, he knows all the tricks of the game when he combines beautiful facial expression with minutely planned action that comes off as a thoroughly believable character – a slob." This is a compliment to Horton's acting skills; in real life he was a neat, particular man.

After the six-week run of *The Odd Couple*, Horton took over the direction of the next play at the Bridgeview Theatre. *Last of the Red*

*Hot Lovers* starred Albert Salmi and Marilynn Horton and critics gave it high praise.

"It is a fast-paced, brilliantly executed farce that has entertained audiences throughout the country, proved itself a hit on Broadway, and in Valparaiso, under the direction of Valparaiso's newest adopted son, Robert Horton, has acquired new verve and polish. By far, it is one of the most technically executed packages put forth on the BridgeVU stage. *Last of the Red Hot Lovers* is Robert Horton's second local attempt at directing. The present play comes on the heels of a seven-week engagement of the Black and White *Odd Couple*, another theatre first starring Junior Waters and Horton himself. Marilynn Horton comes across beautifully. . . Marilynn, the other Horton half is experiencing her 'first' under the direction of Mr. H."[4]

The play ran for four weeks and was followed by yet another production of *The Rainmaker* at the Canal Fulton Summer Arena in Canal Fulton, Ohio from July 11 through July 16. July 25 through August 8 saw him starring yet again in a production of *Oklahoma!* in Toledo, Ohio and a couple of undated references under an unidentified publication snippet entitled "Hollywood" in the *Burris Scrapbook* refer to his preparing for several guest appearances as well as "looking around for another TV series." Indeed, it is at this time that yet another snippet appears in the scrapbook that plans were in the works for a "spin-off" from his "Spy Killer" role in concert with stage producer Mike Merrick and James Sangster under the working title, *The Dexter Style*. The series' premise was centered on the actions of a private detective whose cover was that of running a dress designing business, but it did not come to anything. Robert Horton may have felt a sense of déjà vu, recollecting the *Mark Dolphin* fiasco of 1964, but there is no evidence that the venture with Merrick and Sangster got further than discussions.

Meanwhile, a challenging opportunity in the guise of the musical *1776* arose on a last-minute basis when Bob was approached to undertake the role of John Adams in a production scheduled to take place at the Paper Mill, the State Theatre of New Jersey in Millburn, New Jersey. It was due to open on September 13, 1972 and run through to November 5, 1972.

*With Marilynn in* 1776, *Millburn, New Jersey, 1972. Robert Horton, author's collection.*

1776 first opened on Broadway in 1969 where it was enthusiastically received, enjoyed warm reviews and ran for 1,217 performances. It was made into a movie in 1972, but not released until November 17 of that year. The Broadway musical was nominated for five Tony Awards, and won three, including the Tony Award for Best Musical.

When he accepted the assignment, Robert Horton had very little time to prepare for it. Marilynn was signed to play Abigail Adams, one of only two female roles in the production. It was a tour de force by Bob and as the curtain fell on opening night not only the audience gave him a rousing reception, but the entire cast did too. He later described the play as the most demanding he had ever done, but also the most gratifying.[5]

The play had been running for almost seven weeks when he received word that his father had died on October 24. With almost two weeks left to go, he chose not to back out of the play. Not only would he lose a significant amount of money if both he and Marilynn quit, but there is little doubt that he was not prepared to leave the rest of the cast high and dry, trying to adjust to two understudies in what was a complicated production. He stayed and got on with the show. Exactly what this represented to him emotionally cannot be said. Perhaps he felt that there was no mother to console, and he would only find himself in tension-ridden circumstances with his brother and his family. Perhaps he knew there was nothing he could do, as his older brother would have matters under control. Mead Howard Horton, then, was laid to rest beside his wife at Forest Lawn without his younger son being in attendance.

The cast of *1776* sent flowers to the Horton family, not simply as a mark of respect on the occasion, but as a token of their feelings for Robert Horton. He wrote them a thank you letter in his distinctive hand, addressed to all members of the cast under their role titles, thus:

*"Gentlemen of the Congress:*
*Loyal Custodian:*
*The Ladies:*
*and The Leather Apron*

*A note of thanks for the flowers you so kindly sent to California. I appreciated them, as did my family.*

*My Father lived a full, long and good life. He enjoyed the theater and often traveled great distances to see his son perform.*

*I regret he was unable to see "1776". It is the first production I have ever been in. . . Again, my thanks, for many things – Bob."*

The letter, on heavy blue note paper, is undated. At its head Bob simply wrote his name, *"Robert Horton"*[6]

The early part of 1973 saw him at work in a production of *There's a Girl in My Soup* at the Westroads Dinner Theatre in Omaha, Nebraska. The play ran from January through February and again, he took up the duties of director. On January 11, the *Omaha World-Herald* critic wrote,

"'Play'... lost more than one full day of rehearsal when star Robert Horton couldn't beat the snowstorm to town. It's astonishing how polished Tuesday night's opening was, and the glow was from splendid acting ... Horton is the prissy Britisher whose libido is as swollen as his ego...He was built for the part, playing it like a cross between Rex Harrison and maybe Billy deWolfe with some John Raitt qualities on the side. The carrot-topped actor we know from "Wagon Train" is sleek, handsome and definitely debonair.

HORTON'S TALENTS.

I know that Horton designed the set. And it's one of the best the Westroads has seen in its flexibility and solidity. I know that Horton as director was a hard taskmaster, demanding and a perfectionist. I don't know if this endeared him to the cast. But I do know the results are evident in a tight adult comedy which was excellently blocked and tackled by a talented crew."

That year, 1973, Robert Horton was approaching his fiftieth birthday. The dazzling fame which had accompanied him throughout his five years as Flint McCullough on *Wagon Train* ten years previously, and for a few years afterwards, was waning. Nevertheless, he remained very active and could still draw an audience, witness his appearance in *Catch Me If You Can*, which was presented at the Amarillo Little Theatre for a two-week run in September and October of 1973. The opening night drew an audience of just under 4,000, breaking all previous attendance records.[7] Steve Cornett, a *Globe-News* staff writer interviewed Bob shortly before the play opened, and his article "Ex- 'Wagon Train' Star Finds Variety Playing Stage Roles" explored the changes in Horton's career from world-famous television star to stage actor treading the silo circuit boards. Published in the *Amarillo Daily News* on September 16, Robert Horton is quoted in regard to his *Wagon Train* role,

"It was like working in a shoe factory. You get up every morning, and go to the same place and do essentially the same thing."

Variety in locations and roles mattered to him. He continued,

"For instance, in one year I played in "Man of La Mancha", "Showboat", "Zorba", "Under the Yum Yum Tree", "Carousel", "Picnic","Music Man", and "Girl In My Soup". I ran the gamut in ages from 22 or 23 up to 53. That's variety."

He liked, indeed demanded, good material.

"In television you're always working with what really amounts to bad stuff. We were always looking at our scripts and saying 'My god, how are we going to make this stuff work?'

And 'good stuff' is important to an actor as serious as Robert Horton."

Later, in the same article he observed rather significantly,

"Columbia (Records) thought I might be another Robert Goulet (following his appearance in '110 In The Shade'). But I didn't have an 'If Ever I Would Leave You' in 'Hundred and Ten' like he had in 'Camelot.'"

Again, in the *Amarillo Daily News* of September 22, their critic wrote,

"Catch Me If You Can" is as polished and finely directed a production as has ever been seen on the boards of ALT for a long time. Robert Horton, guest star, plays the part of the confused and confusing bridegroom with that refined, convincing skill that is the brand of a professional. He captured Friday night's audience with the same finesse that marked his popularity on such television series as "Wagon Train" and "A Man Called Shenandoah". As guest star he added to the glitter of a tremendous opening night."

He still retained enough star appeal and influence to embark on a crusade against drunk drivers following a near fatal accident involving a friend. He toured a number of cities with his message through the middle months of 1973, and a lengthy article on his appearances was published in the magazine *Highway Patrol* under the title "Hollywood Personality Joins Crusade Against Drunk Drivers." His considered approach to the problem of drunk drivers, and social drinking was typical of him. He did his research thoroughly and his speaking tour also included making television commercials about the dangers of drinking and driving.

"Jim Stacy, a friend of mine and a fine actor, was involved in an accident. The driver of the car that struck his motorcycle was allegedly under the influence of alcohol or something. Stacy lost an arm and a leg and the young lady with him was killed."

There is no doubt that the accident he referred to made him think, and then act by undertaking a role in the crusade. The writer of the article described Horton as an "easy-to-listen-to speaker and high school kids, college students and civic groups are usually eager to hear what he has to say."

So, while he was forging ahead with his stage career, but no longer in the heady limelight of television, he remained involved in matters which were important to him. Although the material covering his work in the Seventies is much sparser compared to the Fifties and Sixties, there is little doubt that his career on the stage kept him as busy as he wanted to be. Indeed, he said as much to the *Palm Beach Post*'s Amusement Editor Sherry Woods when she interviewed him in March 1970 when he essayed the role of *Zorba* at the Royal Poinciana Playhouse.

"I've reached the stage in my career when I'm no longer killing myself. I'd love to have a new hit on Broadway. If it happens, it will be good for my career. But the desire to pursue that strenuously went away a long time ago."

More and more he took up the reins of the director in the shows in which he starred and that work, too, invariably brought high praise from the critics.

In 1975 he and Marilynn returned to live on the West Coast permanently. They had been house-sitting for a friend, the son of actress Julie Harris, Peter Gorian. Without any intention of buying a home in Los Angeles, they learned that a particular home in Encino was on the market.

In his interview in 1995, with Dwayne Epstein regarding Epstein's biography of Lee Marvin, Horton said,

"We lived in New York from 1963 until 1975. In '75 we came out here. We bought this house (5317 Andasol Avenue) because it was here. We weren't looking for a house. We lived in New York and had a wonderful apartment. But . . . In the back of my head, I was born and reared in Los Angeles, I always thought I would move back here eventually."

Designed and built by the actor George Montgomery, 5317 Andasol Avenue was a single storey ranch-style home on a wide, quiet back street in Encino, close to Encino Park. Bob knew that Montgomery built furniture but was unaware that he built homes. He said,

"My curiosity was piqued when I heard about it (the house) so I went to see it. When I walked in, it was literally love at first sight."

He bought the house, as well as some of Montgomery's furniture and apart from a short period when he worked in New York in the early Eighties, Andasol Avenue was a beloved home to him for the rest of his life. Thus he returned to the city of his birth, to the state he once referred to as "that wonderful place." He continued to pursue his work without interruption. It was as easy to keep up his stage career and other commitments from Los Angeles as it had been from New York. He maintained a schedule which suited him as well as Marilynn. It was not a question of having to work, but of wanting to work. Financially, Robert Horton was very well off. He had made sure, throughout his life, that he was fiscally sound. He employed good business managers and he was careful regarding the agents he chose. In 1952, listed as a leading man in the Players Directory, he was represented by Paul Small Artists, Ltd. By 1962, he was with Ashley-Steiner, Inc., which became Creative Management Associates then subsequently the International Famous Agency. Ten years later this was the agency which still represented Bob. In his interview with Dwayne Epstein regarding his friendship with Lee Marvin, Bob stated that the notorious David Begelman, who founded Creative Management Associates, had been his agent in New York. He was undoubtedly referring to the Sixties and early Seventies, for Begelman left CMA in 1973 to shore up the struggling Columbia Pictures company.

Very little personal family information is extant for this period. Both Horton's parents were dead by the time he and Marilynn returned to California, and his brother's children were grown and starting families of their own. He did, however, involve himself helping his younger "favorite" niece Joan, whose first marriage was breaking up. Joan spoke gratefully of how her uncle "helped me through my divorce". Aware of his niece's problems, he knew enough about the heartache attached to divorce to be of significant help. Their relationship was somewhat closer than those Robert shared with his other family members and he took an active interest in Joan's children. However, a guest book kept by Marilynn cataloging various dinner parties given by the Hortons between 1977 and 1980, records only one dinner given for "The Family". Entries ceased on February 1, 1980, leaving most of the book blank. Nevertheless, it is evidence of a busy social life in terms of entertaining at home for the period covered despite the lack of family involvement.

As the Seventies drew to a close, Robert Horton may have been thinking about slowing down a little. His wife, ten years his junior, was not so ready. At home, in Encino, with his cars at hand and his plane a short drive down the valley, Horton may have felt the attraction of easing his foot off the career gas pedal. It slowly brought about the emergence of what one fan called "the forgotten years". Indeed, in an undated article written by Glenn Lovell for the *Knight News Service* when Horton was fifty-five, Lovell wrote,

"Over the next decade he drifted into comfortable obscurity on the dinner theater and summer stock circuits, finally doing the entire reperatory*[sic]* of American musical classics. Among his favorite credits are "The Music Man," "Show Boat," "1776" ("the most taxing role I've ever done"), and "Oklahoma!" as the no-account Curly.

Looking back over a career that has encompassed everything from some of the best "Alfred Hitchcock Presents" segments to the laughable Japanese sci-fi thriller "The Green Slime," are there any regrets?

"Look, my leaving "Wagon Train" when I did was a calculated risk," Horton explained for what is obviously the umpteenth time. "Maybe it didn't pay off in a big way and maybe I haven't the career I had hoped to have but I honestly have no regrets. If somebody came up to me tomorrow and asked, 'Would you rather have a hit TV series or be in a hit musical,' I'd go with the musical. There's no question in my mind. No question at all."

Those "forgotten" years were the late Seventies and throughout the Eighties. There was a smattering of television appearances;

*Longstreet* in February, 1972, *Police Woman*, with his old friend Angie Dickinson in 1976, and *The Hardy Boys* in 1978, as well as some guest appearances on other shows, like *The Amazing Kreskin* in 1973. He was busy enough in the late Seventies touring on stage, but the wealth of clippings recording those appearances slows to a trickle. His repertoire remained strong, however, and as noted in the *Knight News Service* article, he added a couple of new shows to the list, including the demanding *1776* and the comedy *6 Rooms River VU.*

Furthermore, his name still resonated enough for him to receive an invitation from The White House of President and Mrs. Gerald Ford to attend a function honoring the Emperor and Empress of Japan on Thursday, October 2,1975. The invitation was extended to Robert alone, and the white tie affair took place at ten in the evening. As only "music" was listed on the invitation, and given the time of day, it seems that there was no state dinner involved, simply the opportunity to be present for the entertainment. No doubt other members of the entertainment world were also present along with other notables of the day. Presumably his involvement with the Japanese film industry eight years previously warranted the invitation. He kept the invitation amongst his memorabilia to the end of his life.[8]

There are references to other undertakings as well; a movie to be shot in Spain, perhaps along the lines of the "spaghetti Westerns" made famous by Clint Eastwood. A friend of Bob's, Jan Shepard, herself an actress of note, spoke of Clint Eastwood contacting Bob at some point in reference to such a role, but nothing came of it.[9] On a personal level, other than settling into their home in Encino, very little is extant. Family seemed to play a very small part in their lives and press interest in them also waned, other than to refer, occasionally, to "whatever happened to. . ."

# PART VIII LIFE GOES ON
## Chapter 22
### *As the World Turns and Other Twists*

Nineteen-eighty-two was notable for at least two reasons. It marked Bob and Marilynn's last appearance on stage together, in the comedy *I Do, I Do* at Sacramento's Center Stage Theatre. Among his memorabilia contained in *Scrapbook II*, there is one playbill of this production and two reviews, one of which is distinctly uncomplimentary, citing a number of the critic's complaints about the play, mostly to do with shoddy or inadequate props. One small clipping, lacking any identification, quotes Marilynn. "Everything that could go wrong went wrong," she said, which may explain their lack of interest in preserving more of a record than they did.

Then, later that year, Robert Horton was signed up with the venerable soap opera *As the World Turns*. He was fifty-eight, still

*Bob and Marilynn's final stage appearance together in* I Do, I Do, *May 1982. Author's collection.*

inordinately handsome and still referred to as "the sexiest man alive". The show was broadcast from New York, so the Hortons returned to the East Coast. Robert Horton said, in regard to the show, that it was "easy money". The hours were not demanding, and he did not have to "carry the show." He also said that *As the World Turns* gave him the opportunity to play "a very erudite villain," the first "total villain" role he had ever had. However, no matter what he said, there is something about the work which smacks a little of desperation – daytime television, unbelievable scripts and farcical story lines. There is little doubt that the work brought him face-to-face with his age and a new world order. Many of the actors he had to work with struck him as lazy and slipshod, lacking any kind of discipline or dedication to their art.[1] They were a different generation, twice removed from his, and the work took him a continent away from the home in Encino he loved so much. He didn't need the money. He needed, still, to work, to practice his craft, but the rigors of traveling to perform all over the country had begun to pall. There was no work for Marilynn with *As the World Turns* but together they returned to New York and settled into an apartment on East 68th Street for the duration.

At the time he auditioned for the role of Whit McColl in *As the World Turns*, Robert Horton said that he was also making a movie as well as devising a new night club routine. Nothing developed from either. Three days following the *As the World Turns* audition he was taping the show. He was cast as the husband of Eileen Fulton, the lead actress who had become an institution in the series for over twenty years. In the October 1983 issue of *Soap Opera World* he told writer John Genovese that he felt "blessed" to have worked with Fulton, and subsequently with Betsy von Furstenberg, who took over the role Fulton had essayed for twenty-three years. He said,

"I enjoyed working with Eileen very much. She was very helpful to me from my first day on the show. But in a way it's easier working with Betsy because we're both on the same level – we're actors playing a character, whereas Eileen was Lisa (the character) for twenty-three years." There were, however, rumors that Fulton developed a dislike for Bob and exited the show, which, considering her longevity with it, was a drastic move. In fact, she had a contract dispute with the show's producer Mary Ellis-Bunim which led to her absenting herself sometime in 1983, but not until she had played several months with Bob. She returned to the show in 1984, by which time Horton's character had been killed off.[2] In an article entitled "After Thirty Years in Show Biz, ROBERT HORTON Is Still Going Strong," Horton's longing to return to Encino and the things he loved there was contrasted against his pleasure in the role he had undertaken on *As the World Turns.* Yet, in reading the article, it seems clear that all was not sweetness and light on the set. Horton said,

"My character has never taken off the way I thought it could have." He spoke too of the lack of cohesion regarding the relationships developed between the characters within the scripts, and the lack of discipline among the younger actors on the show, their tendency to improvise versus actually reading and learning their lines.

In the end he completed two seasons with the soap opera. He did not renew his contract. However, he was still active, and he still wanted to be active and a letter secreted in *Scrapbook II* is witness to that. On pink letterhead entitled *La Cage aux Folles* and dated December 12, 1983, it reads,

*"Dear Robert,*

*It was great meeting your [sic]for your "La Cage" audition.*

*I wanted you to know that all the creators of the show, Arthur Laurents, Jerry Herman and Harvey Fierstein and the producers, Allan Carr, Barry Brown & Fritz Holt enjoyed your audition tremendously.*

*They all felt, however, that you looked much too youthful to portray a paternal character…a man who is definitely "fading."*

*I know that they all join me in wishing you continued success in your career and very happy holidays.*

*Sincerely,*

*Stuart Howard."*

Amazingly, this time, his looks worked against him, just as they had way back in the Fifties when he lost the part of a thirty-year old man (when he was aged twenty-seven), although in that case it was more the lack of belief on the part of those auditioning him that he could successfully portray a person of thirty. The letter demonstrates that, at age fifty-nine, he wanted to do something important, was capable of doing something important even if those auditioning him could not see it or give him the chance to prove it. It also confirms that Horton was still in New York at the end of 1983, which may have been due to the contractual obligations he had with *As the World Turns*, as well as his own desire to use New York as a springboard for further acting opportunities.

There is very little by way of concrete information relative to Robert Horton's career on stage or in television in the 1980s but following the disappointment of his rejection for the lead in *La Cage Aux Folles* he happily returned to his beloved home in Encino. He still maintained agents and for a time in the Eighties he was represented by the William Morris Agency, and the man who handled his business was Peter Shaw, Angela Lansbury's husband. They were friends. Peter Shaw had apprenticed with agent Paul Small in the late Forties, ending up in an executive position with them. Robert Horton was first professionally represented by Paul Small Artists, Ltd., who signed him with MGM in 1952, so their relationship was lengthy.[3]

In September 1987 he appeared in an episode of the television series *Houston Knights* and in November 1987, he signed a three-year agency contract with his old friend, Robert Walker, for exclusive representation by Walker's agency, Century Artists, Ltd., which was an indication that he was prepared to work through November 1990.[4] He then had a cameo role in the 1988 remake of *Red River* which starred James Arness and Bruce Boxleitner. Horton played the part of the cattle baron who buys the herd driven to the railroad by Boxleitner. Bruce Boxleitner recalled, in a telephone interview, that Horton remained a true professional. He turned up on time, knew his lines and his scenes were shot without trouble. He did not mix much with the rest of the crew, but there was little need for him to do so. The made-for-television movie, much of it filmed at several locations in Arizona, was aired on April 10, 1988. Robert Horton was by then sixty-four.

On October 1, 1989 he appeared in an episode of *Murder, She Wrote* with his friend, Angela Lansbury, "The Seal of The Confessional". He played the part of a schoolteacher. Later he dismissed the role he played as "unnecessary". His character, he said, was meant to be something of a red herring in the plot, but so much of his part was cut from the final product that he felt that his appearance in it was a wasted effort, rendered unnecessary by the cuts. Even then it can be seen that he cared about his craft and how his participation related to the work in question. This was his last professional appearance in any medium.[5]

The scrapbook kept so lovingly by Betty Burris from the 1950s through the 1980s has practically no content relative to the 1980s. The same is true of several of Bob's personal scrapbooks, including the *Red Book*, and it is, therefore, reasonably safe to conclude that, by the time *Red River* (1988) was filmed, and he appeared in *Murder She Wrote*, Robert Horton was not actively seeking professional roles. In addition, Century Artists, Ltd. was a failing entity, for Robert Walker's colleagues ultimately walked out on him, taking all the company's business.

They formed their own agency in 1994. Why Horton signed with Walker is yet another mystery. Peter Shaw launched his own company, Corymore Productions in 1987, which may explain Horton's move to Century Artists, or perhaps he signed with Walker simply in order to help an old friend.[6]

There is one interview from this period which gives an understanding of Robert Horton's views of the world, at that time, and of his career. In England, where he had enjoyed phenomenal popularity in the late Fifties and throughout the Sixties, an article appeared in the April 15-21, 1989 *TV Times*, a publication which offered TVS and Channel Four viewers a weekly program guide. Entitled "Why Flint Ain't Finished Yet... Thirty-six years ago Robert Horton was the sexiest thing on – or off – a horse. Today, nearly sixty-five, he still gets loyal fan mail from Britain"; it was based on an interview by an un-named writer, an interview occasioned by the re-running of *Wagon Train* in the UK. It said, in part;

"So what became of Flint McCullough? What happened to the rosy future Horton had mapped out? Where is he now? Actually, he was easy to track down - ...

"Now nearly sixty-five, he continues to get loyal fan mail from Britain and other parts of the world....

"His career on Broadway as a musical star didn't take off the way he had hoped it would, back in 1962. 'I left *Wagon Train* because I had other dreams, so to speak. I can't say they have been fulfilled on the level I would like them to have been. But I did most of the things that I wanted to do along the way.'

"He had more than his share of bad luck and mistiming along the way, too.

"*(He)* concentrated on regional theatre *(in the Seventies)* appearing all over the US in musicals with his wife, actress Marilynn Bradley. 'We've been married 29 years this coming December. It's not bad, is it? Especially in this business.'

"His heart is obviously in the theatre and he says he has no regrets whatever about the years he and Marilynn toured the country playing *Oklahoma, Carousel, The Man from La Mancha, There's A Girl in My Soup, Zorba The Greek* and many more. The last musical they did together was in 1982, *I Do, I Do*. . .

"Now, says Horton, a slim, elegant man whose looks have lasted, they're thinking of leaving Los Angeles behind for good and starting anew in Austin, Texas. Property is cheap there, and he can fly his plane in empty skies, drive his beloved Aston Martin and Morgan sports cars on empty roads. . .

". . . and wherever he goes, his fans are sure to find him. The driver who took him to the studios in London in 1968 still writes regularly, and one fan from Bradford flew out to see him last summer – Horton spent the day with her showing her the Hollywood sights. 'One fan wrote me a letter that was so moving saying I'd touched her life in such a way even though I'd never met her, that I've put it in a box of special memorabilia. She told me about a friend of hers, who's probably about eighty now, and how she lives in a mobile home with just her dog for company, and how she lives with memories of me. I put together a packet of pictures I'd had taken over the past couple of years and wrote: "Now I'm about to become a senior citizen, I thought you might like to see what's happened to Bob. This is the way old Bob is now – I'll be sixty-five years old in July." But I didn't get an answer. I hope I didn't hurt those memories. That show has withstood the test of time very, very well. I understand how she must feel. There's a song I used to love to sing, written for a man my age: "Somewhere the years of my youth lie inside me growing old"...It goes on and then it ends up: "because I'm a young man and I don't want to die." Lovely, lovely song. It says it all.'"

There is a great deal within this article which portrays Robert Horton as he truly was, an honest, sincere man who spoke genuinely about his life, his career and his aspirations at the age of sixty-five. They never made the move to Austin, probably because he was too much of a true Angelino and Californian to forsake the place of his birth. There was, too, his deep love for his Encino home.

There were, however, personal events in the late Eighties which deeply affected the lives of Robert and Marilynn Horton. In 1989, aged sixty-five, Bob was ready to retire, and did so. Marilynn, ten years his junior, was not so ready to give up her "career," but she had no choice. She was unable, or ill-equipped to pick up the administrative matters associated with keeping her career active so she was, essentially, forced into retirement with her husband.[7]

Then, even more traumatically, Marilynn lost both her parents, in quick succession. In 1987 Harry Bladd, aged 78, died on February 2, and in 1988 her mother, Fanny Bladd, aged 77, died on August 26. Their deaths were separated by some nineteen months. The death of her mother was particularly devastating to Marilynn. Robert Horton said of her at that time that she "became her mother". He did not mean it as a compliment.[8] He had not enjoyed a positive relationship with either of his in-laws from the very beginning, despite admitting early in his marriage that he envied the closeness his wife enjoyed with her family. When he first publicly alluded to the fact that he was married to a Jewish woman, he spoke generously of the "closeness" of her family and compared it favorably against the state of relationships within his own Mormon tribe.

"Like most Jewish girls, she's extremely close to her family. Any problem involving her parents or even a cousin or an aunt or uncle, is her problem too. It's not that way in my family. We're all individuals, concerned with our individual problems. I like the feeling that Marilynn has brought into our home, the feeling of caring and sharing and of close family ties."[9]

During the years when Bob and Marilynn called New York City home, they visited Marilynn's parents in Boston on occasion, or the parents visited New York. Given the fact that throughout those years, Bob's stage commitments regularly took him all over the country, the opportunities to get together were limited. Once he and Marilynn moved to Encino, in 1975, the Bladd's opportunities to visit Marilynn may have been even more curtailed, but at some point they began to spend at least three months a year at Andasol Avenue, the cold winter months when Boston is an inhospitable place to be. There is one reference to "Mother and Daddy" in Marilynn's Guest Book, dated around January 1978. It can only have been the Bladds, as by that time "Mama" and "Papa" Horton were dead.

As the Eighties drew to a close, the relationship between Bob and Marilynn changed. His retirement, the death of Marilynn's parents and the effect it had on her all played a part. Despite all that was written about the love they bore each other when they married, theirs was, from the start, a volatile relationship. Both were artistic, creative people. From the very beginning, there were arguments, but no matter how much they argued, they always reconciled. Who started the arguments, or why, is neither here nor there. In almost every article published about their union in the 1960s, argument is referred to, almost made to seem a badge of honor. Arguing meant, it seems, being open, honest and upfront with one another. It meant strengthening the bonds between them. Robert Horton spoke of Marilynn's positive influence within their marriage, her participation in business meetings, his consulting her regarding decisions being made within his career. He also constantly referred to what a good marriage they had, how much he loved her, how they always attended to the romance in their lives. He was quick to speak of her talents as a singer and an actress. She had a wonderful voice, he said, his was merely good. He spoke warmly to one reporter about flowers in his dressing room commemorating twenty-four years of being together.[10] Throughout their lives together, he was the decision-maker, the provider, the one who made the rules and organized their lives. In turn, Marilynn was the attentive wife and accomplished hostess who, nevertheless, kept active in the theater through the good offices of her husband. At home she was a meticulous housewife and the beautiful homes they occupied were kept immaculate.[11]

Nevertheless, their relationship altered over the years. Robert's niece Joan described it as "complicated but it seemed to work for them."[12] However, at some point in their life together Robert Horton turned to other women for love and companionship which he seemed to feel was missing in his marriage. He told the woman who he came to call "the love of his life" that he was faithful to Marilynn throughout the first ten years of their marriage.[13] This makes sense. They each had youth and beauty on their side, as well as popularity and success. They were deeply absorbed in each other. During the Sixties, his was a high-profile career, but by the early Seventies it had cooled significantly. He was not in demand in Hollywood, if, given the Wasserman vendetta, he ever would be, and he seemed unable to break back into television. That certainly played a part in his outlook on life. Furthermore, it seems that he and Marilynn had very little else in common, very little to share, beyond the theater. His need for love, approval and validation from women was compelling, and as time marched on he discovered that he lacked those emotions as well as a real companionship within his marriage.[14]

Despite this, he and Marilynn remained together for almost fifty-three years, as well as staying married until the time of his death. Marilynn Horton described herself as the "committed one"[15] in the relationship yet he was the one who, in the end, did everything he could to keep them together.

# Chapter 23
## *The Joy of His Life*

It was toward the end of 1990 when Robert Horton, without seeking it or planning it, met and fell in love with the woman he came to call "the love of his life." How it came about requires some explanation. Throughout his lifetime, but particularly as he portrayed Flint McCullough, the dashing, resourceful and romantic wagon train scout, Robert Horton's early childhood miseries and his steadfast refusal to accept and submit to their limitations inspired countless numbers of his fans to do likewise – overcome adversity. A number of signal examples made it into the press of the day, one in particular concerned a young girl in England in the early Sixties.

Denise Morris, of Aughton, England, was badly injured when she was run over by a truck as a little girl. As a result, she was partially crippled. When *Wagon Train* came to British television in 1958, she fell under the spell of its scout, which prompted her mother to write to Betty Burris, then active with the Robert Horton Friend Club in America. She duly shared Denise's story with Robert Horton, who wrote to the little girl, sending her pictures of his two horses, as her mother had told Betty that her daughter loved horses. Bob encouraged her to take up riding, telling her that it would help strengthen her physically. Then, on his second trip to England in the spring of 1960, he arranged to have her meet him in London. When they met, he told her,

"I think you are a brave little girl and I am proud and happy to have met you."

They met for a second time in mid-May, just before Bob's Royal Command performance. The British press leapt on the story and it was reported nationally.

In 1962, newspapers in England were again full of the fact that he made a point of meeting Denise again. He had written to her from time to time over the course of the intervening two years, and in

May 1962, during his tour of Britain, he and Denise were reunited in Sheffield at the Sheffield City Hall.[1]

There were other such stories, other similar meetings, and it is true to say that for every tale which made the papers, there were probably many more untold, but anyone now reading the hundreds of submissions to his website in the twenty-first century cannot but be impressed by the constant reiteration of the same theme – "You inspired me", "You helped me", "I triumphed because of you". There was, however, one significant story which Robert Horton learned about as a man in his late sixties and which resulted in the formation of a deep and visceral friendship which he called "the joy of his life" and which lasted until the day he died.

He was sixty-six when a story came to his attention which proved to be a catalyst for dramatic change in the course of his life. The story speaks for itself, but it also says a great deal about Robert Horton. It is about a little girl who was born in the mid-1940s, and grew up on a farm in upstate New York. She recounted this story in minute detail and over the course of our correspondence and meetings was utterly candid, open and honest regarding her relationship with Robert Horton. She made few provisos on how her story should be told, the principal one being her wish to remain anonymous. She did, however, agree to being referred to as K.M., a name which was meaningful within her friendship with Robert.[2]

K.M. then, was some twenty years younger than Robert Horton. As she grew she developed a close relationship with her grandmother, who lived with her family. They shared a special affinity, an affinity which is sometimes referred to as "second sight". Occasionally the little girl experienced some of that gift. Her grandmother spoke of such things to K.M., who was a bit of a tomboy, riding horses bareback and running wild about the countryside. She and her grandmother also shared a love of *Wagon Train* when it first appeared on television. They watched it together and both, of course, like millions of others, fell in love with scout Flint McCullough. One day, as they were watching the show, K.M.'s grandmother told her that the love of her life, who resembled Flint McCullough strongly, had died on July 29, 1924. She was certain that his spirit was alive again in the handsome man who portrayed the scout and who had, of course, been born on that very same day. She said to her,

"He was my first love, my dear, and this man will be your last."

One spring day, when K.M. was about thirteen, she and a cousin went out with BB guns to play at *Wagon Train*, as they often did. On this occasion the plan was to ambush a wagon floating down a nearby stream, so with a milk carton substituting for the "wagon," they set off. The milk carton was duly tossed into the stream and each took up a position on either bank, lying flat on the gravel shore with BB guns aimed. K.M.'s cousin fired first. Unfortunately, the BB hit the gravel just in front of K.M, ricocheted into her left eye, and a piece of gravel hit the right eye. Her family rushed her to hospital. It was Palm Sunday.

Several days later, lying in her hospital bed, the girl heard her parents talking with the attending doctor outside her room when they thought she was asleep. The doctor explained that the damage to the left eye was such that he would have to remove it, and that he planned to do so on the Monday immediately following Easter Sunday. She heard him say that the right eye was not much better and that there was a good chance that she would be blind. Stricken with horror, she lay alone, dreadful thoughts swirling in her brain. The prospect of living deprived of her sight terrified her and she ultimately decided to end her life. In the night, when all had gone quiet, she crept out of bed. Her room was on the sixth floor of an old building, and those old sash windows were easily opened. She went to the window, closing the eye which did not have a patch on it so that she might have the courage to heave the window open and jump. She was afraid, but she meant to jump. Then, as she opened her good eye, she saw, standing firmly between her and the window, in full costume, perhaps a little hazy, none other than Flint McCullough, her *Wagon Train* hero. He raised his hand and said, in a very soft, kind voice,

"Don't do this. You are going to have a wonderful life." Then he smiled and faded slowly away. The experience shocked her so badly that she felt her way back to bed, pulled the covers over her head and slept for fourteen hours. When she awoke it was Easter Sunday afternoon and her eye had stopped bleeding. The operation was rendered unnecessary and within a year her sight was fully restored.

Any number of interpretations may be made of this story. That is how K.M. remembers it and that is how she ultimately told it to Robert Horton. As a young woman she had moved to Los Angeles to pursue her own career. There, in her early forties, she married. Over coffee one day she recounted the story to a woman friend who worked in the movie industry and had known Robert Horton. Hearing the story, her friend declared that she ought to tell Robert Horton her tale.

"He'd love to hear it! Write it down and I'll make sure his agent gets it!"

So K.M. wrote the story in a letter to Horton, which he duly received because his agent's secretary put it on top of a pile of correspondence with a note saying "If you read nothing else, read this!" He did read it, and he answered by telephoning K.M. and inviting her to join him and Marilynn for lunch. At K.M.'s suggestion they agreed on the Beverly Hills Hotel's Polo Lounge on Sunset Boulevard. A week later she found herself "sitting in the Polo Lounge across from the most beautiful grey-haired man I had ever seen." That was in December 1990.

He met K.M. alone. Marilynn refused to go with him to meet yet another of his fans, which was regrettable as matters might have taken a different turn had she done so. How Robert Horton felt upon meeting his fan only he knew but the next day he sent her a color photograph of himself on "Stormy Night" inscribed as follows,

"To The Joy In My Life – Robert Horton"

Two weeks later he wrote to tell her that he could not get her out of his thoughts and another lunch date was set.

The meeting grew into friendship, and over the next six months, friendship became real love. When they were together he spoke very little of his life, his family or his career. The time they shared together as two people in love was all that mattered to them.

What he came to love about K.M. is telling. He called her "a happy little thing". Her lack of interest in his storied career fascinated him. He came to understand that she loved him for who he was, not what he had been, or become, or might be. This sincerity had echoes of some of his past relationships. He found it refreshing. He would recount to K.M. arguments he had had with Marilynn and to his astonishment, K.M. often took his wife's side. He could be angry or just moody with her, and she dealt with this behavior either by paying it no mind, ignoring it, or simply by holding him. By his own admission to K.M., it was this kind of warm, reassuring caring of which he had been deprived since childhood; deprived of by his mother and never received adequately from his wives. With K.M. he sought validation as a man and a human being and he found it within this loving friendship. Theirs was a relationship which went through some very traumatic moments, but which never actually died and there is no doubt that K.M. was the true love of his life from the time they met until the day he died, twenty-six years later.

In a special edition of *Globe* magazine published in 1993 entitled "Where Are They Now?" Robert Horton, when interviewed, spoke about the woman he loved, referring to her story obliquely as follows:

"One fan wrote to say that as a child she lost her eyesight," he recalls, "She wanted to commit suicide, but thought about Flint and knew that wasn't something that he would do. She later regained her sight and wrote to thank me."

It is a typically Horton-ish précis of the story which brought them together, but she said he delighted in being able to bring her into the article in this anonymous fashion.

K. M. admitted that she never knew for sure the depth of his love for her. She knew, as Betty Marvin had known before her, that he loved women. Theirs was not a relationship of grand or momentous events. They did little ordinary things together; a trip to Las Vegas, lunch at a favorite restaurant, or simply taking long walks together. Five, six miles at a time, just content to be with one another. He visited her at her tiny studio apartment and gave her little gifts, but he did not make any kind of contribution to her living costs. He showed her the little four-room cottage in Brentwood where he had been so happy. He would often involve her in a day of car washing, getting eight cars a day through the carwash. On the occasion of his seventieth birthday, K.M. bought Robert Horton a poodle which

*In the Valley with friends, mid-Nineties. Courtesy of Babs Hutchins.*

was subsequently named "Gable". She bought the dog because Bob, by his own admission, was too cheap to part with the three hundred or so dollars which Gable cost, even though it was a sum well beyond her budget. "But he wanted it, and I wanted him to have it!" Unfortunately, K.M. and Gable never quite hit it off, although the dog became deeply attached to Marilynn. "It always made me mad that Gable loved Marilynn so, and not me!" laughed K.M., but she never held it against the dog or Marilynn.

On another occasion he hatched a plan to take K.M. flying with him. Together they went to Camarillo Airport where he then kept his Piper Comanche. They cleaned it, tidied it, he tinkered with it. His idea was to fly her up to Santa Barbara for lunch the next day, a short enough flight, but that afternoon he grew anxious and worried. He was sure, he said, that he could get the aircraft into the sky, but he was not so sure that he could, any longer, safely land it.

"It doesn't matter about me," he told her, "I've had a long and full life. But you still have a whole lot of life left to live."

It was the end of his piloting days. It demonstrates how much K.M. meant to him, and it was, of course, an admission to her and to himself of the toll which advancing age was beginning to take on him.

However, K.M. herself, though deeply in love with Bob, was having difficulty living with herself and the guilt brought on by their friendship. She was certain that Bob would not leave his wife for her, and she had her own future to consider. She truly loved her husband but their marriage was in difficulties at that time. She had to decide what to do but without the assurance of a different future she decided to put the relationship on a "friendship only" basis. When she offered Bob simply friendship, he reluctantly accepted the change in status. "Friendship" was really not enough for him, but he was willing to go along with it to keep K.M. in his life. Early in 2001, however, the friendship which he cherished so much came to what they both thought was the end. Caused by a "major blowup," the two split and it was agreed that their friendship was done and finished. Robert Horton was the cause, and he bitterly regretted it, but the situation was such that K.M. said "no more" and turned back to her marriage which was now more settled and content.[3]

# PART IX THE SLOW DEMISE
## Chapter 24
### *The Western Rebirth*

Other developments in the Nineties helped add to the new lease on life for Robert Horton, the lease which had begun with his friendship with K.M. Although he had turned his back on *Wagon Train* and his Flint McCullough character in 1962, he acknowledged later in life that he would probably be remembered most for that portrayal. There was a resurgence of interest in the old black and white Westerns of the Fifties and Sixties, many of which were being re-run on The Western Channel, and various websites sprang up, but there had always been hard core devotees of the genre. One of the leading experts in the field is Boyd Magers, author of numerous books from *Westerns Women* (1999) to *A Gathering of Guns* (2017), a richly detailed anthology of TV Westerns. After a career in radio, Magers established *Video West* in 1977, which, for collectors, is the most respected source for Western and TV movies. He began self-publishing *Western Clippings* in 1994 and maintains its website now. His resume is formidable, and over the past twenty-five years he has moderated over 200 Western Celebrity guest star discussion panels at Western Film Festivals all over the country. It was at one such festival held in Sonora, California, in the late Eighties that Boyd Magers first met Robert Horton, and according to Magers, a casual friendship grew up between them.

The Sonora film festivals drew huge audiences and each featured an award ceremony at which a number of celebrities were honored. Robert Horton was chosen to receive a Lifetime Achievement Award at the Tuolumne County Wild West Film Festival in Sonora in 1993, but when he was told who his presenter would be, Horton, according to Magers "kind of fumed, and said 'Why? He doesn't know anything about me! Why don't you get Boyd Magers to do the introduction?'" Which is exactly what happened and so their friendship was cemented when Magers introduced Robert Horton to the assembled throng. He listed all the aspects of Horton's career, including his lamented appearance in *The Green Slime*, which, to quote Magers, "brought the house down!" Amidst gales of laughter, Magers defused the moment by pointing out that other well-known Western actors had done similar off-beat work.[1] Interestingly Bob's acceptance speech on that occasion singularly omitted any mention of *The Green Slime*. This is what he said, and how he wrote it:

"Thank you very much, Ladies and Gentlemen. And my thanks to the committee of this Film Festival for this honor.

In this wonderful, crazy, unpredictable business I have been extremely fortunate to experience a successful and fulfilling career. To have known the warmth, kindness, and to be truthful, love and devotion that so many of my fans have expressed through the years. To some I was their Hero, to some I was a role model. I had a young man come up to me a few days ago and say, "Mr. Horton, I grew up in a dysfunctional family where I had no role model. I just wanted to tell you that I used you as my role model and that you served me very well. And thank you." We shook hands and I thanked him and he walked away. But he will never know how much that moment enriched my life…To some I was their first crush…crush…do they still use that word? First love; and now there are some who watch my re-runs and with their daughters and now it's the daughter who has the crush. Some of my fans still write on a regular basis, never miss Christmas and always remember my birthday. "My fans" are a part of this business that has touched my life, as I have touched theirs. They are people from many corners of this world. Fans from England who recall the excitement of my performances at the London Palladium. The thrill of being invited to perform at the Royal Command Performance for Her Majesty Elizabeth the Queen, the pomp, the ceremony, the nerves… Nat King Cole forgot the words to "Unforgettable". I was a basket case: singing on the same program as Sammy Davis, Jr., and Nat Cole, not to forget the charm and showmanship of Liberace. It was a night to remember. My own television show in England and Australia.

Special memories here in America. Ralph Edwards' famous greeting at my front door.

"Robert Horton, this is your life." What an honor, what a surprise. Opening night in New York City in the musical One Hundred and Ten in the Shade. Your name in lights on Broadway. To have been a part of the Broadway scene and in the company of Kings and Queens. Richard Burton, Alec Guinness, Mary Martin, Barbara Streisand. What a year. What a memory. Guesting on variety shows with Perry Como, Ernie Ford, Rosemary Clooney, Red Skelton and of course, Ed Sullivan. Headlining in Las Vegas and of course, the television series that opened all of these doors. The years on Wagon Train. A forever part of my life. And the actors that journeyed West with me for five years. Gifted actors with whom I shared the screen, James Mason, Raymond Massey, Ernie Borgnine, Bette Davis, Barbara Stanwyck, Judith Anderson. All Academy Award winners. They will do to ride the trail with.

The wonderful thing about film is that it is a permanent record of an actor's contribution to his time; and the actor at the time of his performance. And because there are people who care about preserving these films I can look back at myself in a Lone Ranger when I was in my twenties, or as Flint McCullough when he was in his thirties, or The Man Called Shenandoah when he was in his forties. Or the executive in *As the World Turns* in his fifties; I could even run A Murder She Wrote of the actor in his sixties. But why bother; I can just glance in a mirror.

I recently was at a Film Festival in Charlotte, North Carolina and they ran an episode of Wagon Train that I had no recollection of ever making. And it was a story that was based on The Mark of Zorro, fencing and all. And I didn't remember it all. But I liked seeing the young Robert Horton. And I liked him.

Well here I am: wearing the jeans I wore in Shenandoah, and a jacket I used in Wagon Train. My hair is no longer red, but it's still here, and whether I look back or enjoy this moment I am fulfilled. The past has become the present. And I thank you for this honor and for sharing it with me."

This meeting in Sonora developed into a lasting friendship between Boyd Magers and Robert Horton. According to Magers

*At the Wild West Film Fest, Sonora, September 1992. L – R: Will Hutchins, Babs Hutchins, Bob. Courtesy of Babs Hutchins.*

Bob loved being part of the festivals and attended many, to the huge delight of the fans. Latterly, however, his ability to be involved in these occasions was affected by increasing ill-health.

"He wanted very much to be there," said Magers."But then he would call and cancel at the last minute, which naturally disappointed the fans, and harmed his reputation. But he really wanted to participate!"

Finally, Magers told him,

"Bob, if you think you can't make it, don't accept the invitation."

Indeed, when Magers, unsure of Horton's health, called him in regard to his possible attendance at a festival in 2007 and was told by Bob of his uncertainty, he simply did not list him as a guest, which was just as well as in the end Bob was unable to attend. Boyd Magers, speaking about Robert Horton, was genuine and sincere regarding his feelings for him. He liked Robert Horton, and had a lot of respect for him, feelings which were undoubtedly mutual. He said of Bob,

"He was a good friend. He had a down-to-earth friendliness, never above it all, no star ego, never encountered that. He was down to earth. He always had time for you. I never hesitated about calling him with questions and that was something I couldn't do with many of the Hollywood people I had to turn to for answers. We became really good friends, I think. And he would always flirt with (Donna) my wife. Well, he would flirt with all women. He knew how to impress a woman, he really did, that was so obvious, even on the 'phone."

Magers also made a point of differentiating Robert Horton from others of the Western genre clique, such as Robert Fuller, Ty Hardin and Clint Walker. His world, said Magers emphatically, was music and musical theater, which was where his friends and social life were concentrated.[2]

The Western Festivals continued to take him out of himself, and he attended several in the ensuing years. There is no doubt that he relished these experiences, even if he found it more and more difficult, physically, to attend. Yet he remained strikingly handsome and well able to cast his spell over the legions of adoring fans who attended the gatherings. He attended the 1996 Film Festival in Knoxville, Tennessee, and the Memphis Film Festival in 1998, where he served on a number of discussion panels. There is no record of his presence at other such gatherings until 2002 when he went to the Western Film Festival in Tombstone, Arizona. He traveled alone to this particular event where, at the age of seventy-eight he found himself surrounded by other aging stars and many adoring fans, but his natural inclination to be solitary left him vulnerable in the hectic modern world of airports and hotels. On this occasion, a woman with whom he had worked in an episode of *A Man Called Shenandoah*, a fellow guest at the gathering, spotted him in the airport departure lounge, asleep, and fearing that he would miss the flight, woke him and helped him board. She said he was "looking a little lost."

That woman, Jan Shepard, a renowned actress who co-starred with Elvis Presley in *King Creole* (1958) and who established a career on television in the Sixties and Seventies is a warm, jolly woman with a lovely smile who, quite clearly, like so many thousands, nay, millions of others, fell under Robert Horton's spell. What she remembers of working with him in that one Western episode, "Plunder," is that he was "delightful" and "professional". What she remembers of their encounter at the airport is that he seemed to need a little help, so she helped him. Helped him board the aircraft, helped him get to the hotel at their destination and helped him check in. Then she made sure that he joined her and her husband, Dirk London (Ray Boyle), at a party with other old troupers in their room that night. It was the start of a beautiful friendship, she says. Happily married to her actor husband since 1954, there was nothing between Jan and Bob but a shared background, common experiences and an ability to find humor in situations, often when others didn't get the joke. Why Marilynn did not attend the 2002 festival is unknown, but she did not. Nevertheless, she was brought into the friendship and subsequently shared it as well.

Over lunch at The Bistro Garden Restaurant in Encino, in June 2017, Jan Shepard spoke lovingly and glowingly of her late friend Bob. She spoke of his magnetism, his good humor. She spoke of

*Bob and Jan Shepard at the Tombstone Western Festival, 2002. Courtesy of Babs Hutchins.*

*Bob and Marilynn at The Golden Boot Awards, August 2004. Courtesy of Richard Gagnon.*

how she and her husband had been guests at the Horton home on a number of occasions and told of how Marilynn and Bob were special guests when she and Dirk celebrated their Fiftieth Wedding Anniversary in 2004. There is no doubt that this friendship helped salve, a little, the hurt of his losses, but it also demonstrates his ability to relate to others and maintain, loyally, friendships based on the simple liking and admiration for one another, as well as shared experiences and memories in and of the same industry. They lost touch toward the end of Bob's life, mainly due to his increasing isolation, but Jan sent a condolence card to Marilynn when she learned of her friend's death. In a phone call with her, Marilynn agreed to get together, but it did not happen. Nevertheless, Jan treasures the memory of her friendship with Robert Horton and had nothing but good to say about him.[3]

In July 2004 Robert Horton celebrated his eightieth birthday and shortly afterwards attended another Western Festival in Tombstone. On this occasion he was the recipient of the much-revered Golden Boot Award on August 7. This award, conceived by the veteran "side-kick" actor Pat Buttram in the early Eighties, was a way to "recognize the achievements of cowboy film heroes and heroines, writers, directors, stunt people and character actors who had significant involvement in the film and TV Westerns."[4]

Introduced by his old friend Robert Osborne of *Turner Classic Movies*, he received the award with grace and dignity. His speech, a short one, is reproduced in full on his defunct website.[5] Robert Horton said,

"Many thanks, Bob O.! Robert Osborne, one very fine fellow. Bob and I met at a small town in Illinois in 1968, a small town that boasted of an excellent regional theatre. And they were very proud of the industry the city was famous for: The Manure Capital of The World! Happily the production we were involved with did not contribute to the city's reputation or its atmosphere.

The year 2004 has proven to be a very special year in my life, full of special celebrations: One, I will soon celebrate being married to my beloved Marilynn for 45 years of wedded bliss; well it wasn't quite 45 years. Two, celebrating the final payment on our mortgage. George Montgomery built our house by the way, the scene of many happy years. Three, an ongoing celebration of my 80th birthday, which took place a week ago.

And now, tonight, being honored with a Golden Boot, joining the special fraternity of actors that I have admired and with whom I have shared the screen for the 62 *[sic]* years I have been a member of the Screen Actors Guild.

However, more important than this trophy, is knowing that you are forever inscribed in Hollywood history: that your contribution has been recognized and recorded and is part of the legacy of Western films, a legacy the Golden Boot is dedicated to preserve, and what a fantastic legacy it is. During the past few years, I have attended many Western film festivals, and I have learned just how important that legacy is to the people of our country. And, what a meaningful and enduring 80th birthday present. I'm very proud, I'm fulfilled, and I have a wonderful sense of completion.

Thank you, and good night."

It was typical of him that he would mention his home, paying off its mortgage and candidly refer to his age, and ever so typical that he would mention Marilynn and their years of wedded bliss. At his side, as he spoke, was his wife. Both are beautifully and appropriately dressed for the occasion, and Marilynn's magnificent Indian jewelry speaks of immense indulgence on the part of her husband. His belt and bolo tie are positively restrained by comparison. There followed festivals in 2005 and 2006, all attended by a coterie of fans who went under the collective name of "Horton's Harem". The 2006 festival was held in Phoenix, Arizona, and here, on March 18, Bob was presented with the "Cowboy Spirit Award" for "embodying the integrity, strength of spirit, and moral character depicted by the American cowboy."[6]

Another development brought about by the resurgence of interest in old television Westerns in general, and in Robert Horton and Flint McCullough in particular, was the establishment of a website dedicated to Robert Horton. A longtime fan, Alicia Williams, created, sometime in the late Nineties, a first version of *The Robert Horton Website*. Horton heard about it from a friend, who described it as "amateurish". He got in touch with Williams. Not at all *au fait* with the rapidly developing world of electronic communications, he nevertheless wanted his name associated with something worthwhile. They discussed the matter and he was persuaded that Williams' motivations were sincere and that her aim was to do him and his career credit. He gave her his blessing and shared with her facts of his professional life as well as a substantial number of photographs.[7]

The website, in its new, more professional guise, was officially established in 2002. It thrived and attracted huge attention from around the world. To this day it carries thousands of comments and tributes from fans of old who were thrilled to discover it, to learn that their hero was still alive and well, and to have the opportunity to communicate with "Flint McCullough." Robert Horton himself never got to grips with the electronic world and disdained computers, although he did, eventually, have a cell phone, but he appreciated the website and how it breathed new life into an old career, so he went along with it. Its content dried up around 2006, and while it is still extant, and carries a brief and poignant acknowledgment of Horton's death in 2016, it is no longer active.[8]

The advent of the Western symposiums helped to divert Robert Horton's attention from the vagaries of aging and brought new people into his life, re-establishing a semblance of a public persona. Unfortunately, by this time, his wife did not share his appreciation of his fans, no matter what guise they came in, although it is fair to say that initially she accepted them as a fact of his life as well as her own.

Throughout his life, particularly as a result of *Wagon Train*, Robert Horton was the object of much adulation; adulation which was demonstrated in the form of individual fan worship and fan club worship and this fan worship followed him until the day he died. It is clear from his own references to them that he valued his fans, and their support. His patience with them and his willingness to meet with them throughout his life is indicative of how much they meant to him, of how much he appreciated their importance to his career, and how much he actually needed their unconditional regard for him. He ultimately became good friends with a number of them. If the extant material from a number of "friend club" newsletters is to be believed, early in their life together, he involved Marilynn to a considerable degree in terms of his communications with various factions of these clubs. Letters from Marilynn, written to the clubs' presidents, reveal a positive outlook on her behalf, and articles written by fortunate members of these clubs who actually met their idol and his wife are glowing in their praise of both, of their friendliness, their kindness and their willingness to meet with and even entertain these "friends". Indeed, the existence of the "Betty Burris scrapbook" bears witness to the kind of friendships which began with fan club membership and developed into real, personal relationships on both sides.[9]

The most active period of the clubs mirrored the most active period of Horton's career, and the largest, by far, was the British fan club. It numbered in the tens of thousands at one point and Robert Horton was at first taken aback by its size and level of activity. In the United States the numbers were not quite so large, but large enough, and there were various regional representations. The membership ranged in age from teenage girls to grandmothers, and there were significant numbers of males represented as well. Many of these people involved themselves in charitable endeavors in the name of the club, and there exists within the fan club material a significant record of the things which were done for boys' clubs, children in hospital, and at least one orphanage which benefitted from the efforts of the fan club members. Robert and Marilynn Horton were very aware of these activities and made their own direct contributions to them.

There are any number of stories about the Hortons taking time to meet their fans when they were on the summer stock circuit in the Sixties and Seventies, and their graciousness is unerringly alluded to. Fan, or "friend" club activity remained fairly active, even into the early Eighties, but the organized entities faded away well before Robert Horton's official retirement. However, with the resurgence of the popularity of old TV Westerns, "old" fans reappeared, and new, younger admirers involved themselves in the Western symposiums which sprang up in the late Eighties and Nineties, so that while the fan clubs disappeared, the fans did not. Far from it.

How Marilynn felt about "the fans" has become a story in itself, but there is little doubt that initially she accepted them as an inevitable part of her husband's success. After all, much later in life, she was able to say to one lady at a Western Festival that she had "the real deal at home."[10]

Nevertheless, by the time they began attending the Western gatherings, their relationship had changed sufficiently for Marilynn to take a less positive view of Robert's fans. She saw them as an imposition, something she was forced to put up with and endure. By the mid-Nineties, she had learned of his relationship with K.M. Fans, and friendships formed through the fan base were, to her, an extension of that relationship. It was the reappearance of those fans en masse, which created more discontent between them.[11]

To read the breathless, excited, gushing reports of dazzled fans at the festivals, who were able to sit with their long-time idol and his wife at dinners, in meetings and in audiences watching the panel discussions, it is easy to be convinced of Marilynn's bonhomie and good humor in these settings and there exists a large body of evidence to show that Robert Horton, throughout his adult life, was loved, respected, admired and thought very highly of by his legions of fans as well as the majority of those who knew him.

Bob certainly valued his fans and referred to them with warm sincerity and affection throughout his life. However, it's not difficult to understand Marilynn's latter-day antipathy toward them and the negative influence they brought to bear on her life. Between them, though, and through their own ability to put on a convincing front for their public they managed to hide the realities of their complicated relationship from all but the very closest of their friends and families.

In the screeds of articles written about the two, in interviews and in panel discussions, when Robert Horton refers to his wife he always does so with admiration and affection. Since Marilynn was seldom asked by the press, except in the very early days of their marriage, about her relationship with Bob, there is very little to go on latterly regarding her side of matters. However, in those early days, Marilynn, when involved in media interviews, was unfailingly supportive and came across sincerely as a young woman deeply in love with her handsome, famous, successful husband. Exactly how they related to one another during their last decades together only they knew, but Robert Horton certainly made sure that, no matter what, he would keep a promise he had made to himself, as well as very publicly, that his fourth marriage would absolutely be his last, and that it would be forever. It is sad, but true, that the ever-present fans' adoration of Robert Horton ultimately drove another wedge between them in the final years of their life together.

# Chapter 25
## *The New Millennia*

With the turn of the century approaching, and a new Millennia dawning, Robert Horton still lived a very comfortable life at his beautiful home in Encino, even if he was without the close comfort of his great love. He and Marilynn, despite everything, remained together. The advancing years, however, were beginning to take their toll, and certain aspects of his life had to be curtailed. That curtailment represented profound loss to him.

The loss of his friendship with K.M. in 2001 upset and distressed him. Another loss he suffered in this period was his ability to fly. There is mention that he made his last flight in 1997, when he was seventy-three, but that is contradicted by his Pilot's Log which shows that he passed a proficiency test in 1992, which allowed him to fly for another two years. If he did fly during those years, he failed to enter anything in his logbook, and given the reality of his realization that he lacked the confidence to fly K.M. to Santa Barbara and back sometime in the mid-Nineties, it's reasonable to assume that when the time came for him to take another flight proficiency test, he simply decided against it. Furthermore, the facts surrounding the sale of his plane indicate clearly that he was no longer the astute pilot he had been, or that his Piper Comanche was airworthy.[1]

At some point in the mid-Nineties, he moved the plane from Van Nuys Airport to Camarillo Airport in Ventura County. He had had an argument with the Van Nuys Airport manager and he had allowed someone else to fly his plane. He withdrew that permission, and then, anxious that the person concerned might have had a spare set of keys made for the Comanche, he decided to relocate it. From Camarillo he moved it to Fox Field, a small airport serving the Antelope Valley in Los Angeles County. The plane sat on a ramp at Fox Field and gathered dust. In 1998, Deputy Sheriff Steve Harbeson of the L.A. Sheriff's Department, while performing a security check at Fox Field as part of his duties, noted what he described as "a derelict plane" there. Harbeson was a pilot. His duty partner, Fred Hill, a black man, was working on obtaining his student pilot's license. Both of them decided that the plane was worth salvaging, despite its dilapidated condition. Harbeson then located Robert Horton via the internet and wrote to him, telling him of his interest in the plane.

On receipt of that letter, Horton called Harbeson, the upshot being that Harbeson rented a small plane, flew to Van Nuys, picked Horton up and flew him to Fox Field. That is undoubtedly the last time Bob flew in a small private plane and may explain the allusion to his last flight being around 1997. According to Harbeson, Bob had not seen the Comanche in several years and had not realized how it had deteriorated. Several discussions about the purchase of the plane followed, but Harbeson and Horton could not come to an agreement on the price, and Harbeson discontinued his negotiations. He looked at several other planes. Meanwhile, Harbeson's partner, Fred Hill, who had not been with him during his meeting with Bob, decided he would like to try one more time, so he called Robert Horton himself. When Horton heard him on the phone, he asked him if he was black. He said that he was. Within minutes he had a deal. Robert Horton told him that he had been raised by a black lady, so he and Harbeson could have the plane for half price. During its purchase, Harbeson and Fred Hill were invited to Andasol Avenue by Horton, where, he said, they were treated graciously.[2] This touching story reflects so much of who Robert Horton was, of how strong Mary Augustine's influence remained in his life. So, in early 1999, the aircraft he had owned for forty years passed into other hands, but he kept a propeller and nosecone which became part of the sale of his Estate in August 2015.

The sale of his automobiles represented yet more loss. He had always had a great love for cars, not the somber black saloons favored by his family, but open sports cars, colorful, sleek and fast. He loved driving and throughout his adult life he always owned a number of automobiles, many of which he acquired early on and kept in pristine condition until the day they were sold. They meant a great deal to him. He declared unequivocally that his cars were there for him to drive, not to show, and he most certainly did drive them fast, and for long distances at times. As his fame grew with *Wagon Train*, journalists were quick to note that he owned at least three different cars, one or two of which were given to him by *Wagon Train*'s sponsor, the Ford Motor Company, when the show made it into the top ten television program ratings. As his ability to acquire cars grew, he added to that stable, owning as many as twelve vehicles at a time. By the time he and Marilynn settled at Andasol Avenue, he kept three automobiles in the home's large garage, while others were garaged with friends. Those he and his wife drove were parked outside the house. Sometime in the Sixties he gave his father one of the cars he had received from Ford, as he also gave his father-in-law a car which belonged to him. Cars, like planes, represented freedom to him, freedom to move about, and get away from the pressures of his life. In an article written for a British magazine, *TV Scene*, published in 1988, he spoke of his twenty-two-year-old drop-head Morgan coupe.

"I have just had it re-sprayed and the interior done. I can't drive it anywhere without people admiring it."

He went on,

"The Aston Martin, the Morgan and my Thunderbird '57 are the favorite of all my cars."

The Thunderbird convertible was a car he drove regularly in the mid-Fifties, and it is seen in a number of promotional press photographs of the day with Horton at the wheel, notably when he went to take horsemanship instruction at Hudkins Stable Ranch, and several times with Jamie, his dog, in the back seat. It may be the car that he famously drove across country to explore the old wagon routes after he got the role of Flint McCullough in early 1957. Over the years, some of the cars changed, but when he finally sold off several in a 2004 auction in Scottsdale, those three favorites were part of the inventory. Later in life he owned others and was especially partial to a 1973 Mercury Cougar convertible, which he still drove when he was in his eighties.[3] Around 1998 he engaged a highly skilled mechanic, David Ritter, who worked at the famed Nethercutt Museum, to prepare his Mercedes Benz 300SL roadster for sale. Ritter was, and is, an expert on Mercedes Benz motor cars and he subsequently looked after all Horton's cars, and helped him sell them, either privately or at auction between 1998 and 2005. Ritter described Horton as friendly and kind. He described his collection of cars as "small, but stylish." An eclectic collection, it represented Bob's own likes, preferences and styles, and demonstrated his excellent taste and knowledge of what was good and collectible. Their sale was yet another landmark on the road to the end, a recognition of the toll of age and time, but Robert Horton made the decision to sell the collection which realized, over that time, a considerable income. It was, undeniably however, another series of losses.[4]

Robert Horton also had a delightful collection of model cars, prominently displayed in his den at Andasol Avenue. It was a significant array, and undoubtedly many were given to him as gifts, as one gives something to "the man who has everything."

One collection he did not sell off was his guns. Early in his life he began collecting old pistols and revolvers, some of which he was notably photographed with at the height of his *Wagon Train* stardom. Many were mounted on wooden plaques and were hung on the walls of his various homes. When he left *Wagon Train*, he asked to keep the revolver he had used, and the collection ultimately contained both that gun rig as well as the rig he used in *A Man Called Shenandoah*. There were flintlock pistols from the 1770s, Colt revolvers from the 1800s and modern handguns such as Walthers, Brownings and Lugers, similar to the weapons used in his spy movies. Some of the guns were given to him as gifts by Marilynn. A valuation carried out in the early 1980s put a total worth of just over $10,000.00 on the collection which numbered twenty-two guns. Only the most modern were capable of being fired.[5]

Though he was no longer in touch with K.M. at this time, his involvement in the Western festivals and friendship with people like Jan Shepard and several of his fans helped to fill some of the void in his life. Perhaps more meaningful, however, was the start of a friendship which came from within his own family. His eldest Horton nephew, Creighton Clark Horton II, approached Robert in the course of a visit in 2003 to his parents' home in San Marino. Creighton, or Creight as he is known, lived and worked in Salt Lake City as a State Prosecutor. He had always admired his uncle although theirs had never been a close relationship. Married, with two daughters, he called Robert and asked if they could visit him. The doors of 5317 Andasol Avenue were flung open, and thus began a warm and happy association which lasted nine years. It undoubtedly filled a void in Robert's life and it must have been as if the rifts between him and his family were healing a little. To Creight and his wife and children, Marilynn and Bob were their "most interesting relatives."[6]

Health problems beset him in 2007, sufficient to prevent him from attending another festival in March in Virginia. He sent his regrets and apologies, especially to the fans who had traveled from England to see him. He described his indisposition as "nothing too serious" although it had been "a bit of a scare" at the time. Now eighty-three, health issues which had dogged him since childhood were coming back to haunt him as well as those brought on by the simple fact of aging. Never a happy or compliant patient at the best of times, these trials of old age only exacerbated all the other demons with which he lived. In May, however, in response to an invitation from his friends, Babs and Will Hutchins, he flew to Boston, Massachusetts to take part in a radio presentation at the Buckley Performing Arts Center in Brockton. He made the effort principally for the Hutchins, whose friendship meant a great deal to him.[7] Later that year he was able to appear at the annual Western Festival in Tombstone though his participation there, especially on the celebrity panel session, seemed muted and low key. Finally, in the latter part of that year, he had to give up an appearance with his friend, Boyd Magers.

In 2008 Bob's agent put out an announcement that Horton would no longer travel to any events or meetings. He was growing tired. The business of traveling was too much, and in essence that is when Robert Horton withdrew from public life. His health was failing and age was taking its toll. Still, he had his beautiful home, several cars which he continued to drive, his mercurial wife and a dog. Gable had, by this time, been replaced by a smaller type of poodle named Teddy B. He was still able to take Teddy B. for long walks, something he enjoyed, for it allowed him the peace and tranquility he coveted.

*Bob's study at Andasol Avenue, c. 2009. Courtesy of the Horton family.*

By this time the Hortons were almost living separate lives, she in her part of their rambling home and he in his. His "part" of the house was where his study and the maid's quarters were located, and as there was no live-in help he slept there, or often in the recliner in his study, which was crammed with memorabilia of his career, as well as photographs of his parents, his brother, all four of his wives and several of his dogs. There were other things which contributed to his decline but principally it was the weight of disappointment, sorrow and loss which represented the burdens of his suffering. He was bereft of the emotional comforts a human being craves; a loving partner, a loving family, a sense of accomplishment and a sense of peace going forward into old age.

Illness reasserted itself in 2008, and it was then that, hearing he was sick, K.M., unable to maintain the silent distance which had existed between them since 2001, got in touch with him to express her concern and continued love for him. After some back-and-forth communication between them, and despite Horton's avowal that he did not want her to see him as an "old fat man," they finally met for lunch and all became as it had been before.

"It was as if we had never been apart," she said, and for a time the resumption of the friendship soothed the pain which both had experienced throughout their long separation.[8] Having this vital friendship restored to him helped ease some of his deep unhappiness, even as he continued to attempt to maintain some kind of relationship with his own family, despite its general lack of closeness. Visits from his nephew Creighton, who retired as a Utah state prosecutor in 2009, occurred, but infrequently. Creighton's mother Anne died in 2008, and her loss was felt acutely by her family. She was a warm, loving woman who had provided a stable home for her children and grandchildren. Of her relationship with Robert Horton little is known, but interestingly she kept a number of newspaper clippings about her famous in-law, and there still exists at least one letter he wrote to her. It was couched in friendly and respectful terms.[9] After Anne's death, Creighton stayed on in the home in San Marino in which he had installed his young family in the early Fifties. As his health deteriorated, his younger daughter, Joan, took up residence with him in order to look after him. There would be no retirement home for Dr. Creighton Horton and Joan looked after him in San Marino until the end. Her uncle asked her if she would do the same for him when the time came. She said she would.[10]

Robert Horton had said that he and his brother had nothing in common, but by now, 2009, his brother was his closest remaining relative so Bob made efforts to try to put their relationship on a more positive footing. Braving the teeming freeways of greater Los Angeles once a month he drove to San Marino to take his brother out to lunch. More often than not these meetings degenerated into arguments.[11] Yet he persisted. In fact, and regardless of what others have said about it, his brother mattered to him. His family mattered to him. It is sad to relate that perhaps, ultimately, Robert Horton meant something to Creighton. He acknowledged to his younger daughter Joan late in his life that he admired Robert for all that he had done in his career, and especially that he had stuck with it and made a success of it. Unfortunately, it seems he never said so to Bob.[12]

Creighton Clark Horton succumbed in May 2012, following several weeks in hospital. His children and grandchildren were scattered from California to Oregon, and Robert Horton got in touch with each of his nephews and nieces to exhort them to visit their father in his final days. Creighton Horton II ultimately spent several days with his father before he died, as did his sister Joan, who had been taking care of her father.[13] He was buried beside his much-loved wife Anne in the Salt Lake City Cemetery. Robert Horton, aged eighty-eight, did not attend his brother's funeral. Quite apart from the fact that his age and ill-health precluded such a trip, he was, of course, "persona non grata" when it came to admission to the Temple. According to his niece he sent a magnificent floral arrangement with a card which read,

"Not friends, but never enemies."[14]

This floral tribute brought about another loss. Urged by the funeral directors to take the many flowers home so that they would not be destroyed by prevailing frosts, Creighton Horton II picked up his aunt and uncle's flowers. Innocently believing that they would appreciate that he had done so, he called to tell them. Unfortunately, his aunt, who answered the phone, was deeply distressed by his actions. For her, the flowers were for "the dead" and should not be removed. She was deeply wounded and declared that, as a result, their friendship had come to an end, forever. It was, he said, a totally unexpected outburst, and it severed the relationship which had meant so much to his uncle as well as to Creighton's own family.[15]

Thus began the dark and final years of Robert Horton's life. By the time the new millennia was twelve years old, Robert Horton was two years away from celebrating his ninetieth birthday. Poor health affected him in sundry ways but he and Marilynn continued to live in their home on Andasol Avenue. Laid out, for all intents and purposes, on one floor, it did not present the kind of difficulties that a more conventional home might have done, and Horton adamantly declared to anyone who would listen that the only way he would ever leave it would be "in a box". With the mortgage paid off, there was no good reason for them to sell and move out.

Nevertheless, Horton was aware of the advancing years. He began to sell off many career-related possessions, some of them to his friend Boyd Magers. No-one in his family appeared interested in these things. Had the family shown any interest, he might have rewarded them with some of his treasures and memorabilia, but it seems that the divide between them was an insurmountable gulf which left both sides sufficiently isolated and beyond any kind of rapport, so that few of the hallmarks of his career found their way into the hands of his relatives.

In the early summer of 2013, one of Robert Horton's fans, a woman in her mid-sixties, and so representative of that generation which "came of age" watching Flint McCullough on *Wagon Train*, sent him a kind of book which she had created, an illustrated story of Flint McCullough. Her name was Eugenia Fredricksen, but she went by the nickname "Corky". Divorced, she continued to live on a small-holding in Washington State with her ailing ex-husband, a professional photographer, and a small herd of horses. It was a matter of convenience for them both. She was a knowledgeable and able horsewoman as well as skillful in the use of digital, computerized photography. She wrote the story and created the illustrations in full color, digitally, using photographs she took of Flint in *Wagon Train* scenes.[16] It was a considerable enterprise, and when he received it, he was duly impressed, despite his mixed feelings about the leading character who he had so happily set aside fifty-one years previously. Too, he wasn't sure about the illustrations, though he did appreciate the work which had gone into them.[17] Two weeks after receiving the book, Robert Horton called its creator. He was able to do so because the return label on its packaging carried a telephone number. He asked to speak to the person who had sent it to him. They talked. She learned that he had not actually read the illustrated story of Flint McCullough, but he wished to thank her for her efforts. Shortly after the book's arrival, Marilynn also called the woman and thanked her for sending the book. She said that it had arrived at a time when Bob was "low in spirit."[18] However, ultimately, Corky became one of a handful of fan friends the family and Marilynn came to refer to as "the delusional fans."[19]

# Chapter 26

## *In The End*

In the end it was a monumental argument which brought Robert and Marilynn's marriage to its absolute nadir at the end of August in 2013. Its outcome was that Marilynn moved out of the lovely home she had shared with Bob for nearly thirty-eight years and out of the life they had shared for fifty-three years. With her went Teddy B.[1]

Robert Horton then found himself on his own, fending for himself. There were, however, others who kept in touch by phone or letters and visits; his great love, K.M., and a handful of loyal friends such as Babs and Will Hutchins and Toby Wolfe. He spoke by phone with those friends, most of whom were elderly and lived far away. He spoke to them of his loneliness, of the fact that no-one in his family came to see him.[2]

One person who did come to spend time with him was Eugenia Fredricksen: Corky. They were in touch from time to time via the phone, and at one point he asked her if she was ever coming to California, expressing the hope that if she did so, they might meet.

In November 2013, Fredricksen did make the trip to Los Angeles and they met, at last, in the lobby of her hotel. It was then that she learned that he was alone and heard from him the reasons why. So began their friendship, and for the next two-plus years, through March 9, 2016, she visited him intermittently.[3]

Robert Horton introduced Fredricksen to K. M., who also made every effort to travel to Encino as often as possible to see him. He understood that K.M. was in no position to be with him on a permanent basis but her periodic visits meant the world to him. The two women liked one another, and grew friendly. Fredricksen found in K. M. a kind, compassionate, generous soul who, while maintaining her friendship with Robert, encouraged him to find some kind of happiness with Fredricksen. She had her own marriage to sustain, a marriage which had improved markedly and now mattered greatly to her. However, she saw a chance for Robert to have someone to care for him in his final years as Marilynn would not, and she could not.[4]

Unlike K.M., Fredricksen had a lively interest in Horton's career as well as his personal life. He willingly answered her questions and shared details of his life with her. As a lonely, old, abandoned man it is understandable that he would, and he did. He poured his heart out to her on many aspects of his career, his marriages and his family.[5]

Eugenia Fredricksen, nevertheless, had those responsibilities at home to attend to so, in fact, being with Robert on a full-time basis was not possible for her. She did, however, help him in a number of matters which he was increasingly incapable of handling himself, such as taking him to doctor's appointments.[6]

Despite living apart from her husband, Marilynn Horton nevertheless maintained an interest in what was going on in his life. She knew about K.M. and Fredricksen and other friends who kept in touch by phone, and from time to time she came by the Andasol home.[7]

By this time Robert Horton had reached a point where, sick of life, all he wanted to do, according to his niece and the friends he told, was to die within the comforting walls of the home he loved so much. Nevertheless, as he told those same few friends, he continued to entertain some kind of hope that his wife might return to him, as she had always done throughout their lives together. He may also have hoped that, if she did not, then K. M. might.[8] For a time, too, he had a hope that his favorite niece Joan might come and look after him in his last years, as she had cared for her father, his brother.[9] In the end, all these hopes were futile.

To the consternation of those of his friends who knew, he refused live-in care, being stubborn, independent and proud, despite the efforts made on his behalf by both K. M. and Fredricksen to find such care. He valued his privacy tremendously. Fredricksen visited him but could not stay for more than a few days at a time. K. M. came too, as often as she could, but there were limitations on her ability to do so. There was no-one to make sure that he ate properly and he spent his time alone, windows shuttered against the daylight, morose and miserable. He avoided doctors'appointments.[10]

2015 brought no improvement in his condition, emotionally, physically or mentally. His mobility was tremendously curtailed. In late January he suffered a fall and was hospitalized briefly. Fredricksen came to stay for a few days, but his emotional state was dire. A subsequent fall only weeks later put him in hospital again. He never returned to his home following that fall.[11] Its repercussions left him hospitalized for several months, and when he finally got out it was to go to an assisted living facility in Sherman Oaks, a move which, according to his niece, K. M. and Fredricksen, Marilynn arranged.[12] She put 5317 Andasol Avenue on the market and arranged for the sale of its contents in August of that year. The sale was handled by Beverley Hills Estate Sales and took place over the course of several days.[12] The house was sold directly to a builder who subsequently demolished it. Within a few months the site was unrecognizable. Now a large, white, two-storey home dominates the lot. Gone is the unique ranch house which once nestled there amidst a glorious garden and was Robert Horton's beloved home for some forty years.[13]

Though he never returned to his home, and he knew it had been sold, Robert Horton never learned its ultimate fate. In November 2015, around Thanksgiving, he fell again, breaking his left hip. Once again he was hospitalized, this time at the Sherman Oaks Rehabilitation Center, and his visitors were principally K. M. and-Fredricksen. Marilynn stopped by for a few minutes once or twice a week, to check on his status, as both K. M. and Fredricksen witnessed. None of his family visited him. Their reasons were their own, but he felt their absence deeply.[14]

Early in 2016, he was moved from the rehab center to hospice care. Some weeks later he refused feeding care. He died on Wednesday, March 9, 2016, in the morning. No-one was with him but Eugenia Fredricksen.[15]

K.M. learned of his passing from Fredricksen. She was living many hours' drive from Encino. Grief stricken and broken-hearted, she was comforted by her husband. Marilynn Horton also called her and K.M. said that their exchange was brief but kind.[16]

According to his own wishes, his body was cremated and his ashes interred in the Rose Garden of the Hollywood Forever Cemetery on April 22, forty-four days after his death. The details were carried out by the Neptune Society. There was no funeral, again, on Robert Horton's own instructions, but the cemetery records are quite clear that one Robert Howard Horton's remains were "scattered" in the Rose Garden on that date. In fact, "scattering" is a misnomer; ashes are buried at least three feet deep. Now he is there, within sight of the famed "Hollywood" sign high up on the Griffith Park escarpment above Hollywood itself, in the company of friends such as Tyrone Power.[17]

There is no memorial to Robert Horton within the cemetery grounds although Robert's oldest nephew, Creighton, has latterly declared an interest in participating in creating a memorial to him. Perhaps this book will also, in some way, serve that purpose.

To the hundreds and thousands of his fans and admirers, a memorial would be more than fitting, and indeed, it would be a travesty if his shining talents were to be forgotten. Not just his talents; his endless struggle to be himself, to be recognized for who he was, to be accepted and loved simply for that. Without a doubt, it was his mother's rejection which set him on the path to prove himself worthy of her love and affection. If she felt his love, it seems she never adequately showed it, and he never adequately felt hers. To this day there are legions of his admirers who long to know more about him. To this day he is loved and venerated by those he touched the most, from the "joy" of his life, to the very least of his fans.

~~~~~~~~~~~~~~~~~~

# EPILOGUE

Throughout his life, Robert Horton was an enigma, and his legacy is no less so. After years of hard work and dedication to learning the art of acting, he finally burst on the entertainment scene like a super nova in 1957, and his star burned brightly for five unforgettable years. Its light slowly diminished when he left *Wagon Train* and went on to a career within the musical theater. The ups and downs of the mid-to-late Sixties were symptomatic of his inability to rekindle the flame, regardless of the reasons behind that inability. In later years he spoke of his enjoyment in theater life, of the rewards which live acting brought him, of the fact that he did not regret the path he chose in 1962, and followed, with some exceptions, until his career came to an end, by his own choice, when he retired at the age of sixty-five. Nevertheless, it is difficult to equate the brilliance of his success between 1957 and 1962 with what followed. Nothing which came after *Wagon Train* compared to the heady heights achieved over those five years. Had he been given just one major movie role in the Sixties, there is little doubt that he would have achieved star status to rank with any of the major players of his day. He was denied that opportunity, and he did what was left to him. His name remained a huge draw in local theaters around the country, because his *Wagon Train* fans came out in droves to see their hero in the flesh. Only then did they discover the depth and breadth of his formidable talents. None of it was enough, tragically, to overcome the barriers placed in his way by Hollywood's implacable blacklisting. How much of that was due to the Wasserman influence and how much was due to Horton's own determination to forge his own career in his own fashion, and his belief that he wielded the power to do so is impossible now to say. How Robert Horton truly felt about how his life evolved will never be known, though in his sixties he did say to one journalist that his career had not been all he had anticipated, but that he had, on reflection, done everything he wanted to do. In his late eighties he said, significantly, that he could have been bigger than Robert Redford.[1] Facts, however, are facts. At one time, and for a good number of years, he was the hottest thing in the entertainment business. When he chose to turn his back on *Wagon Train,* Flint McCullough, Revue Studios and MCA, he never again achieved the star status he had enjoyed in those years. Latterly he spoke of his satisfaction with his career, and his life, but the truth is, it might have been even greater. In the end, his decision to move away from the television series which made his name, to spread his wings in more demanding and versatile ways says much for his character and dedication to his art. Had he had the chance to prove himself on the big screen he would have made an indelible and unforgettable mark on the movie industry and his name would have ranked above all of his contemporaries and become one of the greats of all time. Finally, although he turned his back on the character he created in 1957, there can be little doubt that Flint McCullough was Robert Horton's alter ego. McCullough was all that was best within the man known as Uncle Howard to his family, all that was good in terms of his relationships. He personified everything that Robert Horton sought to be despite the inevitable flaws within his own human persona. Robert Horton, Meade Howard Horton, Jr., had no control over some of the influences which drove him. He always strove to be the better man. He should be remembered for that.

# NOTES

Acknowledgements.

1. Telephone conversation with the author, January 2017 and personal meeting, June 2, 2017.

2. *Scrapbook I*, Author's collection.

3. K.M. interviews, in person, by telephone and via emails, October 2016 – October 2019.

Notes: Part I Chapter 1.

1. *This Is Your Life*, NBC-TV, aired January 22, 1961. Interviews with family members and friends, innumerable articles citing the date over the course of his career.

2. "Secret Confessions", by Beverly Linet, *TV Star Parade*, April 1959.

3. Joan Evans interviews, in person, by telephone and via email, April 2016 – September 2018. All references to her in this chapter are from these interviews.

4. Joseph McMurrin's life is based on information derived from the Biographical Encyclopedia of the Church of Latter-day Saints compiled by Andrew Jensen and published in four volumes between 1901 and 1936.

5. Creighton Horton II interviews, by telephone and via emails, March 2019 – October 2019.

6. Joan Evans interviews, April 2016 – September 2018.

7. Creighton Horton II interviews, March 2019 – October 2019.

8. "From Horse Opera to Soap Opera" by John Genovese, *Soap Opera World*, October 1983.

9. Joan Evans interviews, April 2016 – September 2018.

10. "Miller Sends New Script to Horton," by Hedda Hopper, *Los Angeles Times, November 30, 1959.*

11. *This Is Your Life, NBC-TV, January 22, 1960. "Let Me Tell You About My Boy," by Alice L. Tildesley, TV Movie Screen, August 1961.* Joan Evans interviews, April 2016 – September 2018.


Notes: Part I Chapter 2

1. Joan Evans interviews, April 2016 – September 2018. All references to her in this chapter are from these interviews.

2. "Big Ego, Big Talent," by Robert Johnson, *Saturday Evening Post,* December 30, 1961.

3. Joan Evans interviews, April 2016 – September 2018.

4. "Bob Horton Fights For His Life," by Jane Ardmore, unidentified publication, Spring 1961. "Still Learning The Facts of Life," by Paul Denis, TV Illustrated, June 1958. "The Man Who Runs Uphill," by Jim Cooper, Screenland, May 1958. K.M. interviews, October 2016 – October 2020. Eugenia Fredricksen interviews, October 2017 – May 2019. Also, see Notes 13, 18 and 25 in this chapter.

5. Toby Wolfe interviews, in person, by telephone and via email, May 2016 – May 2018.

6. *This Is Your Life*, NBC-TV, aired January 22, 1960. "Let Me Tell You About My Boy," by Alice L. Tildesley, *TV Movie Screen*, August 1961. K.M. interviews, October 2016 – October 2019.

7. Joan Evans interviews, April 2016 – September 2018.

8. *Robert Horton - Life Story*, Fans Star Library #30, July 1959. "Case Study of a Rebel," by Joyce Gilbert, *TV Picture Life*, 1966.

9. "In Defense of Westerns and Private Eyes," by Jim Morse, *unidentified publication*, c. 1959.

10. "What Women Have Done For Me," by Vi Swisher, *Silverscreen*, October, 1959. K.M. interviews, October 2016 – October 2019.

11. *Robert Horton Life Story*, Mirabelle Magazine, March 9, 1959. *Robert Horton – Story of a Great Star*, by J. M. Nolan, Charles Publications, 1959. Robert Horton - Life Story, Fans Star Library #30, July 1959.

12. USCG records, *Enlistment Contract, Report of Physical Examination and Induction*, February 5, 1943.

13. K.M. interviews, October 2016 – October 2019. Toby Wolfe interviews, May 2016 – May 2018. See also Notes 17, 22 and 23.

14. Creighton Horton II interviews, March 2019 – October 2019.

15. Toby Wolfe interviews, May 2016 – May 2018.

16. "Still Learning The Facts of Life," by Paul Denis, *TV Illustrated*, June 1958. "Bob Horton Fights For His Life," by Jane Ardmore, *unidentified publication*, 1961. "Case Study of a Rebel," by Joyce Gilbert, *TV Picture Life*, March 1966.

17. Toby Wolfe interviews, May 2016 – May 2018.

18. K.M. interviews, October 2016 – October 2019. "The Man Who Steals Your Heart," *TV Year Book*, c. 1958.

19. K.M. interviews, October 2016 – October 2019. Eugenia Fredricksen interviews, October 2017 – May 2019.

20. USCG records, *Enlisted Personnel Qualification Card.*

21. "Flaming Rebel," by Dolores Diamond, *TV Star Parade*, 1958. "One Man Crusade," *Movieland*, February 1958. Eugenia Fredricksen interviews, October 2017 – May 2019.

22. "Those Mixed-Up Years Are Over," by Peter Day, *Picturegoer*, June 13, 1959. "Secret Confessions," by Beverly Linet, *TV Star Parade*, April 1959. "Flaming Rebel," by Dolores Diamond, *TV Star Parade*, 1958. Eugenia Fredricksen interviews, October 2017 – May 2019.

23. Joan Evans, meetings in person, September 11, 2018. Papers, photos and documents she shared with me at that time.

24. "Miller Sends New Script To Horton," by Hedda Hopper, *Los Angeles Times*, November 30, 1959.

25. Joan Evans interviews, April 2016 – September 2018.

26. Creighton Horton II interviews, March 2019 – October 2019.

Notes: Part I Chapter 3

1. "Case Study of a Rebel," by Joyce Gilbert, *TV Picture Life*, March 1966.
2. Joan Evans interviews, April 2016 – September 2018.
3. "Those Mixed-Up Years Are Over," by Peter Day, *Picturegoer*, June 13, 1959. Joan Evans interviews, April 2016 – September 2018. Eugenia Fredricksen interviews, October 2017 – May 2019.
4. "Everybody At Home Was Picking On Me," by Robert Horton (ghost-written), *Photoplay*, February 1959.
5. "Those Mixed Up Years Are Over," by Peter Day, *Picturegoer*, June 13, 1959.
6. "Everybody At Home Was Picking On Me," by Robert Horton (ghost-written), *Photoplay*, February, 1959.
7. Eugenia Fredricksen interviews, October 2017 – May 2019.
8. "Everybody At Home Was Picking On Me," by Robert Horton (ghost-written), *Photoplay*, February 1959.
9. "Alone In A Honeymoon Cottage," by Lee Goff, *TV and Movie Screen*, April 1960.
10. "Bob Horton," *TV and Movie Screen*, June 1960. "What Women Have Done For Me," by Vi Swisher, *Silver Screen*, October 1959.
11. Robert Horton, excerpts from letters written to his mother, dated August 26, 1943 and a second, undated, but probably early September 1943.
12. "Bob Horton Fights For His Life," by Jane Ardmore, *unidentified publication*, 1962.
13. Toby Wolfe interviews, May 2016 – May 2018.

Notes: Part II Chapter 4

1. Harvard School for Boys, Harvard – Westlake School, Wikipedia History. Meeting with Allan Sasaki, School Archivist (now retired), June 5, 2017.
2. *Sentinel Yearbook*, 1942.
3. *Sentinel Yearbook*, 1942. All quotes in this chapter are from *The Sentinel Yearbook*, 1942.
4. Meeting with Harvard-Westlake school archivist Allan Sasaki, June 3, 2017.
5. *This Is Your Life*, NBC, aired January 22, 1961.
6. *Sentinel Yearbook*, 1942.
7. USCG records, *N.C.S. Form No 2719*, January 1943.
8. Joan Evans interviews, April 2016 – September 2018.
9. Creighton Horton II interviews, March 2019 – October 2019.

Notes: Part II Chapter 5

1. Joan Evans interviews, April 2016 – September 2018.
2. *Robert Horton – Story of a Great Star*, by J.M. Nolan, Charlton Publications, London & Liverpool, c. 1959 – 1960. *Burris Scrapbook*, "Robert Horton," *Stardom*, October 1960.
3. USCG records, *Report of Physical Examination and Induction*, February 5, 1943.
4. USCG records, *Enlistment Contract, USCG Orders*, March 17, 1943.

5. "Big Ego, Big Talent," by Robert Johnson, *Saturday Evening Post*, December 30, 1961.
6. Joan Evans interviews, April 2016 – September 2018.
7. Eugenia Fredricksen interviews, October 2017 – May 2019.
8. "Big Ego, Big Talent," by Robert Johnson, *Saturday Evening Post*, December 30, 1961.
9. K.M. interviews, October 2016 – October 2019. Eugenia Fredricksen interviews, October 2017 – May 2019.
10. USCG records, *Application for National Service Life Insurance.*
11. USCG records, *USCG Enlisted Personnel Qualification Card.*
12. USCG Cutter History, *USCGC Shawnee*, 1922, WAT-54.
13. Eugenia Fredricksen interviews, October 2017 – May 2019.
14. USCG records, *Return Medical Certificate*, October 28, 1943.
15. USCG records, *Final Medical Certificate*, March 16, 1944.
16. Joan Evans interviews, April 2016 – September 2018.
17. Robert Horton, *Memphis Film Festival*, panel appearance, 1998.

Notes: Part II Chapter 6

1. USCG records, *Report of the Medical Survey*, March 9, 1944 with 4 endorsements dated March 22 through March 29, 1944. *USCG HQ Medical Office Recommendation*, March 29, 1944. *DCGO, 12th Naval District, Board of Survey Recommendation*, May 25, 1944. *Honorable Discharge Certificate*, June 22, 1944.
2. USCG records, *Honorable Discharge*, June 22, 1944.
3. "Bob Horton Fights For His Life," by Jane Ardmore, *unidentified publication*, 1962.
4. "Still Learning The Facts of Life," by Paul Denis, *TV Illustrated*, June 1958.
5. Creighton Horton II interviews, March 2019 – October 2019.
6. "Making A Business of Success," by Hedda Hopper, *Syndicated, St. Louis Globe Journal*, January 18, 1959.
7. SAG-AFTRA Membership Records.
8. *A Walk in the Sun*, uncut version, author's copy.
9. "Big Ego, Big Talent," by Robert Johnson, *Saturday Evening Post*, December 30, 1961. "What My Wife Does For Me," *Movieland and TV Time*, September, 1966
10. Robert Horton, *Memphis Film Festival*, panel discussion,1998.
11. Robert Horton's *Scrapbook II*, playbill, photos, unidentified reviews.
12. K.M. interviews, October 2016 – October 2019.
13. Eugenia Fredricksen interviews, October 2017 – May 2019.
14. Creighton Horton II interviews, March 2019 – October 2019.

Notes: Part III Chapter 7

1. Robert Horton's *Scrapbook II*, "The Musical Laboratory" by Jay Farber, *unidentified publication* c. 1947. Robert Horton's handwritten notes beside unidentified clippings and photographs.

2. "Still Learning The Facts of Life," by Paul Denis, *TV Illustrated,* June 1958, an observation repeated in more than a score of articles too numerous to mention.
3. Joan Evans interviews, April 2016 – September 2018.
4. Joan Evans interviews, April 2016 – September 2018.
5. Joan Evans interviews, April 2016 – September 2018. Creighton Horton II interviews, March 2019 – October 2019.
6. "I Wish I Could Fall In Love," by Ruth Covington, *TV Star Parade,* c. 1958/59. "Flaming Rebel," by Dolores Diamond, *TV Star Parade, 1958.* "*Robert Horton: From the UM to Stardom,*" *by Frances Swaebley, Miami Herald, Sunday, March 29, 1970.*
7. Robert Horton, *Memphis Film Festival,* panel discussion, 1998.
8. "Why My Marriage Failed,"as told by Robert Horton, *TV and Movie Screen,* May 1958.
9. Robert Horton's *Scrapbook I, Now – The Photo Magazine of Fashion Miami Beach and Great Miami,* Front Cover February 16, 1947. Robert Horton's *Scrapbook II.* "The Musical Laboratory," by Jay Farber, *unidentified publication,*c. 1947.
10 "Why My Marriage Failed," as told by Robert Horton,*TV and Movie Screen,* May 1958.
11. "Robert Horton: From the UM to Stardom" by Frances Swaebley, *Miami Herald, Sunday March 29, 1970.*
12. Toby Wolfe interviews, May 2016 – May 2018.
13. Marvin, Betty, *Tales of a Hollywood Housewife – A Memoir of the first Mrs. Lee Marvin,*New York, NY, iUniverse, 2011, p. 23, p. 24, p. 35.
14. Robert Horton, Dwayne Epstein interview, July 8, 1995. Epstein, Dwayne, *Lee Marvin – Point Blank,* Schaffner Press, Inc., Tucson, AZ, 2013.
15. Meeting with Betty Marvin in Santa Barbara, June 6, 2017.
16. Letters to Robert Horton: From Nolan Harrigan in Long Island, February 11, 1950. From Barry Lundin in New Jersey, February 28, 1950.
17. Robert Horton's *UCLA Graduation Diploma,* August 13, 1949, Author's Collection.
18. Robert Horton's *Certificate of Honors in Theater Arts.* August 13, 1949, Author's Collection.
19. "Wagon Train Hero Is An Intellectual," by Harriet Van Horne, *Washington News (syndicated),* December 8, 1958.
20. Robert Horton's *Scrapbook II* letters. "The Robert Horton Story,"*TV Times (UK),* February 1959. *This Is Your Life,* NBC, aired January 22, 1961.

Notes: Part III Chapter 8
1. Robert Horton's letter to his parents, April 24, 1950. "Bad Luck Couldn't Stop Him," by Sara Lou Harris, *TV and Movie Screen,* c. 1958.
2. "The Robert Horton Story," *TV Times (UK),* February 1959.
3. Robert Horton's *Scrapbook II,* telegram.
4. Robert Horton's *Scrapbook II,* unidentified news clippings re: *Born Yesterday* opening, *Born Yesterday* playbill.
5. Margie Hart, Wikipedia biography and obituary.
6. Margie Hart Obituary.

7. Robert Horton's *Scrapbook II*, unidentified reviews.
8. "On Surreys and Wagon Trains," by Charlotte Phelan, *The Houston Post*, Sunday, June 23, 1968.
9. Betty Marvin's emails to the author, May 2016 – June 2016.

Notes: Part III Chapter 9
1. "TV Close-Up – Robert Horton," by Gwen Carroll, *Movie Mirror*, September 1959.
2. Robert Horton's *Red Book*, movie review clipping, unidentified publication, undated.
3. Joan Evans interviews, April 2016 – September 2018. Eugenia Fredricksen interviews, October 2017 – May 2019.
4. Robert Horton's *Red Book*, Letter from Paul Small of Paul Small Artists, Ltd., February 18, 1952.
5. Robert Horton's *Red Book*, Letter from *MGM* Pictures, February 16, 1952. "TV Close-Up – Robert Horton," by Gwen Carroll, *Movie Mirror*, September 1959.
6. "Little Devil – Robert Horton,"*Hollywood Life Stories*, 1959. "Housewarming!" *Modern Screen*, October 1952.
7. Movie details throughout this chapter were researched through Wikipedia and IMDb records.
8. "Actress Barbara Ruick Files Suit For Divorce" clipping, c. August 1955. "Why My Marriage Failed," by Robert Horton, *TV Movie Screen*, May 1959.
9. Joan Evans interviews, April 2016 – September 2018. K.M. interviews, October 2016 – October 2019.
10. Robert Horton, *Memphis Film Festival*, panel discussion, 1998. K.M. interviews, October 2016 – October 2019. "After 30 Years in Show Biz, ROBERT HORTON is Still Going Strong," by Micki Siegel, Freelance writer, *unidentified TV Guide*, 1983.
11. Robert Horton's *Red Book, Variety*, November 5, 1952.
12. Robert Horton, KSAV Radio interview with Boyd Magers, September 18, 2007.
13. Robert Horton's *Red Book*, Letter to Robert from Dore Schary, February 10, 1953.
14. David Ritter interview, July 2, 2016. "Robert Horton," by Janette Hyem, *TV Scene (UK)* 1989.

Notes: Part III Chapter 10
1. "Flaming Rebel," by Dolores Diamond, *TV Star Parade*, April 1958.
2. Barbara Ruick biographies,Wikipedia, IMDb.
3. Lurene Tuttle biographies,Wikipedia, IMDb.
4. "Why My Marriage Failed," by Robert Horton, *TV Movie Screen*, May 1959.
5. Details regarding *Men of the Fighting Lady* and all other references and statistics concerning Robert Horton's movies throughout this chapter were researched through Wikipedia and IMDb.
6. *USS Oriskany*, Wikipedia.

7. Robert Horton's *Red Book,* unidentified newspaper clipping review, "Robert Horton Latest in Panther Squadron" (working title for *Men of the Fighting Lady* during filming).

8. Robert Horton's *Red Book,* unidentified newspaper clippings of *Men of the Fighting Lady* and *Prisoner of War* reviews.

9. Robert Horton, *Memphis Film Festival,* panel appearance, 1998.

10. Author's collection.

11. "Westward Ho – Mr. Horton," *TV Guide,* August 18 -22, 1958.

12. "Why My Marriage Failed," by Robert Horton, *TV Movie Screen,* May 1959.

13. "Westward Ho – Mr. Horton," *TV Guide,* August 18 -22, 1958.

14. "Westward Ho – Mr. Horton," *TV Guide,* August 18 -22, 1958. "I Like Women," *Stardom,* 1959.

15. "Perfectly Wonderful – Miserably Awful - What It's Like To Date Bob Horton," by Beverly Linet, *TV Star Parade,* December 1958.

16. Lou Valentino interviews, March 2016 – June 2016.

17. "What Women Have Done For Me," by Vi Swisher, *Silverscreen,* October 1959.

18. "Actress Barbara Ruick Files Suit For Divorce," *unidentified,* August, 1955.

19. Barbara Ruick biographies, Wikipedia, IMDb.

20. "Why My Marriage Failed," by Robert Horton, *TV Movie Screen,* May 1959.

21. "Westward Ho – Mr. Horton," *TV Guide,* August 18 – 22, 1958.

22. *Republic Pictures,* Wikipedia, IMDb.

23. Creighton Horton II interviews, March 2019 – October 2019.

24. Joan Evans interviews. April 2016 – September 2018.

25. Inger Stevens biographies, Wikipedia, IMDb.

26. "Still Learning The Facts of Life," by Paul Denis, *TV Illustrated,* June 1958.

27. K.M. interviews, October 2016 – October 2019.


Notes: Part IV Chapter 11

1. Toby Wolfe interviews, May 2016 – May 2018

2. "My Trouble With Women," by Helen Martin, *unidentified publication,* c. 1958.

3. "On All Channels," by Dave Kauffman, *Variety,* June 21, 1957.

4. "Bad Luck Couldn't Stop Him," by Sara Lou Harris, *TV & Movie Screen,* c. 1958.

5. "Robert Horton," From The UM To Stardom," by Frances Swaebly, Drama Editor, *The Miami Herald,* Sunday March 29, 1970.

6. "Westward Ho Mr. Horton," *TV Guide,* September 16 – 22, 1958.

7. *Mr. and Mrs. Hollywood – Edie and Lew Wasserman and Their Entertainment Empire,* by Kathleen Sharp, Carroll & Graf Publishers, NY, 2003.

8. "Horton Scouts TV Dramatic Trends," by Forrest Powers, Staff Writer, *The Minneapolis Star,* Wednesday, February 26, 1958.

9. "Making A Business Of Success," by Hedda Hopper, *Syndicated, St. Louis Globe Democrat,* Sunday, January 18, 1959.

10. Robert Horton, *Memphis Film Festival* panel appearance, 1998.

11. "Politely Stubborn," by Joe Hyams, *TV Guide,* 1958.

12. Untitled Press Release, *TV Illustrated*, March 2, 1958.

13. "By The Method," *The Courier Journal*, February 22, 1959.

14. "Wagon Train and Gunsmoke Vying For Top Honors," *TV Scene, Los Angeles Times*, January 2, 1959. "NBC's Wagon Train Rolled Within 4.2 of Gunsmoke's 44.3.," *Variety*, January 13, 1959. Nielsen Ratings, *Wagon Train*, 38.31, *Gunsmoke*, 36.4, *The Hollywood Reporter*, March 2, 1959. "Wagon Train #1 in Neilsen Ratings," *TV World*, August 1959.

15. Robert Horton, *Memphis Film Festival* panel appearance, 1998.

16. "Bob Horton Will Gross Close To $100,000 On Rodeo Dates Alone This Year," *Los Angeles Examiner*, March 11, 1960.

17. Robert Horton, *Memphis Film Festival* panel appearance, 1998.

18. Toby Wolfe interviews, May 2016 – May 2018.

19. "Wagon Train Co-Star Hard Driving Actor," *unidentified publication*, March 1958.

20. "Making A Business Of Success," by Hedda Hopper, *Syndicated, St. Louis Globe Democrat*, Sunday, January 18, 1959.

21. "Bob Horton Is Happy To Miss Some Trail Rides," by Erskine Johnson, *unidentified publication*, December 8, 1959.

22. *Robert Horton. Story of a Great Star*, by J. M Nolan, Charles Publications (UK), 1959.

23. Eugenia Fredricksen interviews, October 2017 – May 2019.

24. *The Desert Sun*, Palm Springs, February 12, 1959.

25. "Wig Solves Pony Problem," *Lewiston Morning News*, September 1959.

Notes: Part IV Chapter 12

1. James Rosin, *Wagon Train – The Television Series*, Philadelphia, PA: The Autumn Road Company, 2008.

2. Eugenia Fredricksen interviews, October 2017 – May 2019.

3. "Seeing Things," by Hal Humphrey, TV-Radio Editor, *Los Angeles Mirror News*, Monday, May 19, 1958.

4. Nina Foch biography, Wikipedia, IMDb.

5. *TV Movie Scene*, May 1959.

6. Toby Wolfe interviews, May 2016 – May 2018.

7. Eugenia Fredricksen interviews, October 2017 – May 2019.

8. Eugenia Fredricksen interviews, October 2017 – May 2019.

9. Lou Valentino interviews, March – June 2016.

10. "After Thirty Years in Show Biz ROBERT HORTON Is Still Going Strong," by Micki Seigel, NY Freelance writer, *unidentified TV Guide Publication*, c. 1983.

11. Nina Foch Biography, Wikipedia, IMDb.

12. "Entertainment," by Hedda Hopper, *Los Angeles Times*, Saturday, November 22, 1958.

Notes: Part IV Chapter 13

1. Telegram from Piper pilot Don Hart in Lockhaven, PA to Robert Horton at the Terrace Hilton Hotel, Cincinnati on May 15, 1959.

2. "Western TV Stars Pose Problem For Reporter," by Clara Neal, Editor, *Kiowa County Star-Review*, Thursday, June 4, 1959.

3. Joan Evans interviews, April 2016 – September 2018.

4. "Nervous About Flying..." by Harrison Carroll, *Los Angeles Herald and Express*, January 4, 1961.

5. *There's a Girl in My Soup*, playbill profile, J. Pellman Theatre, c. mid-1970s.

6. "Target For Cowboy Horton: A Role In Musical Comedy," by Walter Blum, *TV Log, San Francisco Examiner*, Sunday, October 22, 1961.

7. "Bob Horton Is Happy To Miss Some Trail Rides," by Erskine Johnson, *unidentified publication*, December 8, 1959.

8. Val Parnell, impresario, Wikipedia, IMDb.

9. "Robert Horton...has been offered the highest price ever paid a TV star in England. .." by Charles Denton, *Los Angeles Examiner*, November 20, 1959. "Bob Horton received top salary for the Christmas Show..."*Hollywood Today*, With Sheilah Graham, December 30, 1959.

10. "After Thirty Years in Show Biz ROBERT HORTON Is Still Going Strong," by Micki Seigel, NY Freelance writer, *unidentified TV Guide Publication*, c. 1983.

11. "Entertainment," by Hedda Hopper, *Los Angeles Times*, December 10, 1959.

12. "The Awful Truth About Bob Horton," by Bethel Avery, *Movie Life*, July 1959.

13. Creighton Horton II interviews, March 2019 – October 2019.

Notes: Part V Chapter 14

1. *Grand National Livestock Exposition Horse Show and Rodeo*, Program Star Profile, October 27 – November 5, 1961.

2. "The Bitterest Fight..." by Louella Parsons, *Los Angeles Examiner*, October 10, 1960.

3. "Horton Has Bigger Plans,"*Los Angeles Examiner*, March 23, 1961.

4. *Los Angeles Herald*, February 2, 1960. *Hollywood Reporter*, February 5, 1960.

5. Toby Wolfe interviews, May 2016 – May 2018. Eugenia Fredricksen interviews, October 2017 – May 2019.

6. "Why Husbands Hate Horton," by Chris Collins, *unidentified publication*, c. mid-1960.

7. "Big Ego, Big Talent," by Robert Johnson, *Saturday Evening Post*, December 31, 1961.

8. "Hollywood Tie-Line," by Ruth Waterbury, *TV Channels*, Week of November 27, 1960.

9. "Where Does Wagon Train Head Now?" by Charles Denton, *Los Angeles Examiner*, November 1960. "Wagon Master Bond's Curtain Speech to Co-Star," by Bob Thomas, *Des Moines Sunday Register*, December 18, 1960. "Train Without A Master," by Vernon Scott, *Pittsburgh Press*, December 11, 1960.

10. Robert Horton, *Memphis Film Festival*, panel appearance, 1998.

Notes: Part V Chapter 15

1. "Why My Marriage Failed," by Robert Horton, *TV & Movie Screen*, May 1959.

2. "My Wife, My Love, My Friend," by Jack Canavan, *TV Picture Life,* May 1961.

3. "Entertainment," by Hedda Hopper, *Los Angeles Times,* May 11, 1959. "Robert Horton's Legit Appearance. . . ", *Variety,* June 29, 1959.

4. *Ancestry,* Harry Bladd, Fae Bladd. Toby Wolfe interviews, May 2016 – May 2018. "This Time It's For Keeps," by Ivy Cranford, *TV Screen Life,* Fall, 1960.

5. Norwood Smith biography, Wikipedia, IMDb.

6. Robert Horton, *Knoxville Film Festival,* panel appearance, April 1996. "Bob Horton of '110 in Shade' Rides Home To West Roxbury Wife," by Ward Morehouse, *unidentified Boston publication,* September, 1963. *Brigadoon* playbill profile, St Paul Civic Opera, 1976.

7. "Celebrating The Divorce," *Movie Life,* November, 1960. "Why I Married Bob Horton – Star's Bride Tells Story," *TV Week,* February 8 – 14, 1961.

8. Robert Horton, *Knoxville Western Film Festival,* panel appearance, April 1996.

9. "Why Husbands Hate Horton," by Chris Collins, *unidentified publication,* c. mid-1960.

10. "Keep An Eye On Bob Horton and Marilynn Bradley," by Harrison Carroll, *Los Angeles Herald and Express,* May 4, 1960.

11. "I Want A Girl I Can Chase," as told by Robert Horton, *TV Picture Life,* March 1959.

12. Toby Wolfe interviews, May 2016 – May 2018.

13. Stephen Bladd biography, Wikipedia, IMDb.

14. "Why Husbands Hate Horton," by Chris Collins, *unidentified publication,* c. mid-1960.

15. "Little femme influence there, Bobbo?" *Los Angeles Examiner,* July 19, 1960. Untitled, *Valley Times Today,* by Rich Allen, July 1961.

16. "Bob Horton – Marilyn *[sic]* Bradley," *TV Picture Life,* February 1961.

17. "Bond's Death Halts Horton's Nuptial Plan," by Charles Denton, *Los Angeles Examiner,* November 18, 1960.

18. "Bob Horton Says That Marilynn Bradley Wants To Be Married in Boston," by Harrison Carroll, *Los Angeles Herald and Express,* December 13, 1960.

19. "Nervous About Flying. . ." by Harrison Carroll, *Los Angeles Herald and Express,* January 4, 1961.

20. "Filmland New Year Sad and Glad," by Louella Parsons, *Los Angeles Examiner,* December 30, 1960.

21. *Burris Scrapbook,* unidentified, undated clipping.

22. "My Wife, My Love, My Friend," by Jack Canavan, *TV Picture Life,* May 1961.

23. Joan Evans interviews, April 2016 – September 2018.

24. "Robert Horton: The Night His Bride Fooled Him," by Paul Denis, *TV Picture Life,* May 1961.

25. Creighton Horton II interviews, March 2019 – October 2019.

26. Joan Evans interviews, April 2016 – September 2018.

Notes: Part V Chapter 16

1. James Rosin, *Wagon Train – The Television Series,* Philadelphia, PA: The Autumn Road Company, 2008, p. 44.

2. "Duryea For Wagon Train?"*unidentified publication,* November 11, 1960. "No, Borgnine is NOT replacing Ward Bond..." by Army Archerd, *Variety,* November 14, 1960.

3. James Rosin,*Wagon Train – The Television Series,* Philadelphia, PA: The Autumn Road Company, 2008, p. 45.

4. "In The Air" with Hank Grant, *The Hollywood Reporter,* September 15, 1961.

5. "Wagon Train in $20,000.000 Deal, Switching from NBC to ABC Next Year," *Variety,* October 25, 1961. "Horton Leaving Wagon Train," by John David Griffin, *New York Mirror,* February 8, 1962.

6. Robert Horton, *Memphis Film Festival,* 1998. "Wagon Train tops the charts and according to *Screen World & TV* that's due to Robert Horton's 'derringdo'..." July 1960.

7. "Horton Betting Five Million On Himself," by Charles Denton, *Los Angeles Examiner,* August 28, 1961.

8. Toby Wolfe interviews, May 2016 – May 2018.

9. "Light and Airy" by Jack Hellman, *Variety,* April 24, 1961. "Robert Horton Faces New TV Show With Realistic Confidence," by Margaret McManus, *Sunday News,* 1963.

10. "Horton Betting Five Million On Himself," by Charles Denton, *Los Angeles Examiner,* August 28, 1961.

11. "Robert Horton Forms Production Company,"*Filmland Events,* June 22, 1961.

12. "Marilynn Boils My Bear," by Charlotte Dintner, *TV Radio Mirror,* April 1962. Toby Wolfe interviews, May 2016 – May 2018.

13. "Two Bobs (Kintner & Horton) Cook TV Plot; Wagon Train Star Stays At NBC, Will Compete Against Show,"*Variety,* February 7, 1962. "Bob Horton Expands On His New NBC Deal,"*unidentified publication,* February 9, 1962.

14. "Bob Horton Wants To Sing, Act & Mebbe Even Produce for NBC,"*Variety,* February 28, 1962.

15. "Bob Horton Is Not Happy..." by Shielah Graham, *The Citizen-News,* Wednesday, August 23, 1961.

16. "Robert Horton, NBC-TV Call Off Exclusive Pact,"*Variety,* October 1962.


Notes: Part VI Chapter 17

1. "Horton Plays Homicidal Handyman at Drury Lane..." "On The Aisle" by Claudia Cassidy, *unidentified publication,* May, 1962.

2. "Horton and Wife Star in Charlotte," "The Hortons Charming Actors," by Evelyn Roberts, *Independent Special* Writer, undated. "Singing Good; Music Good," by Emery Wister, News Staff Writer, undated.

3. "Wagon Train Hero Takes Big Chance," by Hedda Hopper, *Los Angeles Times,* May 22, 1962.

4. Robert Horton's *Red Book,* Gower Champion telegram. Unidentified clipping, *Red Book.* Gower Champion biography,Wikipedia, IMDb.

5. Gene Lees, *The Musical Worlds of Lerner and Loewe*, University of Nebraska Press, 1991.
6. Robert Horton's *Red Book*, letters to Robert Horton from Ashley Steiner and CBS, March 1963.
7. "Robert Horton Set For 4 Legit Stints," *Variety*, February 26, 1963.
8. Gene Lees, *The Musical Worlds of Lerner and Loewe*. Lincoln, NE: University of Nebraska Press, 1991.
9. Gene Lees, *The Musical Worlds of Lerner and Loewe*. Lincoln, NE: University of Nebraska Press, 1991.


Notes: Part VI Chapter 18

1. Gene Lees, *The Musical Worlds of Lerner and Loewe*. Lincoln, NE: University of Nebraska Press, 1991.
2. "Horton Sings Way To Broadway," by Wayne Robinson, *The Sunday Bulletin (Philadelphia)* Sunday, October 6, 1963.
3. "Merrick Gets Horton For '110 in the Shade," by Lee Silver, *Unidentified, undated publication.*
4. Inga Swenson biography, Wikipedia, IMDb, *110 in the Shade* profile.
5. Stephen Douglass biography, Wikipedia, IMDb, *110 in the Shade* profile.
6. Agnes deMille biography, Wikipedia, IMDb, *110 in the Shade* profile.
7. David Merrick biography, Wikipedia, IMDb, *110 in the Shade* profile.
8. Harvey Schmidt and Tom Jones biographies, Wikipedia, IMDb, *110 in the Shade* profile.
9. All the cables and telegrams quoted in this chapter are part of Robert Horton's *Red Book* collection.
10. Eugenia Fredricksen interviews, October 2017 – May 2019. Toby Wolfe interviews, May 2016 – May 2018.
11. Letter from Inga Swenson Harris, May 11, 2016.
12. Toby Wolfe interviews, May 2016 – May 2018.
13. "'Shade' Stars Will Sing At Banshees," *New York Journal-American*, Tuesday, March 31, 1964. Inga Swenson biographies.


Notes: Part VII Chapter 19

1. "TV Madness," by Bill Davidson, *Saturday Evening Post,* March 26, 1966.
2. Unidentified clipping, *Burris Scrapbook*, Summer 1962. "Stage Role Given To Robert Horton," by Louis Calta, *The New York Times*, Saturday, October 27, 1962.
3. "Must A Childless Marriage Be Lonely?" by Paul Denis, *TV Mirror*, September 1966. Joan Evans interviews, April 2016 – September 2018.
4. "Bob Likes New York," by Shielah Graham, *Syndicated*, Hollywood, Spring 1964.
5. "You Name It, Horton's Done It," by Bette Markus, Television Editor, *unidentified publication*, c 1971.
6. Tommy Henriech biography, Wikipedia.
7. Robert Horton, *Memphis Film Festival*, panel appearance, 1998.

8. *Mr. and Mrs. Hollywood – Edie and Lew Wasserman and Their Entertainment Empire,* by Kathleen Sharp, Carroll & Graf Publishers, NY, 2003. Eugenia Fredricksen interviews, October 2017 – May 2019.

9. Robert Horton, *Memphis Film Festival,* panel appearance, 1998.

10. Robert Horton, *Memphis Film Festival,* panel appearance, 1998.

11. Boyd Magers, *A Gathering of Guns,* Western Clippings, Albuquerque, NM, 2017. Everett Aaker, *Television Western Players of the Fifties,* Jefferson, NC: McFarland, 1997.

12. "Bob Horton's Wife Tells How She succeeded Where Three Others Failed," *unidentified publication,* c. 1966. *Burris Scrapbook,*unidentified, undated clipping.

13. Robert Horton, *16th Annual Film Festival,* Grand Finale Panel, Charlotte, NC, 1993.

14. Creighton Horton II interviews, March 2019 – October 2019.

15. "I Want Love – Not An Affair," by Bill Tusher, *TV Picture Life,* c. 1960.

16. James Rosin, *Wagon Train – The Television Series,* Philadelphia, PA: The Autumn Road Company, 2008, p. 48.

17. Robert Horton, Dwayne Epstein interview, July 8, 1995.

18. KM interviews, October 2016 – October 2019.


Notes. Part VII Chapter 20

1. "Life of Variety for Bob Horton," *San Francisco Chronicle,* Friday, July 1, 1966.

2. Toby Wolfe interviews, May 2016 – May 2018.

3. Ross Yockey, *New Orleans States,* June 17, 1967.

4. *Robert Horton Friend Club,* unidentified review quoted in the August 1967 edition.

5. K.M. interviews, October 2016 – October 2019.

6. Robert Horton, Brett Homenick interview, 2008.

7. Robert Horton, Brett Homenick interview, 2008.

8. Robert Horton, Dwayne Epstein interview, July 8, 1995.

9. *Robert Horton Friend Club* newsletter, August – September 1968.

10. Robert Horton, Golden Boot Award acceptance speech, 2004.

11. *Robert Horton Friend Club* newsletter, August – September 1968.

12. *Burris Scrapbook* clippings, unidentified but for the handwritten notation '1970'.

13. Joan Evans interviews, April 2016 – September 2018.

14. Creighton Horton II interviews, March 2019 – October 2019.


Notes: Part VII Chapter 21

1. "Robert Horton: Actor left the Hollywood trail for theatre, and has no regrets," by Glenn Lovell, *Knight News Service,* 1979.

2. "It Isn't 'Wagon Train' but Robert Horton Paces Entertaining Playhouse Comedy, "Under The Yum-Yum Tree," unidentified review, July 22, 1970.

3. Author's collection.

4. "How Not To Succeed If You're a Middle-Aged Romeo," by Dorothy Eagen, unidentified publication, July, 1972.

5. "Robert Horton: Actor left the Hollywood trail for theatre, and has no regrets," by Glenn Lovell, *Knight News Service*, 1979. Joan Evans interviews, April 2016 – September 2018. Toby Wolfe interviews, May 2016 – May 2018.

6. Author's collection.

7. "Amarillo Little Theatre Off To An Auspicious Start," *Burris Scrapbook*, unidentified clipping, September 1973.

8. Invitation to the White House in honor of the Emperor and Empress of Japan's visit, White Tie, Thursday evening, 10:00 pm, October 2, 1975.

9. Jan Shepard interview, June 6, 2017.


Notes: Part VIII Chapter 22

1. "After Thirty Years in Show Biz, ROBERT HORTON is Still Going Strong," by Micki Siegel, *unidentified TV Guide*, 1983.

2. Eileen Fulton biography, Wikipedia.

3. Peter Shaw biography, Wikipedia, IMDb. Angela Lansbury biography, Wikipedia, IMDb.

4. Robert Horton's contract with Century Artists Ltd., dated November 16, 1987, Author's collection.

5. Unidentified clipping, Author's collection.

6. Century Artists, Ltd., SDB Partners, Inc. Betty Marvin, *Tales of a Hollywood Housewife – A Memoir of the first Mrs. Lee Marvin*. New York, NY: iUniverse, 2011, p. 203.

7. Toby Wolfe interviews, May 2016 – May 2018. Numerous articles already cited quoting both Robert Horton and Marilynn Horton in regard to her approach to the business side of an acting career.

8. Toby Wolfe interviews, May 2016 – May 2018.

9. "Case Study of a Rebel," *TV Picture Life*, March 1966.

10. "After 30 Years in Show Biz, ROBERT HORTON is Still Going Strong," by Micki Siegel, New York Freelance Writer, *unidentified TV Guide*, 1983

11. K.M. interviews, October 2016 – October 2019.

12. Joan Evans interviews, April 2016 – September 2018.

13. K.M. interviews, October 2016 – October 2019.

14. K.M. interviews, October 2016 – September 2019.

15. Eugenia Fredricksen interviews, October 2017 – May 2019.


Notes: Part VIII Chapter 23

1. *Burris Scrapbook*, Denise Morris letters and clippings, April 1960, May 1962.

2. K. M. interviews, October 2016 – October 2019.

3. K. M. interviews, October 2016 – October 2019.


Notes: Part 1X Chapter 24

1. Boyd Magers interviews, May 20, 2017 (telephone) and in person, May 2018 – October 2019.

2. Boyd Magers interviews, May 20, 2017 (telephone) and in person, May 2018 – October 2019.
3. Jan Shepard interviews, in person, June 6, 2017, October 23, 2019.
4. Golden Boot Website, www.goldenbootawards.com.
5. Robert Horton Website, www.roberthorton.com.
6. 16th Annual Bison Homes Western Festival, March 18, 2006, Cowboy Spirit Award, author's collection.
7. Toby Wolfe interviews, May 2016 – May 2018.
8. Robert Horton Website, www.roberthorton.com.
9. *Fan Club* newsletters dating between January, 1961 and November 1968. USA.
10. *Fan Club* magazines dating between 1958 and 1961. International and UK Fan Club publications.
11. Toby Wolfe interviews, May 2016 – May 2018.
12. K.M. interviews, October 2016 – October 2019. Toby Wolfe interviews, May 2016 – May 2018.

Notes: Part IX Chapter 25
1. Steve Harbeson correspondence, November 2018 – December 2018.
2. Steve Harbeson correspondence, November 2018 – December 2018.
3. Toby Wolfe interviews, May 2016 – May 2018. Eugenia Fredricksen interviews, October 2017 – May 2019.
4. David Ritter interviews, July 2016 – July 2017.
5. Pony Express Sport Shop, Inc., Encino, CA, October 1981.
6. Creighton Horton II interviews, March 2019 – October 2019.
7. Barbara Hutchins interviews, May 2016 – May 2019.
8. K.M. interviews, October 2016 – October 2019.
9. Joan Evans interviews, April 2016 – September 2018. Meeting, September 11, 2018.
10. K.M. interviews, October 2016 – October 2019.
11. Toby Wolfe interviews, May 2016 – May 2018.
12. Joan Evans interviews, April 2016 – September 2018. Creighton Horton II interviews, March 2019 – October 2019.
13. Creighton Horton II interviews, March 2019 – October 2019.
14. Joan Evans interviews, April 2016 – September 2018.
15. Creighton Horton II interviews, March 2019 – October 2019.
16. Eugenia Fredricksen interviews, October 2017 – May 2019.
17. Toby Wolfe interviews, May 2016 – May 2018.
18. Eugenia Fredricksen interviews, October 2017 – May 2019.
19. Joan Evans interviews, April 2016 – September 2018.

Notes: Part IX Chapter 26
1. K.M. interviews, October 2016 – October 2019. Toby Wolfe interviews, May 2016 – May 2018. David Kestenbaum, Esq., telephone interview, March 2020.

2. K. M. interviews, October 2016 – October 2019. Toby Wolfe interviews, May 2016 – May 2018. Barbara Hutchins interviews, June 2016 – May 2019.

3. Eugenia Fredricksen interviews, October 2017 - May 2019.

4. K.M. interviews, October 2016 – October 2019.

5. Eugenia Fredricksen interviews, October 2017 - May 2019.

6. K. M. interviews, October 2016 - October 2019.

7. K. M. interviews, October 2016 - October 2019.

8. K. M. interviews, October 2016 - October 2019. Toby Wolfe interviews, May 2016 – May 2018.

9. K.M. interviews, October 2016 – October 2019. Eugenia Fredricksen interviews, October 2017 – May 2019. Toby Wolfe interviews, May 2016 – May 2018.

10. K.M. interviews, October 2016 – October 2019.

11. K.M. interviews, October 2016 – October 2019. Eugenia Fredricksen interviews, October 2017 – May 2019. Toby Wolfe interviews, May 2016 – May 2018.

12. Beverly Hills Estate Sales advertising "Sale of The Estate of Robert Horton," August 2015.

13. Joan Evans interviews, April 2016 – September 2018. Creighton Horton II interviews, March 2019 – October 2019. Author's research, contacting and meeting the builder concerned, personal visits to Andasol Avenue.

14. Eugenia Fredricksen interviews, October 2017 – May 2019. K.M. interviews, October 2016 – October 2019. Joan Evans interviews, April 2016 – September 2018. Creighton Horton II interviews, March 2019 – October 2019.

15. K.M. interviews, October 2016 – October 2019. Eugenia Fredricksen interviews, October 2017 – May 2019.

16. K.M. interviews, October 2016 – October 2019.

17. Author's research, telephone discussion with a representative of The Neptune Society which handled the burial, July 2016. Two personal visits to the Hollywood Forever Cemetery in January 2017 and June 2017 which involved two separate discussions with the cemetery director who confirmed the dates and internment details.


Notes: Epilogue.

1. Eugenia Fredricksen interviews, October 2017 – May 2019.

# BIBLIOGRAPHY

## INTERVIEWS and DISCUSSIONS.

Boxleitner, Bruce. Interview via telephone, September 26, 2016.

Epstein, Dwayne. Interview with Robert Horton, July 9, 1995. Shared in its entirety with the author.

Evans, Joan. Interviews and discussions by telephone, via email and in person. April 2016 – September 2018.

Fredricksen, Eugenia. Interviews and discussions via email. October 2017 – May 2019.

Homenick, Brett. Interview with Robert Horton, 2008. Shared in its entirety with the author.

Horton, Creighton. Interviews and discussions by telephone and via email. March 2019 – October 2019.

Horton, Marilynn. By telephone, January 2017 and in person, June 2, 2017.

Hovey, Theodore. Discussions via telephone and via email July and September 2016, and in person January and June 2017.

Hutchins, Barbara. Interviews and discussions by telephone, via email and in person. May 2016 – May 2019.

Kestenbaum, Esq., David. Interview and discussion via telephone, March 2020.

K. M. Interviews and discussions by telephone, via email and in person. October 2016 – October 2019.

Livyatan, Asi. Discussions via telephone, text and in person. February 2016 – June 2017.

Magers, Boyd. Interviews and discussions via telephone and in person. May 2017, May 2018, October 2019.

Marvin, Betty. Interviews and discussions via email, May and June 2016 and in person, June 6, 2017.

Ritter, David. Interviews and discussions by telephone and via email. July 2017 – July 2017.

Sasaki, Allan. Discussion via telephone, March 2016 and in person June 3, 2017.

Shepard, Jan. Interviews in person, June 6, 2017 and October 23, 2019.

Valentino, Louis. Interviews via telephone and email, March 2016 – June 2016.

Wolfe, Toby. Interviews and discussions by telephone, via email and in person. May 2016 – May 2018.

# BOOKS

Aaker, Everett. *Television Western Players of the Fifties.* Jefferson, NC: McFarland, 1997.

Blum, Daniel. *A Pictorial History of Television.* Philadelphia & NY: Chilton Company Book Division, 1959.

Bowman, Peter. *Beach Red.* New York, NY: Random House Press, 1945.

Brode, Douglas. *Shooting Stars of the Small Screen.* Austin, TX: University of Texas Press, 2009.

Connor, Jim. *Hollywood Starlet: The Career of Barbara Lawrence.* USA: SLP Publications, 1977.

Epstein, Dwayne. *Lee Marvin – Point Blank.* Tucson, AZ: Schaffner Press, Inc., 2013.

Jensen, Andrew. *Latter-Day Saints Biographical Encyclopedia of the Church.* Salt Lake City, UT: Deseret New Press, Andrew Jensen History Company, 1901 – 1936.

Lees, Gene. *The Musical Worlds of Lerner and Loewe.* Lincoln, NE: University of Nebraska Press, 1991.

Magers, Boyd. *A Gathering of Guns.* Albuquerque, NM: Western Clippings, 2017.

Marvin, Betty. *Tales of a Hollywood Housewife – A Memoir of the first Mrs. Lee Marvin.* New York, NY: iUniverse, 2011.

Nollen, Scott Allen. *Three Bad Men John Ford, John Wayne, Ward Bond.* Jefferson, NC: McFarland, 2010.

Rosin, James. *Wagon Train – The Television Series.* Philadelphia, PA: The Autumn Road Company, 2008.

Settel, Irving & Laas, William. *A Pictorial History of Television.* New York, NY: Grosset & Dunlap, Inc., 1969.

Sharp, Kathleen. *Mr. and Mrs. Hollywood – Edie & Lew Wasserman and Their Entertainment Empire. New York, NY:* Carroll & Graf Publishers, 2003.

Speed, F. Maurice. *The Western Film and T.V. Annual.* London, England: Macdonald, 1960.

Summers, Neil. *The First Official TV Western Book.* Vienna, WV: Old West Shop Publishing, 1987.

Summers, Neil. *The Official TV Western Book,* Old West Shop Publishing, WV, 1989.

*Picture Show Annual.* London, England: Fleetwood House The Amalgamated Press, Ltd., 1956.

# ARCHIVES

Burris, Betty. *Scrapbook,* 11 x 14 x 5, 1952 – 1980's. K.M.

Horton, Robert. *The Red Book Album of Memorabilia,* Red leather cover, gold embossed, 14 x 18 x 5, 1940's – 1980's. Boyd Magers.

Horton, Robert. *Scrapbook I,* Brown leather cover, 11 x 16 x 4, c.1946 – 1950. This also contains a blue pocket file folder holding numerous clippings, photo copies of clippings and articles, and some playbills, and parts of playbills dating from the 1970's and 1980's. Author's Collection.

Horton, Robert. *Scrapbook II,* Tooled brown leather cover, very worn, 11 x 16 x 3, c.1946 – 1950. Author's Collection.

Horton, Robert. *Scrapbook III,* Brown leather photograph album, 8.5 x 11, 1950's – 1960's. Author's Collection.

Horton, Robert. *Scrapbook IV,* Black3-ring binder photograph album, 8.5 x 11, 1945 – 1970's. Author's Collection.

Horton, Robert. *Scrapbook V,* Green leather cover, large portraits annotated by Robert Horton, 11 x 16 x 3, 1940's – 1950's. Author's Collection.

Horton, Robert. *Scrapbook VI,* White vinyl 3-ring binder, press clippings of singing acts, 11.5 x 8, 1960's – 1970's. Author's Collection.

Horton, Robert. *Scrapbook VII,* Brown leather album inscribed "Bob Horton" in gold on the front and in gold inside front cover "Vaya Con Dios." Articles specifically related to his love life, 14 x 18. 1950's – 1960's. Boyd Magers.

Horton, Robert. Clippings covering *Wagon Train* years. Clipping services identified - Allen's Press Clipping Bureau – Los Angeles, San Francisco, Portland, Seattle. Central Press Bureau, Pittsburgh. McFadden & Eddy Associates, Hollywood. Sylvia Norris, Hollywood, clippings pasted on both sides of each page, 14 x 18 x 6. 1957 – 1962. Boyd Magers.

Horton, Robert. *The Sentinel,* The Harvard School Yearbook, 1942. Author's Collection.

Horton, Robert. *U.S. Coast Guard Records,* Application from join-up to medical discharge, 1943 – 1944. Author's Collection.

Horton, Robert. NBC's *This Is Your Life script,* January 1961. Author's Collection.

Horton, Robert. *Pilot's Log,* Piper Comanche N59RH, 1961 – 1994. Author's Collection.

Horton, Robert. *Playbills and theater programs,* Acquired from Robert Horton's Estate as well as individually, 1940's – 1980's. Author's Collection.

Horton, Marilynn. *Guest Book,* Record of guests and dinners at 5317 Andasol Avenue, 1979 – 1982. Author's Collection.

# DOCUMENTS

Robert Horton's Graduation Certificate from The Harvard School, June 12, 1942. Author's Collection.

Robert Horton's Honorable Discharge Certificate, June 22, 1944. Author's Collection.

Robert Horton's UCLA Graduation Diploma, August 13, 1949. Author's Collection.

Robert Horton's UCLA Certificate of Honors in Theater Arts, August 13, 1949. Author's Collection.

Robert Horton's Invitation from Queen Elizabeth II to perform at The Royal Command Performance in London, May 16, 1960. Author's Collection.

Robert Horton's Certificate of Congratulations for being a Selected Representative Artiste on the Occasion of The Royal Variety Performance, May 16, 1960. Author's Collection.

Marriage Certificate facsimile, Robert Horton to Marilynn Bradley, December 31, 1960. Author's Collection.

Robert Horton's Century Artists, Ltd. contract, November 16, 1987. Author's Collection.

Robert Horton's passport, ID page. Copy.

## FAN CLUB PUBLICATIONS.

Author's Collection.

United States:

*Horton Highlights.* January 1961. Annual re-cap.
*Horton Highlights.* January 1962. Annual re-cap.
*Robert Horton Friend Club.* November 1965 Newsletter.
*Robert Horton Friend Club.* December 1965 Newsletter.
*Robert Horton Friend Club.* November 1966 Newsletter.
*Robert Horton Honored Star.* February 1967 Newsletter.
*Robert Horton Friend Club.* February 16 – March 1, 1967 Newsletter.
*Robert Horton Friend Club.* April 1967 Newsletter.
*Robert Horton Honored Star.* May 1967 Newsletter.
*Robert Horton Honored Star.* June 1967 Newsletter.
*Robert Horton Honored Star.* July 1967 Newsletter.
*Robert Horton Friend Club.* September – October 1967 Newsletter.
*Robert Horton Friend Club.* November 1967 Newsletter.
*Robert Horton Friend Club.* January 1968 Newsletter.
*Robert Horton Friend Club.* February – March 1968 Newsletter.
*Robert Horton Friend Club.* April – May 1968 Newsletter.
*Robert Horton Friend Club.* August – September 1968 Newsletter.
*Robert Horton Friend Club.* October – November 1968 Newsletter.
International Fan Club:
*International Fan Club Bulletin.* August 1958.
Britain:
*Robert Horton British Fan Club. 2nd Edition.* March 1960. His copy.
*Robert Horton British Fan Club. 3rd Edition.* May 1960.
*Robert Horton British Fan Club. 4th Edition.* August 1960. His copy.
*Robert Horton British Fan Club. 5th Edition.* March 1961. His copy.

## TELEVISION, PANEL DISCUSSIONS, RADIO

*This Is Your Life.* Televised by NBC on January 22, 1961. Recorded at NBC Studios on January 18, 1961. Robert Horton's copy. Author's Collection.
*Hollywood Backstage.* Syndicated television series, 1964 – 1967. Author's Collection.

*The Amazing World of Kreskin.* Canadian Television, Ottawa, Canada, January 17, 1972. Author's Collection.
Interview re: *As the World Turns,* 1983 – unidentified. Author's Collection.
*Tuolumne Wild West Film Festival, Lifetime Achievement Award,* Honoree, Sonora, Tuolumne County, CA, September 24 – 26, 1993. Author's Collection.
*Charlotte Film Festival.* Panelist, Charlotte, NC, 1993. Author's Collection.
*Knoxville Film Festival.* Panelist, Knoxville, TN, 1996. Author's Collection.
*Memphis Film Festival.* Panelist, Memphis, TN, 1998. Author's Collection.
*Golden Boot Awards,* Honoree, Tombstone, AZ, August 7, 2004.
*KSAV Radio Interview with Boyd Magers,* September 18, 2007. Author's Collection.

## LETTERS AND TELEGRAMS
Author's Collection
Horton, Robert. Letter to his mother, Chelta Horton, Los Angeles, CA, May 11, 1941.
Horton, Robert. Letter to his mother, Chelta Horton, Los Angeles, CA, May 9, 1943.
Horton, Robert. Letter to his mother, Chelta Horton, Los Angeles, CA, August 26, 1943.
Horton, Robert. Letter to his mother, Chelta Horton, Los Angeles, CA, c. September 6, 1943.
Horton Family. Telegram to Robert Horton, Coral Gables, FL, April 7, 1947.
Winnie, John Ross. Letter to Boyd Smith, Yale University, New Haven, CT, March 8, 1948.
Horton, Mead and Chelta. Telegram to Robert Horton, Coral Gables, FL, April 15, 1948.
Jerry _____. Letter to Creighton Horton, San Marino, CA, April 15, 1948.
Hearn, G. Edward. Letter to Dean Charles Sawyer, Yale University, New Haven, CT, September 12, 1949.
Daves, Delmer. 20th Century-Fox Inter-office memo to Jim Ryan, Hollywood, CA, October 20, 1949.
Harrigan, Nolan. Letter to Robert Horton, Los Angeles, CA, February 11, 1950.
Lundin, Barry. Letter to Robert Horton, Los Angeles, CA, February 28, 1950.
MH, Production Director. Letter to Robert Horton, New York, NY, April 18, 1950.
Horton, Robert. Letter to parents, Mead and Chelta Horton, Los Angeles, CA, April 24, 1950.
Blood, Bill. Telegram to Robert Horton, Los Angeles, CA, June 13, 1950.
Ebeling, Betty and Walker, Bob. Telegram to Robert Horton, Atlantic City, NJ, July 11, 1950.
McConnor, Vincent. Letter to Robert Horton, Atlantic City, NJ, July 24, 1950.
Henreid, Paul. Letter to Robert Horton, New York, NY, October 25, 1950.

Nayfack, Nicholas – Loews, MGM. To Robert Horton, Beverly Hills, CA, February 16, 1952.

Small, Paul. Letter to Robert Horton, Hollywood, CA, February 18, 1952.

Schary, Dore. Letter to Robert Horton, Hollywood, CA, February 10, 1953.

Horton, Robert. Letter to Ed Zinneman, Hollywood, CA, May 24, 1954.

Reed, Donna. Letter to Robert Horton, Hollywood, CA, October 5, 1954.

Raisin, Bob. Letter to Robert Horton, Hollywood, CA, December 17, 1954.

Ruick, Barbara. Telegram to Robert Horton, Los Angeles, June 22, 1955.

_____, Edina and Gar. Letter to Robert Horton and Inger Stevens, Hollywood, CA, November 26, 1956.

Horton, Robert. Letter to Allan Miller, Hollywood, CA, September 23, 1957.

Hart, Don. Telegram to Robert Horton, Cincinnati, OH, May 15, 1959.

Horton, Robert. Letter to his British Fan Club, London, England, March 1960.

Horton, Creighton and Anne. Telegram to Robert Horton, Hollywood, CA, January 18, 1961.

Melnitz, William W. Letter to Robert Horton, Studio City, CA, April 27, 1961.

Loevinger, Lee, US Dep of Justice. Letter to Robert Horton, Hollywood, CA, August 31, 1961.

Kintner, Robert. Telegram to Robert Horton, Studio City, CA, September 27, 1961.

Bergstrom, Pat. Letter to Robert Horton, Chicago, IL, June 21, 1962.

Horton, Robert. Letter to father, Mead Horton, Los Angeles, CA, June 1962.

Champion, Gower. Telegram to Robert Horton, Columbus, OH, August 23, 1962.

Smith, Ray. Telegram to Robert Horton, Jackson, MS, October 11, 1962.

Smith, Ray. Telegram to Alan J. Lerner, New York, NY, undated, but c. March 1963. Champion, Gower. Telegram to Robert Horton, Columbus, OH, August 23, 1962.

Kosson, Daniel H. Letter to Robert Horton, New York, NY, March 18, 1963.

Champion, Gower. Telegram to Robert Horton, Boston, MA, September 9, 1963.

Merrick, David. Telegram to Robert Horton, Boston, MA, September 9, 1963.

Rodgers, Richard. Telegram to Robert Horton, New York, NY, October 24, 1963.

Schmidt, Harvey and Jones, Tom. Telegram to Robert Horton, New York, NY, October 24, 1963.

de Mille, Agnes. Telegram to Robert Horton, New York, NY, October 24, 1963.

Strasberg, Lee and Paula. Telegram to Robert Horton, New York, NY, October 24, 1963.

Hopper, Hedda. Telegram to Robert Horton, New York, NY, October 24, 1963.

Young, Gig and Elaine. Telegram to Robert Horton, NY, October 24, 1963.

MacRae, Gordon and Sheila. Telegram to Robert Horton, NY, October 24, 1963.

Heyward, Leland. Telegram to Robert Horton, New York, NY, October 24, 1963.

Goulet, Robert. Telegram to Robert Horton, New York, NY, October 25, 1963.

McGlohon, Loonis. Letter to Robert Horton, New York, NY, December 3, 1963.

Rodgers, Richard. Letter to Robert Horton, New York, NY, December 12, 1963.

McGlohon, Loonis. Letter to Robert Horton, New York, NY, August 25, 1964.

Horton, Marilynn. Letter to Pearl Wolf, Secretary, March 13, 1968.

Horton, Robert. Letter to Fan Club, June 1968.

Horton, Robert. Letter to the cast of *1776*, November 1972.

Howard, Stuart. Letter to Robert Horton, New York, NY, December 12, 1983.

Horton, Robert. Letter to a fan named Danny, address unknown, December 12, 1993.

Swenson, Inga. Letter to Aileen Elliott, Cochranville, PA, May 11, 2016.

Chenault, Cynthia (Cindy Robbins). Email to Aileen Elliott, Cochranville, PA, May 12, 2016.

Marvin, Betty. Emails to Aileen Elliott, Cochranville, PA, May 2016 – June 2016.

## PERIODICALS

"Actress Barbara Ruick Files Suit For Divorce," *unidentified publication*, August 1955.

Allen, Rich. Article re: renting Norman Luboff home in Studio City, *Valley Times Today*, San Fernando Valley, CA, July 1961.

"Amarillo Little Theater Off To An Auspicious Start," *Catch Me If You Can*, *unidentified review clipping*, September 1973.

Anderson, Janette and Bob. "A Man For All Seasons," *Traildust*, Spring 1994.

"Appaloosa Holds Heart of Hollywood's Horton," *The Appaloosa Journal*, March 1960.

Archerd, Amy. "No, Borgnine is NOT replacing Ward Bond," *Variety*, November 14, 1960.

Ardmore, Jane. "Bob Horton Fights For His Life," *Unidentified publication*, Spring 1961.

Avery, Bethel. "The Awful Truth About Robert Horton," *Movie Life*, July 1959.

Barnes, Clive. New York Music Critic, *Unidentified publication*, 1992.

Bingham, Joe. Review of *The Spy Killer*, Television Review, *unidentified publication*, December 1969.

Blum, Walter. "Target For Cowboy Horton – A Role in Musical Comedy," *TV Log, San Francisco Examiner*, October 22, 1961.

"Bob Horton – Marilyn*[sic]* Bradley," *unidentified clipping*, February 1961.

"Bob Horton Expands On His New NBC Deal," *unidentified clipping*, February 9, 1962.

"Bob Horton Hits Back At Critics," *San Diego Union*, c. 1963 - 1964.

"Bob Horton Suspended for Missing "Train," *Variety*, October 7, 1960.

"Bob Horton Wants To Sing, Act and Mebbe Even Produce for NBC,"*Variety,* February 28, 1962.

"Bob Horton Will Gross Close To $100,000 On Rodeo Dates Alone This Year,"*Los Angeles Examiner,* March 11, 1960.

"Bob Horton's Wife Tells How She Succeeded Where Three Others Failed,"*unidentified publication,* 1966.

"Bob Horton,"*TV & Movie Screen,* June 1960.

"By The Method,"*The Courier Journal,* February 22, 1959.

Calta, Louis. "Stage Role Given To Robert Horton,"*New York Times,* October 27, 1962.

Canavan, Jack. "My Wife, My Love, My Friend,"*TV Picture Life,* May 1961.

Carroll, Gwen. V Close-Up – Robert Horton,"*Movie Mirror,* September 1959.

Carroll, Harrison. "Keep An Eye On Bob Horton and Marilynn Bradley,"*Los Angeles Herald & Express,* May 4, 1960.

Carroll, Harrison. "Bob Horton Says That Marilynn Bradley Wants To Be Married in Boston,"*Los Angeles Herald & Express,* December 13, 1960.

Carroll, Harrison. "Nervous About Flying,"*Los Angeles Herald & Express,* January 4, 1961.

"Case Study of a Rebel,"*TV Picture Life,* March 1966.

Cassidy, Claudia. "Horton Plays Homicidal Handyman at Drury Lane," On The Aisle, *unidentified publication,* May 1962.

"Celebrating the Divorce,"*Movie Life,* November 1960.

Collins, Chris. "Why Husbands Hate Horton,"*unidentified publication,* c. mid-1960.

Cooper, Jim. "The Man Who Runs Uphill,"*Screenland,* May 1958.

Cornett, Steve. "Ex-Wagon Train Star Finds Variety Playing Stage Roles,"*Amarillo Daily News,* September 16, 1973.

Covington, Ruth. "I Wish I Could Fall In Love,"*TV Star Parade,* c. 1958 – 1959.

"Cow-rousing…All's quiet on the western front – for the moment,"*Los Angeles Examiner,* October 21, 1960.

Cranford, Ivy. "This Time It's For Keeps,"*TV Screen Life,* Fall 1960.

Davidson, Bill."TV Madness,"*Saturday Evening Post,* March 26, 1966.

Day, Peter. "Those Mixed Up Years Are Over,"*Picturegoer,* June 13, 1959.

Denis, Paul. "Must A Childless Marriage Be Lonely?"*TV Radio Mirror,* September 1966.

Denis, Paul. "Still Learning The Facts Of Life,"*TV Illustrated,* June 1958.

Denis, Paul."Terror in the Skies,"*Movieland and TV Times,* June 1961.

Denton, Charles. "Robert Horton Has Been Offered Highest Price Ever paid TV Star in England,"*Los Angeles Examiner,* November 20, 1959.

Denton, Charles. "Horton Fights On and Off The Screen,"*Los Angeles Examiner,* February 1960.

Denton, Charles. "Bond's Death Halts Horton's Nuptial Plan,"*Los Angeles Examiner,* November 18, 1960.

Denton, Charles. "Where Does Wagon Train Head Now?" *Los Angeles Examiner*, November 1960.

Denton, Charles. "Horton Betting Five Million On Himself," *Los Angeles Examiner*, August 28, 1961.

Diamond, Dolores. "Flaming Rebel," *TV Star Parade, 1958*.

Dintner, Charlotte. "Marilynn Boils My Bear," *TV Radio Mirror*, April 1962.

"Don't Pin Him Down," *Screen Spotlight*, July 1960.

Du Brow, Rick. Regarding the relationship with Ward Bond, *Unpublished UPI press release*, April 29, 1960.

Durham, Louise. Regarding the signing to *I Picked a Daisy*, *Indianapolis News*, August 1, 1963.

"Duryea for Wagon Train?" *unidentified clipping*, November 11, 1960.

Eagen, Dorothy. "How Not To Succeed if You're a Middle-Aged Romeo," *unidentified publication*, July 1972.

Farber, Jay. "The Musical Laboratory," *unidentified publication*, c. 1947.

*The Flamingo Nightclub* lawsuit, *Los Angeles Examiner*, September 1966.

Franklin, Rebecca. Interview with Horton on how he got into acting, *Unidentified publication*, 1964.

Freeman, Donald. "Point Of View" "Bob Horton Hits Back At Critics," *The San Diego Union*, Undated.

Genovese, John. "From Horse Opera to Soap Opera," *Soap Opera World*, 1983.

Gilbert, Joyce. "Case Study Of A Rebel," *TV Picture Life*, March 1966.

"The girl who gets Robert Horton for a husband. . ." *Screen Stars*, June 1959.

Goff, Lee. "Alone In A Honeymoon Cottage," *TV & Movie Screen*, April 1960.

Grant, Hank. "In The Air," *The Hollywood Reporter*, September 15, 1961.

Graham, Sheilah. Interview re: flying lessons, *Citizen News*, March 12, 1959.

Graham, Sheilah. "Bob Horton Received Top Salary for Christmas Show," *Hollywood Today*, December 30, 1959.

Graham, Sheilah. "Horton To Do British TV," *The Citizen-News*, March 2, 1961.

Graham, Sheilah. "Bob Horton Is Not Happy," *The Citizen-News*, August 23, 1961.

Graham, Sheilah. "Bob Likes New York," *Hollywood Today*, Spring 1964.

Griffith, John David. "Horton Leaving Wagon Train," *New York Mirror*, February 8, 1962.

Harris, Sara Lou. "Bad Luck Couldn't Stop Him," *TV & Movie Screen*, c. 1958.

Hellman, Jack. "Robert Horton Throwing Away Opportunity," *Variety*, April 24, 1961.

"His Interest in TV Led to Film Contract," *Worcester Sunday Telegraph*, October 5, 1952.

"Hollywood Personality Joins Crusade Against Drunk Drivers," *Highway Patrol*, 1973.

Homenick, Brett. "Cult Classic Commander," *G-Fan*, Winter 2009.

Hopper, Hedda. "Entertainment," *Los Angeles Times*, November 22, 1958.

Hopper, Hedda. "Making A Business of Success,"*Syndicated St. Louis Globe-Journal,* Sunday January 18, 1959.

Hopper, Hedda. "Entertainment,"*Los Angeles Times,* May 11, 1959.

Hopper, Hedda. "Miller Sends New Script To Horton,"*Los Angeles Times,* November 30, 1959.

Hopper, Hedda. "Entertainment,"*Los Angeles Times,* December 10, 1959.

Hopper, Hedda. Interview about The Royal Command Performance, *Los Angeles Times,* May 1960.

Hopper, Hedda. Regarding His Suspension, *Los Angeles Times,* October 15, 1960.

Hopper, Hedda. "Bob Horton's Introducing His Fiancé To Friends Tonight,"*Los Angeles Times,* December 21, 1960.

Hopper, Hedda. "Wagon Train Hero Takes Big Chance,"*Los Angeles Times,* May 22, 1962.

Hopper, Hedda. "Horton Gets New Broadway Musical,"*Los Angeles Times,* August 1, 1963.

Horton, Marilynn. *(Attributed to)* "Why I Married Bob Horton – Star's Bride Tells Story,"*TV Week,* February 8 – 14, 1961.

Horton, Marilynn. *(Attributed to)* "I Never Thought He'd Marry Me!"*Movie Mirror,* September 1961.

Horton, Robert. *(Attributed to)* "Why My Marriage Failed,"*TV & Movie Screen,* May 1958.

Horton, Robert. *(Attributed to)*"Everyone At Home Was Picking On Me,"*Photoplay,* February 1959.

Horton, Robert. *(Attributed to)* "I Want A Girl I Can Chase,"*TV Picture Life,* March 1959

"Horton "Eye" Star,"*The Hollywood Reporter,* July 23, 1968.

"Horton Has Bigger Plans,"*Los Angeles Examiner,* March 23, 1961.

"Horton's Flying – More Dangerous Than Dean's Driving?"*Unidentified publication – clipping,* November 1960.

"Horton's Girl Sulks,"*Minneapolis Sunday Tribune,* January 10, 1960.

"Horton's Legit Appearance,"*Variety,* June 29, 1959.

"Hortons Make Oklahoma! Beautiful Evening Here,"*The Tribune,* July 1966.

"Housewarming!"*Modern Screen,* October 1952.

Hull, Bob. Interview regarding Horton's rodeo appearances, *Los Angeles Herald and Express,* Fall 1958.

Hull, Bob. "ABC's "Foreign Exchange First Class Thriller,"*The Hollywood Reporter,* January 15, 1970.

Humphrey, Hal. "Seeing Things,"*Los Angeles Mirror News,* May 19, 1958.

"Husbands Hate Robert Horton,"*American Weekly,* March 15, 1959.

Hyam, Janette. "Robert Horton,"*TV Scene (UK),* 1988.

Hyams, Joe. "Politely Stubborn,"*TV Guide,* 1958.

"I Like Women,"*Stardom,* 1959.

Interview re: nightclub work, *Houston Chronicle,* February 1967.

Interview regarding Horton's background, career, *The Palm Beach Post,* March 1970.
Interview with Horton when he visited Pittsburgh, *The Pittsburgh Press,* 1958.
Interview with Marilynn re: her "surprise" marriage, *TV Picture Life,* December 1961.
"It Isn't Wagon Train But Robert Horton Paces Entertaining Playhouse Comedy 'Under The Yum-Yum Tree'," *unidentified publication,* July 22, 1970.
J. Pellman Theatre, Playbill profile, mid-1970's.
Johnson, Erskine. "Bob Horton Is Happy To Miss Some Trail Rides," *unidentified publication,* December 8, 1959.
Johnson, Robert. "Big Ego, Big Talent," *Saturday Evening Post,* December 1961.
Kauffman, Dave. "On All Channels," *Variety,* June 21, 1957.
"Life Story," *Mirabelle, Morrison & Gibb Ltd.,* July 1960.
Linet, Beverly. "Perfectly Wonderful, Miserably Awful," *TV Movie Life,* December 1958.
Linet, Beverly. "Secret Confessions," *TV Star Parade,* April 1959.
Lovell, Glenn. "Actor Left the Hollywood Trail for Theater, and has no regrets," *Knight News Service,* 1979.
Lucas, Gail. Nightclub Review, *Citizen Journal,* February 17, 1965.
"MCA To Suspend Robert Horton Unless He's Back on Wagon Train by Tomorrow," *Variety,* October 5, 1960.
"The Man Who Steals Your Heart," *TV Yearbook,* 1958.
Mann, Helen. "Still Learning The Facts of Life," *TV Illustrated,* June 1958.
Martin, Helen. "My Trouble With Women," *unidentified publication,* c. 1958.
Markus, Bette. "You Name It, Horton's Done It," *unidentified publication,* c. 1971.
McManus, Margaret. "Robert Horton Faces New TV Show With Realistic Confidence," *Sunday News,* 1963.
Morehouse, Ward. "Bob Horton of '110 in Shade' Rides Home To West Roxbury Wife," *unidentified Boston publication,* September 1963.
Morse, Jim. "In Defense of Westerns and Private Eyes," *Unidentified publication,* 1959.
*Murder She Wrote, unidentified clipping,* c. 1990.
"NBC's Wagon Train Rolled Within 4.2 of Gunsmoke's 44.3," *Variety,* January 13, 1959.
Neal, Clara. "Western TV Stars Pose Problem For Reporter," *Kiowa County Star-Review,* June 4, 1959.
"New Rodgers-Lerner Musical Rescheduled," *New York Herald Tribune,* April 1963.
Nolan, J. M. "Story of a Great Star," *Charles Publications,* 1958.
*Now – The Photo Magazine of Fashion Miami Beach and Great Miami.* February 16, 1947.
O'Brian, Jack. Article re: flying. *New York Journal-American,* January 24, 1961.
"One Man Crusade," *Movieland,* February 1958.
Parsons, Louella. "The Bitterest Fight," *Los Angeles Examiner,* October 10, 1960.

Parsons, Louella. Re: the Horton wedding. *The Los Angeles Examiner,* December 30, 1960.
Phelan, Charlotte. "On Surreys and Wagon Trains,"*Houston Post,* June 23, 1968.
"Plan To Wed,"*Unidentified Los Angeles newspaper,* June 1946.
"Playhouse Personality,"*Atlantic City Reporter,* August 12, 1950.
Powers, Forrest. "Horton Scouts TV Dramatic Trends,"*The Minneapolis Star,* February 26, 1958.
"Presents Never Presented,"*Los Angeles Examiner,* December 24, 1959.
Re: His pilot qualifications, *Sunday-Register Iowa TV Magazine – Des Moines,* June 18, 1961.
Re: *ABC-TV Movie of the Week, The Spy Killer* and *Foreign Exchange,* early 1970.
Re: Annual Palm Springs Mounted Police Rodeo, *The Desert Sun,* February 12, 1959.
Re: Back injury, Persian Room cancellation, *unidentified clipping,* mid-1965.
Re: Dates with Cindy Robbins,*TV Star Parade,* March 1960.
Re: The death of Ward Bond, *Los Angeles Examiner,* November 11, 1960.
Re: His extra-curricular acting activities, *Detroit Free Press,* March 13, 1960.
Re: His friendship with Nina Foch, *TV Movie Screen,* May 1959.
Re: His meeting with fan Denise Morris in England, *unidentified press clippings, (UK),* April 1960.
Re: His second meeting with fan Denise Morris in England, *unidentified press clippings (UK),* May 1962.
Re: Horton turning down *Unsinkable Molly Brown* role, *unidentified clipping,* 1962.
Re: Horton's disputes on the set, *Los Angeles herald,* February 2, 1960.
Re: Horton's disputes on the set, *The Hollywood Reporter,* February 5, 1960.
Re: Move to Studio City home, *Los Angeles Examiner,* July 19, 1960.
Re: Psychoanalyses, *TV & Movie Screen,* September 1959.
Re: Purchase of land in Malibu, *unidentified clipping,* mid-1965.
Re: Robert Horton's feelings about Bond, Westerns,*The Hollywood Reporter,* May 24, 1960.
Re: *Wagon Train's* rise to the top of the charts, *Screenworld and TV,* July 1960.
Re: Bond's Death, *Los Angeles Examiner,* November 11, 1960.
Re: His relationship with Ward Bond,*The Hollywood Reporter,* May 24, 1960.
Report re: adjustment to WT contract,*Variety,* January 1960.
Report regarding Horton's search for an Appaloosa horse, *Lewiston Morning Tribune,* August 1958.
"The Robert Horton Story,"*TV Times (UK),* February 1959.
"Robert Horton – The Little Devil,"*Hollywood Life Stories,* 1959.
"Robert Horton Forms Production Company,"*Filmland Events,* June 22, 1961.
"Robert Horton Introduces – Robert Horton Life Story,"*Mirabelle Morrison & Gibb, Ltd.* March 1959.
"Robert Horton Latest in Panther Squadron,"*unidentified clipping,* c. 1953.

"Robert Horton Life Story - #30,"*Fans Star Library, Amalgamated Press,* July 1959.

"Robert Horton Set For 4 Legit Stints,"*Variety,* February 26, 1963.

"Robert Horton Tested,"*Hollywood Nite Life,* April 5, 1946.

"Robert Horton, NBC-TV Call Off Exclusive Pact,"*Variety,* October 1962.

"Robert Horton,"*Stardom,* October 1960.

Roberts, Bill. "A Smash,"*The Houston Post,* March 1967.

Roberts, Evelyn. "Horton and Wife Star in Charlotte,"*unidentified publication,* unidentified date.

Robinson, Wayne. "Horton Sings Way To Broadway,"*The Sunday Bulletin, (Philadelphia)* October 6, 1963.

Salisbury, Lesley. "Why Flint Ain't Finished Yet,"*TV Times (UK),* April 1989.

Siegel, Micki. "After 30 Years in Show Biz, ROBERT HORTON is Still Going Strong," New York Freelance Writer, *TV Guide,* 1983.

Silver, Lee. "Merrick Gets Horton For '110 in the Shade,"*unidentified publication,* unidentified date, but c. August 1963.

"Shade Stars Will Sing at Banshees,"*New York Journal-American,* March 31, 1964.

"Star Bright Wants It Light," *The Hollywood Reporter,* February 3, 1961.

Star Profile, *Grand National Livestock Exposition Horse Show and Rodeo Program,* October 27 – November 5, 1961.

St. Paul Civic Opera, *Brigadoon,* Playbill profile, 1976.

Swaebley, Frances. "Robert Horton: From UM to Stardom,"*Miami Herald,* March 29, 1970.

Swisher, Vi. "What Women Have Done For Me,"*Silverscreen,* October 1959.

Tildesley, Alice L. "Let Me Tell You About My Boy," *TV and Movie Screen,* August 1961.

Tomkies, Mike. "Sure, I Would Marry Again,"*National Enquirer,* May 1959.

*Trieste Festival of Science Fiction Films. Variety,* July 10 1968.

Trent, Susan. "Love's Young Dream,"*Unidentified publication,* c. 1953.

Tusher, Bill. "I Want Love – Not An Affair,"*TV Picture Life,* c. 1960.

"Two Bobs (Kintner & Horton) Cook TV Plot; Wagon Train Star Stays at NBC, Will Compete Against Show,"*Variety,* February 7, 1962.

Untitled press release re: Horton's problems with *Wagon Train* scriptwriters, *TV Illustrated,* March 2, 1958.

Van Horne, Harriet. "Actor Cowboy Reads Books Too," *syndicated, New York World Telegram and Sun,* c. 1958.

"Wagon Train and Gunsmoke Vying For Top Honors," TV Scene, *Los Angeles Times,* January 2, 1959.

"Wagon Train Co-Star Hard Driving Actor,"*unidentified publication,* March 1958.

"Wagon Train in $20,000,000 Deal, Switching From NBC to ABC Next Year,"*Variety,* October 25, 1961.

Wahls, Robert. "Footlight – Meet Bob – Not Flint,"*unidentified publication,* February 1964.

Waterbury, Ruth. "Hollywood Tie-Line," *TV Channels,* November 27, 1960.

"Westward Ho – Mr. Horton," *TV Guide,* August 18 – 22, 1958.

"What does this hard-riding "scout" do in his spare time?" *St. Louis Globe Democrat,* October 26, 1958.

"What My Wife Does For Me," *Movieland & TV Times,* September 1966.

"What Women Have Done For Me," *Silver Screen,* October 1959.

"Where Are They Now?" *Globe,* 1993.

"Who The Hell Does He Think He Is?" *Los Angeles Mirror News,* January 1958.

"Wig Solves Pony Problem," *Lewiston Morning News,* September 1958.

Wilson, Earl. Interview regarding singing lessons, *New York Post,* c. October 1963.

Wister, Emery. "Singing Good, Music Good," *unidentified review,* unknown date.

## PERIODICAL REVIEWS

Apone, Carl. Review of *Carousel, Pittsburgh Press,* July 1963.

Best, Bob. Review of *Picnic* at The Little Theatre, Sullivan, Kansas, reproduced in the *Robert Horton Friend Club Newsletter,* August – September 1968.

*Catch Me If You Can* Review, *Amarillo Daily News,* September 16, 1973.

Eder, Shirley. Nightclub Review, *Downtown Monitor,* November 25, 1964.

Fanger, Don. UCLA *Daily Bruin,* March 23, 1949.

Flamingo Nightclub Review, *Las Vegas Sun,* August 1967.

Flamingo Nightclub Review, *Los Angeles Times,* August 1967.

Flamingo NightclubReview, *unidentified item,* reproduced in *Robert Horton Friend Club Newsletter,* August 1967.

Flamingo Nightclub Review, *Las Vegas Review,* August 1967.

Fortridge, E. Review of his performance on the *Perry Como Show, Boston Herald,* January 21, 1960.

Foley, Griffin. Review of Sydney, Australia Chequers nightclub act, *Sun Telegraph,* July 1967.

Gardiner, John. Review of *Guys and Dolls* Detroit performance, *Windsor Daily Star,* September 9, 1959.

Guptill, S. Carleton. *Picnic* Review, *The News (Kennebunkport)* August 1969.

Hobdy, D. J. Review of *Oklahoma!* at Houston Music Theatre, *unidentified publication,* reproduced in the *Robert Horton Friend Club Newsletter,* August – September 1968.

Kelly, Kevin. Review of *110 in the Shade, Boston Sunday Globe,* September 22, 1963.

Kessell, Norman. Review of Sydney, Australia, Chequers nightclub act, *Sun,* July 1967.

*Kismet* Review, *The Sacramento Bee,* July 27, 1971.

Mann, Sydney. Review of Sydney, Australia, Chequers nightclub act, *Mirror,* July 1967.

Murdock, Henry T. Review of *110 in the Shade, The Philadelphia Inquirer,* September 1963.

Nightclub Review, *Detroit Emergency Press*, November 17, 1964.

Nightclub Review, *El Paso Herald Post*, February 1965.

Review of *Brigadoon*, *St. Paul Pioneer Press*, April 1967.

Review of his performance at The London Palladium, *Daily Herald (UK)*, December 28, 1959.

Review of *Oklahoma! The Plain Dealer*, July 1966.

Review of Robert Horton and wife Marilynn performing together in UK. *Musical Express (UK)*, May 19, 1961.

Review of Sydney, Australia Chequers nightclub act, *Sydney Entertainment Review*.

Review of *The Return of the Texan*, *Variety*, November 5, 1952.

Reviews of *Men of the Fighting Lady* and *Prisoner of War*, *unidentified clippings*, c. 1954.

Staff, Charles. Review of performance in *The Pajama Game*, *Unidentified Indianapolis Newspaper*, 1968.

*There's a Girl in My Soup* Review, *Omaha World-Herald*, January 11, 1973.

*There's a Girl in My Soup* Review, *The Charlotte News*, August 1969.

Thompson, Howard. *The Green Slime* review, *The New York Times*, May 22, 1969.

Veitch, Jock. Review of Sydney, Australia, Chequers nightclub act, *Sun-Herald*, July 1967.

White, Matt. Review of Sydney, Australia, Chequers nightclub act, *Mirror* July 1967.

Yockey, Ross. Review: Robert Horton at *New Orleans Municipal Auditorium Summer Pops*, *unidentified publication*, June 17, 1967.

## INTERNET

IMDb

Wikipedia

# APPENDIX 1: HIS BODY OF WORK

This list is by no means fully comprehensive. It cannot be. However, it represents the best which research can produce. The years Robert Horton spent on the stage particularly throughout the Seventies and Eighties cannot be fully documented as to number of appearances, where and when or for how long, but his repertoire is well known. Based on his general modus operandi, that is, taking work which suited his lifestyle and gave him maximum freedom and flexibility, he may only have worked three to four months out of each year, although there were exceptions, namely *As the World Turns* in 1982-83. He did not need to work for money. He worked for the personal challenge, satisfaction and professional validation he gained.

# APPENDIX 2: FILMOGRAPHY

Robert Horton was a contract player with *MGM* from 1952 through 1954.

*A Walk in the Sun.* As Pvt. Joe Jack. *20th Century Fox,* December 25,1945

*The Tanks are Coming.* As Captain Horner. *Warner Brothers,* October 31, 1951.

*Apache War Smoke.* As Tom Herrera. *MGM,* September 25, 1952. (Known as *Apache Trail* prior to release).

*Return of the Texan.* As Dr. Harris. *20th Century-Fox,* December 4, 1952.

*Pony Soldier.* As Jess Calhoun. *20th Century-Fox,* December19, 1952.

*Story of Three Loves.* Uncredited. *MGM,* March 5, 1953.

*Bright Road.* As Dr. Mitchell. *MGM,* April 17, 1953. (Known as *See How They Run* prior to release).

*Code Two.* As Russ Hartley. *MGM,* April 24, 1953.

*Arena.* As Jackie Roach. *MGM,* June 24, 1953.

*Prisoner of War.* As Francis Belney. *MGM,* May 4, 1954.

*Men of the Fighting Lady.* As Ensign Neil Conovan. *MGM,* May 7, 1954.

*The Man Is Armed.* As Dr. Mike Benning. *Republic Pictures,* October 19, 1956.

*The Green Slime.* As Captain Jack Rankin. *MGM,* in USA May 21, 1969. (Known as *Battle Beyond the Stars* during production).

# APPENDIX 3: MADE FOR TELEVISION MOVIES

*The Man Who Bought Paradise.* As Danny Paris. CBS, January 17, 1965.

*The Dangerous Days of Kiowa Jones.* As Kiowa Jones. MGM/ABC-TV, December 25, 1966.

*The Spy Killer.* As John Smith. ABC-TV, November 11, 1969.

*Foreign Exchange.* As John Smith. ABC-TV, January 13, 1970.

*Red River.* As Mr. Melville, the cattle buyer. MGM-UA Television, April 10, 1988.

# APPENDIX 4: TELEVISION

The first period of his television work, in New York, is recorded on a sheet of New York Life Insurance letterhead in his mother's handwriting. Despite my own research, some of these listings produced nothing definitive which confirmed Bob's participation. Nevertheless, Chelta Horton's notes must be given some credence, especially when supported by other mentions, several attributed to Bob himself.

*Magnavox Theatre* from New York. One Season, 1950. 7 shows, nothing listing Bob.

*The Danny Thomas Show. Colgate Four Star Review. Motorola TV,* October 11, 1950 as a football player.

*Suspense.* Live television plays broadcast on *CBS* from New York. No listing of Robert Horton from October 1950 through May 1951 that I could find. He may well have been un-credited in the first two, but several mentions of this series credit him with the lead in the last show in which he appeared. Furthermore, it seems that Robert Stevens, the director, gave him these parts because he liked what he saw and he liked how Bob acted. According to Bob, he was recommended to Stevens by Paula Strasberg of the Actors Studio. The time period for these appearances had to be late 1950 through early 1951. Beverly Linet, who met him in September 1951 at a cocktail party for Barbara Britton, reported that she had seen him in the *Suspense* play "Vamp Till Dead," playing the part of a chauffeur.

*The Ed Sullivan Show* broadcast from the Boston Opera House, November 19, 1950. Skit. Ed Sullivan himself found the record of Bob's appearance.

*Ford Theatre,* CBS Television. "Another Darling" As Brian Farragut. December 1, 1950. Live TV show in NYC. First Fan Mail.

*Studio One,* CBS Television, Nothing from October 1950 – April 1951.

*Fire Side Theatre* aka *The Jane Wyman Show.* General Television Enterprises. No listing of Bob from October 1950 through May 1951.

*Henry Morgan Talent Show.* No listing for Bob, 1951.

Bob was signed to Warner Brothers in early 1951. He made *The Tanks Are Coming* for them which involved filming on location in Kentucky through June 1951.

"From Such a Seed". As – unknown. *Chevron Theatre,* MCA/Revue Productions, May 16, 1952.

"Tenderfoot". As the Tenderfoot. *Lone Ranger TV Series,* ABC, November 25,1954.

"Portrait of Lydia". As Greg Howell. *Ford Television Theater,* NBC, December 16, 1954.

"Mr. Sargent and The Lady". As Sonny Sargent. *The Ray Milland Show,* CBS, February 17, 1955.

"The Margaret Browning Story". As Joe Schofield. *The Millionaire,* CBS, February 23, 1955.

"Story of Nora Fulton". As Moon Franklin. *Public Defender,* CBS, June 2, 1955.

"The Will to Survive". As Jack Barrell. *Studio 57,* Revue Productions, January 18, 1955.

"Call from Robert Jest". As Pete. *Studio 57,* Revue Productions, March 29, 1955.

"The Milwaukee Rocket". As – unnamed. *Matinee Theater,* NBC, December 13, 1955.

"Kings Row". As Drake McHugh. *Warner Brothers Presents,* 7 episodes, NBC, 1955 – 56.

"The Black Road". As David Ederly. *Studio 57,* Revue Productions, February 21, 1956.

"Betrayed". As Fred. *Lux Video Theater,* NBC, April 19, 1956.

"Danger at Clover Ridge". As Forest Ranger Norm Keller. *Cavalcade of America,* ABC, May 8, 1956.

"Girl on the Run". As David Lynch, *Celebrity Playhouse,* Screen Gems, May 29, 1956.

"Decoy". As Gil Larkin. *Alfred Hitchcock Presents,* Revue Studios, NBC, June 10, 1956.

"False Prophet". As Cpl. Tom Vaughn. *Crossroads,* ABC, June 29, 1956.

"Phone Call for Matthew Quade". As – unnamed. *Climax!,* CBS, July 5, 1956.

"Another Sky". As – unnamed – with Inger Stevens. *Matinee Theater,* NBC, July 25, 1956.

"Crack of Doom". As Mason Bridges. *Alfred Hitchcock Presents,* Revue Studios, NBC, November 25, 1956.

"Helldorado". As Morell, the gambler. *Sheriff of Cochise,* Desilu Productions, December 7, 1956.

"Mr. Blanchard's Secret". As John Fenton. *Alfred Hitchcock Presents,* Revue Studios, NBC, December 23, 1956.

*Playhouse 90.* CBS Television, 1956 – 1960. *Nothing showing Bob 1956 -1957.*

"Bottle of Wine". As Wallace Donaldson. *Alfred Hitchcock Presents,* Revue Studios, NBC, February 3, 1957.

"Tongue of Silver". As The Traveler. *Matinee Theater,* NBC, March 15, 1957.

"The Water Skier". As Chuck Conway. *Code 3,* Rab Co TV Productions, June 25, 1957.

"Last Will and Testament". As George Cook. *George Sanders Mystery Theater,* Screen Gems, NBC, July 20, 1957.

*Wagon Train.* As Flint McCullough. Revue Studios/NBC/MCA, Seasons 1 – 5, 189 Episodes. First aired September 18, 1957, "The Willy Moran Story" (#1) through May 16, 1962, "The Nancy Davis Story" (#186). Robert Horton appeared in 103 episodes up to and including #186.

"The Last Rodeo". As Jim Cherburg. *General Electric Theater,* Revue Productions, CBS, December 7, 1958.

"The Disappearing Trick". As Walter Richmond. *Alfred Hitchcock Presents,* Revue Studios, NBC, April 6, 1958.

"Much Ado About Nothing". As Benedict. *Matinee Theater*, NBC, with Nina
Foch, May 19 & 20, 1958.

"A Delicate Affair". As Tad Spencer. *Studio One in Hollywood*, CBS, July 28,
1958.

"The Last Dark Step". As Brad Taylor. *Alfred Hitchcock Presents*, Revue Studios,
NBC, February 8, 1959.

"No Place To Hide". As Danny Barnes. *The DuPont Show with June Allyson*,
Four Star Television, CBS, December 21, 1959.

"Jeff McLeod, The Last Reb". As Jeff McLeod. *Startime*, Hubbell Robinson
Productions, NBC March 1, 1960.

"The Man". As Howard Wilton, The Man. *Theater 70*, ATV, (UK), September
10, 1960.

"Hooked". As Ray Marchand. *Alfred Hitchcock Presents*, Revue Studios, NBC,
September 25, 1960.

"The Choice". As Horace. *The Barbara Stanwyck Show*, ESW Productions, CBS,
April 17, 1961.

"The Perfect Accident". As – unnamed. *US Steel Hour*, Armstrong Circle Theater, February 21, 1962.

"Mission of Fear". As – unnamed. *US Steel Hour*, Theatre Guild, CBS, April 3,
1963.

*Mark Dolphin*. As Mark Dolphin, pilot filmed but never aired, 1965.

*A Man Called Shenandoah*. As Shenandoah, Bronze Productions/NBC TV, 1
Season, 34 Episodes, September 13, 1965 through May 16, 1966.

"Field of Honor". As Jim Collins. *Longstreet*, ABC-TV, February 17, 1972.

"The Lifeline Agency". As Frank Armitage. *Police Woman*, NBC, November 23,
1976.

"Sole Survivor". As Alan Kline. *The Hardy Boys*, Universal Television, ABC,
January 29, 1978.

*As the World Turns*. As Whit McColl. CBS, 1982 – 1983.

"Heads I win, Tails You Lose". As – unnamed. *Houston Knights*, Columbia
Pictures Television, CBS, September 22, 1987.

"Seal of the Confessional". As Jack Hutchings. *Murder She Wrote*, Universal
Television, CBS October 1, 1989.

# APPENDIX 5: VARIETY SHOWS; STAGE, TELEVISION AND RADIO

*The Steve Allen Show*, NBC, September 22, 1957.

*The Lux Show hosted by Rosemary Clooney*, NBC, April 10, 1958.

*Suspense Radio Theater*, CBS, as Tom Dooley, December 7, 1958.

*The Hollywood Bowl Family Night*, Hollywood Bowl, Hollywood, CA, July 17,
1959.

*Andy Williams Special*, "Music from Shubert Alley", NBC, November 13, 1959.

*The Perry Como Show*, NBC, January 20, 1960.

*The Tennessee Ernie Ford Show,* February 13, 1958, March 19, 1959, March 17, 1960, March 23, 1961.

*Sunday Night at the London Palladium,* The London Palladium, London, England, December 27, 1959.

*Robert Horton Saturday Spectacular Show,* Pre-recorded on December 29, 1959, aired on ATV, January 2, 1960.

*Royal Command Performance for the Royal Variety Show* at the Victoria Palace, London, England in the presence of Queen Elizabeth II, May 16, 1960.

*Sunday Night at the London Palladium,* The London Palladium, London, England, May 7, 1961.

*The Robert Horton Show,* Hammersmith Gaumont Theatre, London, England, May 13, 1961. The show then went on the road for two weeks throughout the UK. Marilynn appeared with Bob for three numbers each night, May 13-27, 1961.

*The Robert Horton Show,* The Hippodrome, Birmingham, England, May 14, 1961.

*The Robert Horton Show,* Guildhall, Portsmouth, England, May 15, 1961.

*The Robert Horton Show,* The Gaumont Theatre, Cheltenham, England, May 16, 1961.

*The Robert Horton Show,* Coulston Hall, Bristol, England, May 17, 1961.

*The Robert Horton Show,* The Odeon, South End, England, May 19, 1961.

*The Robert Horton Show,* The Gaumont Theatre, Lewisham, England, May 20, 1961.

*The Robert Horton Show,* The Regal, Hull, England, May 23, 1961.

*The Robert Horton Show,* Civic Hall, Sheffield, England, May 24, 1961.

*The Robert Horton Show,* The Globe, Stockton, England, May 25, 1961.

*The Robert Horton Show,* The Apollo, Manchester, England, May 26, 1961.

*The Robert Horton Show,* City Hall, Newcastle, England, May 27, 1961.

*The Robert Horton Show,* The Empire, Liverpool, England, May 28, 1961.

*The Red Skelton Hour,* CBS, April 16, 1963.

*On Broadway Tonight,* CBS, August 12, 1964.

*The Ed Sullivan Show,* CBS, November 17, 1963, June 7, 1964, April 3, 1966, March 5, 1967.

*Stump The Stars with Diana Dors.* CBS, February 4, 1964.

*Summer Pops Season,* Municipal Auditorium, New Orleans, Louisiana, June 16, 1967.

*Chequers Nightclub Show,* ABC (Australian Broadcasting Company), broadcast July/August 1967.

*The Joey Bishop Show,* ABC, September 1, 1967.

*The Amazing World of Kreskin.* Canadian Television, Ottawa, Canada, January 17, 1972.

*Radio/TV Classics Live!* Buckley Performing Arts Center, Brockton, MA, May 4 – 5, 2007.

KSAV Radio interview *with Boyd Magers,* September 18, 2007.

Bob also appeared as a guest on many talk shows, several quiz shows and other variety shows throughout his career.

# APPENDIX 6: THEATER

*I Give You My Husband.* As Jerry Walker. Jewel Box Theater, Los Angeles,12 week-run starting January 1946.

*Streamliner.* As Peter Drake. University of Miami, October 28 – 29, 1946.

*Accent on Youth.* As Dickie Reynolds. University of Miami, December 4, 1946.

*Mr. Mick Hangs A Moon.* As Chuck. University of Miami, January 22 – 23, 1947.

*Golden Boy.* As Joe Bonaparte, The Golden Boy. University of Miami, April 8 – 12, 1947.

*Uncle Fred Flits By.* As Narrator. *UCLA* Summer School, July 23 – 26, 1947.

*Lilacs and Ticker Tape.* As Higgins. *UCLA* Summer School, July 1947.

*The Little Foxes.* As Horace Giddens. University of Miami, September 4, 1947.

*Night Must Fall.* As Danny. University of Miami, April 14 – May 15, 1948.

*Thunder Rock.* As Streeter, supply plane pilot. Campus Theatre 170, UCLA, 1948.

*Footprints on the Ceiling.* As a dancer. UCLA, June 28 – July 3, 1948.

*Three Men on a Horse.* As Al. UCLA, July 15 – 16, 1948.

*Twelfth Night.* As Antonio. Campus Theatre 170, UCLA, November 28 – December 11, 1948.

*The Hasty Heart.* As Yank. Campus Theatre 170, UCLA, March 19, 1949.

*Harvey.* As Dr. Raymond Sanderson. Atlantic City Players, Week of June 30, 1950.

*Born Yesterday.* As Paul Verrall. Atlantic City Players, Week of July 10, 1950.

*On The Town.* As the announcer. Atlantic City Players, Week of July 24, 1950.

*The Respectful Prostitute.* As Fred Clarke. Atlantic City Players, Week of July 31,1950. Held over for five weeks.

*Picnic.* As Hal Carter. The Ring Theatre, Los Angeles, June 1955, Northland Theater, Detroit, June 1959, The Little Theater, Sullivan, June 1968, Cherry County Playhouse, Traverse City, 1968, Theater Under the Stars, Kennebunkport, August 1968. Other appearances in this role are undocumented.

*The Rainmaker.* As Starbuck. The Ring Theatre, Los Angeles, July 1956, Canal Fulton Summer Arena, Fulton, July 1972, The Barn Dinner Theatre, St. Louis, July 1976. Other appearances in this role are undocumented.

*The Man.* As Howard Wilton, The Man. Drury Lane Theatre, Chicago,May 20, 1962 for six weeks.

*The Odd Couple.* As Oscar Madison and as Director. Bridge VU Dinner Theatre, Valparaiso, May – June 1972, The Plantation Dinner Theatre, St. Louis, October – November, 1976. Other appearances in this role are undocumented.

Other plays he has been credited with are *All My Sons, Death of a Salesman, Cat on a Hot Tin Roof* and *The Price*. Research has, however, produced no specific supporting information such as critiques, articles or playbills, although these plays are mentioned in Bob's profile within an undated playbill for *Sabrina Fair*.

## APPENDIX 7: MUSICAL THEATER REPETOIRE

Those in which he appeared with Marilynn are denoted with the initials MH. He performed in these shows variously from 1959 until 1982.

*Guys and Dolls.* As Sky Masterson, with MH.

*Brigadoon.* As Tommy Albright, with MH.

*Oklahoma!* As Curly, with MH.

*Carousel.* As Billy Bigelow, with MH.

*110 in the Shade.* As Starbuck. Boston, Philadelphia, September 1963. New York – Broadway October 1963 – August, 1964.

*The Pajama Game.* As Sid Sorokin, with MH.

*Sabrina Fair.* As Linus Larrabee, Jr.

*Same Time Next Year.* As George, with MH. Directed by Robert Horton.

*There's a Girl in My Soup.* As Robert Danvers, with MH.

*1776.* As John Adams, with MH. First played this in 1972, Sep 13 through November 5, taking on the role at short notice.

*6 Rms. Riv Vu.* As Paul Friedmann, with MH. Directed by Robert Horton.

*Zorba.* As Zorba.

*Man of La Mancha.* As Don Quixote, with MH.

*Kismet.* As Hajj, with MH.

*Show Boat.* As Gaylord Ravenal, with MH.

*Catch Me If You Can.* As Daniel Corbin, with MH. Directed by Robert Horton.

*I Do, I Do!* As Michael, with MH.

*Under the Yum Yum Tree.* As Hogan, with MH.

*The Girl in The Freudian Slip.* As Dr. Dewey Maugham.

*The Music Man.* As "Professor" Harold Hill.

He has also been credited with appearing in *Pal Joey*. Research has not brought to light anything more concrete than Bob's own mention of hoping to star in a Broadway production of the show.

## APPENDIX 8: NIGHTCLUB ACTS

Elmwood Casino, Detroit, November 1964.

Tommy Henrich's, The Diamond Room, Columbus, February 1965.

La Fiesta Supper Club, El Paso, March 1965.

Shamrock Hilton, Houston, date unknown, but c. 1965.

The Continental Room, International Club, Houston, February 1967.

Chequers Nightclub, Sydney, Australia, June 28 – July 19, 1967.

Flamingo Room, Flamingo Hotel, Las Vegas, Nevada. August 10-31, 1967. There is a mention of an engagement in Canada, but research has brought nothing to light.

# APPENDIX 9: RECORDS AND ALBUMS

"Shenandoah" / "Maria". PYE single (UK)1960.
*Sunday Night at The London Palladium.* PYE EP (UK) 1960.
"Roll Along Wagon Train" / "Sail Ho". PYE single (UK) 1960.
"The Girl That I Marry" / "Time After Time". PYE single (UK) 1960.
*The Very Thought of You.* Columbia Records, LP 1964.
*110 in the Shade.* RCA LP 1964, with the original Broadway cast.
*The Man Called Shenandoah.* Columbia Records, LP 1965.

# APPENDIX 10: RODEOS, LIVESTOCK SHOWS, PARADES AND CAUSES

Last, but not least, were the countless numbers of rodeos and livestock shows which Bob attended as a result of the fame he gained as Flint McCullough in *Wagon Train.* These appearances were numerous; he earned extraordinary appearance fees and astonished most audiences by riding into the arena, dismounting and singing. He never wore the Flint McCullough costume. He also headed up some fund-raising campaigns (his name was a huge draw) and starred in two of the country's most prestigious holiday parades, The Rose Bowl and Macy's Thanksgiving Parade. There is no comprehensive list of the rodeos he starred in, but the following helps to indicate their span, which began in 1957 and ran through the end of 1961.

Santa Fe Rodeo, Santa Fe, NM, as Grand Marshall, Fall 1957.
March of Dimes, Launched 1958 fund-raising campaign in Louisiana, January 25, 1958.
Harris County Junior Sheriff's Association Show, "Night of Stars," Houston, TX, April 9, 1958.
National Cystic Fibrosis Foundation Fund Drive, as Honorary Chairman, launched May 1958.
Paddleboard Days, Catalina, CA, as Commodore of "The World's Longest Paddleboard Race, August 17, 1958.
Caldwell Night Rodeo, Caldwell, ID, as the Rodeo Star, August 8 & 9, 1958.
Lewiston Annual Round-Up, Lewiston, ID, as the Rodeo Star, September 4 & 5, 1958.
Riverside Diamond Jubilee Parade, Riverside, CA, as Grand Marshall of the Jubilee Parade, October 5, 1958.
Macy's Thanksgiving Day Parade, as the featured star, November 27, 1958. Arbitron rating of 27.7 topped all records for any daytime show at the time.

19th Annual Palm Springs Mounted Police Rodeo, Palm Springs, CA, as Grand Marshall, February 7 & 8, 1959.
Phoenix Rodeo, Phoenix, AZ, as Grand Marshall, March 12 through 15, 1959. This broke all records to date.
Holmes Championship Rodeo, Cincinnati, OH, as the Rodeo Star, May 14 through 16, 1959.
Rodeo World Championship, Columbus, OH, as the Rodeo Star, May 21 through 23, 1959.
Tulsa Annual Charity Horse Show, Tulsa, OK, as the Rodeo Star, May 26 through 30, 1959.
13th Annual Alabama State Fair, Birmingham, AL, as the Rodeo Star, October 10, 1959.
Texas Prison Rodeo, Huntsville, AL, as the Rodeo Star, October 19, 1959.
Sandhills Hereford and Quarterhorse Show, Odessa, TX, as the Rodeo Star, January 1960.
St. Paul Winter Carnival Torchlite Parade, St. Paul, MN, as Grand Marshall, February 6, 1960.
Houston Fat Stock Show & Rodeo, Houston, TX, as the Rodeo Star, February 24 through March 6, 1960.
New Mexico State Fair, Albuquerque, NM, September 23, 1960.
Arkansas Livestock Exposition & World Championship Rodeo, Little Rock, AR, as the Rodeo Star, October 3 through 8, 1960.
72nd Annual Pasadena Tournament of Roses Parade, January 2, 1961.
Fort Madison Rodeo, Ft. Madison, IO, as the Rodeo Star, September 8, 1961.
34th Annual Ak-Sar-Ben Stock Show and Rodeo, Omaha, NE, as the Rodeo Star, September 22 through October 1, 1961.
Grand National Livestock Exposition Horse Show & Rodeo, Cow palace, San Francisco, CA, the Rodeo Star, October 27 through November 5, 1961. Robert Horton's appearance there set an all-time attendance record.

# APPENDIX II: WESTERN FESTIVALS AND SYMPOSIUMS

This listing is based on all available evidence including several of Robert Horton's own programs.
Desert Circus, Palm Springs, CA, 1986.
Tuolumne Wild Film Festival, Sonora, Tuolumne County, CA, 1992.
Tuolumne Wild West Film Festival, Lifetime Achievement Award, Sonora, Tuolumne County, CA, September 24 – 26, 1993.
Charlotte Film Festival, Charlotte, NC, 1993.
Knoxville Film Festival, Knoxville, TN, 1996.
Memphis Film Festival, Memphis, TN, 1998.
Hopalong Cassidy Festival, Cambridge, OH, 2001.
Western Film Festival, Tombstone, AZ, 2002.

Lone Pine Film Festival (14th Annual), Lone Pine, CA, October 10 – 12, 2003.
Warren Earp Days Western Book Exposition, Willcox, AZ, July 10 – 13, 2003.
Reel Cowboys, Silver Spur Award, Sherman Oaks, CA, 2003.
Western Legends Round-Up, Kanab, UT, August 24 -29, 2004.
Golden Boot Awards, Honoree, Tombstone, AZ, August 7, 2004.
Bison Homes Festival of the West, Phoenix, AZ, March 17 – 20, 2005.
16th Annual Bison Homes Western Festival, Cowboy Spirit Award, Phoenix, AZ, March 18 – 21, 2006.
Western Film Festival, Tombstone, AZ 2007.

# APPENDIX 12: ROLES HE HAD TO DECLINE OR HE REFUSED.

Due to his *Wagon Train* obligations, his dislike of the material, or unacceptable contractual conditions.

Verbatim quotes from *Clippings I* and *II* and the *Burris Scrapbook*

November 1957. "Offered movie role by London's James Woolf – "Ride The Rough Wind" to be filmed in Tunisia."
November 1957. "Offered the lead in "An Urge to Love," an upcoming Broadway musical slated for April, 1958. Production, musical by E. Robert Fitzsimmons."
February 1958. "Slated to play "Curly" in St Louis Opera's version in summer."
March 1958. "Slated to play opposite Nina Foch in "The Girls of Summer" in Eastern summer stock."
April 1958. "Talk of his doing a movie about the Air Force with Dan Duryea."
May 26 1958. "Offered the starring role in "City of the Dead" to be made in London in August 1958."
July 14, 1958. "Horton asked for four weeks off to star in "The Rainmaker" at Chicago's Edgewater Beach Playhouse in August."
September 28, 1958. "*US Steel* working a deal to star Robert Horton as an Irish revolutionary in "A Day In Fear"."
September 16, 1958. "In discussions with Theater Guild executives regarding an upcoming Broadway musical."
October 1, 1958. "Offered lead opposite Gwen Verdon in "Redhead" on Broadway."
January 20, 1959. "Sydney Box, English producer, wants Horton to star in "All Through The Night" by George Thrapp, to be filmed in England."
February 9, 1959. "Horton considering a two week personal appearance tour under Granada TV auspices."
March 2, 1959. "Negotiations underway for Horton to co-star with Richard Burton in "The Bramble Bush" being produced by Milton Sperling for Warners."

April 1, 1959. "David Merrick, after hearing Horton sing on the Tennessee Ernie Ford Show offered him the starring role in a musical version of Eugene O'Neill's "Ah Wilderness"."

April 21, 1959. "Morton Da Costa and Robert Flyer talking to Horton about "Saratoga Trunk" musical on Broadway."

August 4, 1959. "Efforts made by *DuPont Show of the Month* to get Horton to star in "Body and Soul"."

September 23, 1959. "Still in negotiations with James Woolf to star in a feature film."

October 12, 1959. "Signed to star in "An Occurrence at Owl Creek" for *Alfred Hitchcock Presents.*"

October 9, 1959. "Wanted by *US Steel Hour* for a play, "Solid Gold Bathtub"."

November 30, 1959. "Offered starring role in "The Misfits" with Marilyn Monroe and Clark Gable by Arthur Miller, the playwright." In the end Bob and Miller couldn't agree on the interpretation of the character.

February 5, 1960. "Ford Theater *Startime* in the offing for Bob Horton."

March 10, 1960. "British TV wanted Horton to return to star in a 90 minute version of *The Rain Maker.*"

April 27, 1960. "Horton bypassed the lead in *Oklahoma!* with CVG for three weeks to stay in Europe and take his first vacation in years."

April 29, 1960. "Offered a co-starring role with Burt Lancaster and Jimmy Stewart in *The Way West.*"

May 25, 1960. "British producer-director Stanley Donan interviewed Horton to star in *Man Running* for Columbia."

July 21, 1960. "Robert Horton to play one of the leads in *US Steel Hour's* "The Yum-Yum Girl" to be filmed for airing next October."

September 13, 1960. "David Merrick offered Horton the top male role in his Broadway production *Lili.*"

November 8, 1960. "Horton received a query about availability to star in *My Geisha.*"

November 15, 1960. "Horton cancelled plans for a Christmas TV show in London in order to work straight through the holidays on *Wagon Train.*"

November 22, 1960. "Jean Dalrymple has offered Robert Horton the male lead in her New York City Center revival of *Showboat* which she'll produce in April. Horton is trying to arrange shooting schedule of *Wagon Train* in order to accept the offer."

November 24, 1960. "With Robert Horton's *Wagon Train* schedule up in the air because of Ward Bond's death, he may be able to cut loose to accept Jean Dalrymple's offer to star in New York City Center in her revival of *Showboat.*"

February 4, 1961. "Edwin Lester wants Bob Horton for his star in *Guys and Dolls* this summer for Civic Light Opera."

February 18, 1961. "Robert Horton tuning up the pipes to have a go at the stage in New York in August. He's been offered a co-starring spot with Dorothy Shay in *Guys and Dolls* at the New York City Center."

March 29, 1961. "If his *Wagon Train* schedule permits Bob Horton will title star in a New York City center revival of *Pal Joey* starting May 25."

April 26, 1961. "With only one more season to go in *Wagon Train* Horton explained in Hollywood why he's resisting a new 5 year contract. He's hoping to land a part in the Richard Rodgers – Alan Jay Lerner Broadway musical *Queen For A Day.*"

May 15, 1961. "Robert Horton, while in England is talking a two picture deal with Associated British Picture Corporation. Pact would go into effect upon completion next year of Horton's contract with Revue Studios."

June 14, 1961. "Robert Horton has set a pact with Pye Records for a new album."

August 31, 1961. "Bob Horton's all hipped up about a new Portia Nelson – Scott Holtzman musical *Wander Guy.*"

November 3, 1961. "Robert Horton is a candidate for the lead in Meredith Wilson's next Broadway musical, *The Understudy.*"

November 1961. "Bob Horton is perusing the script of a musical version of *The Prisoner of Zenda* which producer Edwin Lester wants to put on Broadway."

November 13, 1961. "Lew Wasserman studying a request from Bob Horton to take off from *Wagon Train* in time to accept an offer to star on Broadway in *The Underworld*, a musical kind of *Untouchables* based on the life of gangster Dion O'Banion."

January 5, 1962. "Robert Horton will star in a mobster musical *Underworld* on the Big Street if current discussions work out."

February 8, 1962. "Bob Horton's wish to star in a Broadway musical now sees him with a choice of three. He'll meet with Vincent Donahue regarding *Underworld*, then with Don Driver and William Stone regarding their musical adaptation of Somerset Maugham's *The Reverend Miss Jones* and finally, with Richard Rodgers regarding starring role in the new musical he is writing with Alan Jay Lerner." (Which was *I Picked A Daisy*).

February 19, 1962. "Bob Horton had to turn down the co-starring role in Marilyn Monroe's next picture *Something's Got To Give*. Seems Horton okay'd the deal if 20th Century-Fox could guarantee that the picture would be finished by August when he plans to go into the Broadway musical *Underworld*. Studio's answer was that with Marilyn Monroe heading the cast it couldn't even guarantee the film would be started by then."

February 28, 1962. "Robert Horton sitting on an offer from Alan Lerner to head to London to play the original Richard Burton role in *Camelot.*"

Undated, but c. summer, 1962. "Unreasonable". As for movies, he (Robert Horton) said, "From my standpoint the things they wanted from me recently were unreasonable. Most of the offers had a no-Broadway clause for two years after the film was made. I turned down "Molly Brown" because Metro wanted such a clause in the contract."

# Aileen J. Elliott
## Author

I was born in Edinburgh, Scotland in 1947 and grew up with my twin sister, older and younger sisters and younger brother in a close-knit family. I was educated at James Gillespie's High School for Girls and the Edinburgh College of Art.

I emigrated to the US in 1967 and was first married in 1968. I followed a career in the travel and hospitality industry and over time, and because I was asked to, I often wrote for newspapers and magazines. I always enjoyed writing and entertained myself creating short and long stories as well as a number of lengthier fiction novels. This biography is my first introduction to the world of serious writing and publication. Its subject is close to my heart and I hope fervently that I have done a great man – a great star – justice.

Printed in Great Britain
by Amazon